Hearts, Minds, Voices

Hearts, Minds, Voices

US Cold War Public Diplomacy and the Formation of the Third World

JASON C. PARKER

OXFORD
UNIVERSITY PRESS

OXFORD
UNIVERSITY PRESS

Oxford University Press is a department of the University of Oxford. It furthers
the University's objective of excellence in research, scholarship, and education
by publishing worldwide. Oxford is a registered trade mark of Oxford University
Press in the UK and certain other countries.

Published in the United States of America by Oxford University Press
198 Madison Avenue, New York, NY 10016, United States of America.

© Oxford University Press 2016

Library of Congress Cataloging-in-Publication Data
Names: Parker, Jason C., author.
Title: Hearts, minds, voices : U.S. Cold War public diplomacy and the formation
of the Third World / Jason C. Parker.
Description: New York, NY : Oxford University Press, [2016] |
Includes bibliographical references and index.
Identifiers: LCCN 2016011858 (print) | LCCN 2016032458 (ebook) |
ISBN 9780190251840 (hardcover : acid-free paper) | ISBN 9780190251857 (Updf) |
ISBN 9780190251864 (Epub)
Subjects: LCSH: United States—Foreign relations—Developing countries. |
Developing countries—Foreign relations—United States. | Cold War—Diplomatic history. |
United States—Foreign relations—Philosophy. | United States—Foreign relations—1945–1989. |
Decolonization—Developing countries—History—20th century. | Race—Political aspects—United
States—History—20th century. | Race—Political aspects—Developing countries—History—20th
century. | Developing countries—Politics and government—20th century. | Developing countries—
Foreign relations—20th century. | BISAC: HISTORY / Modern / 20th Century. | HISTORY /
United States / 20th Century. | SOCIAL SCIENCE / Media Studies.
Classification: LCC D888.U6 P27 2016 (print) | LCC D888.U6 (ebook) | DDC 327.73009/045—dc23
LC record available at https://lccn.loc.gov/2016011858

1 3 5 7 9 8 6 4 2
Printed by Sheridan Books, Inc., United States of America

Some material in the book has been adapted from previously published work: Jason Parker, "Crisis
Management and Missed Opportunities: U.S. Public Diplomacy and the Creation of the Third World,"
in *The United States and Public Diplomacy: New Directions in Cultural and International History*, edited
by Kenneth Osgood and Brian Etheridge, Brill, 2010; and Jason Parker, "Cold War II: The Eisenhower
Administration, the Bandung Conference, and the Reperiodization of the Postwar Era," *Diplomatic
History* 30, no. 5 (2006): 867–892. By permission of the Society for Historians of American Foreign
Relations and Oxford University Press.

CONTENTS

PREFACE AND ACKNOWLEDGMENTS

This book explores an unintended consequence of the unwanted intrusion of an unnerving conflict. It represents a powerful moment in a tragic story—and arguably that story's bright spot. Just as most of Shakespeare's tragedies are not yet tragedies if one stops reading by Act III, the present book tells of the unexpected rise but stops before the disappointing fall. But it is less a Shakespearean tragedy than a Columbian one. It unfolds during the first half of the Cold War, but its central development—postwar decolonization—belongs on the longer timeline of European overseas empire that began in 1492. It thereby ranks as a world-historical moment whose reverberations are felt well into the present day. Among these is the rise of what Vijay Prashad calls the Third World Project—itself the fruit of the dialogues of decolonization and the superpower conflict in these decades, an interactive creation process that forged the Third World's "imagined community." Such communities coalesce around internal qualities that bond their members—but also around shared opposition to external factors. In this case, Global North public diplomacy tried to spread the Cold War into this still-forming entity. In doing so it provoked a reaction that fused preexisting currents to form a community, one built in large part around rejection of the Cold War that Washington and Moscow so insistently tried to introduce. The result was not one but two new cartographies—one drawing the postcolonial atlas of sovereign nation-states, the other revealing three "worlds" including the newborn Third—born of an undesired collision and a vibrant global conversation.

This study had its genesis in the events of September 11 fifteen years ago. Just as that day reshaped global affairs for years to follow, it has reverberated through scholarship since then, as scholars have struggled to make sense of the temptations and limitations of modern-day empire as practiced by actors from the United States to ISIS. Among the questions that haunted the United States in the wake of the attacks was a poignant perennial: "Why do they hate us?" The question pointed to a topic that had only caught scholars' attention in a sustained way during the years just prior: public diplomacy, or the attempt to shape foreign opinion in ways that serve a government's own national and strategic interests. Excellent recent studies have shed much light on twentieth-century US public diplomacy, but few of them pay extended attention to US Cold War outreach to the Global South. Most recent scholarship on US–Global South relations, meanwhile, focuses on interventions and intrigues rather than appeals and outreach. That Venn-style gap in the literatures impedes our ability to address the question. It leaves obscure the decades of US outreach that sought to neutralize such hatred by presenting a positive image of the United States, and to generate sympathy among both elite and mass audiences abroad.

This project originally set out less to answer that question than simply to fill that gap: to reconstruct the lost history of America's attempts to present itself and its policies to the Third World. Along the way, it evolved into something larger. The book's eventual thesis—that the Cold War began as a binary ideological showdown but evolved into a multiparty colloquy—grew as the archives revealed that the conceptual entity of the Third World owed its evolution in considerable measure to the Cold War campaigns to win over its inhabitants. The ideal of solidarity among the imperialized had coursed through South–South, diasporic, and "Pan" circuits for decades. But it was not until the Cold War forced the geopolitical-ideological question that the imagined community of the Third World coalesced around three pillars: nonalignment, economic development and modernization, and the transracial "spirit of Bandung."

Given the pejorative baggage that in many minds attaches to the term "Third World" these days, it is easy to forget that in its time it was the proverbial wave of the future, a well-nigh divine destiny. As Andrew Rotter notes, "key leaders of Third World nations, particularly . . . Sukarno [and] Nehru, appropriated the idea of the Third World and claimed it as a source of power." Since the Cold War most consistently inserted itself into the Global South via public diplomacy, it unwittingly played a role in midwifing that imagined community into existence, by persuading peoples there that they shared more with each other than they did with the Global North's bipolar conflict. The importance of public diplomacy is further evidenced in the energy with which new-state Global South actors themselves jumped into the fray. Their conversations in response to Global North appeals gave discursive shape to the Third World project.

My hope is that in like fashion this book will be a conversation catalyst in its own right, contributing to the scholarly debate and spurring further research into the nexus of Cold War public diplomacy, race, development, and decolonization. I embarked on the project hoping to have learned from the process of writing my first book some valuable lessons for writing the second. But I found to my chagrined surprise that only a precious few such lessons actually obtained. The one that looms largest is the importance of support of various kinds, without which this book would not exist. I wish especially to acknowledge, and profoundly to thank, the Smith Richardson Foundation, the Truman Library Institute, the Fulbright Foundation, the Mershon Center for International Security Studies at Ohio State University, the Mellon Foundation, the University of Michigan Bentley Historical Library, the West Virginia University Eberly College of Arts and Sciences, and the Glasscock Humanities Center and the PESCA program at Texas A&M University for the grant and fellowship support that enabled me to research and write this book.

In addition to funding support, a number of venues also provided this project with a series of intellectual homes along the way. Especially as its thesis expanded and evolved, this project benefitted from time spent at West Virginia University, the Mershon Center, the Universidad de San Andrés in Buenos Aires, Aix-en-Provence, the International Seminar on Decolonization at the Library of Congress, and Texas A&M University. Friends and colleagues at all of these sites helped the project to reach this fruition. I am particularly grateful to Liz and Ken Fones-Wolf, Katherine Aaslestad and John Lambertson, Matt and Annastella Vester, Joe and Marta Hodge, Richard Herrmann, Peter Hahn, Mitch Lerner, Eduardo Zimmerman, Marcelo Leiras, Daniel Friel, Jean-Christophe and Magali Strategias, Maite Monchal, David Vaught, Lisa Cobbs, Kate and Jeff Engel, Terry Anderson, Brian Linn, Andy Kirkendall, Angela Hudson, Brian Rouleau, Kate Untermann, Glenn Chambers, Josh Shifrinson, Will Norris, and Dom Bearfield.

I am also grateful for the chance to have presented and discussed this work at a number of places away from home, where the conversations were not only intellectually enlivening in their own right but also helped me to think through the evolution of my thesis. Among these, several stand especially tall: the International Security Studies colloquium at Yale, the Rothermere American Institute at Oxford, the American History Seminar at Cambridge, the Center on Public Diplomacy at USC, the Center for Cold War Studies at UC-Santa Barbara, the Hall Center at the University of Kansas, the International Studies Seminar at the University of Colorado, the Eisenhower Lecture at Gettysburg College, the Kennedy Center at BYU, the End of Empires symposium at Brown University, the Belgrade NAM symposium at the Serbian National Archives, and the State Department Historians' Office. At the above sites and elsewhere I am indebted to friends and colleagues who supported, challenged, and improved the project along its long way: Bob McMahon, Andrew Preston, Nigel Bowles, Nic Cheeseman, Kate Epstein, Nick Cull, Salim Yaqub, Sheyda Jahanbani, Tom Zeiler, Andrew Johns, Sandra Sousa, Rob Rakove, Scott

Lucas, Bevan Sewell, Svetozar Rajak, and Arne Westad. I am also deeply ap-
preciative of SHAFR colleagues who have in various ways—and whether they
realize it or not—helped this project along over the years: Ken Osgood, Erez
Manela, Matt Connelly, Justin Hart, Mary Dudziak, Michael Hunt, Kathryn
Statler, Jim Meriwether, and the phenomenal Carol Anderson.

Special thanks are due to those whose support went above and beyond
what anyone could reasonably expect. In Washington, DC, locals and
decolonization–seminar participants alike made this project better. All of the
"seminarians"—especially Dan Branch, Miguel Jerónimo Bandeira, Michael
Collins, Paul McGarr, Gez McCann, Elisabeth Leake, Ryan Irwin, Lien-Hang
Nguyen, Paul Chamberlin, Chris Dietrich, Emma Hunter, Chris Lee, Lucy
Chester, Chantalle Verna, Yasmin Khan, Birte Timm, Abou Bamba, Daniel
Immerwahr, Jess Chapman, Frank Gerits, and Jeff Byrne—taught me much.
As did my fellow seminar faculty leaders Roger Louis, Dane Kennedy, Philippa
Levine, Sudhir Pilarisetti, Marilyn Young, John Darwin, Jen Foray, and Lori
Watt, with whom it has been an honor and a joy to work these last ten sum-
mers. Local friends Miriam and Will Cunningham, Meredith Hindley, Sarah
Snyder and Danny Fine, Jim Siekmeier and Catherine Tall, Seth Center, Gregg
Brazinsky, Josh Botts, Lindsay Krasnoff, Todd Bennett and Kath Rasmussen,
and Cindy Ray offered critiques, encouragement, and companionship in great
measure; and I owe the "Rum Summiteers" Channa Threat, Adam Howard,
Steve Galpern, Aiyaz Husain, and Tanvi Madan an extra shot of smooth, well-
aged gratitude. Aiyaz and Meredith, in fact, are joined by Jessica Stites Mor
and Leena Dallasheh in the category of those to whom I am indebted perhaps
most of all, for the crucial, inspiring roles they played at make-or-break moments in the process. I am deeply grateful for the patience, support, and brain-
play offered by all of the above in making this book happen. Its errors are solely
my own.

My professional debts also include my editor Susan Ferber, with whom
as before it has been an unqualified pleasure to work, and to the anonymous
OUP readers whose critiques helped me to strengthen the book. I am also
very grateful to my research assistants Ansley Hopping, Jeff Crean, and Mike
Fasulo, for their hard and outstanding work. Finally I wish to thank the archi-
vists without whom our work is not remotely possible: the staffs at the Library
of Congress, NARA, and the Truman (especially Randy Sowell, David Clark,
Lisa Sullivan, and the much-missed Liz Safly), Eisenhower (especially David
Haight and Valoise Armstrong), and Kennedy Presidential Libraries.

Final and very deepest thanks go to my family, to whom this book is dedicated: to Océane and Logan, who went from grade-schoolers to teenagers
on three continents over the course of this project and were mostly joyous

troopers along the way; and to Pascale, who has been more supportive and understanding, even through the toughest times, than anyone historian or not has a right to ask for. I can never thank them enough, and can only hope that the book and its attendant adventures serve as some small compensation for time lost and trials endured.

Hearts, Minds, Voices

Introduction

In the Beginning Was the Word

> Rhetoric [was] a generative principle of Cold War politics.... A cold war is, by definition, a rhetorical war, a war fought with words, speeches, pamphlets, public information ... campaigns, slogans, gestures, symbolic actions, and the like.
> —Martin J. Medhurst, *Cold War Rhetoric* (1997)

The Cold War began as a bipolar confrontation, but it evolved over time into a multipolar conversation. The slow-motion transition from World War II's Grand Alliance to the superpower standoff extended the low-level hostilities that had characterized relations between West and revolutionary East prior to the war. Each side claimed to have the better formula for modern industrial society. In 1945, with most of Europe lying in destruction and with death, enmity, and exhaustion weighing on its surviving peoples, the task of reconstituting such societies in the ruined lands—caught as they were between the victorious rivals and their competing prescriptions—loomed impossibly large. In this sense the nascent Cold War, while a thoroughly strategic and ideological struggle, was more than a contest for power between nations. It was also, often self-consciously, a battle to shape the future within nations. It promised as much to redraw the geopolitical map contested by the two poles as to remold human society for the modern era—and it did so at a moment of millennial awakening among diverse peoples seeking their own destinies and their own share of that era's bounties.

In the years immediately after 1945, Washington and Moscow had both located ground zero of this contest—the fulcrum of potential war-making power—in Europe. But if the signature developments of the early Cold War, such as the Marshall Plan and the Berlin Airlift, took place there, it is notable that some of the earliest clashes between the erstwhile allies-cum-adversaries unfolded on the Eurasian periphery: Iran, Greece–Turkey,

Indonesia, Indochina, Israel–Palestine, and Korea. If the frontlines were in Berlin, the flanks too could be identified on the map—and be seen to be moving further outward over time. This owed in part to both sides' belief in the universality of their formulae, and to the ways that the clash incorporated geopolitics alongside matters of internal societal organization. It owed as well as to deepening American and Soviet awareness that Europe's prospects were connected in myriad ways with her overseas possessions, then advancing toward decolonization–strengthening the conclusion over time that the non-European world was a crucial battleground.

The war had terribly shaken the European empires, many parts of which had been rumbling for decades prior. As the impact of Europe's destruction leached into her overseas possessions, which in 1945 still covered one-third of the Earth's land surface, her colonial subjects took stock. The metropoles' orgy of mutual destruction called into question their right to rule themselves, much less peoples overseas. Moreover, the war-borne suffering of Europe was not dissimilar in kind from the past and present privations in the empires abroad. World War II, to an even greater extent than its predecessor, thus undercut all manner of Western claims. Postwar residents of Africa, Asia, the Middle East, and the Caribbean who looked up at European flags grew louder in questioning the colonial regimes under which they lived. They looked for answers in the dueling northern hemisphere models for the way forward from poverty to modernity, but with an added dimension—seeking a way out from under European rule. This left them naturally suspicious of the competing American and Soviet claims, which seemed but two sides of a single phenomenon: a "pan-European" project to continue the global domination that dated back to Columbus.[1]

These areas were, moreover, enormously diverse and widely scattered, from the western hemisphere to Africa to the Asian rimlands. They had only in common that they were neither West nor East in the superpower clash, that they suffered European imperialism past or present, and that their inhabitants were nonwhite and mired in poverty. The independence of these European-ruled areas constituted an epochal moment in world history, as the three decades after 1945 saw the number of sovereign nation-states double and then nearly double again. It constituted as well one of the great global challenges of the Cold War, which in many of these environs was anything but a "long peace."[2] In places like Korea and Vietnam, the intrusion of the Cold War into local decolonization struggles could render them tragically, unrecognizably bloody. Such sites taught lessons. Nationalist leaders fighting for independence could see in them the potential of the superpower clash at best to open channels of aid and alliance, but at worst to produce horrific local violence, suffering, and war—the last of these possibly of the nuclear variety as the two poles expanded their arsenals to doomsday proportions.

Yet most of the peoples in these areas experienced the superpower clash neither as the much-feared mushroom cloud nor in the abundantly violent way that Vietnam and Korea did. They instead experienced it as what came to be called public diplomacy—as a multifront media war, launched by the superpowers in pursuit of strategic and psychological gains, to win them over. The not-infrequent episodes of espionage and armed intervention in decolonizing and underdeveloped areas held higher stakes for local life and limb. But public diplomacy was the more sustained presence, one intruding upon and influencing the day-to-day conversations of these lands and peoples in historic flux. Both Washington and Moscow exerted themselves strenuously—in the phrase coined later, during the Vietnam War—to "win hearts and minds." Abetted by the latest technologies of mass communications, the United States Information Agency (USIA) and its Soviet counterparts spread their competing gospels to increasingly wider—and often interested but skeptical—audiences across the decolonizing and impoverished Global South. Reception there was mixed. The promise of social and material progress, enshrined in the dueling prescriptions, enticed the new states seeking to grow their economies after the European flags came down. But they were deeply and justifiably wary of being drawn into Cold War machinations.

Moreover, on the whole they disagreed that the conflict was a greater threat to the non-European world's future than were colonialism, white supremacy, and poverty. The region had long wrestled with these curses, at home and through expatriate circuits abroad. A range of intellectuals including W.E.B. DuBois, George Padmore, Rabindranath Tagore, Saad Zaghlul, José Enrique Rodó, and others less well known had from the early decades of the twentieth century denounced their imposition on the daily lives of subject peoples. Historian Minkah Makalani notes that many of these thinkers, especially on the radical left, detected early on the connections linking their scattered struggles.[3] These *cris de coeur*, whether voiced at home or in diasporae, helped to cement these struggles' importance long before the Cold War public diplomats showed up. The latter gradually discovered that this conviction would sharply limit the marketability of their messages. However, if the persuasiveness of these superpower media campaigns often fell short of Washington's hopes, their pervasiveness was inarguable. As historian Nicholas Cull notes, the USIA *was* the Cold War in much of the Third World.

The non-European world responded to this media war by joining it. Once circumstances—above all the achievement of sovereignty—allowed, many major new states built public diplomacy apparatuses of their own. These enabled a Nehru, Nasser, or Nkrumah to join the conversation created by the superpowers' information campaigns within his borders, fusing them to the discussions already flowing there—and to project the resulting ripostes as his country's own two cents beyond them. Public diplomacy campaigns in radio, print, film, and interpersonal exchange acted as a prestige-multiplier for the new states, many of which made it a priority even as they lacked the resources to address pressing domestic needs. Like a new flag, a desk in the United Nations General Assembly, a national airline, an Olympic team, and other accoutrements of sovereignty, such campaigns affirmed a new state's arrival on the world stage. It permitted charismatic leaders to bolster their domestic and regional stature, to advance their agendas, and to jockey against one another for primacy on yet wider planes. At times and in particular theaters, this output exceeded that of the USIA or the Eastern bloc, though those two produced a greater total volume worldwide. By 1960 the two superpowers' media outreach, supplemented by that of their respective allies, competed with a half-dozen or more non-European voices at any given site in the Global South.

This Global South engagement with the East–West war of ideas teased out its differences with both, as well as the different strains, and at times cross-purposes, among the new actors' agendas. These non-European contributions to the discussion, now pulsing unhindered through circuits of their own rather than piecemeal at the forbearance of colonial officials, revealed common ground on some of the most fundamental and consequential issues in play. One of these was the conviction that the Cold War posed an existential threat, as its nuclear dimension threatened human extinction and its military gamesmanship menaced the fragile new states. A related notion was that for all its destructive potential, the Cold War and its twin devils of "Yankee imperialism" and "communist subversion" were lesser concerns than was a declining but stubborn European colonialism. That colonialism, in turn, was inseparable from "racialism" and white supremacy. The need for the abolition of the evil systems created in their name, on display from South Africa to the American South, provided the point of perhaps the greatest unanimity among the new actors. Finally, a further legacy of empire—underdevelopment and poverty—ranked as arguably their highest priority and as a point of high solidarity. Of the three issues, only the nuclear dimension of the first ranked as truly novel; Global South thinkers had identified, and decried, key aspects of the others since at least the turn of the century. They now drew upon this cultural capital to formulate the response that coalesced in the postwar moment, as these issues meshed into a rough consensus among the new actors, uniting them despite the evident diversity in their ranks.

Their efforts at hashing out these interlaced issues, in the context of a cacophonic media war, resulted in an historic unintended consequence. In the late 1940s, as the Cold War was beginning in earnest and the first wave of decolonization crested, US public diplomacy all but ignored the lands outside Europe in order to concentrate on that strategic prize. Yet the definition of the struggle and the doctrine for waging it entailed a logic that soon led outward to the decolonizing areas, whose transitions could fuse with the Cold War to destructive result. Neither Washington nor Moscow could define precisely this huge area, but both came gradually to believe in its strategic importance. Accordingly, they dispatched their public diplomats to carry the Cold War into this geopolitical and intellectual space between the poles. They discovered, within less than a decade, that its inhabitants had their own responses to the global conflict that supposedly defined their lives and prospects. In a manner akin to historian Erez Manela's Wilsonian Moment, once Cold War public diplomacy came into direct and daily contact with the intellectual currents already coursing through the non-European world, it added fuel to a dynamic, interactive process there. That process led its inhabitants to stake out a perimeter around the common ground of what historian Vijay Prashad calls the "Third World project," whose center was an erstwhile shared agenda and whose interests they voiced to each other and to the Global North.[4] The act of carrying the Cold War outside of its main European theater into these Asian, African, Middle Eastern, and Latin American environs, via public diplomacy meant to win over non-European hearts and minds, helped to create a non-European geopolitical bloc—and, in the contemporary words of Guinean Foreign Minister Louis Lansana Beavogui, a "spiritual family."[5] US public diplomacy in areas outside Europe was meant to woo peoples there to the western side. Instead, by persuading them of their common interest in seeking to transcend rather than join the Cold War, it helped to cultivate the concept and entity of the Third World.

This book traces the history of American public diplomacy outside Europe during the first decade and a half of the Cold War and its inadvertent role in fostering the entity of the Third World. It examines the simultaneous drawing of two new global maps: that of decolonization replacing the European empires with Asian, African, Middle Eastern, and Caribbean nation-states, and that of the Cold War dividing the globe first into two and then into three "worlds." Public diplomacy provided a kind of connective tissue between the two cartographies. Its spread beyond Europe—first gradually and by two actors, then massively by multiple ones—was an index of the widening Cold War and of that conflict's conceptual limitations to which non-European actors responded. As decolonizing peoples became a center of USIA attention, they themselves began deploying public diplomacy to assert a different view of world affairs, one identifying racism and colonialism as the greater causes of tension than was the Cold War, and ranking nonalignment and economic development as higher priorities than that conflict.

Although the scholarly literature on public diplomacy has grown remark-
ably in the last decade, it has by and large remained focused on the First and
Second Worlds.[6] Most scholarship on the Global South, meanwhile, only
touches upon the topic in passing. This book presents a set of case studies in
US public diplomacy in the Global South, focusing on information campaigns
around particular Cold War crises, initiatives, and developments. It seeks to
answer a number of interrelated questions, and thereby to capture the full
scope and deeper meaning of the worldwide media war. How did Washington
make its Cold War case to win over the non-European world at moments of
flux, crisis, and opportunity? What does the evolution of that case—and the
expanding number of both listeners and responders—suggest about the role
of public diplomacy in the Cold War and in the genesis of the Third World?
What, if any, larger lessons emerge from the interplay of decolonization and
the superpower conflict, and for strategic international communications in the
present-day world it made? The book recounts particular campaigns with an
eye to the evolving terminology, theory, technologies, and techniques of US
outreach to decolonizing and impoverished areas—and to the ways in which
populations there responded by asserting a different view of their place within
global affairs.

The case studies span the first three US presidential administrations of the
postwar era of decolonization. They were selected from among dozens of possible cases to sample the full range of moments, places, and themes that public
diplomacy eventually helped to fuse into the Third World. World War II had
bequeathed a large, unwieldy overseas information apparatus to the Truman
administration. As historian Justin Hart has shown, wartime information operations had notable practitioner-champions such as Archibald MacLeish, for
whom the "empire of ideas" was key to America's global role, and the concept
remains important to understanding public diplomacy's intellectual history.
Washington was, however, torn about the propriety of propaganda in peace-
time, and with the Cold War yet to take shape, the Truman administration
dismantled much of this machinery and disregarded the rest. But adversar-
ial relations with the Soviets, looming over a precarious Europe, prompted
Washington to reconsider. Gradual recognition of the importance of mass
outreach led the Truman team to reanimate its efforts in that vein, above all
in support of the Marshall Plan. This concentrated on Europe to the virtual
exclusion of the rest of the globe, despite the Truman Doctrine having in principle expanded the conflict worldwide.

The first application of the doctrine outside Europe, the Rio Pact binding the western hemisphere against communist incursion, did little to
prompt supporting information activities, notwithstanding the US public
diplomacy infrastructure already in place in Latin America. Nor did the

historic achievement of South Asian independence in the first wave of decolonization—coming on the heels of the British withdrawal from the eastern Mediterranean that prompted the doctrine, and amidst a recurring sterling crisis—suffice to widen noticeably the scope of active US outreach into these newly sensitive corners of the Cold War world. It would take, in the wake of Mao's triumph in China, the outbreak of war in Korea—the latter itself a decolonizing area—to convince the Truman administration to deploy information activities seriously outside Europe. Administrative chaos hamstrung the endeavor. Washington reorganized its information machinery four times during the Truman years, which ended without its ever achieving philosophical coherence or organizational efficiency. It had, though, broken out of Europe and thus began, however unevenly, expanding the United States' mental map of the Cold War.[7]

Eisenhower—who along with Kennedy was the most fervent devotee of public diplomacy among the postwar presidents—resolved the administrative chaos through the establishment of the USIA in August 1953, and he directed the agency to continue looking southward. These were, in an important sense, the formative years of American Cold War public diplomacy. They were also, not coincidentally, a watershed in the emergence of the not-yet-named Third World. There, in places like Guatemala, information operations were a central piece of Ike's New Look strategy to counter communism on the cheap. In Washington's eyes, the Guatemala intervention paid dividends beyond that country's borders. Despite little evidence of success, the USIA used it prominently in anticommunist media programming in other impoverished parts in the hemisphere and beyond. In the latter areas the first wave of decolonization had ebbed, but another was building—as was the impatience of African Americans in the Jim Crow South and the assertiveness of the emerging nations of the Global South. The Bandung Afro-Asian Peoples Conference of April 1955 hinted at the changing landscape. It connected, in broad though blurry strokes, with moments such as the *Brown v. Board of Education* Supreme Court decision to mark what historian Tim Borstelmann calls a "sea-change" in global race relations. Evidence of this change piled up in a series of subsequent events. The Anglo-French failure at Suez hastened Europe's retreat from empire; Ghana became the first of many sub-Saharan countries to win its independence, starting the second wave of postwar decolonization; and the Little Rock Crisis brought Jim Crow violence to vivid life in world media. The Eisenhower administration tended, by and large, to view these events through "Cold War lenses." But the USIA perceived these other currents, and above all noted that Washington and Moscow were no longer alone on the public diplomacy field in the Global South, where new actors had begun deploying their own forces in the battle for sympathies abroad.

The Kennedy administration consummated both the organizational revamp and the operational focus on what Kennedy called "the southern half of the globe" and what some, notably in France, were starting to call the *tiers-monde*. The overhaul brought the agency's first celebrity head in Edward R. Murrow and elevated its role in the foreign policy decision-making process higher up than under Eisenhower. This enabled Murrow to apply the New Frontier's Global South geopolitical emphasis to USIA operations. Under him, the agency further expanded its infrastructure and activities in Africa and Latin America, the latter increasingly seen as an impoverished kindred spirit to the Afro-Asian world despite its own decolonization being more than a century past. Especially after Castro's revolution in Cuba, Latin America also served as a primary target for the administration's evangelists of moderniza- tion. The two converged in the Alliance for Progress, the centerpiece of agency programming in the hemisphere and a staple of its output elsewhere. The Alliance telegraphed the US conviction that underdevelopment was the most important element binding together the disparate corners of the Global South.

However, USIA activities surrounding other key events there signaled awareness of other "glues." Of these, nonalignment, decolonization, and race were the most prominent. They were manifested in such events, respectively, as the Belgrade Conference, the Congo Crisis, and the struggle for freedom around the Black Atlantic—including its theater of operations in the US South. By the time of Kennedy's assassination, the USIA had so promoted his Third World agenda in the Global South that he was inseparable from it in many minds there—with consequent worry that its promise would go unful- filled after his death. The Kennedy years nonetheless mark a milestone in the maturation of US public diplomacy—as well as that of Global South actors, whose media operations reached a critical mass with the cresting of decolo- nization and civil-rights activism and with the founding of the Non-Aligned Movement (NAM) at the heart of the Third World project. That project had not, by this 1963 bookend, reached its full fruition. Nor had issues such as apartheid, Vietnam, or the New International Economic Order as yet come to exert a dominant influence on the project, as they would during its subsequent phases. But by the early 1960s the Third World project had, to borrow Winston Churchill's phrase, reached the "end of the beginning"—a moment in which its first full iteration became recognizable to all parties north and south.

The definition of that project is therefore at the core of this story, but as with "public diplomacy" and other key terms herein, it had an evolving, com- plicated, and contested meaning. When French demographer Alfred Sauvy first coined the term *"tiers-monde"* in 1952, it sketched a cryptic southward vision, one just beginning to perceive the degree to which the decolonizing areas of the world did not—would not, ought not—fit into the Manichean schema that the Cold War had imposed. Most of Africa, Asia, and the Middle East belonged to the category; Latin America and parts of the Caribbean, not apparently or necessarily so. Sauvy's term resonated with his French audience, as it recalled the *tiers-etat* of the Revolution.[8] This intimated that the decolonizing areas were seizing control of their own destinies, as the peasantry had done in 1789. That heritage helped it to become a more recognized trope in French, especially after philosopher Jean-Paul Sartre published a foreword to Frantz Fanon's *Wretched of the Earth* in 1961 (translated into English the same year), giving the term its widest audience to that point.[9]

It did not come into widespread usage in Washington for years afterward. The variety of terms US officials used to describe the vast, amorphous area suggest the competition among its defining qualities: the Afro-Asian bloc, the Bandung Group, the Uncommitted or Neutralists or Non-Aligned, the Under- or Less-Developed Countries, the Emerging Nations, the Under-developed South. It is perhaps fitting that the father of containment, George F. Kennan, would be among the first US officials to use the term "third world" in this vein—tellingly, in a despatch from the 1961 NAM Conference—in US diplomatic correspondence.[10] By the time he did so, its meaning had been discussed on the international plane for half a decade in the new nations' own media outreach. Among its defining qualities were a stance of Cold War nonalignment; a need for economic development to overcome the poverty that imperial rule had left behind; and an often implicit, vaguely romantic sense of nonwhite solidarity. Since part of the mission of this book is to historicize this Third World as it emerged from the worldwide conversation of Cold War public diplomacy, this study seeks to avoid anachronistic usage of the term. For the sake of varying its prose, this book uses terms like "Global South" and "non-European world"—perhaps equally dicey—to denote what Sauvy had in mind.[11] But this is also intended to drive home the point that if American and Soviet public diplomacy had originally, and inadvertently, helped to engender and nurture the concept of the Third World, its philosophical evolution and its geographic expansion to include the western hemisphere were due not to Sauvy nor solely to the superpowers but to these areas' inhabitants themselves.

A main venue of this evolution was public diplomacy, though that term, unlike "Third World," is used anachronistically in this study. Although it can be found in diplomatic documents dating back to the eighteenth century, its modern coinage dates to 1965. It signifies the effort to shape foreign public opinion in ways that serve a national strategic interest. The term entails a variety of techniques and timeframes, from short-term mass-media print and audiovisual output around pivotal events, to longer-term, often smaller-scale outreach. Like Third World, the concept of public diplomacy evolved during these years, in keeping with the range of activities it entailed—none of which fit perfectly with its title and some of which remained in tension within it. Pre-1965 Washington documents refer to Information Operations or Activities, whose various dimensions are labeled Propaganda, Political or Psychological Warfare, and Cultural Diplomacy.[12]

The last of these included some of the best-known American outreach of the Cold War, such as the Fulbright Exchange program, the tours of "jazz ambassadors" like Louis Armstrong, and Richard Nixon's impromptu "kitchen debate" with Nikita Khrushchev at the 1959 American National Exhibition in Moscow. The kitchen debate highlights the sometime-subtle differences between public and cultural diplomacy, as it used "cultural" items to make an ideological point to a mass audience; in scholar Heonik Kwon's phrase, "material goods readily available in American society . . . were powerful rhetorical devices for selling American political ideals overseas."[13] Although "cultural diplomacy" is sometimes used as virtually a synonym of public diplomacy, it is more properly understood as a subset of it—under the latter's umbrella and more often oriented toward a generalized goodwill rather than winning a specific strategic or policy point. Cultural diplomacy on the whole uses different tools and timelines, deploys different and often more nuanced content via a "softer" approach, and has different impacts. As often as not, as historian Penny Von Eschen's *Satchmo Blows Up the World* shows, these do not make the point or produce the consequence that Washington intended. This inadvertence is also the case in the present study, which takes advantage of the outstanding scholarship on cultural outreach to focus instead on the USIA's crisis- and event-driven news "spin" and image management.[14]

The spectrum these labels suggest points to the identity crisis with which US public diplomacy struggled during its formative years. Its activities ran the gamut from skullduggery to marketing to journalism. They could be found across the various shades of propaganda: "black," or un- or falsely attributed disinformation often spread via covert operatives; "white," or verifiable journalistic information spread via public officials and sources; and "gray," or when in practice the lines and sources blurred. The tension therein was mostly resolved by the late 1950s, though it never fully disappeared. Moreover, for the first fifteen years of the Cold War, public diplomacy was kept at the margins of national security decision-making. Its practitioners were seen as salesmen not strategists, propagandists not policymakers. But even the skeptics agreed on a fundamental rationale for undertaking postwar public diplomacy. Given a world war that had entailed the mass mobilization of whole societies and a revolution in mass communications, the "publics" of the globe were bound to play henceforth a different, and larger, role in world affairs. As the American playwright and wartime propagandist Robert Sherwood put it in 1943, "we think today in terms of peoples rather than nations."[15] Outreach to them could not replace traditional diplomacy, but it constituted at the least a vital supplement to postwar statecraft.

Yet the skeptics had a point. A permanent problem so haunted the enterprise that one could reasonably doubt the wisdom of undertaking it at all. The permanent problem, put succinctly, was the gap between word and deed—between "spin" and policy. Persuading foreign audiences of American goodwill and goodness could be a difficult task if US policies or practices seemed to point in the opposite direction. Even when the gap could be finessed, a permanent question lingered: whether or not any such persuasion was taking place. Determining whether public diplomacy was achieving its objectives is no easier for historians looking back than it was for public diplomats at the time. What might be called the "hearts and minds, stomachs and eyeballs" problem vexed the USIA. It was easy to track the penetration of American consumer culture overseas, by counting Coca-Cola bottles and Hollywood movie tickets sold.[16] It was—and is—devilishly harder to detect a mind persuaded or a heart won over. As Murrow put it, "no cash register rings when a man changes his mind." It is telling, and ironic, that he was speaking at a time when the USIA's audience research operations were their most sophisticated to date. By the end of Murrow's tenure, USIA studies had grown both finer-grained and wider-scoped. Nonetheless, an incontrovertible answer to public diplomacy's permanent question—"Is it working?"—eluded analysts then as scholars now.

This study offers one answer to this ongoing question. It is less concerned with whether public diplomacy perceptibly helped or hurt US efforts to achieve strategic objectives in a given situation. It reconstructs the information campaigns in these case studies, recounts Washington's contemporary assessments of effectiveness, and offers some critical, tentative judgments in retrospect. But effectiveness is less its concern than the way in which US campaigns carried the Cold War into the Third World and, in doing so, helped to coalesce the latter entity. That coalescence can be traced in the explosive rise of public diplomacy by non-European actors themselves, offering an answer to the permanent question: Global South countries, mostly experiencing the superpower conflict as a media war for hearts and minds, joined that war as soon as circumstances allowed. Their actions speak as loud as they wished their words to. They made external media outreach a national priority even when they lacked the resources to address their pressing internal needs. This suggests that despite the lack of conclusive evidence that public diplomacy could produce tangible strategic results, these leaders—no less than those in Washington and Moscow—believed that it could. All parties, in other words, acted as if public diplomacy was both effective and important enough to pursue. This suggests that judgments of its success, whether contemporary or retrospective, are something of a chimera. All of the actors herein committed to the enterprise, believing it to be worthwhile even if evidence of success was wanting. The media explosion left a thronged arena for public diplomats of all stripes, and the global conversations in this raucous forum helped to midwife the postwar Third World project.

A number of smaller patterns and themes in US public diplomacy and in non-European responses to it helped to drive this major one. Across the first decade and a half of the Cold War, US public diplomacy underwent a set of important shifts. Some were concrete, others abstract, and all were more or less gradual. One was organizational: from chronic administrative chaos to relatively smooth-functioning order. A related shift was, for lack of a better term, philosophical: from public diplomacy being an afterthought in foreign policymaking to having a seat at the national security table. Another was operational: from improvisation to sophistication in both output and research. Still another was tonal: from bombast and propaganda to persuasion and, to the extent possible, evenhandedness. But the most important for the purposes of this study was geographical: from Europe to everywhere else. A number of patterns and practices mark the progress of these shifts, merging them at times in surprising ways. American public diplomacy in the non-European world was strongly and consistently pro-UN, for example. It emphasized historic American anticolonialism, the slow but gradual improvement of US race relations, American support for economic development, and steadfastness in the Cold War.

These could be a tough sell. Competing and proliferating media voices rebutted these themes with references to US alliances with European colonialists, to the bloody intransigence of Jim Crow, to the omnipresence of American business, and to the risk that steadfastness might lead to war. The USIA sought, where possible, to deploy "native voices" as proxies to address these issues and, to the extent that success could be divined, it often found such campaigns to be among the most effective. Its audiences encompassed both the proverbial masses and an array of targeted "niche" sectors in Global South societies. The niches were a subject of much greater USIA focus there than in Europe. This was in part because they tended to show more interest in racial and colonial issues—arguably the two greatest challenges that USIA faced in the Third World—than did mass audiences. But both tended to pay enough attention to these that they became the core of the Third World critique, further fleshed out by nonalignment and development, of the Global North fixation on the Cold War. If the physical creation of its own public diplomacy infrastructure provided the Global South with a medium through which to respond to the US treatment of these topics, the resulting discussion on those networks aided the philosophical coalescence of the messages embedded in the Third World project.

These themes emerge in the roughly chronological range of the case studies presented in this volume. The selected cases represent points of contact between USIA efforts to win hearts and minds, and the major currents of the Third World project. They represent, as well, the range of American approaches to navigating those currents. In some cases the USIA effort was massive and sustained; in others, such as in the proxy campaigns, episodic and understated. Though it might seem at first glance counterintuitive, the apparent inaction of the latter, behind-the-scenes, "hands-off" campaigns is itself revealing. What the USIA chose to cover, moreover, was as suggestive as how it covered them. Many episodes that in retrospect appear significant in the creation of the Third World project appeared much less so at the time and were underplayed or absent in USIA output. Others such as Bandung, whose significance was perceived at the time, received the proxy-campaign, "backstage" treatment. In either instance, the USIA left at least a partial opening to be filled by the media outreach of Global South actors. That outreach informed the choice of case studies herein, since these episodes featured several of the most important non-European actors to join the public diplomacy fray and thereby nurture the discursive maturation of the Third World.

Some of the elements central to the broader Third World project, such as apartheid or Vietnam, are noted here only in passing because their apogees came after the period studied concludes. Others, including Sputnik, that were key to the USIA's Cold War, are left out. This choice underlines the argument that such moments—despite the USIA's best efforts—often simply mattered less to non-European leaders than did Third World issues. One subject that did matter to them—the home-front violence of Jim Crow—is included as a case study despite not being "foreign," because the USIA correctly gauged it as having special resonance in the nonwhite world abroad. In all cases the text presumes a familiarity with the historical narrative and therefore offers only a minimal recap, focusing instead on the USIA outreach surrounding the event in question. The case study structure necessarily means that this book is neither longitudinal nor comprehensive in its treatment of what the USIA said to the non-European world during the Cold War. It is, rather, a curated selection meant to tease out larger meanings of what the United States sought to say— and what the Third World, as it took shape, said back.

The case study structure, finally, is intended to enable this study to connect with and contribute to several different areas of scholarly interest. Most obvious is the literature on US public diplomacy, in which Cull's excellent history occupies a central place. His study follows a different design; as he found after exhaustive digging, "a crisis-driven structure of public diplomacy . . . simply did not fit the archival record of the USIA."[17] The present book does not dispute the utility of this approach in understanding the history of the agency or

of public diplomacy writ large. But it contends that the crises and campaigns
herein connect dots revealing how the agency's efforts contributed to the evolution and American awareness of the Third World concept on the Cold War
landscape. This study shares Cull's purpose of putting public diplomacy on
the scholarly map alongside a raft of recent works doing so. While its structure
necessarily sacrifices depth for breadth, the choices are meant both to recover
the largely overlooked history of public diplomacy as a feature of American
Cold War strategy and to glean its role in the "creation story" of the Third
World project.[18]

This book also seeks to further the internationalization of postwar histo-
riography, as well as the "transnationalization" of the study of both the Cold
War and the Third World. It does so within certain limitations. The archival
sources and framework of this project limit its ability to do much more than
present Global South agency as seen from Washington. A fuller accounting of
its expression in Third World public diplomacy would require those nations'
archives, and hopefully future scholars will test this book's argument in them.
But these limitations do not foreclose the opportunity to advance a thesis
about the interaction of that Global South agency beyond its borders and with
its times—above all with the Cold War that did so much to define them and
that the Global North tried so insistently to introduce. It extends and refines
the thesis of historian Odd Arne Westad's magisterial *The Global Cold War* by
arguing for a different kind of Global North "intervention" in the formation of
the Third World. Cold War public diplomacy, because it was more commonly
experienced and practiced by Global South actors than was military intervention, offered an accessible medium for fleshing out the Third World project.
Moreover, it draws attention to the extent to which Global South actors saw
that project as part of the Cold War stakes denoted by historian Melvyn Leffler
(quoting Cold Warrior George H. W. Bush): a battle "for the soul of mankind."
It draws, furthermore, on scholarship regarding the key role of the international plane in the cultivation and leveraging of non-European nationalism,
and it complements work on the Global South debate on the definition and
direction of the Third World project by focusing on public diplomacy's role
therein. Finally, it affirms the importance of print-capitalism in facilitating the
rise of modern nationalism, since in like fashion the mass-media transnation-
alism of multiactor Cold War public diplomacy nurtured the imagined community of the Third World.[19]

The entity that emerged from that conversation ultimately dashed the hopes
of its avatars. Its very existence was nonetheless remarkable and of signal importance in understanding the dynamics of postwar history. Conceiving of
the Cold War as a multipolar conversation offers little comfort to its sufferers,
from Southeast Asia to Central America, for whom it was a bloody and tragic

affair. But it allows for the differing perspectives and priorities between South and North on the geopolitical, existential, and indeed philosophical stakes of the postwar period and acknowledges the active participation of both hemispheres in the discussion. As decolonization drew one new set of lines on the atlas, US and Soviet Cold War public diplomacy inadvertently spurred the process of drawing another. When the Global South responded to this battle for hearts and minds by joining their voices to it, they bridged the two processes and in a sense completed both. East and West had proposed competing visions for their new lives as independent nation-states, but these failed to accommodate the currents the South held most dear: nonalignment, economic development, anticolonialism, and antiracism. These coalesced in the multipolar, international battle for sympathy and solidarity to form Sauvy's Third World. But it would not be Sauvy who gave the term its fullest definition. Instead its inhabitants themselves did, finding enough common ground in the term to merge their regions upon it apart from East and West—forming an entity that redefined the Cold War in a quest to transcend it.

Absent at the Creation

The Truman Administration's Public Diplomacy Outside Europe

If I could control the medium of motion pictures, I would need nothing else in order to convert the entire world to Communism.
—attributed to Joseph Stalin in 1942 conversation
with Wendell Willkie

The decolonization of Asia, Africa, and the Caribbean constituted one of the great global challenges of the Cold War, and it posed a particular challenge to those members of the Truman administration whose charge it was to engage the public diplomacy front of that conflict. This was in part because all three constructs—the Cold War, public diplomacy, and the decolonizing non-European world—were themselves fluid and evolving in the immediate post-war years. The Truman years were in some respects the formative phase of these concepts, as well as of their infrastructural and technological dimensions. While the latter two, respectively, hampered the execution of US public diplomacy and refined the power of audiovisual mass media to drive mass politics, it was the conceptual evolution that arguably would be the more important legacy. The significance of these years lay not only in the maturation of an American "empire of ideas," but also in similar ideational evolutions in the actual empires of the day. At a minimum, the confluence created a new arena in which the Cold War could be fought. That enlarged geopolitical and communications arena, moreover, would increasingly encompass those tropical and subtropical areas outside Europe that were still ruled either from western capitals, or by western capital.

Less immediately certain, however, was the extent to which the March 1947 Truman Doctrine—perceiving a "totalitarian" challenge that was simultaneously material, ideological, and strategic—applied to these areas. Truman's rallying of American opinion to the Cold War fight led inevitably to the matter of proverbial hearts and minds at home and abroad. This, equally inevitably, led to the deeper question: *whose* hearts and minds? On the home front, the answer was straightforward: those of the American public.[1] Abroad, the first answer was "Europe's," but reflection took this further. The diagnosis on the continent, after all, was that poverty, deprivation, and suffering would lead those hearts and minds into the communist trap, which when snapped shut would endanger Western well-being. Similar suffering, compounded by the oppressive politics of colonial regimes, was widespread in the world outside Europe, which was presumably just as susceptible to the radicals' call. The ever-widening definition of "hearts and minds" led naturally if gradually to further questions: who are these non-Europeans, what if anything do they have in common, and how can they be reached and won over to the US side?

The Truman administration's public diplomacy among these populations with few exceptions started late, lacked coherence, and suffered from chronic bureaucratic turmoil. The end result—playing "catch-up," and not terribly well—actually redounded to US advantage, as Washington thereby stumbled into an effective minimalist stance during the early postwar years. Case studies in Latin America, South Asia, and the Korean regional theater, plus an overview of the Point Four program of US aid and development assistance, illuminate the lunging American grasp of a public diplomacy practiced essentially as a reactive measure, whose main opportunities were missed and whose main consequences were unintended. Each case accents a key aspect of early-stage US public diplomacy. Latin America had already been the site of such activities for a decade by the time the Cold War started and thus represented the default template for non-European areas. South Asia was the first area of the European empires to win its postwar independence, marking the beginning of the era of decolonization. Both of these episodes transpired during the first of four Truman-era reorganizations of US information operations—an ongoing structural chaos that helps in part to explain the haphazard US outreach to the two areas. Yet it is the rest of the explanation that points to their larger significance. Washington saw neither area as being connected to the other, nor much integrated into the nascent Cold War, notwithstanding the Truman Doctrine, which on its face drew them willy-nilly into it. But the Truman team's information outreach, surprisingly in retrospect, moved slowly at best and hardly much at all in this direction. The doctrine's logic brought these areas inside the fold, but its halting public diplomacy made no special effort to speak to them—until Point Four began to fuse them together on Washington's mental map, under the rubric "underdeveloped." The belated realization that other actors—above all the Euro-imperial powers and the Soviets—*were* addressing them prodded Washington and colonial nationalists alike to begin rethinking the geostrategic and intellectual space that was neither East nor West and to seek ways to reach out in hopes of winning it over.

Background and Backyard: US Public Diplomacy
in Early Cold War Latin America

World War II taught Washington the importance of what was usually called propaganda, or political or psychological warfare, which had been extensively used in theater military operations.[2] After the war, however, the dismantling of the machinery of US public diplomacy ratcheted down along with the broader American war effort. The institutional headquarters was in the Office of War Information (OWI), and its constituent parts the Voice of America (VOA) and the US Information Service (USIS), which had carried out the bulk of the OWI's overseas activities. A major bureaucratic reshuffling at war's end— the first of four during the Truman years, each under a different director— sent the USIS and VOA, along with some residual "overt-operations" functions of the OWI and the Office of Inter-American Affairs (OIAA), into the Interim International Information Service (IIIS). This in turn was folded into the Department of State, alongside its newly created Office of International Cultural Affairs and International Press and Publications Division. The covert-operations side was housed in the newborn CIA and charged with waging psychological war.[3] Starved for funding and unloved in their new quarters, the wartime entities' new position raised questions about their posthostilities mission and degraded what institutional memory still survived. The IIIS's greatest remaining asset was its head: Assistant Secretary of State for Public and Cultural Relations William Benton, former advertising executive and consultant to Nelson Rockefeller's Office of Inter-American Affairs. Benton was one of several key figures to have concluded during the war that public diplomacy needed to be central to postwar American foreign relations and that it needed to be conducted "comprehensively."[4]

As US–Soviet tensions rose and gave the Cold War a more visible shape in a series of 1946 crises, public diplomacy came back—partly due to Benton's constant prodding—to the Truman team's attention. The crisis in Greece and Turkey that precipitated the Truman Doctrine subtly underlined the "public" aspect of the emerging Cold War—or rather, suggested the role that publics might play in it. Senator Arthur Vandenberg famously captured this in his comment to Truman that the president would have to "scare the hell out of the American people." Support from the American public would obviously be necessary to undertake the conflict. But given the very rough sense of what victory in that conflict would look like, so too would foreign publics have to be won over.

As with the August 1941 Atlantic Charter it echoed, the ultimate writ of the Truman Doctrine was a matter of some uncertainty. In both cases, the main audiences were friends and foes in Europe. Hence the doctrine's support for "free peoples who are resisting attempted subjugation" meant those subjugated by the communism of its adversary rather than by the imperialism of its allies. But the main audience was not the only one. As nationalists across the Global South heard the doctrine, they posed uncomfortable questions to US representatives abroad. Forcing such clarifications made clear that even if the United States prioritized Europe in the Cold War, Europeans were not the only ones listening to American pronouncements—or for that matter to Soviet-sponsored propaganda, which was by all accounts already much more elaborate, expansive, and effective both within and outside Europe.[5] By comparison, from the Truman Doctrine through the first year of the Korean War, US public diplomacy proceeded haltingly, unevenly, and often unproductively or counterproductively outside Europe. The mechanical difficulties of executing effective public diplomacy at this early stage were compounded by conceptual difficulties, the uncertainties of the early Cold War, and the metamorphosing European empires.

The Truman administration thus came only slowly to realize the importance of public diplomacy in waging the nascent Cold War. The doctrine did make indirect reference to it; the second charge in its indictment of totalitarianism was "a controlled press and radio" that allowed the minority to subjugate the majority. But most of the administration's attention to the subject in 1947 focused on its shape and purpose in theaters of hot war and on the home front during hostilities.[6] Beyond this, what outreach the administration did actively undertake—Marshall Plan publicity, TROY, the expansion of VOA—added up to a slapdash, ad hoc public diplomacy. These also focused on Europe to the exclusion of the rest of the world. This made sense given the presumption of the Cold War as a conflict centered on that continent, but the logic of the doctrine, and the Cold War sparks it generated, ensured it would not be confined there.

Indeed, though the eastern Mediterranean was the Truman Doctrine's declared focus, the first formal installation of US Cold War national security doctrine was closer to home. Latin America was the first region to be drawn into the system of Cold War alliances and in some respects served as a model for those that followed.[7] Moreover, it offers an interesting test case for US public diplomacy, since it had been the target of Washington's first forays into cultural diplomacy during the 1930s. In historian Justin Hart's phrase, "the State Department clearly intended to use Latin America as the 'laboratory' for honing an approach that it would eventually deploy worldwide."[8] Its bicultural centers in Latin American cities were ostensibly nonpolitical entities whose mission was cultural outreach and exchange.[9] This was entirely and explicitly by design. As Ben Cherrington, head of State's Division of Cultural Relations put it, his shop must "not be allowed to become 'a diplomatic arm or a propaganda agency.'" As historian Frank Ninkovich notes, in keeping with State's view of "relations with its Southern neighbors as a problem in the dynamics of cultural lag," cultural outreach was the logical starting point and manifested Washington's desire "to point cultural relations in the direction of modernization"—something that would return to the forefront of US policy for Latin America during the Kennedy years, in the form of the Alliance for Progress.[10]

Yet their political subtext was easy enough to perceive, and World War II brought it fully to the surface. A large part of the United States' problem in Latin America since 1898 had been the image of the bullying, greedy Yankee. Cultural outreach was an essential companion to the Good Neighbor Policy, whose purpose was to repudiate both the fact and the image. After the fall of France made real the possibility of an Axis incursion into the hemisphere, the FDR administration created the OIAA under Rockefeller's leadership. Its remit included cultural diplomacy, on grounds that, as Rockefeller put it, "'intellectual imperialism, the imperialism of ideas, was at the moment just as serious a threat to the security and defense of the hemisphere as the possibility of a military invasion.'" His advisor Benton agreed and strongly advocated going beyond retail-level cultural diplomacy to incorporate mass media into a broader campaign to counter German influence in Latin America.[11] The mission had thus shifted—from the "soft" 1930s outreach highlighting US qualities and Good Neighbor sympathy under the banner of Pan-Americanism to a wartime mix of soft and "hard" campaigns aimed at the strategic containment of Germany.

At first glance, Latin America would appear to have been the ideal extra-European site to practice US public diplomacy. Even the timing seemed propitious, as the region swung away from dictatorship in a promising postwar moment of reform.[12] In places such as Guatemala reformist governments were theoretically open to partnership with a Good Neighbor Uncle Sam bringing a message of common interests. In the event, this was not the case. Even with physical and media networks—of sorts—in place, and even given the precedent of a mission that included both soft-sell cultural outreach and harder-sell undercutting of a geopolitical rival, US public diplomacy in Latin America was slow to act upon the Cold War that had been declared in the Truman Doctrine. Instead, it followed the traditional model of interstate affairs: as something executed between diplomats and largely leaving the mass public out of the equation, other than the literate strata of the population reading high-level diplomacy after the fact. Whatever Benton's vision of public diplomacy's role, the United States listlessly promoted the Cold War to its southern neighbors.

In their reports back home, US officials did pay close attention to Latin American press coverage of such geopolitical happenings—but what is striking was the degree to which American diplomats merely reported that coverage rather than influence it. The diplomats built relationships with select editors and reporters, but this was the extent of US efforts to shape Latin American public opinion beyond a generalized feel-good Good Neighbor sentiment. Cultural diplomacy predominated at the binational centers. In activities there, geopolitics was at best an afterthought left to embassy underlings. Washington's information activities in Latin America focused consistently on elites, which goes some way toward explaining the inattention to mass outreach regarding Cold War developments like the Truman Doctrine and the Rio and Bogotá Pacts. Ninkovich points out that before Rockefeller and the OIAA, US officials such as Richard Pattee were convinced of " 'the striking role of the intellectual minority in Hispanic American nations [which] is undoubtedly the point of departure for any contact with public opinion in the American Republics. It is too little recognized that public opinion as such is nonexistent outside the limited circle of the intellectuals.' " Even after the OIAA was founded, this stance remained the default: "Officers like Pattee questioned whether it was even possible to reach the [Latin American] masses directly. 'We are faced with the very difficult problem of ascertaining whether there is such a thing as an articulate, coherent mass of rural population in a given country.' "[13] This approach yielded some ground to mass outreach in Latin America during the 1950s, but it never disappeared. In the 1960s it returned with added vigor there and in rest of Global South in an expanded form of niche-targeting that aimed at narrow but influential tranches of opinion.

Embassy reports about the impact of the Truman Doctrine in Latin America concentrated on its reception in print media, with officials showing no discernible efforts at shaping or spinning it. The day before Truman's speech, the US ambassador in Uruguay gave a sense of the local landscape. A weekly publication ran a series quite "out of character," warning that a new phase of "American colonialism and imperialism" was likely at hand, thus marking the end of the Good Neighbor as Truman consolidated postwar gains.[14] Yet a survey of embassy reports after the speech revealed less such concern. Indeed, several despatches said that the Truman Doctrine and the unprompted coverage of it in the hemisphere galvanized a Latin American anticommunism and sharpened a sensitivity to communist propaganda. The US Ambassador to Chile wrote Truman that the doctrine "has enormously increased your popularity [as] the press here has played up your speeches and actions." Another despatch pointed out a Brazilian editorial arguing that, the Cold War having been declared, the Americas should line up on the right side by calling a conference to showcase the "common accord" of hemispheric peoples.[15] Despite the lack of any discernible US efforts to reach the Latin American masses on these issues, elite reactions like this lent momentum to US plans for just the sort of hemispheric conference that the Brazilian editors had called for.

The September 1947 Rio Conference produced the first of the major Cold War alliances, the Rio Pact, which united the hemisphere in ostensible anti-communist solidarity. In terms of public diplomacy, it followed the Truman Doctrine pattern by remaining an elite-level conversation conducted across the Americas among diplomats and journalists.[16] That conversation quick-ened as the conference approached. Washington did pay some attention to the choreography of the conference, with an eye to opinion in Latin America and beyond. One official foresaw that Rio "would of course be a superb op-portunity to dramatize the solidarity of [the] hemisphere." Another sug-gested finessing the itinerary of Truman's upcoming South American tour to "emphasize the cooperative angle [and] avoid the impression among Latinos of monopolising [sic] the show." Neither comment suggests that the masses were the target audience. As the conference approached, the Latin American press split roughly into two factions: one critical of it on either ideological and particularist-nationalistic grounds, and one supportive in the name of Cold War and hemispheric solidarity.[17]

US officials kept close tabs on both. The first appeared to be winning a PR battle that the United States was hardly fighting.[18] Aside from conversations with editors, American diplomats did little to press the case for Rio to Latin American publics even as the conference was underway. In contrast, the com-munist side often "personalized" their propaganda. Brazilian military officers, for example, discovered planted in their barracks pamphlets blasting the Rio Pact and exhorting Brazilian soldiers to resist it. The "campaign of informa-tion against the American invaders" was hyperbolic—but it was, compared to the elite-focused US approach, more tailored and sophisticated in its reach.[19] These qualities did not add up to communist success in altering Brazilian policy. To the contrary, insofar as US diplomats could discern, such bombast may have hardened the Latin American regimes' anticommunist resolve. But the difference between American and communist approaches to public diplomacy was nonetheless clear. To borrow a military metaphor, the United States was using occasional "dumb bombs"—headlines broadly dropped on the newspaper-reading, decision-making swath of the population. Meanwhile, the communists used the press in addition to "smart bombs" targeted at key members of select audiences by, for example, literally leaving messages on their pillowcases. The steps involved in the latter operation bespeak its sophis-tication. Identifying such target audiences as the officer corps—individuals at the core of domestic power in Latin America—and discreetly getting word to them under the noses of barracks guards suggest the communists' greater forethought and execution at this stage. If activities of this kind, whether targeting niche- or mass sentiment, did not ultimately sway Latin Americans to the communist side—if indeed, they backfired—they nonetheless made US activities look amateur in comparison.

American diplomats reported this to Foggy Bottom, but did little to change their practices in the months between Rio and the founding of the Organization of American States at Bogotá, Colombia, in March 1948. Riots outside the proceedings offered yet another instance of what US officials called "communist and subversive provocation" in stirring up trouble—and in giving inadvertent advantage to the US side.[20] The most charitable reading of this public diplomacy passivity was that it was a deliberate strategy of "rope-a-dope"—that it would backfire and evoke among the Latin American masses deep revulsion against the radicals. While there was some evidence of such revulsion, nothing suggests it was the fruit of deliberate US public diplomacy strategy.[21]

US success in this regard is perhaps best seen as a happy accident. It was, indeed, less American success than communist failure, as the latter's overreaching happened to produce a result favorable to Washington. To the extent that both sides defined "success" as the pulling of Latin American regimes to one pole or the other, the United States had the easier task, requiring the mere inertia of retaining the elites' generally pro-American status quo. Blithe optimism about the US performance could become detached from growing anti-Yankee sentiment concomitant with a gradual rise in the regional popularity of communism as Latin Americans sought to define their place in the emerging Cold War order. That rise looked to continue, moreover, within and beyond the hemisphere when Stalin, six months after the Truman Doctrine and two months after Rio, activated the Cominform. As Hart writes, this worried Foggy Bottom that communist propaganda would neutralize the monies spent on the Truman Doctrine and the Marshall Plan; afterward, "both Congress and the White House started to take information policy much more seriously."[22] The "happy accident" got some of Truman's public diplomats rethinking the Cold War in Latin America around the Rio and Bogotá meetings. They began gleaning a deeper interpretation: the PR war was real. It would have to be fought if the Truman Doctrine was to be upheld—and it was one the United States was losing in its very backyard.

First Wave: Messaging the Decolonization of South Asia

Halfway around the globe, events in 1947 would reinforce this same conclusion. South Asia was not the first colonial area to proclaim its independence in the wake of World War II, but it was by far the largest, richest, and most populated—and among the first to be achieved in peaceful collaboration, rather than violent confrontation, with the metropole. The wartime protestations of the likes of Winston Churchill notwithstanding, most parties from Delhi to London to Washington saw South Asian independence to be virtually inevitable, though its precise course was uncertain. The subcontinent encompassed a dizzying array of confessional, ethnic, and linguistic divisions, peace among which had been maintained by the British Raj, but the dividing lines obeyed no particular geographic logic. By early 1947 British withdrawal was certain, and independence thus imminent. But how peaceful the transition to independence and its aftermath would ultimately be and what cartographic shape it would take were matters of deep confusion and deeper concern.

The Roosevelt administration had pressed Britain to grant independence to India during the war and the United States continued to support that process in the region, although this was not how it often appeared to South Asians on the ground.[23] The process, as seen through American eyes, was not without its worries. Violence and turmoil might bode ill for decolonization processes envisioned elsewhere. The "partition" solution endorsed in June 1947 by both the viceroy Lord Mountbatten and the Indian National Congress sought to head off such a tragedy, with what would prove to be a notable lack of success. Perhaps most important, the Indian leadership, especially Jawaharlal Nehru, was little loved in Washington. Most US officials saw Nehru as effete, diffident, and unreliable, even absent the possibility that his political affiliations made him a Trojan horse for communism.[24] They recognized that significant global attention was focused on South Asia as decolonization approached, even if by and large the superpowers' attention was not.[25] That global interest made it a test case of the US Cold War doctrine still taking shape, and at least an implicit challenge to the limitations of the Truman Doctrine. The doctrine's declaration that the United States would "support free peoples who are resisting attempted subjugation by armed minorities or by outside pressures," did not *ipso facto* include Indians—but it would presumably do so if those Indians, once independent, fell under a communist regime.

Even before the doctrine, some Truman administration officials grasped the importance of winning over Indian public opinion as independence drew near, figuring that if nothing else this would help to check Nehru's less-desired tendencies.[26] Previous outreach had been unevenly effective in reaching its main targets among the Indian leadership. US officials had frequently had trouble placing items in Indian newspapers since much USIS output was "not particularly adapted to Indian interests," although library programming had proven valuable given "the political situation, with all its historical implications, [which] has focused attention of the Indian political leaders on American history," especially the Founding and the Civil War, which many

Indian leaders saw as analogous to their struggles regarding independence and partition.[27] US public diplomats in India offered to help reach that mass audience on behalf of both US and Indian interests. American statements of support for Indian independence sought to do just that.[28]

Yet two things stand out, and not only for their resemblance to the patterns in Latin America. As in Latin America, US efforts were limited to print media and to a far lesser extent radio—and in both media, US activity was less robust than that sponsored by the Soviets. Partly as a result, State analysts reported that the Indian press was "probably the most anti-American in the world outside the East bloc"—which meant that little of the lethargic US information program was being republished in local print media.[29] While some of this anti-American bent was due to the Soviet cultivation of Indian journalists, it also stemmed from Indian suspicion of the United States as the ally of the British and to disgust over its Jim Crow practices.[30] These efforts sparked a local debate about the ultimate aims of American policy, as they did in Latin America. US consular officials reported that even among Indians inclined to be sympathetic, concerns about American designs ran deep: "Now that [we are] the world's leading power, certain sections of the Indian press have transferred their professional bitterness toward Britain to the U.S. . . . Releases dealing primarily with American democracy in the abstract will [thus] be treated with suspicion by large numbers of Indian editors."[31]

This was true beyond press circles. Many members of the Indian leadership questioned the American approach to the Cold War and its implications for India. In language certain to resonate in a country on the cusp of decolonization, one Indian commentator decried the Truman Doctrine as "dollar imperialism out to colonise as much of the world as it can." The brother-in-law of Pandit Nehru told the US information officer at Bombay that "the tombstone of the United Nations [will read] 'Here lies UN, Killed March 12th by Harry Truman.'"[32] Indian fear that the doctrine would kill the institution in its infancy, or would provide a cover for imperialism of a new but no less powerful kind, was genuine. But the Truman Doctrine elided something even more basic. It proposed to stand with "subjugated peoples against totalitarian (communist) domination," while managing to sound obtuse and noncommittal regarding peoples subjugated by imperialist domination. It thus drew the world map along East–West lines, but was vague about the North–South split that was at least as much on the minds of colonial nationalists. The latter, after reflection, began redrawing the map themselves, in ways that would reject the Truman Doctrine and the Cold War, and assert instead the unity of those southern latitudes that both had left behind.

In India itself, an event dedicated to such "redrawing"—the often-overlooked Asian Relations Conference of April 1947—seems to have escaped

the attention of US information personnel on-site. While Nehru's neutralism was much more salient in the view of the Truman team—and indeed
in Nehru's as well, for whom it was the basis of a truly independent foreign
policy—the end of "white" rule over the "brown" subcontinent was nonetheless accompanied by overtones vaguely echoing America's own uncomfortable
racial realities. The Asian Relations Conference suggested that South Asian
independence would have an unavoidably racial tinge to it. At the conference
this even seemed to overshadow neutralism, which was more implicit than explicit, especially compared with the "racial" identity grounded in the glories
of a shared Asian civilization and foregrounded in Gandhi's repeated use of
the term "coolie" in his remarks at the meeting. In the aftermath of the conference, as scholar Itty Abraham shows, participants began to transcend the
inherited imperial legacy of thinking in "racial logics" of "Asian civilization"
and to emphasize the centrality of neutralism-nonalignment in Indian diplomacy. Race, accordingly, moved largely to the margins of Nehru's rhetorics
of neutralism, both toward the wider world and toward India's peers in the
first wave of decolonization. But it could never stray too far from the center of
American relations with the nonwhite world, whose interest in and antipathy
for Jim Crow could only rise. This was especially the case in India, even more
so than with parts of Africa at this point, given the budding mutual affinity
between the leaders of the Indian civil disobedience and African American
civil rights movements.[33]

This intellectual landscape helps to explain why US public diplomacy surrounding the arrival of independence was so understated. Aside from pro-
forma statements of support channeled through local press elites, the US team
concluded that its interests at the climactic moment were best served by a
public diplomacy determined to "first, do no harm." This was not an unreasonable conclusion, but it ceded the field to the communists who had thus far
been waging the PR fight far more actively and comprehensively. Moreover,
after the transfer of power, US officials in New Delhi and Foggy Bottom began
to wonder if their stance had in fact been the worst of both worlds: neither
winning over Indian opinion, nor pulling off the anticolonialist "good-guy"
role. At a minimum, officials pondered whether Indian independence had
been a missed public diplomacy opportunity. While Indian officials thanked
Washington for what in retrospect was quite understated support—and began
wrestling with their own public image problems, stemming from the partition
violence—US diplomats wondered what if any goodwill that approach had
achieved, especially given that by year's end some voices had begun to blame
the United States for that violence.[34]

On closer inspection, it becomes clear why the limited US forays in public
diplomacy in Latin America and the colonial world were always an uphill

battle. No matter what American officials said about particular cases of de-colonization or about nonwhite peoples generally, communist propaganda ensured that US shortcomings—especially related to racial matters—were always at least equally prominent. In India, for example, the State Department found that among the "Stereotyped Conceptions of the US" were "unfavor-able [ones] which find some acceptance [through] Soviet-inspired propaganda [which] portrays the US as an imperialist partner of Britain and a country that practices racial discrimination."[35] Though US civil rights activism had not yet coalesced into a high-profile movement, instances of racial terror were common enough that Soviet public diplomats never wanted for material. As historian Mary Dudziak puts it, this was well-known enough in the Truman administration that it felt obliged to begin paying increased attention to civil rights in large measure because "other countries [were] paying attention to domestic American racism."[36] Nor was this attention confined to decoloniz-ing peoples abroad, nor strictly one-way. The concurrent cresting of African decolonization and civil rights activism in the next decade would bring the issue to its apogee before world publics. But at this early stage, the problems it posed to US public diplomats were becoming ever more clear and would aid them in being among the first American Cold Warriors to remove their "Cold War lenses."[37]

In the wake of the Holocaust and a race-tinted war in the Pacific, sensibili-ties about such matters were raw. The lynching of black veterans in Monroe, Georgia might have been little remarked on in earlier decades. In 1946 it was noticed around the globe. It became a *cause célèbre,* along with such embar-rassments as the continued segregation of the American capital. By 1950, the Truman administration would submit an *amicus curae* brief on behalf of the NAACP's *Brown v. Board of Education* lawsuit because of the national "image problems" that racism was causing in the global Cold War contest for allegiance. Were there no communist propagandists, well-earned bad press of this kind would still have deeply stained the American image abroad. But such operatives, both in the main battleground of Europe and the emerging battlegrounds of Europe's empires, worked assiduously to ensure such stories reached the widest possible audience.

In this way, public discourse about racial and other issues relating to the decolonizing world helped to show the Truman administration the impor-tance of the worldwide PR battle. Subsequent administrations would gradu-ally be persuaded of the greater importance of these issues than Cold War ones to the peoples of the Global South. However, as evidenced in late-1940s South Asia and Latin America, persuading the masses of American good faith via *public* diplomacy was practically an afterthought to the tra-ditional, private kind. As a consequence of the sharpening hindsight about this approach, 1948 saw formal American public diplomacy first begin to take shape on a more global scale. This conceptual evolution would soon find expression in a legislative milestone. In the view of Truman's National Security Council, this effort was primarily reactive in nature. But its importance would grow over time, as the administration concluded that the months since the Truman Doctrine had marked the arrival of "psychological warfare" worldwide.[38] The terminology reflected the hardening Cold War mindset, revealing that Washington was beginning to see not only the conflict's scope widening beyond Europe, but also its rising stakes and the need for new means to win them.

This analysis animated the debate about the US Information and Educational Exchange (Smith-Mundt) Act, which Congress passed in January 1948, authorizing funds to disseminate abroad "information about the United States, its peoples, and policies."[39] The act wrote the charter for the overseas information and cultural activities that collectively constituted US public diplomacy. It thus reorganized the ad hoc arrangements Benton had inherited from the war or created since and further articulated their Cold War mission.[40] While that machinery would undergo two more iterations before Truman left office, and a third, more lasting one with the 1953 founding of the USIA, it would henceforth rest on a base of variable but mostly dependable Congressional support. For proponents like Benton, that support had arrived just in time.

Mere weeks after India's independence, Benton had resigned his post, and the East bloc launched the Cominform. If, as Nicholas Cull writes, "'containment' [had] provided a clear logic to retain and expand U.S. information" activities, and thus was instrumental in securing the passage of Smith-Mundt, the contemporaneous Cominform launch underscored the importance of the information front.[41] But the two sides did not trace that front across the world map in exactly the same way. Nor did other powers such as the United Kingdom, which notwithstanding its near-bankruptcy maintained an overseas-information service three times the size of the USIS. In the view of public diplomats gearing up to sell the Marshall Plan in Europe in late 1947, their mission still focused overwhelmingly on East and West.[42] This was the communists' priority as well—but by this point the Soviets had also been propagandizing for more than two years as far afield as the Middle East, Brazil, and French Africa. Although Washington would soon designate certain areas outside Europe, including South Asia, a "danger zone" in terms of overall American strategy and hence in terms of public diplomacy, these were still seen as ultimately peripheral.[43]

Winning Hearts By Teaching Hands? Point Four and the Maps of the Underdeveloped World

The small footprint and afterthought nature of US public diplomacy in Latin America and South Asia reflected Washington's Europe-first focus. But implications drawn at European front lines influenced American thinking about the superpower standoff worldwide. Above all were worries that, given the right conditions, the standoff might spread even absent Soviet military expansionism. Chief among such conditions was the deprivation that had wracked Europe since the war. But if poverty under European flags on the continent was something new, poverty under European flags in the empires was a longstanding problem, indeed practically a way of life. This was a preoccupation of Global South intellectuals like Raúl Prebisch, whose 1949 paper "The Economic Development of Latin America and Its Principal Problems" fueled conversations as it circulated widely among imperialized peoples.[44] If the communists could prey upon the poor amid the rubble of Europe, they might be able to do the same elsewhere. In this way, the problem of poverty linked far-flung regions to each other and to the Cold War.

It pointed, moreover, to the psychological dimension of the conflict. Poverty ground away the morale of vulnerable populations. The Truman Doctrine and Marshall Plan addressed the problem in Europe, but its geographical and psychological limitations were obvious and could turn these assets into liabilities. Latin Americans wondered where their equivalent aid was, and colonial peoples looked askance at Washington's bolstering of the metropoles. As the evidence mounted that the Soviets had stepped up their propaganda war, the Truman team feared that even if the United States matched their media efforts, the limitations of its message might prove too much to overcome in underdeveloped areas outside Europe.

The solution was the Point Four program, which would deploy economic and technical assistance to underdeveloped areas in what was, not counting the Marshall Plan, to date the largest US government "foreign aid" program in history. It would showcase Western expertise, generosity, and partnership in the economic development—the not-yet-coined "modernization"—of impoverished parts of the world. The program would flesh out long-term American Cold War strategy beyond its military and nuclear aspects. By naming poverty as a strategic concern, it expanded the Cold War map across the globe in ways the Truman Doctrine had only hinted at.

The initiative thus played an underappreciated role in the conceptual coalescence of a proto-Third World defined above all by its shared underdevelopment.[45] As might be expected given its origins—its outlines would be first sketched by a veteran public diplomat—Point Four also influenced the evolution of US Cold War public diplomacy, though in unexpected ways. Like its descendants, the Peace Corps and the Alliance for Progress, Point Four would seem inseparable from its public image dimension. Unlike them, however, outreach was at first quite understated, because its resources were focused on instruction rather than persuasion. The latter took time to gel. When it did, in combination with the Korean War, it began the reorientation of the medium, message, and targets of US public diplomacy decisively away from Europe, or rather added new territory to the strategic map.

As of late 1947, US public diplomacy had achieved uneven penetration and limited depth outside Europe. In November, State officials circulated the administration's proposed "US Information Policy Statement," which recommended responding aggressively to the Soviet propaganda onslaught. The western hemisphere desk noted that the proposal, like current practice, was "particularly tailored to meet conditions in Europe." In Latin America, as the Truman Doctrine–Rio Pact episode showed, this was by design: "For us to 'flavor' the news for this area with too piquant a sauce will . . . be self-defeating." But this left public diplomats grasping for ways to counteract the Soviets' charges "without descending [to] distortion and invective."[46] Those charges were multiplying. In the Middle East, popular interest in news about the expanding American role, which Washington "does not supply . . . will be supplied by others who remain ready, willing, and able." Above all this meant Radio Moscow's Arabic-language programming, "a frequent source of articles [for] the Arabic press," and one that rarely passed "without an attack on American policy and motives [such as] the concept of American 'dollar imperialism.'" Meanwhile, in the Far East, the US public diplomacy presence was more extensive—eighteen posts in six countries, compared to sixteen in all of the Middle East, Africa, and South Asia—but in locations such as Saigon, its challenge was less about answering communist propaganda than it was overcoming "rigid censorship by the French colonial government."[47]

More worrisome for US officials was the absence of an overarching positive message—and the prospect that the communist propaganda surge drowned what was being conveyed. In places such as India and Iran, where American news agencies were few on the ground, field reports affirmed that US public diplomacy was just barely holding the line, by running interference with local journalists. This usually was a defensive move against Soviet charges excoriating all things American while exalting Moscow as the "bulwark of true Democracy and the true champion of the interests and independence of small nations." At other sites, such as French North Africa, British, French, and Arab media reinforced the US image as essentially greedy and self-interested: "News of the [political] advance of others causes the North Africans to feel somewhat impatient at their comparatively stagnant status [and their] disappointment with the UK and the USA [is] in proportion to what they do not do in that direction."[48]

The absence of a positive message to counter these unfavorable currents prompted American official Benjamin Hardy to sketch the Point Four concept. Drawing inspiration from his earlier stint as an OIAA Press Officer in Brazil, Hardy recounted that "in fall 1948 I began to wonder what new move the US could make in the 'cold war' which would enable us to capitalize on the advantage gained [from] the Marshall Plan [and] make further gains in winning world opinion to our side." Hardy conceived what he called a "democratic manifesto" that would, in a sense, expand the Marshall Plan outside Europe. Interestingly, he "had not thought of singling out the underdeveloped areas as the exclusive focus of the program," though he felt these held promise too.[49] Lamenting the US approach to the Cold War as too "negative," Hardy urged that a new initiative be announced in Truman's inaugural address. Noting that parts of the policy infrastructure were already in place, Hardy argued for their use in "a dramatic, large-scale program that would capture the imagination of peoples of other countries and harness their enthusiasm for social and economic improvement to the democratic campaign to repulse communism." This "would require skillful planning and a spirited, effective information program," but it had the potential "to convince the common people of the world that we are on their side."[50]

Hardy's idea found favor as it circulated through Washington channels. Foggy Bottom supported it on grounds of its Brazil rather than its Marshall roots: "[It] would be wholly consistent with [our] attitude [toward] the problem of economic development in underdeveloped countries. [Its] value . . . in promoting economic and social progress and in generating goodwill among common people toward the U.S. has been amply demonstrated." The projection of the New Deal abroad further burnished its appeal. Truman later reflected that it embodied the belief in the "power of government [to foster economic progress.] It was important to say in effect that, the New Deal having just been ratified at home, the United States was willing to help other peoples achieve their own New Deals."[51]

Observers made the same connection. In a reelected Democratic administration, this could only strengthen its charm. This, too, harmonized with Hardy's concept of a democratic manifesto. Making the case that the New Deal was the prized fruit of democratic solidarity, an early draft of the Inaugural held that "we are experiencing one of the rare mass movements of history, in which people all over the earth are stirred by a common impulse. The people of virtually all countries, of all races and tongues, by common consent are determined to better their conditions of life." At a meeting with Truman *consigliere* Clark Clifford, Hardy wove these themes into an outline of the proposed program. Clifford came away persuaded that it was "just the thing."[52]

Truman agreed. He made Point Four the climax of his inaugural address's quartet of "major courses of action . . . for peace and freedom" in positive opposition to communism.[53] Unlike the Truman Doctrine which had named "communists" just once (and only in connection to Greece), this speech repeatedly named its nemesis in making the case for the superiority of the US formula for democracy and development, and the need to apply it on behalf of the "more than half the people of the world . . . living in conditions approaching misery [whose] poverty is a handicap and a threat to them and to more prosperous areas." However, like the Truman Doctrine, the speech referred to the importance of media in the global contest, recognizing "all who want relief from the lies of propaganda." It also disavowed its European cousins: "The old imperialism—exploitation for foreign profit—has no place in our plans."

Anecdotal evidence found that the proposed program had struck a chord. A roundup of US press comment included "[voices which] praised its [positive] 'propaganda value' in the Cold War."[54] The State Department found the overall verdict positive but mixed:

> This is understandable, since the address on the one hand in effect declared ideological war by frankly [stating] for the first time . . . that communism is bad per se, and on the other hand laid heavy stress upon the U.S. desire for peace and a constructive program for social and economic improvement abroad . . . The Address . . . properly understood, will go a long way toward accomplishing the objective of winning wide popular support.[55]

The Policy Unit went on to recommend that "media and information officers abroad [should] conduct a sustained and consistent effort to show in ways most convincing to the mass audience that each of the major [American] policies and undertakings is a peace-building project in itself."

Before such convincing could begin, a number of practical and philosophical issues required attention. Most important, there was as yet no actual Point Four program or even legislation—only Truman's rhetoric, whose reverberations would surely weaken over time absent policy action. The audiences for that rhetoric also had to be identified, so that they could be reached once a policy was in place. Finally, that message had to be tuned to broader US strategy without giving the impression that US aid would be conditioned upon loyalty to Washington.[56] The main immediate audiences were domestic elites, above all Congress, and foreign masses and elites alike. Selling Point Four required a pitch that would be anticommunist enough for the former without being too Cold War for the latter. The home front was in some respects the more important audience at this early stage, but the foreign audience could never be forgotten.[57]

The nature, contours, and full scope of that overseas audience were still fuzzy. Poverty was its primary trait, but a geographical concentration outside Europe was a close second. In his message supporting the Point Four legislation, Truman acknowledged the eagerness "of Africa, the Near and Far East, and [parts] of Central and South America . . . to play a greater part in the community of nations" but whose "grinding poverty and lack of economic opportunity" held them back. This "constitute[d] one of the greatest challenges of the world today."[58] Congress agreed and passed the legislation.

Despite Truman's sketch of the geographic parameters, its conceptual borders remained fluid. A 1950 Public Affairs Institute pamphlet "Helping People Help Themselves," for example, listed Nova Scotia alongside India and Jamaica as underdeveloped candidates for Point Four. The pamphlet did, however, note the anticolonial nationalism in the latter places and the ways it could affect aid programs: "Rising or resurgent nationalism will play no small role in a program of development. . . . In the colonial empires of East and West Africa nationalistic movements are growing with vigor."[59] This sentiment distinguished decolonizing hard-poverty tropical areas from the likes of Nova Scotia, but was still blurry. Assistant Secretary of State George McGhee in the *Department of State Bulletin*, informally instructing personnel worldwide, listed the "underdeveloped areas" as including Greece and Turkey, along with "Iran, the Arab states and Israel, Afghanistan, Ceylon, Burma, South Asia, and most of the African continent," though not Latin America. A December 1949 world map published in Point Four public diplomacy materials identified three groupings: the "developed, intermediate, and underdeveloped" worlds.[60]

Point Four's principal target was the peoples in the underdeveloped world, which included both sovereign countries and "dependent areas," that is, colonies of Europe. How to engage them was a delicate question, as the administration went about articulating the mission and assembling the machinery of Point Four. US officials noted that communist attacks on the initiative peaked after the inaugural address and again when its legislation passed, charging that since the "metropolitan powers 'are doing nothing' to assist dependent areas," the United States was pursuing its own "imperialistic designs on these areas." Other voices, communist and nationalist, "charge[d] that we are simply backing up the imperialist powers."[61] Nor could Washington answer by again pushing the anti-imperial theme, since this perturbed European allies.

Partly for this reason, the highest-profile Point Four activity would occur in independent nations, even though colonial areas were "the most underdeveloped parts of the world."[62] US public diplomats planned to spread word of Point Four's achievements in the former in hopes of winning admiration in the latter, since "the broad objectives of Point Four . . . are the same for dependent areas and independent states." Output would emphasize American cooperation with international organs like the UN and with "peoples" themselves, in view of "the importance of publicity emphasizing the program as one designed primarily to benefit the people of underdeveloped areas," ultimately including dependencies.[63] The importance of Point Four publicity went well beyond the underdeveloped areas directly served. Truman assistant David Lloyd anticipated that before long "we ought to have a couple of outstanding examples of resource development in underdeveloped countries which are directly attributable to Point Four. The value of such pieces as to the practical and propaganda aspects of the Cold War would be tremendous." His colleague Philander Claxton concurred that such favorable opinion would positively influence foreign "reactions to the character of total American foreign policy."[64]

While there was broad consensus on the importance of the public dimension, some continued to argue for the primacy of the domestic audience. As the legislation was being drafted, the State Public Affairs Office (PA) had jealously guarded its claims of authorship of the Point Four idea, pointing to PA's "very extensive information program" on its behalf. But PA's principal writ was stateside opinion, and even as it boasted of home front output, the office lamented the difficulty in matching this overseas, in part due to the nature of the "underdeveloped" audience abroad. A January 1950 Point Four booklet—published by PA for English-speaking audiences—described its "geographic scope" as "most of Latin America, Africa, and Asia including the Middle East [which] should be considered underdeveloped areas." A speech by Truman aide Walter Salant named that same grouping as being "of vital importance," though implicitly distinct from "the U.S. and Free World as a whole." Tellingly, Salant also signaled the role of Western media in raising their inhabitants' consciousness of their underdevelopment and their expectations for overcoming it.[65] Media overseas would necessarily play a major role in the Point Four initiative addressing this.

As Point Four moved toward implementation, the administration held high hopes for its publicity potential. Acheson wrote Truman that "the worldwide response to [Point Four] has been a significant feature of a notable year in international affairs. . . . [It has] captured men's minds and raised their spirits in the midst of postwar discouragement." Hayes noted that it was "our best answer to . . . in the words of Nehru . . . 'the apathy of despair' and the 'destructive rage of the revolutionary.' Point Four offers to the neglected peoples of the earth a tangible hope for the future."[66] In March, the Senate affirmed the need to "initiate and vigorously prosecute a greatly expanded program of information and education among all peoples of the world," since communist propaganda "cannot be beaten back by arms and money alone." This echoed Acheson's statement that month to the Senate Foreign Relations Committee: "Democracy is on trial for its life . . . including [in] those areas of the world we call 'underdeveloped.' These areas include parts of Latin America, Africa, the Middle East, and the Far East, where two-thirds of the world's people live, many of them in the shadow of hunger, poverty, and disease."[67]

Point Four would form the core of the effort to win them over against the communist gambit for their allegiance. Over the course of 1950, the Truman administration sought to realize this potential, embedding Point Four within the "Campaign of Truth" that Truman announced in April. But a number of new obstacles arose, even as older ones persisted. The "expectations gap" between the Inaugural rhetoric and what Point Four could quickly and reasonably accomplish meant that the program might "give way to disillusionment and even resentment."[68] The European-dependent areas also continued to vex. Though many of the highest-visibility projects would be in independent states such as Ethiopia and India, others went to colonies via the Marshall Plan's Economic Cooperation Administration and thus via the metropoles, limiting the United States' ability to engage colonial peoples directly. State officials lamented that the "psychological, emotional, [and] spiritual atmospheres and conditions" produced by "'colonial status'" in these areas "quicken[ed] distrust. In North Africa Arabs are saying, 'the Europeans get all the tractors. What does any Arab get?'" Suspicions of this kind lent credence to the steady barrage of Soviet charges that Point Four was either a bankroll for continued European imperialism or a mask for the American version.[69]

A further complication lay in the turf war between the USIE and the Technical Cooperation Administration (TCA) over the content of Point Four media products. Whereas public diplomats aimed to win hearts and minds, TCA sought to teach brains and train hands. Hence it favored instructional and educational materials—"public understanding"—over the inspirational messages and exhortatory uplift—"public persuasion"—that USIE wanted. The split reflected a fundamental difference of mission between the agencies, which would go unresolved for almost a year.[70] In certain cases, disseminating know-how instead of propaganda allowed American officials to circumvent host-state restrictions on the latter. In Iran, where both the populace—"a hatred of foreigners, especially Westerners, is the dominant political fact [here]" –and the regime were hostile, an inspector reported in late 1951 that "because of prohibitions on propaganda, our information man, Wells, has resorted to almost pure point IV-type [*sic*] work using all of his media . . . for educational [and technical] materials . . . Wells [says] this is the only sound informational approach. People just aren't interested in how virtuous the

U.S. is and how heinous the Russians." Even out in the field, the turf war continued: "Strangely [TCA and USIS] had not come to an agreement for point IV to draw on USIS facilities though Wells is anxious so to serve."[71] One consequence, USIE reported, was that "in one village [so close to the] USSR–Iran border that Russian troops could see that a film show was in progress . . . two hundred [villagers] attended the showing" of such films as *How Disease Travels* and *Kill the Louse.*[72]

A focus on such minute things as lice could make it difficult to connect Point Four aid to bigger Cold War themes. Yet Washington held fast to the conviction that Point Four reinforced the natural American advantage in the psychological Cold War: it served, for some at State, as evidence that the American creed was in sincere harmony with the foreign masses' desire for "progress in a responsible, orderly, peaceful fashion." In August Truman's National Security Council (NSC) affirmed that Point Four, "an important political and psychological measure," was "an integral part of U.S. long-range foreign policy as well as a valuable support for current national security objectives."[73] State reaffirmed that its presentation abroad, though, had to refrain "from looking like a demand for appreciation of American largesse" and instead to emphasize "a sense of participation" among the peoples concerned. This reflected the USIE's central themes of cooperation and partnership, as did its consistent foregrounding of the UN and its emphasis on community self-help.[74] In practice, then, much of the Point Four outreach left the connection to the ideological struggle implicit. Unlike much Campaign of Truth output, which erred on the side of bombast, the message of Point Four in the psychological Cold War was left understated.

Although its audience-research tools were less sophisticated than they would be a decade hence, what US public diplomats could glean suggested that Point Four's embedded themes were reaching, if not quite swaying, foreign audiences. Testimonials from individuals, as well as rebuttals in communist propaganda and real-world reactions, were taken as evidence that "USIE is reaching the masses . . . intelligently and effectively."[75] As always, reach was easier to measure than effectiveness, and almost certainly exceeded it as public diplomats sent Point Four media deep into Global South towns and countrysides. In Latin America, film trucks took Point Four into the far reaches of Paraguay, while TCA Director Dr. Henry Bennett toured the continent, the Institute of Inter-American Affairs arranging for extensive radio and print media coverage.[76] The penetration was deep enough to prompt communist propaganda responses, such as the article in Costa Rica accusing Point Four of being a plot to extract natural resources. It was broad enough that a Salvadoran newspaper described feeling invaded by "army of técnicos on the march." However, to the extent that Latin American approval of Point Four was detectably on the rise, the State Department's intelligence bureau (INR) found that it was more so in elite circles where "response . . . has been generally favorable, but in only a few instances enthusiastic. Public response has most often been apathetic."[77]

Elsewhere, opinion split less between sectors than within them. Ambivalence characterized much elite and mass sentiment alike. US public diplomacy had first sought to persuade South Asian public opinion that Point Four's deeds, though slow in coming, would eventually match its words.[78] But the gap persisted. A Bombay weekly lamented that " 'Point Four was a message of cheer and hope to the forgotten man. As months rolled by, it became apparent that the common man was over-optimistic." This, in turn, fed the perception that the program's idealistic facade was just a snake-oil sales-pitch that would entrap India in the Cold War.[79] In sub-Saharan Africa, what mass opinion analysts could detect was scant but favorable—aside from communists, some "tribal" nationalists, and French residents, who were the most resistant. In the Middle East, public reception varied by country but on the whole followed a trajectory similar to South Asia. A campaign of Arabic-language print material, along with contacts between US officials and members of the Egyptian government and press, had helped to make the atmosphere "favorable." However, INR found that "while public interest remained relatively slight, there was a substantial current of opinion, which, while welcoming . . . aid, remained suspicious and resented having Egypt described as 'underdeveloped.' "[80]

This pointed to the conceptual and operational delicacy of selling Point Four: its raison d'être was underdevelopment, but the problem had to be addressed in ways that didn't offend its putative beneficiaries. The Rockefeller Committee Report found that nationalist pride meant that not only peoples but also "governments, which have only recently emerged from colonial subjection, still are suspicious and even resentful of outside aid." Such predilections were spread unevenly across a wide and diverse swath. The study counted one billion souls in the underdeveloped world, making it more populous than "either the United States or the Soviet Union, and which has all the regions: Latin America, Africa, the Middle East, South Asia, Southeast Asia, and Oceania."[81] But nationalism pulsed through its newly sovereign corners as well as its long-independent ones. Washington's principal public diplomacy tactic was, in effect, to ride it—endorsing it explicitly or subtly, and stressing the cooperative aspect of US aid policy.

For example, the Point Four Information Committee recommended that the independence of Libya in 1951 be used in media output as "an excellent peg for the Department to [publicize] its policy toward Africa and the national aspirations of African peoples." The International Information Administration's (IIA) Committee on Content told public diplomats to convey US "comradeship" with Asians against communism—"a new imperialism [that is] threatening Asia."[82] These messages were reinforced across various media. The story of Dr. Albion Patterson's collaborations with Paraguayan farmers, for example, appeared in both English- and Spanish-language output in 1951.[83] The US embassy in Cairo emphasized that "Point Four agreements and achievements in other countries are also continually publicized in order to create a more favorable climate toward Point Four in Egypt." The next year, USIE produced the educational-poster series "'Point Four in Action' . . . stress[ing its] cooperative aspects [and] showing typical projects in Africa, the Middle East, and Latin America."[84]

As the Truman years ended, reception in the field was still difficult to gauge with any precision, though actors on both sides proceeded as if their campaigns were both important and effective. A *New York Herald Tribune* reporter traveling in the Mideast noted the region-wide media duel: "Wherever Point Four operates, the good words for it are matched and sometimes outmatched by the mudslinging it receives."[85] There, as in South Asia and Latin America, nationalist and communist propaganda counterattacked. Paraguayans who happened to see Dr. Patterson's story, for example, might have subsequently seen the pamphlet titled "The Imposition of Truman's Plan of War of Point 4" rebutting it.[86] US public diplomats felt they had the upper hand in many places. In India, for example, the intense cultivation of press contacts and a new, popular, PR-savvy ambassador helped to drive positive coverage and placement of USIS materials in local media. In Ethiopia, an enthusiastic host government prodded the press to cover Point Four approvingly and extensively. In Lebanon, the use of town-hall meetings and print-rhetoric presenting Washington's preferred themes got a warm local response.[87] Ultimately, though, the impact on hearts and minds was uncertain. As the *Herald Tribune* reporter put it: "In the absence of quick and concrete results, the importance [of aid] is often unappreciated. . . . Nobody can doubt that Point Four is bringing some good to a lot of people, but . . . its net effects in terms of changing Arab public opinion toward the U.S. . . . for the better is a question that cannot positively be answered."[88]

More certain and more significant was the impact of the Point Four campaign upon the borders of the underdeveloped zone on Washington's mental atlas. In a speech to the April 1952 National Conference on International Economic and Social Development, Acheson noted the overlay between the "technological revolution" that underdeveloped countries sought to join and the "revolutionary ferment of nationalism. As a result of the turbulence [of] these two powerful forces, there is no longer a question as to whether or not there will be profound changes in these under-developed parts of the world. That question is settled."[89] The speech updated American progress in fulfilling Truman's Inaugural. Acheson again distanced Washington from European imperialism, obliquely blaming it for underdevelopment. But he acknowledged that the "revolutionary ferment" was more than reactionary anticolonialism. It was also a response—nationalist if not strictly "anticolonial"—to poverty, and it transcended all manner of geographic, ethnolinguistic, ideological, and other divisions. An early draft alluded to "the peoples of the underdeveloped areas of the world—in Asia, in Africa and the Middle East, in Latin America . . . stirring and awakening after centuries of . . . subjection to outside domination." State objected to language which "strongly criticized old colonial practices" on grounds that it would encourage "extreme nationalists" and offend allies, and the terms were watered down.[90] But the lands in question were not. The conference left American officials "delighted," as Truman aide George Elsey exulted that US "public information officers [would] have enough to chew on for months."[91]

Nor was the administration alone in naming underdevelopment a pressing concern, an ideologically tinged contest, and an organizing principle of geopolitics. The *Economist* in 1953 acknowledged the imperfections of the label but the reality of the grouping and the stakes:

> There is practically universal agreement that the "backward" or "underdeveloped" countries of the world (no one has discovered a really satisfactory alternative to these invidious and question-begging epithets) need to be helped along the path of economic progress much faster . . . [Their] increasing awareness of Western standards is politically explosive and would be so even were Communism entirely uninterested in exploiting it.[92]

The growing consensus at all four points of the compass that underdevelopment was a bond fed naturally into the sense of a contest for its loyalties as rival prescriptions for development were beamed southward. But it also raised the possibility that the new grouping—perhaps spurred by the contest—might decide otherwise for itself.

War in Korea had sharpened the urgency of Point Four. If Korea confirmed the militarized prophecies of NSC-68, it also led the Truman administration to redouble Point Four—not least because the war announced in bloody fashion that the Cold War had leached out far from Europe and turned hot in the bargain, making socioeconomic progress on the periphery all the more vital. As Truman put it in September 1950, three months into the fighting in Korea:

> Communist propaganda holds that the free nations are incapable of providing a decent standard of living for underdeveloped areas . . .

Point Four will be one of our principle ways of demonstrating the complete falsity of that charge ... [Korean] aggression ... has underlined the importance of the Point Four concept ... There is a direct relationship between strengthening underdeveloped areas and strengthening the free peoples of the entire world.[93]

But new independents like India and Indonesia drew a different lesson. The war spurred them to refine neutralism into something held in common, as yet indeterminate, and to stand upon it to assert a role in settling the conflict. The notion of a "Third Force" first came to prominence during Korean War diplomacy in September 1950, thanks to the two Asian independents. US observers found it a recurring tendency in their later diplomacy.[94] The combination of underdevelopment, independence, and the Cold War could thus harden the impoverished world against not one but both poles. It made the malady of underdevelopment, and its Point Four cure, all the more important for the afflicted collective that both were helping to bring into being.

The gestation was a slow one, and not only in the Global South. In the early years of the Cold War, the recurrence of crisis around the periphery defined most broadly—from Greece to South Asia to South America—had sufficed to stir only the peripheries of American strategy. In a sense, missed opportunities there underlined retrospectively the importance of public diplomacy. Washington initially did little to change its First-World-first habit regarding both message and audience, even as postwar public diplomacy conceptualization and infrastructure continued to grow by fits and starts and to expand further after Smith-Mundt in 1948. Crises in Europe—the main theater and highest priority of US strategy—eclipsed the lands outside it. From spring 1947 until summer 1949, episodes and crises outside the continent were secondary, not just in the sense of lesser importance but of positive subordination. The transfer of power in India and the guerilla war in Malaya, for example, weighed much more heavily on Washington for their impact on British power than for their import as harbingers of race-inflected nationalism, shifts in the regional strategic balance, an awakening of the world's have-nots, or of decolonization per se.

However, the logic of the Truman Doctrine and Cold War-charged events outside of Europe pulled American attention there. Slowly and unevenly, US public diplomacy followed. Not until 1950 would US officials term parts of the Cold War periphery a "danger zone": impoverished areas of strategic importance whose loyalty and stability were unsure. Even after the designation was applied, such areas remained a secondary focus of American strategy until the outbreak of the Korean War. This helps to explain what is striking in retrospect: the opportunities Washington missed to make the West's case at this early stage. In large measure, the notion of a Cold War threat to the sprawling "Afro-Arab-Asian world" foundered on the fact that the concept was itself still inchoate until underdevelopment began to give it definition—and even then, the machinery through which Washington might address it was a work-in-progress.

The regional cases of Latin America and South Asia show how that geopolitical concept, and the public diplomacy methods and messages addressed to it, began taking shape between the Truman Doctrine and the Korean War. Latin America was the site of the earliest US outreach outside Europe, while South Asia was the earliest postwar area to leave European rule—and both, to borrow Sherlock Holmes's phrase, were dogs that did not bark. The containment doctrine implied the two areas' import in the Cold War conflict and suggested that for all their evident differences they had at least this in common. Yet Washington was slow to convey this to the masses in either place. It only began to do so once underdevelopment connected them to the conflict—and to each other—amid intense competition in the information arena. The Truman team had been quick to identify the threat of the "monolith" but slow to act on it among non-European hearts and minds.[95] The result was that Washington fell into a minimalist approach to public diplomacy, which perhaps ironically proved more effective than aggressive outreach might have done. This stance would soon be abandoned in the hot war in Korea. But it left legacies regarding institutional setup, modes of strategic public relations, and intellectual frameworks for treating decolonization and its transnational chaperones, race and poverty, in the new arena in which the Cold War could be fought—and into which the conflict's own logic would inexorably lead it.

| 2 |

Hearts and Minds on New Frontlines

The Public Diplomacy of the Korean War in Asia

> Aggression has to be met, for it endangers peace. At the same time, the lesson of the past two world wars has to be remembered and it seems to me astonishing that, in spite of that lesson, we go the same way. The very processses of marshaling the world into two hostile camps precipitates the conflict that it had sought to avoid.
> —Jawaharlal Nehru, Columbia University, October 1949

By 1950, Washington had become convinced of the need to join the battle for hearts and minds. As part of the shift in American strategy that produced NSC-68 that winter, the Truman team committed to a Campaign of Truth that sought to regain the PR initiative by coherently and aggressively pressing the American case, and improving American standing, in foreign eyes. While the Truman administration can be faulted for not thinking ambitiously enough about the importance and means of carrying the campaign to non-European audiences, this was an understandable failing—and only a partial one, given the extra-European targets of Point Four. But over the eighteen months after the Point Four announcement, much of Washington still saw many such audiences as being essentially outside the Cold War. Moreover, beyond this outsider status, they had little enough else obviously in common besides poverty and the shared experience of European rule. Notwithstanding the administration's "globalizing" rhetoric of the conflict, the Cold War threat to these areas was medium- to long-term and more or less abstract at that. Even if the organizational chaos of Truman-era public diplomacy machinery had not hindered outreach to the Global South, the conceptual muddle of this vast amorphous area and its distance from the communist menace discouraged any such large-scale effort.

The Korean War changed the abstract threat into a concrete one. Following on the heels of Mao's triumph in China, Kim Il-Sung's invasion left no doubt that the Cold War could spill over into areas far from the European heartland and into decolonizing areas such as the Korean peninsula. While the most pressing threat was military, the war also brought a difficult test on the information front. Hart notes that "the crises in China and Korea precipitated a complete overhaul of U.S. information policy [as] the explosion of revolutionary nationalism in Asia posed a fundamental challenge to the content, if not the form, of U.S. public diplomacy, [confronting officials with] the toll that years of Europe-first policies had exacted on America's image in the non-Western world."[1] With the exception of the Office of War Information (OWI) at its wartime height, the volume, diversity, and audiences of public diplomacy in the regional Korean war zone were novel in US information experience. In one sense it offered a chance to put the Campaign of Truth into action. But in addition to illustrating such overarching themes were more immediate concerns—above all that the need to gain hearts and minds on the Korean ground had to be closely integrated with military operations. Simultaneously, beyond the peninsula Washington sought to use the war to showcase the American commitment to Asian allies, and especially to the United Nations, against the threat that the now-militarized Cold War might spread further.

American officials were not the only ones to notice this threat. The role played by Global South actors in both the formal and the public diplomacy of the Korean War helped to make the conflict a watershed in the competition for hearts and minds. Three months into the fighting, Indonesian Foreign Minister Mohammad Hatta called for a "third way" in the Cold War, one that would build on the neutralist stance his country shared with India and that both believed could inoculate Asia from further violence better than US or UN arms or alliances could. Nehru agreed, seeing in the conflict a chance for neutralism to prove its mettle before sympathetic audiences near and far. He agreed as well with Washington on the importance of the United Nations in solving the conflict, although they differed on the centrality of "Arab-Asian" audiences' role in this solution. For both the Truman administration and Global South nationalists alike, the Korean War connected a number of dots, whose traces suggested that such a grouping might be starting to take shape. As the site where the Cold War first turned into large-scale hot combat, Korea put a premium on public diplomacy both in and around the war zone. The trials and errors of the Truman years, born of the need to battle the communists for hearts and minds previously disregarded, bequeathed both the machinery of public diplomacy to its successor and, more importantly, the second draft of a new geopolitical entity in the Global South at which that machinery could be targeted. Just as the containment doctrine had created the European locus of a geographical zone known as the "Free World," the Korean War revealed the need to coordinate US public diplomacy in the diverse parts of the non-European world then being slowly brought together in the Washington mind as the soon-to-be-named Third World. It was a construct that peoples there would before long embrace, embellish, and repossess.

A Marshall Plan of Ideas: The Campaign of Truth, NSC-68, and Hot War in Korea

The unambiguous entry of the Cold War into an area far outside Europe re-oriented American thinking about the scope and nature of the superpower conflict. The communist takeover of China in late 1949, along with Soviet acquisition of the atomic bomb and the launch of McCarthy's crusade, prompted Washington to undertake a major shift in US Cold War strategy. In response to the one-two-three punch of communist menace in Eurasia and on the home front, the Truman administration spent the early months of 1950 drafting NSC-68. The document envisioned an apocalyptic clash of ideology and strength, and it called for more muscular measures than the previous version of containment. Instead, it prescribed active confrontation in what had become a "total" conflict. In April Truman approved NSC-68, sketching the American posture for an ominous new phase of Cold War geopolitics.[2]

Among its overarching conclusions, NSC-68 made more explicit the re-definition of the Cold War as a test of offensive strength rather than a matter of semidefensive siege. It went much further than the Truman Doctrine both in terms of its geographic reach outside Europe, especially into Asia, and its psychological dimension there and elsewhere. Consequently, the machinery of US public diplomacy was again retooled for the enlarged mission. NSC-68 found that the Soviets held a significant advantage on this front. In order to counter it, the team drafting NSC-68 expected to ask for $155 million to be earmarked for "foreign propaganda."[3] Even this, they feared, might be insufficient to match the national communist parties' talent for "propaganda, subversion, and espionage" and to counter the success of the Kremlin's message: "Its peace campaigns and its championing of colonial peoples . . . in the free world these ideas find favorable responses in vulnerable segments of society. They have found a particularly receptive audience in Asia." By comparison, NSC-68 suggested that US Cold War public diplomacy had thus far suffered from the lack of a coherent and unified narrative regarding the values of American society.[4]

Truman sought to address this in his April 20, 1950 announcement of the Campaign of Truth. The campaign would reach both domestic and foreign audiences, and it would represent a systematic rebuttal to the continuing on-slaught of communist propaganda.[5] It would, in particular, counter commu-nist lies about American intentions and avow the superiority of free societies to audiences in critical areas fighting to establish or protect such societies. In one sense it marked the return of Benton's influence to the information arena, since in his first speech as a new Senator on March 22, 1950, he had called for a "Marshall Plan of Ideas," which became the basis of the campaign.[6] It would, in a way, be the public face of the still-secret NSC-68 strategy. In ad-dition to its cameo appearances at home, the campaign was set to become the focus of short-term US output abroad in short order. It led to, among other things, the overshadowing of some longer-term and "softer" forms of outreach, notably much of Washington's cultural-diplomacy programming. As scholar-practitioner Richard Arndt observes, "the Campaign of Truth had four goals: create a healthy international community and unite it behind U.S. lead-ership; present the U.S. fairly and counter lies; stress America's peaceful inten-tions as well as its preparedness for war; and reduce Soviet influence. Culture or education did not appear in [this] program."[7]

The campaign's timing was particularly interesting regarding the non-European world. Like NSC-68, the campaign became the "battle plan" during an actual shooting war partly as an accident of its timing. When fighting broke out in Korea on June 25, 1950, it seemed to vindicate the vision of the Cold War that NSC-68 had laid out mere months before—and for Truman, it seemed as well to vindicate his doctrine, as he described Korea as "the Greece of the Far East."[8] In a similar fashion, the campaign held that an aggressive psychological and information strategy would be key to overall victory in the Cold War con-flict, including in its "hot zones" wherever they might appear. The President's Advisory Committee on Information found that Korea showed that Truman's call for the campaign was "even truer now than when you gave utterance to it, because of the aggression in Korea [which] has made it all the more im-perative that we intensify our effort." The chair of the Advisory Committee on Educational Exchange concurred: "Korea serve[s] as a tragic illustration of why the Campaign of Truth should be put into effect immediately." While as historian David Krugler shows, the invasion "overshadowed plans to imple-ment the Campaign," it also "invigorated" such public diplomacy arms as the VOA "with new purpose," accelerating the expansion and experimentation in American output.[9]

Korea thus presented the first real testing ground of the revamped American strategy—including public diplomacy—in the Cold War outside Europe. The nearly constant state of crisis in-theater during the first year of the war made improvisation important to public diplomacy and led to the revival of old, and in some cases the invention of new, forms of outreach. Precisely because part of the rationale for going to war in Korea was its "demonstrator" or "showcase" effect, which would prove American reliability around the region and indeed the world, the use of Korea in US public diplomacy offers an index of how the Truman administration saw the relationship between that outreach and over-all US strategy in the heat of crisis. Finally, the challenge was acute given not only the relentlessness of communist public diplomacy but also its apparent success; by most accounts, in part by virtue of their head start, the communists were winning the PR war in Asia.[10] By the war's first anniversary, the admin-istration had experimented with more and different public diplomacy tech-niques on the ground in Asia, as well as drawing lessons for organizing such efforts back in Washington.

On the eve of the Korean War US public information efforts in East Asia, beyond a scattering of Fulbright affiliates around the region, consisted of VOA and intermittent print-centric outreach. VOA was finding a sizable au-dience but having an uneven effect; in the words of one assessment its "anti-communist propaganda [was] overdone," and marked by too much "triviality in picturing local US conditions." Complementary experiments—such as mailing USIE materials in plain wrappers to private individuals in main-land China—were underway and looked promising.[11] But there as elsewhere around the Asian littoral, the lack of consistent, centralized messaging across media from Washington left US efforts at best somewhere short of coherence and at worst virtually inapplicable to local conditions. In the Philippines, for example, a lack of trained personnel, the tendency of popular media like film and radio to operate out of sync with less accessible text media, and the failure to work within local idioms and priorities undercut US success. In September 1950, the International Information Administration (IIA) would establish one of its three Regional Service Centers (RSC) in Manila. Before the RSC came online, US print output in Asia was limited and rarely timely due to lack of any local production facilities.[12]

For US public diplomats, Kim's invasion of the south provided a vivid il-lustration for the campaign and prompted its accelerated deployment to areas—including Korea—which had been designated as crucial to its success-ful execution. The importance of the public sphere to the outbreak of war was noted at the time. A month before the June 25 invasion, US Ambassador John Muccio had pleaded with Secretary of State Dean Acheson that USIS cover-age of American security commitments not omit Korea: "These omissions are always noted here in Korea, and they add to the sensitivity and fear of the Korean government and Korean citizens" and could encourage belligerence from across the 38th parallel. Acheson himself had authored the most famous such omission in his January 1950 speech excluding Korea from America's "defense perimeter." The State Department sought to preempt the regional damage the speech might do, carefully editing the tape before its VOA broad-cast in the Far East—Krugler notes that journalist Eric Sevareid "complained 'it was the most remarkable effort to protect a public official from himself that Washington [had] seen in years'"—but the subsequent invasion proved Muccio correct.[13] It also showed American officials that it was not always possible—nor, they concluded, necessary—to link particular instances like Acheson's speech or a given battlefield engagement to the overarching cam-paign. Much of the US public diplomacy in-theater was run by the military as an adjunct to war operations.[14] Much of the rest in Korea itself, and all of its offshoots deployed around the Asian littoral, was run by diplomatic public affairs personnel on-site. Both arms made use where possible of the campaign and gleaned instructive experiences about public diplomacy's place in overall American strategy.

Within Korea, the war prompted a response of American outreach to both North and South Korean military personnel and civilians alike. On the day of Kim's invasion, the IIA later reflected, "USIE-Korea was a far-flung orga-nization with experienced local personnel and equipment necessary for con-ducting a hard-hitting information and educational exchange program. By the third day of the war a large part of American personnel had been evacuated to Japan." Most soon returned to undertake an altered mission: "field opera-tions . . . modified to emphasize war and morale news" from mobile and rear-echelon facilities. This mission could be the difference in the battle zone, as "when the enemy was less than five miles from Taegu [and] a misinterpreted military directive resulted in a ROK order to [evacuate] all civilians . . . [the] USIE was a lone, if loud, voice exhorting the people to stay. USIE promptly succeeded in stemming the panic, and Taegu remained the second-largest functioning city in Korea."[15]

The Pentagon requested that information activities in-theater be integrated into military command in hopes of sustaining the morale of civilians caught in the fire zone. This was by necessity, given the absence of military public out-reach resources: "In the first few months of war, before these [Army Psywar] units were established in Korea, USIE provided the shock troops, and later the cadre, in the 'hot' information effort." But the blurring and shifting lines of combat meant frequent overlap of audience and message—and consequent bureaucratic skirmishes.[16] Most military-run public diplomacy had as its goal the demoralizing of North Korean troops and the bolstering of South Korean troops and civilians. The VOA, balloons, pamphlet-drops, and comic books were the main media used—cheap to produce and easy to "piggyback" onto military operations. These complemented the routine dissemination of "USIE news [via] radio, [mobile] public address sets, printed or mimeographed hand-outs, leaflets, bulletin-boards, and motion pictures . . . throughout the critical summer of 1950, when rumor and panic were the chief USIE targets." This performance, impressive given the circumstances, in both its military and civilian guises in the months between Kim's invasion and the September counterattack at Inchon, did not sugarcoat the dire prospects of those months.[17]

This is not to say that US public diplomats, both military and civilian, did not "spin" for effect. Three weeks into the war, the VOA, for example, broadcast the sunny assessment that "the military situation had gone 'exactly according to historical precedent'—that the aggressor always wins the first battles but 'inevitably loses the last battle.'"[18] A July 1951 study compared VOA English-language broadcasts in the Far East before and after Kim's invasion. It found that in the latter period, programming "became more hard-hitting and outspoken [and] made more frequent allusions to the conflict between the democratic and communist worlds ... [with] more partisan and less factual material than before [the war started]." Preinvasion broadcasts in both English and Cantonese were "persuasive and dramatic" in tone, an approach "replaced by the condemnatory which was applied to communist aggression and tyranny" once the combat had been joined. However, even the bombast was intermittently tempered by larger strategic concerns. Foggy Bottom instructed VOA to refrain from "explicitly associating the USSR with responsibility for the invasion" in the week after it, and even over the next month opted not to directly charge Moscow, instead "using a variety of thinly coded phrases and news items to blame the Soviets" indirectly.[19]

In hindsight, two things are most striking about the public diplomacy of the first three months of the war. First, the need to practice it in an actual theater of combat and address it to both military and civilian audiences demonstrated that Washington's instincts were basically correct about the importance of public diplomacy at times of crisis. The first NSC foray into the subject had been to game-plan psychological and information operations for a war zone and for a war-footing at home.[20] Experience in the first months of pell-mell crisis in Korea seemed to confirm the essential correctness of integrating public outreach with military missions in real time. However, the Korean crucible also demonstrated that effective public diplomacy required its own, dedicated mechanism for the civilian sector before and after—not just during—hostilities. Unfortunately for the United States, at the moment the war had broken out that mechanism had been disorganized at best, and the months of constant crisis leading up to Inchon offered little opportunity to reorganize it.

The second aspect, which extends beyond the Inchon landing, is the way in which the war was treated in public diplomacy around the region. A survey of the guidance documents and correspondence between Washington, Korea, and US outposts in East Asia provides a sense of the themes, messages, targets, and spin applied to US coverage of the crisis. Given that part of the original rationale for the strong American response had been to present the region and the world an example of American resolve and UN unity, the actual treatment of the Korean message as US fortunes ebbed and flowed is instructive.

Early outreach around the northern Pacific littoral presented the war as a showpiece of the American commitment to Asia and especially to the United Nations. Indeed, a plan to use internationally known American actor Jimmy Stewart in a pro-war PR campaign was scrapped because "this would not [have] enough of a UN flavor."[21] Multilateralism had from day one been the center-piece of US outreach. Within three weeks of the invasion, USIE had produced a newsreel titled "United Nations Aids the Republic of Korea" and screened it in more than twenty languages worldwide.[22] Like the Jimmy Stewart plan, the original cut of the film found too much US and not enough UN for inter-nal critics: the visuals "overwhelm[ed] the viewer with the feeling that this *is* primarily a U.S. action. Physically it is, but psychologically the participation of other countries . . . should be given much greater emphasis [as this] would have greatly strengthened the propaganda emphasis. . . . I feel very strongly that this picture will fail to do the job adequately [in, e.g.] India and Burma." The revised final cut set an agency standard for the "positive type of output . . . most effective in winning support for U.S. and UN policies in Near Eastern, South Asian, and African countries," far more so than "atrocity" films that public diplomats doubted "would have any pronounced effects upon Nehru and his colleagues with the ideas of orienting India toward the West."[23]

Supplemental guidance from Foggy Bottom to Far Eastern posts kept the UN theme central, while connecting it in locally tailored coverage to US actions in Formosa, Indochina, and the Philippines. In Formosa, public diplomats were told to emphasize "that by this impartial act [of military re-sponse the] US is creating situation of peace in Far East and is neutralizing a sterile conflict which is draining strength of China." For Indochina and the Philippines, emphasis was put on how US actions extended "existing US policy to raise shield protecting peace, freedom, and orderly progress of na-tions and peoples involved." This emphasis guided USIS-Manila's dissemina-tion of a record amount of newspaper column inches, stepped-up production of booklets and pamphlets in English and Tagalog, the rebroadcast of speeches by Truman and the US Ambassador, and the "heavy use of cartoons."[24]

But the message could be a tough sell. US public diplomats in Indochina and around the region conveyed the disheartening local reactions to the war's out-break and underlined the difficulty of the task they faced.[25] Not least of their problems was that the United Nations was losing on the battlefield. Events were outrunning any attempt at damage control. The State Department informed its public diplomats that it would depart from the prewar pattern of weekly message-dissemination—instead directing its guidance ad hoc to capitalize on opportunities and minimize damage where possible—and stressed the need to follow the given plan of action. This included the need for factual reporting of hard news, for putting defeats in perspective, and for propping up Korean morale. Perhaps more telling, Foggy Bottom stressed the need to obscure any extra-Korean involvement that might emerge, and to emphasize Nehru's recent statement on the importance to the non-European world that the UN succeed in resolving the crisis.[26] In other words, US public diplomacy sought to minimize the strategic dimension of the crisis by avoiding drawing in other hostile powers and simultaneously to maximize the longer-term advantage of being on the right side of the non-European world in the conflict. The latter's sensitivities were much in mind on both sides of the Cold War, as shown in the choice of terms of approbation, with each side accusing the other of "imperialism" and "colonialism" in Korea and elsewhere.[27]

Two of the principal themes animating US public diplomacy in the first months of the Korean conflict—peace and multilateralism—were above all reactions to communist media campaigns. A third—American unity in support of the war effort—was just as heavily stressed, though it was less a response to communist charges. The Soviets had launched a campaign they called the "peace offensive," which connected to some longer-standing Soviet tropes. As with the Campaign of Truth, the Korean War provided a media opportunity for the superpowers each to claim its side had basically been right all along. Truman sought to counter the peace offensive and to sound the chosen American themes in a speech about the Korean situation.[28] On the ground in Asia, however, American public diplomats perceived that however they used such outreach, their success in the region was dependent on events on the battlefield: "For general world use we should emphasize we are still trading space for time. Indications tide turning in our favor [are] still premature." USIS and consular officials in Asia were directed to stress Korean popular support and allied-Asian government support for UN efforts, along with other regional stories such as the anniversary of Indonesian independence and the expansion of VOA operations in Indochina. Even if the themes resonated to varying degrees in Taipei, Manila, or Saigon, military success was thus far elusive, undercutting them. Nor could the Soviet adjuncts to the peace offensive—continued attacks on "Yankee racism and imperialism"—be ignored. The fear that racism was America's "Achilles' Heel," as Truman had put it, haunted the administration as the United States waged war against a nonwhite enemy.[29]

The six weeks surrounding the September 15 Inchon landing saw a mood swing of sorts among US public diplomats. Describing what it called a "critical stage," the State Department on August 17 lamented the status quo and the lack of spinnable news. The best that could be done, officials concluded, was to hold to broader abstractions they hoped would resonate, to stress atrocities and civilian suffering at the hands of the communists, and to avoid giving the impression of a turning tide so as not to raise unmeetable expectations. Indeed, a deeper fear seemed to be taking root in the Truman administration: that Korea was merely a microcosm of looming defeat in the larger war for hearts and minds.[30] The success at Inchon and after suggested that perhaps conditions had changed. As news from Korea got better, though, US public diplomats on the whole remained restrained, especially concerning possible regional analogies: "Do not," field personnel were instructed, "repeat NOT draw comparisons [between Indochina] and the Korean situation." American officials in the region feared that the Vietminh might spin US success in defending the "independence" of Asian people to their advantage in their struggle against Paris and its puppet Bao Dai regime. By the end of the month, events were generating cautious optimism. This was reflected in the continued emphasis on such items as allied-Asian contributions to post-Inchon success, a message disseminated especially through the expanded distribution of comic books and cartoon posters.[31]

The Truman administration was determined to press the information offensive, and it raised the volume on two aspects of its message to the non-European world. US information personnel were instructed to give heavy play to Truman's restatement of US interests in Korea as a means of rebutting charges of American imperialism in Asia. US support for anticolonialism and reconstruction there, "with particular emphasis on the collective character of the program," was the first aspect. The second was renewed attack on "imperialism" in language attuned to Asian ears, using a trope that US public diplomats would continue to deploy for the next decade: "Soviet imperialism really [is the] new colonialism." In addition, stronger emphasis was placed on tailoring broad themes communicated from Washington to local conditions assessed by personnel in the field.[32] As northward-advancing US/UN forces succeeded on the battlefield, US public diplomats sensed and pressed their advantage. In addition to the battlefield momentum, they finally had the mechanical abilities to do so too. The RSC in Manila was now operating at full speed, producing printed materials for quick distribution around the region, in order to, in the words of one field report, "stimulate [Asian] nationalism and at the same time attack Soviet imperialism [via this] sort of [a] visual VOA."[33]

The entry of Chinese forces into combat after US troops crossed the Yalu River ended the latter's momentum and greatly complicated both the military and public diplomacy calculations. At first, in keeping with the longstanding policy of de-emphasizing any possible widening of the military-strategic sphere of the war, US officials downplayed the participation of Chinese troops, but communist propaganda soon began to make China's participation widely known. American public diplomats were guided to reply along particular lines, while still prudently hedging their bets: "Avoid staking US prestige on all-out victory . . . ditto for China, let them keep face . . . avoid empty threats [and] divert word attention from this nexus."[34] Emphasis would remain on the message that the US/UN posed no threat to China or its interests but only sought "to help the Korean people create an independent nation for themselves." Closer to the combat now rolling back southward, US military propaganda blanketed civilians with leaflets titled "A Time for Courage Not Despair" and the invaders with material urging defection, highlighting the UN role, and asking "why die for China and Russia?"[35]

State officers at the time were contemplating a simpler template for information operations—"punch-lines that would stick in the audience's mind"— which would apply the Korea case around the region. However, alliance realities soon led this impulse into "awkward problems since, for example, the horrid words 'freedom' and 'independence' are apparently excluded from the vocabulary of American officials in Indochina."[36] That is, the number of usable punch lines available was limited. Moreover, the Chinese onslaught deepened the US public diplomats' tendency to hedge their bets: "Demolish Sino–Sov[iet] charges of UN or US aggressive intent and depict current developments in Korea as a renewal of previously frustrated COMMIE aggression. Re-emphasize on all occasions fact that action in Korea is UN action . . . Avoid giving China and Soviets propaganda ammunition for their 'imperialist aggression' theme." Perhaps most striking of the latter was the finessed retraction of Truman's November 30 comments about the possibility of using the atomic bomb on the peninsula.[37]

Others among these directives included a reinvigorated psychological counteroffensive at the global and regional levels, and a more finely tuned one at the country level. On the former, the end of November saw not only the attempt to limit the military and public diplomacy damage of the Chinese onslaught, but also a broad stock-taking of the year on both fronts. Consular officials in Europe and the Near East were asked for local reactions to the Chinese offensive. Public diplomats around the Asian littoral were asked to collect local examples of printed communist propaganda to be forwarded to Manila for analysis and riposte.[38] This required careful handling in other American outposts, especially as the Chinese offensive ramified. In the Philippines, for example, officers were told to "avoid reports [of] disgruntlement [among] Filipino troops" as the momentum swung against the United Nations. In Korea proper, the emphasis on the United Nations, on battlefield minutiae, and on the bigger Cold War picture produced a curious circumstance in VOA programming: "While the broadcasts . . . were permeated by the event of the Korean War, the country on whose soil it was fought heard very little about itself." Overall, the end of 1950 and with it the end of the first six months of the "tennis match" Korean War elicited Washington's determination to keep the conflict at the center of the big picture. In its December 6 guidance, State notified its officers that "forthcoming proposals, statements, and actions will lend themselves to making clear that Korea is only part of the total problem."[39]

By late 1950, American public diplomats were convinced of the nuanced nature of their task in Asia. Korea had its uses in the global spotlight, but any such use had to be carefully considered in the local and regional contexts as well. For example, US propaganda about its aid in the reconstruction of Japan, presented as a sign of American good faith and stake in Asian success, caused friction among Asian neighbors who had recently suffered at Japanese hands—and who had no particular sympathy for Japanese suffering or enthusiasm for salving it. In Korea the picture appeared less fraught—until the open Chinese entry into the war, which raised fears and hopes among, for example, Indochinese who knew they might be next. The extent to which the State Department was more preoccupied with how Korea "played" outside the peninsula and region than within it is quite striking. The year-end assessments focused at least as much on Europe as on neighboring East Asia, let alone on the broader non-European world.[40] That is, even after six months of war and eight months of the attempt at a concerted public diplomacy campaign, the Truman administration proceeded according to their basic strategic calculus: Asia had shown its Cold War volatility and thus importance, but Europe was still ground zero.

However, there is some evidence that this was the moment when Washington began to see a more nuanced global picture. The lessons accumulated outside Europe, from the Truman Doctrine to the Yalu River counterattack, joined with those inherited from World War II led policymakers to conclude that the undertaking of combat to protect non-European areas from communism was not enough by itself to win those areas over, no matter how skillful the public diplomacy. Rather, a more comprehensive policy and rhetoric was needed. These would have to encompass not just the airy "defense of the free world and peoples" but also combine economic development via Point Four, political progress as in India and Indonesia, and cultural outreach into an overall psychological strategy in the non-European world.[41] Moreover, frustration over US shortcomings thus far seemed to have risen as high as the now-apparent stakes. Benton wrote Acheson to lament that "the stepup of the [Soviet] propaganda attack . . . seems to me almost as dismaying as the [Chinese] attack. . . . For all its recent expansion of educational and information exchange, State still hasn't pitched its sights to the level of a great national-defense operation in this field—nor even close to it. . . . I am far more troubled even than I was some months back by our failures in this area."[42]

Stalemates and Stabilities: Washington, the Peninsula, and the Region

Within the next few months of early 1951, the military situation on the Korean peninsula stabilized along battle lines that would last with minor adjustments for the rest of the war. The stalemate offered the chance to apply the lessons that had been gleaned about US strategy and the place of public diplomacy in it. Attention to the foreign–public sphere had officially been part of American foreign policy since the Smith-Mundt Act of 1948. It had been given a theme in the Campaign of Truth and applied across most of the board since the spring of 1950. Yet having been tested in Korea, it seemed to have just barely passed. Too many moving parts, as well as an inability to reliably measure success, hindered the enterprise even as its importance rose in most American eyes. By 1951 most parties agreed that information activities were important, but none could say for sure whether these activities were succeeding.[43] The fact that these operations were not better integrated into foreign policymaking compounded the hindrance. Finally, the Chinese revolution and the Korean War had made American public diplomacy's earlier inattention to the non-European world look foolish in hindsight and in dire need of redress as the reorganization of public diplomacy's institutional infrastructure—the fourth such during the Truman years—proceeded in early 1951.[44]

The first wartime inklings that yet another overhaul was required had stirred in the aftermath of the Inchon landings. A rethinking of both message and means, in and near the war zone, was underway by year's end.[45] This would attempt to resolve the understandable though unfortunate tensions between "informational" and "cultural" activities, and between Washington directives and local realities. Continuing confusion over bureaucratic responsibilities, and the turf wars it generated, drove the discussion as well. The ongoing search for a usable metric of public diplomacy effectiveness was another source of dissatisfaction for the Truman administration, as indeed it would prove to be for its successors.[46]

The creation of the Psychological Strategy Board (PSB) in April 1951 moved both public diplomacy and the non-European world closer to the center of American foreign policymaking. The PSB represented an attempt at resolving bureaucratic battles over day-to-day operations, combined with abstract ideation about strategy and how to "sell" it, and with the improved program oversight needed to make the sale.[47] In enumerating the categories and themes to be addressed, it ranked as one target "dominant attitudes [which] cut across national, economic, and cultural groupings: nationalism . . . racial consciousness [and] familiarity or the lack of it with representative institutions." This and the rest of the taxonomy of targets would guide the PSB's first task: "It must begin with an idea, a very definite idea, of our political warfare plans, in order to know what masses of men it is supposed to move where, when." Even then, it would face the permanent public diplomacy problem of the gap between word and deed: the PSB "would always have to live with the anomaly of having control only over the secondary instrument for getting the results it is supposed to achieve."[48] NSC-68 had recommended the establishment of the PSB a year earlier, which helped give impetus to Truman's push for the Campaign of Truth. But it had done so in line with the administration's Europe-first focus. Since that recommendation, Korea had enlarged the scope. In addition, the PSB was meant to oversee more than just public diplomacy; it would also cover most other forms of Cold Warfare. However, the fact that public diplomacy had come closer to bureaucratic parity with those other forms as peer activities on the PSB was a significant step, even if the Board itself ultimately proved to worsen the national security team's administrative headaches.

Looming large among these was the basic ambiguity about whether information activities were best conducted as PR, diplomatic, or covert operations. This ambiguity was only partially resolved by the PSB, since a deep bureaucratic confusion underlay the operational and definitional ones. As Edward Lilly wrote in a study of "Psychological Operations 1945–51" just shy of the PSB's first birthday:

> PSB is now facing up to its major problem: to develop a psychological strategy with which all agency operations can be coordinated. The old issues have again raised their heads ... State and JCS are now using psychological operations to establish a precedent for the larger issue. In war, will State or JCS control the preparation of national policy? ... PSB's existence has been too brief to solve these hoary problems.[49]

As a practical matter in the field, this bureaucratic infighting in Washington was but one impediment to public diplomacy operations in Korea, which had plenty of its own, and arguably greater, challenges to overcome. But by the midpoint of the war, US information officers on the peninsula and in the region felt they had done passably so, at least regarding operational challenges if not philosophical ones.

If these more abstract difficulties persisted, the day-to-day problems subsided as officials applied the lessons of the previous year to the growing strategic standoff. For example, after Seoul changed hands for what proved to be the final time in late September 1950, US public diplomats had returned to find their facilities destroyed: "Just a few days after the city was retaken, key operations were returned to Seoul. Here the new problems were how to operate in a bombed, shelled, and burned-out city [against a] stark background of hunger, destruction, cold, and insecurity. Within four weeks, however, USIE again had a smooth-working [expanded] operation. . . . New, improved publications [such as] a weekly pictorial news poster were inaugurated" as was new and up-to-the-minute radio programming. The information team credited this, and their performance under fire, to their dispersed prewar network: "There were USIE centers in all key cities even before the war. By reorganizing them as the war . . . moved back and forth, they were easily converted into operational HQ. In addition to shelter, these centers had [equipment and an] experienced Korean staff. Thus at all times there was continuity in USIE efforts in spite of evacuations, returns, and re-evacuations." Knowing that the battlefield stalemate might turn out to be temporary, US public diplomats took the biggest lesson for operating in war zones like Korea: "The most definitive conclusion that can be drawn . . . is that the normal information program must be geared for swift changes if it is to function in a war situation . . . [it must be] flexible, motorized, and decentralized . . . The moral for other USIE operations threatened by Communist military attack would seem to be 'scrounge, hoard, motorize, and decentralize.'"[50]

At the same time, both this combat-adjacent approach and outreach in more peaceful areas required a large-scale, and thus much less mobile, production center safely out of enemy range, as well as localized knowledge of regional target audiences. The RSC in Manila employed a small army of translators to fill these needs. By early 1951 the center was producing pamphlets and posters by the millions, and by the anniversary of the invasion was running at full capacity:

> Graphics—posters, cartoons, photos—and the printed word reduced to its simplest form are the most important ways of reaching the great Far Eastern audience. The need is for printed material produced in great volume, and tailored to the particular race and culture involved. As an example, one of [the Manila] RPC's first efforts was the cartoon book entitled *When The Communists Came*, which told the story of the Communist occupation of a Chinese village. Some 600,000 copies of the book were produced in eight different languages.[51]

The eight languages were among the nearly twenty in which US public diplomats in Asia routinely published visual media. The *IIA Newsletter* in June 1951 noted that "as an example of the complexity of the language problem in making the Campaign of Truth effective, in the Philippines alone, it is necessary to print a given piece of copy in eight different dialects to cover the country."[52] The US information teams in Korea and elsewhere in Asia had reason to feel, in short, that they had surmounted the logistical challenges of doing public diplomacy, even under live-fire hostility, and had the tools by this point in the war to accomplish their mission.

Officials back in Washington—including the squabbling factions of the PSB—were less convinced. The inability to find reliable metrics for success bedeviled the enterprise everywhere, perhaps nowhere more so than in Korea.[53] Output, in short, did not equal outcome. A report to the PSB found the psychological-warfare picture of which public diplomacy was a part to be troubling, military-heavy at the expense of civilian and diplomatic affairs, and lacking in "overall strategic planning . . . operations are completely ad hoc and suffer from lack of planning . . . Themes and appeals are mixed up to the point that they cancel each other out. In addition, there is so much leaflet and loudspeaker activity that the enemy suffers from 'propaganda fatigue.'" In a metaphor that would recur, the analysis found that the campaign "suffers from the 'shotgun approach.'"[54] A concurring opinion lamented along similar lines that "it doesn't seem that we have much psychological strategy as distinguished from tactics in Korea. We have never enunciated what our terms and objectives for peace are. In diplomacy you keep these things secret, but in psychological strategy the whole point is to make at least the minimum objectives public. That is how you win minds."[55]

Officials in the field saw "ad hoc" as a feature rather than a bug, and unavoidable—a rapid-response, crisis-driven consequence of the hot-war context. As for propaganda fatigue, this was a reflection of the conscious choice to err on side of volume, itself in turn a reflection of the success-metrics problem. But field officers acknowledged that the bureaucracy's clashing views were, in part at least, rooted in the difference between strategy and tactics. They concurred, moreover, that there were messaging problems in both. Certain of these had persisted since the invasion. Terms and tropes such as "democracy" and "independence" continued to complicate American outreach—not only for the apparent hypocrisy of underlying US policy, but also for reasons of local preconception. One group of information officers in an unnamed Asian country, for example, "found that the use of the word 'democracy' was of tremendous importance . . . but . . . in American propaganda was a double-edged sword since the meaning assigned to the word locally was a Communist one."[56]

The IIA Committee on Content recommended, in effect, counterattacking the other side's terminology. This was intended to move the battle from Western hypocrisies to Eastern ones and potentially resolve some of the lingering philosophical and strategic flaws in US outreach in Asia. The Committee's report guided public diplomats to expropriate the communists' language to convey the American message: "In the *New Asia* the *inevitable* course of history is toward *liberation* from *oppression*. The *people of Asia* are *struggling* to secure *national fulfillment, peace, and progress.* This is a revolution to achieve and guarantee the rights and needs of people everywhere . . . [and one] which the U.S. *shares in* and *supports* with a spirit of *comradeship.*" On a two-column chart of "What Asians Want" and "What USIE Output Must Tell Asians," the report detailed the themes and terminology to be deployed:

> *National Fulfillment*—It belongs to you as a right. You must win it. It is inevitable because the March of History is towards liberation from oppressors. Your brothers in this continuing revolution stand by your side. *Peace*—As so often in past, peace is once again threatened by oppressors and imperialists. But the will and determination of the peoples of Asia will triumph. The U.S. supports the people of Asia in their struggle to achieve this peace. *Progress*—Oppression has been and is the obstacle to progress in Asia. To achieve the social and economic progress which is Asia's right and heritage will be a long and hard trek. But free men, working together, as equals, will succeed.[57]

Finally, in what would become a staple of US output over the next decade, "a *new imperialism is threatening* Asia and all of the world." Truman's Point Four address had sought to distance the United States from the imperialism of its European allies. Now, making explicit a theme embedded in the Campaign of Truth—and risking those allies' displeasure by doing so—US public diplomacy would charge the communists with that sin. In drafting his spring 1952 followup address, Truman's team argued over "the question of how the President should describe the desire of the people of Asia and Africa to control their own destinies." The drafters found "mutually satisfactory language" partly by emphasizing US support for the UN in such matters—and by pointing to the war in "Korea [as] everlasting proof that we meant it."[58]

Korea thus played a starring role in both the reappropriation of the communists' language and in the foregrounding of the United Nations in US outreach outside Europe. The communist powers' media campaigns let neither go unchallenged. The May 1952 issue of a USIS publication widely distributed in the Middle East, *USA News Review*, reported that "Soviet propaganda urg[es] Arabs to look upon Communists in the Korean War as the 'champions' of Asian and African peoples in the struggle for freedom and independence from Anglo-Americans. By propagandizing under the guise of a struggle for peace, the USSR is . . . encouraging militant nationalism among these peoples against the West."[59] A typical US reply could be found in a special issue later that year, highlighting the United Nations with emphasis on the communists' diplomatic intransigence at Turtle Bay, and the multinational army—implicitly championing "Asian and African peoples"—fighting on Korea's behalf. USIS coverage downplayed the diplomatic efforts of the Arab-Asian representatives—*actual* such "peoples"—at the United Nations, because most of these were neutralist in nature and thus at odds with US policy.[60] But it accepted the premise that the principles and forces in play in Korea defined the world struggle in microcosm, and the notion that control of its language would shape discussion of world affairs in the near future.

Two particular issues complicated this endeavor over the second half of the war. Both bacteriological warfare and POWs made for sharp communist attacks, discreetly coordinated among Soviet, Chinese, and North Korean officials, on the US–UN side.[61] The charges stuck well enough to force US public diplomats to expend considerable resources rebutting them over the protracted course of armistice talks. Beginning in early 1952, the communists accused the UN Command of using bacteriological weapons in North Korea and Manchuria. Soviet and Chinese propaganda featured photographs and descriptions of fissured shells and canisters alleged to carry infected insects into enemy territory. In an ironic twist, US officials noted that in some of the photographs, the burst canisters were themselves "propaganda bombs" used to drop leaflets. By mid-March, one-fifth of external Chinese radio broadcasts emphasized these accusations, while downplaying the communists' refusal to permit neutral inspections of the alleged crime scenes.[62] American officials fretted that the campaign seemed to be gaining traction among neutrals both in and outside of Europe.[63] To counter, the Truman information team echoed Acheson's viewpoint that "we must do anything we can to get the international committee to make the request of the commies to permit inspection," and to do so very visibly, as there was "a great deal of propaganda value in this."[64] The continued Chinese refusal to allow inspections, even when suggested by a bona fide neutral like Nehru, undergirded US rebuttal of the charges, which after burning bright for three months largely faded by summer.

However, by summer 1952, the stalemate over POWs had become the centerpiece of communist outreach.[65] Given the tennis-volley nature of the frontline combat during the first year or so of the war, the question of what to do with captured soldiers and civilians dated back to its beginning. It was only when armistice negotiations began, however, that the issue took center stage in both formal and public diplomacy. At its heart was the matter of "forced repatriation." This involved returning home POWs classified as enemy combatants, embedded in captured populations that also included "foreign" conscripts and civilians caught on the wrong side of the moving front lines, who did not wish to go home. The memory of Stalin's treatment of repatriated Soviet soldiers after 1945 led most American officials, including Truman himself, to stand on precaution and principle against repatriation. They believed that this might net a Cold War PR coup—and the practical dimension loomed large as well, since UN forces held roughly ten times as many communist POWs as vice-versa, a battlefield imbalance that could be decisive for the communist side.[66]

The difficult and protracted discussions of the issue between the belligerents indirectly reflected much of the debate within the Truman team. All parties were deeply aware that neither the battlefield-logistical nor the principled dimensions of the question could truly be severed from its propaganda one. The issue became a proxy for the stakes of the conflict and for the claims each side's output made about its society and way of life. Chinese propaganda, for example, presented a photograph of smiling African American POWs with the caption "[they] are happy with their treatment at the hands of the Korean People's Army and Chinese volunteers. For the first time in their lives, they find themselves treated as equals."[67] On another page of the same issue could be found photos of 1937 Japanese atrocities at Nanking, to remind the audience of that particular US–UN ally. The Americans, for their part, gave heavy coverage to rebuttal—"press, photographs, motion-pictures, radio," and an ROC-sponsored speaking tour of Southeast Asia by a select group drawn from the 14,000 Chinese POWs who had refused repatriation, chosen "freedom . . . and delivered first-person accounts of life under communism."[68] The POWs held a prominent place in both sides' media output, as in their armistice diplomacy, for the duration of the war, subsiding only after a number of key factors—the inauguration of Dwight Eisenhower as president and the death of Stalin among them—resolved the issue and sped up ceasefire negotiations.

The prospect of armistice invited speculation as to the reconstruction and rehabilitation of the country. US public diplomacy underscored efforts to physically rebuild and psychologically bolster not just Korea but its neighbors. During the first few months of 1953, VOA told Far East audiences the story of one Col. Munske's efforts to "rehabilitat[e] war-torn [Seoul] and car[e] for its homeless [and orphaned] population[s]." Another program, a Mandarin broadcast titled "Faithful Wife," sought to bring the ideological struggle literally home. The weekly drama "tells of how the serene and tranquil existence of the House of Li was shattered because one of its members turned toward Communism." In Korea itself during this period, twenty separate VOA programs continued to place "special emphasis . . . on the UN collective action in Korea." The multilateral angle was among other things a roundabout way of reinforcing the universality of the struggle for freedom. This also found expression elsewhere, such as in a winter program titled "Battle Without Armor" that told the story of one Korean's "lonely struggle for religious freedom and civil rights" against communist domination.[69]

The theme of cooperation, especially of the inter-Asian variety, in the name of overcoming wartime suffering and poverty underpinned much American outreach in the last year of the war. VOA personnel in the field interviewed

Filipino soldiers in Korea to gather "radio letters home" which were beamed to the Philippines, connecting the soldiers with their families and villages back home—and with the region's collective role in holding the anticommunist line. Beyond manning the battlefront, the Filipinos also served to underline the mutual aid that marked so much US public diplomacy coverage of the war effort in the region:

> Again and again VOA correspondents just back from the war front have described over the air the many ways Philippine soldiers and others of the UN Command are helping Korean civilians help themselves. They are lending a hand in rebuilding houses, in restoring ravaged land, and in fighting insect pests and the spread of disease. They have taught the Koreans to use peat—plentiful in some areas—to heat their homes. They have shown them new ways of farming, have brought new seed and fertilizers, and helped them repair their damaged water works. [In a followup broadcast] President Rhee expressed also his country's gratitude for Filipino soldiers' devotion to the cause for which the war is being fought [and] for their spirit of comradeship with the Korean people.[70]

The effort to build a community in Asia that was avowedly part of the Free World—a construct by now in regular use in American conversations on strategy—was not limited to that region. In one sense, this was an ironic development. War in Korea had brought the need for US–UN-led multilateral unity to the forefront of Washington's mind and the foreground of its outreach in that country. However, in short order it had extended this imperative elsewhere, far beyond the Korean peninsula. In part this was driven by the implications of Point Four, whose focus on poverty and development helped to draw attention beyond the battle zone to other vulnerable, impoverished areas.

It was driven, moreover, by the tenor of conversations in Asia about the way forward from the Korean War. After crossing the Yalu, China blasted what it called Indian attempts to be the "voice of Asia" leading an "Asia for the Asians" movement—something Nehru himself publicly rejected, though American officials like John Foster Dulles were skeptical of the disavowal.[71] These efforts, combined with the relentless and spreading communist public diplomacy onslaught, forged a larger dynamic: the evolution of Washington's own understanding of the global conflict and of the American attempt to explain it to others. By the middle of the decade, both Cold War sides as well as those nonsuperpower actors caught in between would prioritize this mission and its Global South targets. But the antecedents of this could be found as early as the war's first days. A commission reviewing USIE activities noted in June 1951 that in hindsight, Soviet public diplomacy activities "in North Korea prior to the [war] . . . point out, by example, the need for shifting the emphasis in the operation of the program to other parts of the world."[72] Nor were the Americans and Soviets the only ones, in the wake of Korea, to look further afield. Historian Cary Fraser writes that the Lebanese ambassador to Washington, in a conversation with State officials a few years later, said that the tandem of Palestine and Korea had led "the Arab nations to make common cause with the Asian and African states. The Korean War had provided the impetus for this collaborative process."[73]

The undeniable, active interest of those "other parts"—most visible in the Arab–Asian nucleus' Korean diplomacy at the UN—by itself offered a reason to pay attention to how US messages about Korea played elsewhere and to increase US messaging to those areas. Korea persuaded the Truman admin- istration of the Cold War's full and expanding dimensions outside Europe.[74] The Korean War also persuaded the Arab–Asian cohort of its stake and role in the expanding Cold War. The Truman team created the PSB in an attempt to reorganize itself to master its own strategy and messaging—and to woo wavering parties at the UN and beyond. In the event, the PSB proved inad- equate to the task. But its creation suggested that the psychological dimen- sion of American strategy, including public diplomacy of much wider scope, would have a higher profile in Washington and in the world abroad as the war in Korea wound down.

The PSB was thus the "institutional" aspect of Cold War public diplomacy to coalesce in the late Truman years, but its other aspects—namely its con- ceptual dimension and its geographical reach—did as well. Truman's public diplomats steadily expanded their operations outside Europe; by fall 1951, for example, VOA was broadcasting in forty-six languages, doubling its output in a year.[75] His information team had also gradually learned the importance of tracking their messages, to better discern which were having the desired effect. In the course of this research, some US officials noted the lateral connections between, for example, Nehru and Sukarno, and began to identify the "Arab- Afro-Asian" grouping gestating around the still-murky concept of "neutral- ism" even before either term had come into common usage.[76] In the summer of 1952 the NSC found that US outreach to those areas had failed to persuade their peoples that the US–Soviet confrontation was of greater importance than white colonialism.[77] The confluence of racial, colonial, and economic clashes within the ideological matrix of the Cold War prompted a reassess- ment of the geostrategic atlas. American efforts, however halting or clumsy at this early stage, to win hearts and minds in the world conflict led all parties to rethink the postwar dynamic. The timing is perhaps only coincidental but is definitely suggestive. Just as American diplomats, public and otherwise, were concluding around 1952 that the "bipolar" world contained the makings of a still-forming third entity, Sauvy coined "Third World" in a French publication. Within a decade the term would begin gaining currency in the capitals of East and West—and across the awakening South as well.

Most scholarship that touches on Truman-era public diplomacy character-izes it as late-starting, ham-handed, ad hoc, fundamentally reactive, and mar-ginally effective at best—and this was in its highest-priority targets in Europe. Areas outside the continent were given even shorter shrift, as the above Asian examples suggest. This reflected Washington's fundamental preoccupation with Europe and its inclination to view events both there and beyond almost exclusively through the prism of the Cold War. Thus even when issues of race relations and colonialism appeared on the administration's mental horizons, they were seen more in various tints of red than in black, brown, yellow, and white—a conceptual prism that privileged the anticommunist struggle over the anticolonial one, and which goes a long way toward explaining the scat-tershot nature of the Truman team's information operations. This conceptual shortcoming was not the only reason for the lack of public diplomacy coher-ence. Another was technical, as new communications technologies of varied speed and reach emerged for spreading the American word. Still another was the ongoing tension between information operations and cultural diplomacy. Complicating all of this was the basic organizational problem highlighted in the Korean theater: the sheer number of government actors in play. Three months into the war, one study identified "twenty-seven agencies or parts of agencies . . . concerned with psychological warfare. [It was] the most talked of and least prepared for activity in Washington."[78] Hence the lack of coher-ence and uncertain effectiveness were arguably as much mechanical and "or-ganic" problems as conceptual ones. Collectively these prevented an effective response to many of the most pointed accusations levied in communist infor-mation activities, most infamously and enduringly those related to the POWs and to bacteriological warfare.[79]

American experiments in public diplomacy between the Truman Doctrine and the endgame of the Korean War left behind important legacies. As the Truman years came to a close, US public diplomats sought to reorient their activities in ways that would improve their chances of success—and to do so across a much broader canvas beyond Europe. Chief among the improve-ments envisioned was the drive to tailor programming locally through the training and use of area specialists and "natives," and through the tracking of media consumption and message reception on the ground.[80] This would be part of a switch to country-specific programs, in contrast to the one-size-fits-all approach of the Campaign of Truth. As one report intended for incoming

Eisenhower administration officials put it, "in the vernacular this means ex-
changing the shotgun for the rifle [and] it is a further long step toward enabling
us to take the 'offensive' in the war of ideas." In related fashion, the reorganization of the IIA and especially its media activities would "'speak' overseas
more through the voice of indigenous groups."[81] In an interesting reflection
on the world status quo, the same report wondered if the "rifle" could even
do the job. Lamenting the American shortcomings in public diplomacy and
a vaguely neutralist, racially inflected Global South—coalescing in the post-
Korean War landscape, in ways not the case only a few years earlier—it seemed
that "we are not really trying to win" and that the reorganization of the US
public diplomacy apparatus would in the end be insufficient to do so. The
writer, had he known it, might have taken solace in the fact that the incoming administration—and, more significantly, the awakening Afro-Asian-Arab
world in the aftermath of the Korean lesson—had other plans.

Pawns, Proxies, and Pressing the Case for the Free World

The USIA and Eisenhower's New Look

The State Department deals with governments. The USIA deals with peoples.
— "Study of USIA Operating Assumptions," USIA Report,
December 1954

The quagmire in Korea took a prominent place in the 1952 presidential campaign and drove debate about the American posture in the Cold War. This included public diplomacy, still unlabeled as such, but the failures of which were central to Eisenhower's critique of Truman. The general argued that American shortcomings on this front and the Korean one were both organizational and conceptual. This was at least in part a consequence of Truman's inattention to the subject. His launch of the Campaign of Truth notwithstanding, Truman had mostly left the task up to his bureaucracy, herding the public diplomacy cats toward his newly created Psychological Strategy Board (PSB) and hoping this would lead to greater PR success worldwide. It did not. Instead, the PSB exacerbated the worst features of the bureaucratic standoff and did too little to settle the matter of what role public diplomacy should have in policymaking.[1] Added to the Korean stalemate, this meant that Eisenhower's attacks were substantially more on the mark than most election-year rhetoric. He was well-suited to make such attacks stick. Eisenhower was a true believer in the psychological warfare at the core of US information activities, and his belief was of a piece with his vision of the superpower conflict. The approach proposed in NSC-68 and embodied in Korea had been costly, inconclusive, and perhaps unnecessary. A "new look" deploying public diplomacy at the frontlines, Eisenhower argued, was an essential and inexpensive means of executing American strategy. His position resonated with the information personnel he inherited. As IIA head Robert Johnson put it during Eisenhower's first summer as president, "[our message] should be a *positive* one of hope, of faith, of promise. It should not confine itself merely to parrying . . . the hammer-blows of Communist propaganda. . . . An information program that [does this] may well be the margin between shooting war and ultimate peace."[2]

The suasion of hearts and minds on a fully global scale now ranked amid Washington's highest strategic priorities. It enshrined a psychological approach to Cold War foreign policy and required better machinery for its pursuit: the August 1953 creation of the United States Information Agency (USIA). This did not end all the bureaucratic battles, nor overcome residual suspicions in parts of Foggy Bottom, about the targets, approach, methods, and effectiveness of public diplomacy. But it was very much in keeping with Eisenhower's Cold War doctrine. It was, moreover, scalable to ever more distant corners of the globe, including in the far, extra-European reaches of a Free World undergoing an unmistakable but indeterminate metamorphosis. There, American analysts found, the "profound political and psychological changes" stemming from anticolonial nationalism, racial awakening, and economic underdevelopment would greatly affect the US ability to achieve Western objectives, as "the political and social forces at work are not basically sympathetic to Western values."[3] The first Eisenhower administration assigned the USIA the mission of bolstering that diffuse entity and ensuring strong ties between it and the Cold War West. That entity, partly in response to this campaign, was increasingly finding its own voice and using it to push back against being conscripted into the Cold War.

The Eisenhower administration's public diplomacy improved in most measurable respects upon that of its predecessor. It did, like all American outreach, suffer from the two "permanent" impediments to that exercise: the gap between words and deeds, and the lack of a foolproof metric for assessing success. But its operations helped Washington to grasp that the postwar landscape was beginning to change rapidly and the United States thus found itself playing catch-up in areas heretofore mostly overlooked. The Eisenhower team's game plan hinged on two concepts: to unite the Free World in part by exposing the menace of "Red Colonialism."[4] The plan proved untenable because of flaws in the American understanding of both—and because of Global South actors' avowal of a different agenda altogether. The administration was right about the power of the word "colonialism" but wrong about the US ability to deploy it convincingly, and by the start of Eisenhower's second term his team would go back to the conceptual drawing board. Although Europe was still the linchpin, the continents outside the Continent became inexorably more important to the USIA during these years. By the late 1950s they outshone Europe in terms of public diplomacy resources deployed, just as their transformation was becoming more difficult to manage. This reflected the tectonic changes afoot, above all a global race revolution. Even as the president revamped and institutionalized American public diplomacy, gave it an honored place in his national security apparatus, and practiced it in innovative ways, the successes it found outside Europe, in sites from Guatemala to Bandung, proved fleeting—especially among those nations newly free that were then changing the global Cold War landscape.

Organizing for Total Cold War: The Creation of the USIA

The Eisenhower administration's reorganization of the US public diplomacy apparatus shaped how particular case studies outside Europe, in Guatemala and at Bandung, unfolded. The psychological approach to the Cold War in some ways merely refined a key Truman administration conclusion: "In critical areas . . . [we] should conduct with greater vigor, political warfare operations as an integral part of its overall strategy, in order to reduce communist and neutralist influence [and] combat anti-American propaganda."[5] In other ways, though, it foregrounded that approach to such an extent that US strategy overall took on a different cast. This was revealed in the bureaucratic shake-up of the administration's first year, of which public diplomacy was a prominent part. Upon taking office, Eisenhower appointed the President's Committee on International Information Activities (PCIIA, or Jackson Committee) to study the subject.[6] The committee's recommendations, along with those of the President's Committee on Governmental Reorganization (or Rockefeller Committee), guided the ascension of public diplomacy in US national security policy. Reflecting the president's desire to use both new and old media in innovative ways, his desire to wage the Cold War on the cheap, and his conviction that the conflict was above all a moral and psychological struggle, the Jackson Committee suggested a number of priority areas: reorganizing the policy and public diplomacy machinery both in Washington and at outposts abroad, expanding its intelligence and research capabilities, privileging a "country focus" in output, and acquiring greater country experience and program latitude for officers in the field.[7]

Chief among the changes recommended by the Jackson and Rockefeller Committees and enacted by the president was the creation of the USIA. The USIA was built around a core consisting of the IIA and VOA and incorporating related agencies' activities.[8] The consolidation coincided, at first glance perhaps paradoxically, with decentralization of operations. The rearrangement placed greater responsibility on officers in the field, who gained latitude and who reported to newly appointed regional directors. Henceforth "country plans" would be generated on-site, with guidance from and review by the roving regional directors and ultimately Foggy Bottom. The plans would draw, as appropriate, on the two key themes the USIA laid out for 1954: free world unity and the peaceful use of atomic energy, tailoring one or both to local conditions. As the agency reported to Congress, "the criterion in each instance is 'Does it help support and explain our foreign policy in terms of others' legitimate aspirations?'"

Although this clarified the operations and even the mission of US public diplomacy in key ways, it complicated other aspects. Friction with the State Department—a perennial problem—continued to be an issue. The reorganization removed some points of contention, but could not overcome the persistent belief among many professional diplomats that information personnel were mere salesmen out of their league in the realm of national security.[9] Eisenhower's endorsement of the USIA's mission helped, as did the creation of a dedicated research arm and the insistence of its first director Theodore Streibert on a firewall between his shop and the CIA.[10] But this momentum was to a large degree offset by low morale in the ranks—largely the fruit of ongoing McCarthyite attacks on the agency—and extending even to his own Secretary of State John Foster Dulles. Dulles exhibited a marked lack of enthusiasm for the endeavor; he feared that the wrong kind of output would lead foreign peoples to believe that the United States offered a blanket endorsement of their aspirations.[11]

Eisenhower shared this concern to a degree, but he was nonetheless determined to present the new American message to the world, so much so that he elected not to wait on the restructuring to act. The death of Stalin in March 1953 was an unmissable opportunity to make a "dramatic psychological move," in the words of C. D. Jackson, Eisenhower's special assistant for psychological warfare. Soviet Premier Georgi Malenkov concluded the same thing, calling for peace in a speech to the Supreme Soviet on March 16. He thereby, in historian Kenneth Osgood's phrase, "had stolen Eisenhower's thunder." The United States attempted to steal it back one month later. Eisenhower's "A Chance for Peace" speech, as Osgood relates, waged the Cold War in the guise of seeking to transcend it; the speech "sought to identify world hopes for peace with US aims in the Cold War, to define a hope for the future that could sustain free world morale . . . it was a skillfully executed exercise in political warfare designed to wrestle the peace initiative away from the Kremlin [and] was a dress rehearsal for the administration's notion of psychological strategy."[12] The PSB, via the IIA and VOA, ensured that the speech was heavily covered in various media the world over.

Seeking to reclaim the vocabulary of "peace," however, pointed to the linguistic difficulties Washington faced. As the Jackson Committee put it, " 'Cold War' and 'psychological warfare' are unfortunate terms. They do not describe the efforts of our nation and our allies to build a world of peace and freedom. They should be discarded in favor of others which describe our true goals."[13] In the "Chance for Peace," Eisenhower and his team sought just this sort of terminological transcendence. Over the course of the decade, though, the attempt to achieve this would reforce a rethinking—and a remapping—of the Cold War world.

The reorganization was only the first step to solving the many problems facing American public diplomacy. Not least among these was that the field was starting to become crowded. Although the Americans, Soviets, and British had the largest media presences, new players like India's Nehru and Egypt's Gamal Abdel Nasser had joined the fray, presaging the Global South public diplomacy explosion to come. When Nasser, for example, launched the "Voice of the Arabs" radio broadcast to mark the first anniversary of the Egyptian revolution in 1953, he made sure that its signal could reach not only much of North Africa but also South and Southeast Asia. In the realm of international radio broadcasting, the total number of hours broadcast in all areas had risen to nearly seven thousand per week.[14] Measuring what figures like this meant presented another quandary. Tools for such measurements had been developed in a domestic and frequently nonpolitical context; whether they could be profitably applied to foreign and ideological questions was an open question. Finding and refining such tools, and especially determining which ones were best applied to various subsectors of foreign publics, preoccupied researchers from the inception of the USIA.[15]

In addition to the challenge of picking the right medium was that of tuning the message for local contexts. That which Eisenhower had sought in the "Chance for Peace" was not necessarily seen as the one to emulate six months later, especially outside Europe; as one USIA analyst put it, "in the present situation . . . creating realistic fear of the Kremlin is more important than creating admiration of America or its institutions. It will be enough if a listener in India, e.g. comes to feel that his present way of life is threatened by Soviet imperialism."[16] It was increasingly clear that the fledgling USIA had to set priorities in its outreach: identifying foreign audiences and subsectors within them, and then matching the tools to the targets. This would be vital outside Europe, where the "political warfare tactics of Soviet leaders [include] exploit[ation] of Asian and African nationalism, in order to gain allies and make economic, political, and military difficulties for the Western powers."[17] Such differentiation was crucial. As an NBC News editorial put it, "the real curse of the information service . . . is the close supervision of people thousands of miles away in Washington who have little awareness of local conditions and try to give the Finns and the Filipinos the same treatment."[18] The country-focus approach was intended to address this, but its implementation would take time.

All this was further exacerbated by the precise division of public outreach labor between overt and covert operations. The latter played a prominent role in New Look strategy, and both would be overseen by the new Operations Coordinating Board (OCB). But Streibert's firewall notwithstanding, their jurisdictional lines inevitably blurred. To put it most simply, the USIA was to cover the white-to-gray end of the public diplomacy spectrum, while the CIA and covert-operations personnel covered the gray-to-black. In practice, there were so many shades of gray that the two agencies' efforts frequently overlapped and in some instances were practically inseparable. This would prove especially true in the non-European world, where—given the death of Stalin, his successors' overtures to colonial nationalists, and the critical mass of those nationalists' collective self-assertion—the Jackson Committee's cultivation of the new USIA would bear the most fruit.

The Jackson Committee recognized that the Cold War could not explain or accommodate all the forces at work in Asia, Africa, the Middle East, and Latin America. But it insisted that these forces were important to the United States insofar as they connected to American Cold War interests. Most salient of these forces were nationalism and race, which interlaced with the communist threat in ways that would challenge US public diplomacy and indeed US strategy generally. The Eisenhower administration was not unaware of the broader, world-historical dynamics of race and decolonization independent of the Cold War.[19] However, it took as a given that these dynamics would never, in practice, operate independently of the conflict. That is, in the administration's view, even the repeated glimmers of insight that, say, Nasserite nationalism or transnational racial sensitivities were strong and even dominant forces in a particular situation did not neutralize communism's ability to hijack them sooner or later. Thus in case after case, from Guatemala to Bandung, the insight that something else was at work was sublimated to the imperative of seeing the world through Cold War lenses, shaping short-term policy choices accordingly. Partly in consequence, in those two cases, the US public diplomacy performance and record were mixed: short-term basic success, but longer-term setbacks, missed opportunities, and repercussions. However, the longer-term effect of USIA campaigns touching these events and issues, and the agency's attempts to plumb audience replies to them, was to prompt American officials to see the global postwar landscape anew.

"Guatemala Makes A Friend": The USIA and the Coup

Neither the spy-game drama nor the realpolitik nature of the 1954 US intervention in Guatemala should overshadow its simultaneous role as PR maneuver. Although Korea and Europe consumed most of the new administration's foreign attention, Latin America was the subject of one of its first high-profile trips abroad. The Jackson Committee concurred with US officials who averred that "the importance of Latin America to the U.S. has been generally overlooked in the information program, and the presentation of the American viewpoint through information media [has been] neglected."[20] The president sent his brother Milton, an expert on the region, on a tour of Latin America in the summer of 1953. The trip was heavily promoted by US public diplomats, and USIS materials on it could be found in Latin American media for weeks afterward. The coverage also included a short film released the next spring titled *Visiting Good Neighbors*. A test screening to Latin American nationals deemed that "the film achieved its objectives of promoting friendship and unity in the Americas, [and] reassuring Latin Americans of U.S. interest," though it was less successful in its attempt at "forestalling excessive expectations of U.S. aid." On balance this seemed a good start at inoculating the hemisphere from what the USIA and NSC saw as "a continuing danger from communist activities in the Caribbean area."[21]

Washington worried, however, that this might prove insufficient to counter the threat of such activities in Guatemala. There, Jacobo Árbenz Guzmán's agenda of nationalization and land reform, and his openness to East bloc ties, signaled to the administration a possible communist foothold in the Americas. In its earliest months in office, the Eisenhower team took stock of its predecessor's efforts—or what the holdover ambassador called "a public affairs program by indirection . . . an attempt . . . to infuse into local leaders of public opinion the ideas which [we] desired to get across." The NSC ordered a comprehensive campaign to drive Árbenz from power, a campaign in which information warfare—especially its "gray" variety—would play a vital part.[22]

By early 1953, an IIA field report found that that front of the campaign was faltering. Although the American message—equal parts friendliness toward Latin America in the abstract and hostility toward communism and the Árbenz government in reality—was being reliably transmitted via a majority of press and radio outlets, a strong anti-American and pro-communist countercampaign seemed to be gaining ground. The Guatemalan government, ostensibly independent but possibly communist-affiliated agencies, and foreign governments including Argentina and Poland were pushing back. Assessing why domination of the media environment was proving so difficult to achieve, the IIA named "ignorance of the masses," "blindness or apathy of the upper classes," "exaggerated nationalism," and widespread illiteracy as the main obstacles. But all was not lost: "The steps the Mission has taken in the press to paint Communism truly and to counter the Big Lie are on the right course."[23]

The administration viewed these actions as essentially responding to a threat, and, since it was failing to draw in regional allies, not a terribly effective one. The solution, outlined in the June 1953 country plan for Guatemala, was to move quickly to tilt the media landscape in Washington's favor. The task was twofold: first, to show the Guatemalan people the immediate danger of communism, connected abroad but embedded within; and second, to identify their interests with democracy, freedom, and the United States. The principal vehicle would be the independent press, supplemented with niche outreach to teachers, students, and government and labor officials.[24] The main target was Guatemala's people, not its government. The distinction would shrink before largely switching as the crisis mounted over the next year. As it did, the US strategy would come to encompass all three stripes of propaganda—white, gray, and black—and would come to override most other public diplomacy priorities in mid-1954. A rise of gray and black variations was partly due to cutbacks at USIA, which left the agency less able to achieve its assigned objectives. These then fell to the spies to carry out, with Eisenhower's and the Dulles brothers' blessings. Nonetheless, public diplomacy was central to the American attempt to preempt the crisis beforehand, to resolve it once begun, and to manage its aftermath. This last task unexpectedly proved an exercise in damage control, as an intended object lesson to communists everywhere netted instead, as historian Max Paul Friedman shows, a backlash of unintended consequences for US image management.[25]

Although anti-Árbenz planning had been underway since the previous summer, the US counteroffensive—public diplomacy and otherwise—began in earnest in March 1954. At the Caracas meeting of the OAS that month, Dulles stressed the communist threat to Latin America, recently staved off in British Guiana but not killed outright. Guatemala was the only country present to vote against the Caracas Declaration—understandably, since the document was a thinly veiled allusion to the situation there.[26] The USIA sought to make hay out of the vote, to little avail. Hemispheric public opinion, as far as US officials could discern, thought Árbenz a "'home-grown' revolutionary" in a regionally familiar mold, or thought his transgressions paled next to the American "economic imperialism" of United Fruit. These sentiments proved difficult to dislodge. Even the ventriloquistic technique of "cross-reporting Latin American opinion"—for example, planting stories in a Chilean newspaper which were then reprinted elsewhere in Latin America with Chilean attribution—proved unsuccessful. "The Agency's speical [*sic*] coverage team at the Caracas Conference fed out a continuous flow of news, backgrounders, photos, and recordings, concentrating on the anticommunist resolution and Guatemala's lone opposition. . . . These materials were disseminated by all field offices throughout the conference with good placement," as were TV and film coverage.[27] The agency redoubled its efforts, to ensure saturation across the hemisphere, and worked around restrictions imposed by the Árbenz regime on operations in Guatemala itself.[28] USIA officials sought to set the regional tone for Caracas by a steady playlist of anticommunist and anti-Árbenz themes in the Latin American press. Denying the organic nature of Árbenz's political success, US public diplomats blasted the international communist conspiracy for victimizing the Guatemalan masses and for taking advantage of "Latin Americans' immaturity and irresponsibility."[29]

US officials took the opportunity to relay their message to the far corners of the hemisphere, where it was folded into specific country plans for information activities—all the while taking care to leave few if any fingerprints in their Caracas- and Guatemala-related efforts. The Caracas meeting itself had met with varied responses in the Latin American press. In some capitals, it was the logical fruit of the Rio Pact and not terribly controversial, although even close American allies bristled at the implication that the nonintervention clause, so carefully enshrined in the OAS charter, was revocable if the communist threat grew large enough. Indeed, at Caracas, public and traditional diplomacy bled together. Dulles combined back-room dealing with podium grandstanding, twisting arms to overcome the fact that "there was more fear of U.S. interventionism than of Guatemalan communism." Sympathetic actors around the Americas caught the signal and moved to isolate local communist forces.[30]

Washington stepped up its PR offensive in May when news broke—with help from CIA Director Allen Dulles—of a shipment of Czech weapons to the Árbenz government. Guatemala claimed neutrality while Foster Dulles claimed vindication. The secretary echoed his brother in talking up the threat, seeing "Peril to [the] Panama Canal," as the *New York Times* headline put it. Árbenz argued that his attempts to secure arms from the United States had been rebuffed and that his own country's security—including its disputed borders with British Honduras—required the imported weapons. The public aspect of the transaction alarmed the Policy Planning Staff (PPS), which noted that it set "a bad example inside the Hemisphere, suggesting alternatives to dependence on the U.S." The bad example, moreover, promised to worsen. It might, imagined the State Department's PPS, lead "Latin Americans [to] identify themselves with Little Guatemala if the issue should be drawn for them . . . as a contest between David Guatemala and Uncle Sam Goliath."[31]

Dulles and the CIA, often via the state press of allies like Somoza in Nicaragua, warned that the imported weapons were a prelude to aggression. The Guatemalan government parried such headlines right back, denouncing in a Panamanian newspaper Washington's "vast campaign [of] false information" such as charges that a Soviet outpost had been established on the isthmus.[32] The vast campaign spread its message via all available mass media, including an impressive array of cartoon and poster art. More than two hundred press and radio items were prepared and placed. One hundred thousand pamphlets, twenty-seven thousand posters and cartoons, and the film *Caracas: Resolution and Reality* were distributed throughout the Americas.[33] In a telling division of labor, however, the USIA let the CIA handle the lion's share of public outreach in Guatemala. USIA headquarters directed all branches in the hemisphere to give the Guatemalan crisis its full attention, especially after the Czech arms story broke. The other branches' freedom of maneuver contrasted with the limitations at ground zero. A joint USIA-Embassy message from Guatemala City reported home that it was "exploiting normal media channels to maximum possible under present conditions." Those conditions were worsening palpably; USIA personnel at the binational center suffered "harassment and intimidation" by Guatemalan agents. The solution lay in funneling intelligence to be used in media materials to the embassy in Honduras, from which it could be deployed to counter unfriendly foreign reporting and communist propaganda theater-wide.[34]

The coup and intervention were confused, almost farcical, and, as they proceeded, they seemed in Washington's view a close-run thing. A week after Armas's small invasion force had crossed the border, the USIA lamented that the United States was losing the PR war. The "successful global communist propaganda campaign" was taking its toll on operations; "our hard-hitting anti-communist program," broadcast over El Salvador's 50,000 watt radio station, had been "drastically circumscribed," while Agence France Presse was spreading "anti-American stories."[35] Seeking to fight fire with fire as the offensive got underway, the CIA jammed the Guatemalan government's radio broadcasts, replacing them with "local" voices aimed at confusing the public and paralyzing the military. Both mass and niche audiences were targeted in these in-theater information activities during the Guatemala crisis—especially those conducted by the CIA, which had three particular audiences within the mass public one. Their importance was in inverse proportion to their size. The largest of these was the rank-and-file of the military, numbering thousands; the next was the top tier of the officer corps, numbering hundreds at most and in practical terms perhaps only dozens; and the smallest was Árbenz and his immediate circle.

Much of the American public diplomacy output at all four levels—masses, military, officers, Árbenz—was raw propaganda gray or black. But even the white variation showed little hesitation about taking sides. Within Guatemala, efforts were hamstrung by government censorship and by foreign news agencies playing the "ventriloquist" card back: they had a "marked tendency . . . to cross-report reactions adverse to the U.S. and to select comment out of context." A Cuban radio network found itself virtually hijacked by the USIA, becoming the vehicle of pro-invasion forces as of early June. Testifying to the administration's sincerity when it said that Guatemala would have a critical "demonstrator" effect, both Cold War sides ratcheted up their PR campaigns, and various interested parties paid close attention. The USIA reported a "continuous clamor" on Moscow radio; one *Pravda* article on the crisis was broadcast thirty times.[36] In many areas, "communist propaganda found ready acceptance." The NSC pondered "the best means of publicizing the fact that the Árbenz government had been directed from Moscow, as a means of counteracting the Communist propaganda line that the United States had intervened in the internal affairs of Guatemala."[37] Even in areas where public opinion showed greater equanimity, the episode "produced an unusual amount of comment"— most of it critical of the United States. In both the New World and the Old, the American hand was "universally believed" to be behind the invasion; "the situation in Guatemala . . . appear[s] to be injuring the good name and prestige of the U.S. in Latin America and Europe, if not also throughout the underdeveloped areas of the world." The demonstrator effect, indeed, seemed to be backfiring: "All this plays into the hands of the communist propagandists, and as it injures the U.S. in foreign eyes it strengthens the communist movement."[38]

Further attesting to the Eisenhower administration's belief in the demonstrator effect, Guatemala retained the spotlight for months after the coup. The spinning continued unabated. From Washington's perspective it had no choice but to do so, as evidence trickled in that Latin Americans had bought precious little of the spin during the coup. Even a month after it, with Armas firmly installed, a "large measure of skepticism . . . characterizes [foreign] public reaction to the Guatemalan situation."[39] On the ground in Guatemala, as before, the CIA took the lead, with the USIA close behind. Langley began assembling evidence of Árbenz's communist ties. These proved extant but largely ephemeral. Undeterred, the CIA took what they did find—including "Marxist" books from Árbenz's library, some of which had recently been removed from USIS libraries on those same subversive grounds, and offered it as proof that the coup had been in the right. In this the CIA had reasonably enthusiastic help from the local media, which perhaps had the new regime's autocratic mien in mind. They thus aided the USIA's Guatemala station, whose programming aimed at bolstering the Armas regime. The USIA concentrated on documenting, via film, photograph, and oral accounts, "communist atrocities" under Árbenz. This entailed a hearty retrospective spin on the previous regime's activities, "re-educating" those suspected of having been infected by it, and urging confidence in its successor.[40]

However, it became increasingly clear to the USIA that a tactical win in Guatemala might end up netting strategic losses elsewhere. The agency concluded that the answer lay in convincing foreign audiences of the organic nature of the coup: "The principal objective . . . should be to create the conviction throughout the world that the Guatemalan people found communism evil and utilized all means at their disposal" to evict it. But the imperative of "inducing more vigorous [indigenous] anti-communist activities" in Latin America, as the OCB put it in July, would require more than just public relations. Positive policy tweaks and actual activity that would help to, for example, eradicate illiteracy would be key. These were key to overcoming "the continued predisposition [abroad] to believe in U.S. imperialism."[41] Such a predisposition was not helped by the obvious American hand in the series of juntas after the coup: Foggy Bottom wrote to the Embassy that the latter's "decisive role in this dispute should be obscured publicly, otherwise it will be used by anti-U.S. elements to detriment U.S. objectives [sic]."[42]

Elsewhere in Latin America and beyond, similar outreach had some success. "After initial shock . . . conservative and moderate public opinion tended to become less critical [as Guatemala's appeal to the United Nations] aroused strong criticism. . . . A few countries made efforts to guide public opinion along lines more favorable to US." Argentina's state-controlled press most notably repudiated the "camouflaged enemy" of communism, thus finding themselves by default on the US side. But nationalist and leftist voices there and elsewhere maintained a pro-Árbenz line, continuing to denounce the United States. The lasting impression of the US role would depend, analysts concluded, on "the policies of the [Armas] regime, especially with respect to the 'reforms' of the past decade." Outside the hemisphere, the United States simply lost the battle of headlines. Washington was tarred with the brush of imperialism and colonialism in western Europe and in its recent and current colonies—that is, in places where those terms carried heavy, painful weight. A left-leaning Arab newspaper blasted that "'direct intervention' in the affairs of other countries was replacing the older US policy of only 'indirectly supporting' European Imperialism as in Asia, Africa, and the Middle East."[43]

The USIA stared deeply at the tea leaves, decided that they augured badly, and increased its activities in hopes that the Armas regime would improve the intervention's reputation in retrospect. "The Agency will continue to give high priority to Guatemala during what undoubtedly will be a long period of rehabilitation . . . in addition to Guatemala there is urgent need for a marked step-up in the information program for the hemisphere."[44] This mission took various forms far afield: the cartoon series *The Liberation of Guatemala* ran in 869 newspapers in forty-six countries. On a more thematic level, two hundred thousand copies each of six pamphlets and posters outlining the role of private investment in Latin America were planned for distribution in winter 1955. Two anticommunist cartoon strips produced by the agency appeared in more than three hundred Latin American newspapers, and dozens of anticommunist "dramatic radio shows" pulsed through hemispheric airwaves. Such media were deployed to achieve a twofold task: exposing "Soviet penetration of the Americas," and "counteracting [same with a] campaign on the pro-democratic side, [emphasizing] what must be done to preserve liberty."[45]

As of December 1954, however, success was still elusive. By that point, as Friedman notes, the CIA had "paid for articles in the world press from Denmark to Japan, from India to the Vatican"—to virtually no avail.[46] The USIA had known what the episode ultimately proved—that "propaganda can never be better than policy"—and realized how steep their uphill climb was. During the invasion and coup, at just the moment the military effort "seem[ed] to be failing," the agency had told the OCB's Working Group on Latin America "that until we have a strong, forward-looking, dynamic economic policy for Latin America, it is difficult for USIA to explain and defend our policies." The USIA encouraged the quick development of such a program, having seen afresh in Guatemala the near-impossibility of their job without it: "The principal problem will be to find the means of associating the US with the aspirations of the peoples of Latin America. . . . To win the support of the peoples as well as the governments for our major policy objectives is a task of enormous and long-range proportions."[47] As 1954 ended, the agency reported that it would continue to emphasize both negative and positive outreach, highlighting Atoms for Peace, the Rio Conference, and the Milton Eisenhower report. Among the activities planned for the new year was, on the June anniversary of the coup, the hemisphere-wide distribution of the film that had been shown across Guatemala, celebrating Vice President Richard Nixon's postcoup visit to that country: *Guatemala Makes a Friend.*[48]

Uncertainty about the effectiveness of these operations, and more fundamentally about the USIA's mission itself, prompted a sweeping study circulated in national security circles around Christmas 1954. The data had been collected since just after USIA had opened its doors and continued during and after the Guatemala coup. They made for a frustrating read. The report affirmed the importance of reorganizing public diplomacy and of integrating it into the national security machinery. But the study ended by confirming its starting premise: "Many of the essential problems confronting the Information

Program have not changed very much throughout its history. The big questions arise again and again and are not easily answered."[49] The study undertook the long overdue act of comprehensively examining public diplomacy's operating assumptions and daily exertions. Although some officials had earlier wrestled with these questions, the changed institutional, ideological, and international setting gave a different tenor to the self-examination this time around. In so doing, it began what would become a long-range research program into the effectiveness of information activities, albeit one made harder by ongoing operations in places like Guatemala, the success of which was difficult to glean at this stage.

The study suggested that many of "the big questions aris[ing] again and again" were primarily mechanical. But most of the conceptual big questions were of somewhat newer vintage and in profound flux. In issues touching upon race or colonialism, in particular, world discourse was evolving fast. The Cold War framework simply did not fit the great challenges of world affairs as seen from many areas of the non-European world. Indeed, that framework seemed a positive distraction. At a minimum this suggested that Americans ought to proceed carefully when deploying it. Warnings about the evils of communism often resonated little—or did so in the wrong direction when they implicitly bolstered European rule as necessary to Cold War victory: "In colonial areas political considerations often require USIA to ignore the native population and to concentrate on the European minority." There were practical considerations too: "It is impossible to reach 'the guy with the loincloth in the jungle.' "[50]

Beyond the technical challenge—to say nothing of the racist condescension—of reaching the loincloth-clad, one public diplomat in the study phrased the dilemma this way: "What is the reaction of the Vietnamese on a statement about freedom from Communism without saying anything about freedom from the French?" Nor could the color dimension be ignored. The study found that race continually undercut US appeals: "*The position of the Negro* is considered throughout USIA to be *America's major point of vulnerability, particularly in dealing with non-white peoples.*" Domestic progress might be turned to US advantage: "Color is a bond among peoples. Feature stories dealing with Negro progress in US are good output for West Africa." But even this could backfire if handled wrong: "Commonsense assumptions may not reflect area knowledge, as in the judgment that Arabs identify themselves with the colored peoples and therefore would enjoy Negro victories in boxing matches." Above all, on issues of race and colonialism, loomed the problem of the gap between words and deeds: for example, the "US vote in the UN on Morocco offsets American claims of advocating colonial independence."[51]

This complicated picture was, in a sense, the beginning of wisdom for American public diplomacy: institutionally, it had begun to know what it did not know. Wrestling with race and colonial issues on a world stage that might not share the Cold War framework of both the East and West was profoundly difficult. The challenge of understanding and relating to foreign audiences on a variety of fronts—but especially these two—was complex: *"USIA does not know very much about the areas about which it should know most.* Basic communication studies are needed in Asia precisely because mass media are just beginning to develop: 'The more important a country is policy-wise, the harder it is to do research.'" Partly as a result of the 1954 study, research would henceforth be made absolutely central to USIA activities. Moreover, this knowledge of one's lack of knowledge did not impeach the underlying conviction, shared by Eisenhower and his public diplomats alike: the paramount importance of foreign peoples, not just leaders or states. As one official observed in the study, "'you saw what the masses [in] India did. They got freedom from Britain. They must be important. There's considerable pressure from below." India was not the only place from which pressure from below was rising. There and elsewhere across South and Southeast Asia, nationalist leaders channeling such pressure began finding allies in one another, and formalizing the effort to coalesce into something yet larger.

Voting By Proxy: Neutralism, the Color Curtain, and Bandung's New World Map

At virtually the same moment that the USIA self-study was being read in Washington, some of its prophecies and conclusions were being made manifest in Asia. Its prescriptions too could be observed in the months that followed, in Washington's response to the landmark meeting of the Afro-Asian Peoples Conference at Bandung, Indonesia. There the Eisenhower administration produced a refinement of what one might call "covert information operations"—that is, a campaign with no espionage or paramilitary component, but one just as covert and invisible to most observers. The Bandung Conference presents a second revealing case study in the Eisenhower administration's first-term public diplomacy outside Europe.

Unlike Guatemala, no violence attended the event. But what Bandung shared with the crisis in Central America was the possibility of high Cold War stakes and the certainty that any public US role in playing for them had to be minimized to the fullest extent possible. In the Guatemalan case, Washington had taken great though ultimately futile pains to cover up its involvement in and support for the coup. At Bandung, Eisenhower's public diplomats faced the challenge of making a case on a number of tricky subjects and in a forum to which the United States was not invited.[52] The fact that the

US and its Euro-imperial allies were unwelcome meant that American objectives would have to be pursued through friendly third parties in attendance. If the Guatemala crisis had seen Washington advance a pawn on the Cold War chessboard, Bandung would require instead the use of a proxy player to move any pieces. Though similar on the surface, the two roles differ in important respects, most of all in the latter's relative autonomy and implied "peer" or "ally" status. This was especially vital in the realm of public diplomacy. Given the spectrum of white-gray-black information operations, the cultivation of reliable proxies was of huge importance. At Bandung the refinement of this approach paid off handsomely, and the USIA would use it again during this administration and its successors.

In late 1954, Indian Prime Minister Jawaharlal Nehru and Indonesian President Sukarno announced their intention to convene representatives from a score of new independent nations and colonies to the Asian-African Conference at Bandung, Indonesia. Twenty-nine countries ultimately sent delegations to the historic conclave, which resonated widely through both elite and mass cultures across the Global South.[53] The Bandung Conference posed a diplomatic challenge to both Cold War camps, but perhaps more so to Washington than to Moscow.[54] The conference took place amid a fresh crisis in China, an ongoing quandary in Indochina, and a "sea-change in American and international race relations" bookended by the *Brown v. Board of Education* decision and the Montgomery Bus Boycott.[55] The conference's announcement of an embryonic Afro-Asian-neutralist bloc presented a potential paradigm shift in international affairs; the attendance of China heralded a possible opening for communist expansion. Either constituted a troubling scenario. The latter prospect additionally bore the ominous possibility that China would use its position as both a communist and nonwhite nation to challenge Nehru's neutralism and lay claim to leadership of both of those blocs.

The administration paid sustained attention to Bandung, which posed a minor threat to the administration's foreign policy goals—a threat Washington took seriously and averted thanks to well-executed public diplomacy. Upon receiving the December 29, 1954 announcement of the Afro-Asian Conference, the Eisenhower administration began to brainstorm a reaction. The announcement came in the context of the seemingly endless crisis in the region, to which the United States had previously responded with the creation of SEATO in September 1954. The Bandung proposal, to its authors at least, was a response to the response. Nehru sought to promote neutralism-nonalignment and the "Five Principles of Peaceful Coexistence" (*panscheel*)—and to serve the more practical purpose of countering the Pakistani–American alliance that threatened those principles and Indian security as well.[56]

Sukarno's hosting of the conference signaled his desire to bolster his domestic standing and to share the "neutralist" spotlight, in the process gathering support for his effort to evict the holdout Dutch regime in West Irian.[57] Beyond such country-specific objectives, the collective Bandung agenda—which included anticolonialism, disarmament, and development, among other transnational priorities—made clear its overarching purpose as an ideological and realpolitik answer to regional turmoil. Moreover, its potential symbolic significance was obvious. Although it was not history's first gathering of imperialized peoples, it was the first to engage them as independent (or soon-to-be) sovereign actors, and it invigorated, though perhaps more in retrospect than in the moment, a romantic sense of Afro-Asian destiny just as global race revolution was stirring. As Nehru put it in an address to the conference, "the links that bound the Asian and African countries together in earlier ages had been sundered in their more recent history of foreign conquest and annexation. The New Asia would seek to revive the old ties and build newer and better forms of relationship." Bandung intensified, in historian Christopher Lee's words, "the *feeling* of political possibility presented through this first occasion of 'Third World' solidarity, what was soon referred to as the 'Bandung Spirit.' "[58]

Bandung first appeared to Washington as both a realpolitik and propaganda threat. Assistant Secretary of State Walter Robertson warned Dulles that he "should be giving thought to it. It is a vehicle of Communist propaganda." Nor was this the only potential problem. The specialist pointed out the contrast between the upcoming US-sponsored "Bangkok Conference with mostly whites and a few Asian people, and their [Bandung] conference would be practically all colored." This was a matter of no small concern, though not of overwhelming worry, for Washington; as Congressman Walter Judd told the president after a tour of the Far East, "every single nation out there has as its #1 concern national independence . . . [and] they are afraid that the United States will stay with the white people."[59] On the other hand, the prospective Bandung would not, as seen from Washington, be totally without positive qualities. It might, for example, turn out to be a superficially feel-good and quickly forgotten exercise, a salve to Afro-Asian pride but strategically meaningless. But most of its potentialities were more ominous than auspicious. As Dulles put it to selected Chiefs of Mission, the "Department seriously concerned eventual implications and most interested to avoid damaging effects this conference [*sic*]."[60]

Dulles opined to the NSC on January 5 that Bandung "raised interesting problems [and] would involve important decisions for the United States." Ignoring for the moment its military and nuclear implications, Dulles presented the Afro-Asian meeting in PR terms. He was more sanguine than his aide about its propaganda impact: "The voice of the free world"—channeled through pro-Western Asian countries in attendance—"should be able to blanket the voice of Communism at the Afro-Asian meeting." This PR focus did not obscure the larger strategic picture of the region, within which the conference might raise a host of basically symbolic issues. At any rate, in terms covering both strategy and public relations, Dulles concluded elliptically that "there were still many unresolved problems" that the meeting would pose to the United States, since so much was still unknown.[61]

To address these problems, the OCB formed a working group on the Afro-Asian Conference. The group's charge was the "development of courses of action to promote U.S. objectives" regarding the Bangkok and Bandung meetings, which were overwhelmingly information related in nature. The group's terms of reference directed attention to three points, beginning with the need to harmonize policy regarding the meetings. Second, the group was to prepare materials for Bandung regarding "Soviet-Chinese aggression and imperialism . . . so as to place Communist Bloc countries . . . psychologically on the defensive."[62] Third, the group was to create channels through allies to the conference. Finally, time was short; the group's report was due in mere weeks. The group gleaned some leads from the December 29 announcement: the conference did not seek to create a regional bloc; dialogue would be nonbinding; and economic issues, self-determination, and the nuclear arms race were paramount.[63] From this, the OCB concluded that "most states [would] use the Conference to further their private aims or for prestige purposes . . . [Pakistan, e.g.], is enthusiastic about using the Conference to embarrass Nehru." Japan "wishes to use [it] to end its 'isolation from the mainstream of Asian politics." Meanwhile, the Philippines should "be encouraged to attend to provide a means of keeping the U.S. closely informed . . . and to provide a friendly nonneutralist spokesman." The Philippines had another use as well. To the extent that colonialism would be in the dock, USIA analysts thought, the former US colony manifested the American commitment to anticolonialism.[64]

The announcement that China would attend altered the equation. For one thing, the OCB deduced, an active role by Beijing turned the anticolonialism theme to communist advantage. As one official put it in a report titled "Exposing the Nature of the Afro-Asian Conference": "[Bandung], with Chinese Communist participation will present the grimly amusing spectacle of world communism holding itself up as the protagonist of local nationalist movements and anti-colonialism."[65] Moreover, American options for "turning [this plan] against them" were limited. Since the United States would not be present, Washington could only approach Bandung from afar, on a "moral and psychological level [from which to] expose the Soviet colonial-imperial pattern which uses China as its agent in Asia." The OCB passed its findings to the USIA so that it could produce materials to "discredit the Conference and create an atmosphere that it is a Communist propaganda maneuver."

This psychological war-gaming, however, had to wait. An ongoing policy review at the State Department left the US stance on the conference in limbo and prevented a decision on how to "use ... available materials on Soviet colonialism in connection with [Bandung]."[66] In addition, although China had fixed Bandung on Washington's radar, the conference agenda and possible US responses remained blurry. OCB official Kenneth Landon reported on February 7 that things were coming into focus. A list of possible Bandung agenda items included anticolonialism, nuclear matters, economic development, color discrimination, and Chou En-Lai's five principles. These suggested that the agenda would be deliberately "non-controversial ... so that it can be made to appear ... that when Afro-Asian nations meet together without the 'war-mongering' Western democracies that peace prevails."[67] The OCB sketched several options in reply. The means for executing them were few; Landon pointed out that the United States "will have to work through its friends, propaganda, [or] public statement." One option was a high-level goodwill statement and hope for political and economic progress for the attendees. Another was "saturation" anticommunist USIA programming in "affected countries." Finally, friendly attendees could be briefed beforehand, and serve as proxies on-site: this would "enable them ... to unmask the real purposes of the Communists at the conference and ... disturb [its] pseudo, peaceful, and unanimous atmosphere. In the inevitable discussions on colonialism they should be prepared to raise questions regarding the new colonialism of communism."[68]

This strategy governed US moves regarding Bandung throughout February and March. At Bangkok, the SEATO Council sent salutations to Bandung and demonstrated the "transmitter" role of the friendly Asian governments. The statement asked Pakistan, Thailand, and the Philippines to convey "cordial greetings to the other 17 free countries" at Bandung, as well as a shared dedication to peace, equal rights, and self-determination. This represented "one occasion on which information aspects had been taken into account in [SEATO] decisions."[69] Channeled through SEATO's Asian voices, the message sought subtly to reinforce the point about "Communist colonialism." Making that point through SEATO gave at least an outside chance at making a convincing case. As even Dulles would later note, for Nehru and most outside Europe, Soviet colonialism lacked the racial dimension necessary to qualify for the term.[70] The message had the added virtue, in US eyes, of not committing Washington to economic aid. This was an important hedge. Anything more substantial on the point might be construed as unsubtle bribery or might hurt feelings, among any slighted Bandung conferees and people elsewhere, notably in Latin America. Moreover, it was not at all clear that Congress would approve whatever foreign aid promises might be made. Finally, such rhetoric on the cheap underlined the basic message that the United States, uninvited, would accept that status and remain uninvolved.

The effort to project the image of a helpful, hands-off, supportive-yet-resolute United States nonetheless ran some risks. Among them was the possibility that despite the conference's purposely nonpolemical agenda, Nehru or Chou might have other plans. Either was capable of generating turbulence. The timing posed an additional risk. As Bandung drew near, the administration pondered whether 1955 was a window of opportunity or an omen of failure regarding relations with neutralist countries. UN Ambassador Henry Cabot Lodge wrote a skeptical Senator William Knowland that currents were running in American favor: "In the last two years the Soviet propaganda output has declined both in quantity and effectiveness . . . [and this] has registered even among the so-called Cold War neutrals."[71] Updating the NSC on those neutrals' forthcoming attendance at Bandung, CIA Director Dulles stated that "a very odd assortment" of twenty-nine nations would attend the conference, whose "nearest common denominator . . . was a recent experience of Western imperialism." While "it was very obvious that the Conference would present many opportunities for exploitation in Communist propaganda . . . the outlook for the West was perhaps not as pessimistic as it might seem" due to the presence of pro-Western Asian countries. Preparations by OCB "to counteract hostility to the U.S." and the possibility of a battle between Nehru and Chou also tempered the risk.

Whether Lodge was correct that the communists had blown their chance, Eisenhower's team had come to a decision. When nationalism, neutralism, and communism met at Bandung, the United States would "stress an offensive rather than defensive approach."[72] This would entail "taking steps . . . not only to prevent the Communists from exploiting the Conference to [our] detriment, but also to turn the Conference to the positive benefit of the free world." An OCB game plan of March 28 prescribed these steps. The plan started with the work of INR and the Working Group in assessing "Communist intentions, and [giving] suggestions for countering." These were distributed to US officials abroad, with instructions to consult with invitee governments and friendly attendees. Regarding the latter, "efforts will be made to exploit [the Bangkok message]" through the Thai, Pakistani, and Philippine delegations. Other US posts—notably in Japan and Turkey—were working along similar lines.[73] At home, members of the American press were briefed, which "appear[s] to have been instrumental in setting the public tone." Plans for USIA coverage abroad, including cooperating with British counterparts, had also been put in place.

Given the "discreet" offensive strategy, any high-level engagement would require great care. Nelson Rockefeller, the administration figure most connected to foreign aid issues, had proposed in March that Eisenhower give a speech on these issues "before Bandung." Dulles, however, argued that timing of such a speech was too tricky. If given too close to the conference, it would be perceived as an American attempt to interfere. In addition, the US position on these issues had still not taken firm shape, certainly not firm enough to write "a major Presidential speech [on] subjects which are . . . delicate to deal with . . . [and] which are not yet fully resolved at the highest levels."[74] As a compromise, it was decided that the administration's weekly press conference would state the American position: praise for the "constructive progress . . . being made toward the elimination of colonialism." This was to accompany Washington's main spin regarding Bandung: "The only powers today that are seeking to extend a dominating control over other peoples in the time-worn pattern of colonialism are the *Communist powers*."[75] If the methods were subtle, the message was not: western colonialism was dying a natural death, while "eastern" colonialism was spreading.

Dulles continued to ponder the wisdom of a high-level pronouncement. Any reference to economic aid, for example, "will have people think we are going to have a massive Marshall Plan and they will get their hopes too high," which would leave non-Asian countries feeling left out. Moreover, Dulles thought Rockefeller's recommendations regarding colonialism were fairly empty and blind to the racial subtext: "[Dulles] said colonialism to the Asians means rule of whites over blacks."[76] In the event, Washington stuck with its chosen PR course. Eisenhower both approved Dulles's approach and soothed his concerns, instructing his secretary of state to address the Bandung Conference informally during an April 17 press conference, in profoundly banal language. The statement lauded Bandung as a venue for the affirmation of peaceful solutions to Asian crises, naming the ongoing Chinese offshore-islands controversy as one such. This, in turn, would advance the cause of "social and economic advancement . . . responsible self-government, and durable national independence" beyond Asia alone.[77]

Events on the ground in Bandung proceeded more or less as the United States had hoped. Allied voices pressed American concerns, covered in turn by sympathetic journalists (many of them Americans) and relayed to USIA for heavy rotation in regions outside Europe. The administration's immediate post-Bandung analysis focused mainly on the strategic implications, but did not overlook this public diplomacy dimension. The State Department's Office of Intelligence Research (INR) offered some preliminary conclusions. First, the conference showed "that there is an Asian-African consensus . . . strong enough to discourage Communists, neutralists, or anti-Communists from splitting it." Yet "no single regional leader emerged," notwithstanding Nehru's and Chou's best efforts. The meeting constituted a psychological milestone as well. The prospect of Afro-Asian partnership, either ad hoc or formal; the assertive unity of the pro-Western Asian countries; and the end of "a lingering sense of inferiority" might combine to create a stronger and friendlier region, even one "more ready to cooperate with the West."[78]

Dulles, in a report to the Cabinet on April 29, declared that Bandung was on balance a gift to Washington. With a few small changes, he said, its final communiqué "was a document which we ourselves could subscribe to [and he] listed about eight points of [it] which were consistent with our own foreign policy." Better still, this went beyond the public American stance; the secretary said that "even [the Bandung document's] references to colonialism were in accord with what we feel in our hearts," although they were unable to say this publicly.[79] Dulles stated that Bandung was a win in other respects as well: "The Conference was a very severe reverse for Mr. Nehru . . . Chou [by contrast] achieved a certain personal success," but did so only by striking a concilia-tory, not confrontational, pose—and one mocked in gendered terms on-site by key US ally and proxy Carlos Romulo: "They [Chou and Nehru] remind me of a debutante and her mother at a coming-out party."[80] The administra-tion had feared that Chou would present the United States as aggressor and China as liberator in East Asia, "and thus gain a green light to . . . start violence in the Formosa area. Just the opposite occurred." This laid the groundwork for a cease-fire in the ongoing offshore-islands crisis and even positioned the United States favorably in related negotiations. Finally, Dulles reported that as per the US plan, "the friendly Asian countries put on an amazing performance at Bandung with a teamwork and coordination of strategy which was highly satisfying."[81]

Best of all, thanks to the pro-Western Asian participants, any reference to colonialism condemned not only its Western version but by implication "the more recent evil of Communist colonialism" as well. A May 11 CIA memo further enumerated "Post-Bandung Thoughts." Like Dulles, the CIA found that the "Western friends" had done "a most admirable job" and were proud of it; indeed, "they were inclined to take credit for the fact that the confer-ence was not a propaganda triumph for Chou En-lai," nor, as feared, for Nehru. US actions should now take advantage of the "psychological climate [the pro-West powers] created at Bandung," to avoid any "apparent intransigence on our part," and "to find a formula for restoring Nehru's pride."[82] Washington thought that Nehru "[saw] himself as the leader of all Asia" but had been shown at Bandung not to be, which if played right could redound to American ad-vantage. The US Embassy in Jakarta, the closest American eyes to the action, seconded this evaluation of Bandung as a Western win and explored its larger ramifications.[83] The picture was mixed. Romulo, for example, while helping to imprint the Western position on the conference proceedings, excoriated American support for "Western colonialism [whose] age . . . had come to an end." However, as historian Augusto Espiritu notes, this did not elicit "even a sign of displeasure from Washington," perhaps in large measure because the Eisenhower administration felt the conference on the whole had turned out, partly thanks to Romulo's exertions, to be a pleasant enough surprise where American interests were concerned.[84]

In key respects, Bandung seemed to vindicate the Eisenhower team's basic approach to much of the non-European world: a focus on covert or psychological operations, hints at economic aid, the use of pro-American proxies, and where possible a light touch. Bandung repaid this approach in spades. Those aspects of the conference that the administration sought to orchestrate went as planned; even those parts over which Washington had no control, such as Chou's conduct, ended up netting an American advantage as well. Soviet propaganda, for its part, confirmed this implicitly by denying it explicitly: "American propaganda has not achieved its goals. . . . The results of [Bandung show] the extent of the magnitude of changes which have taken place in Asia," and the decline of the Western position there.[85]

Bandung did not produce an American epiphany. But it did prompt officials to begin to see the Free World differently. As C. D. Jackson wrote that autumn, "the U.S. has definitely not sorted out its own thinking, torn between a) our instinctive anticolonial feelings and b) playing ball with our colonial allies. . . . The combination has made our policy contradictory, confusing, and at times almost irresponsible." The context raised the stakes of this incoherence, Jackson went on, at the United Nations where "the ghost of colonialism hovers over the chamber at all times, and is in complete control of the thought processes of the Asians, Mideasterners, Africans, and Latin Americans— and, with reverse English, the Europeans" as well. Nor was Jackson alone in his assessment. As Dulles and Eisenhower heard from African American Congressman Adam Clayton Powell, who had attended Bandung in a nonofficial, journalistic capacity, "colonialism and racialism must be eradicated as quickly as possible in our foreign policy. . . . The timetable for freedom was no longer within our control—Bandung had stepped it up, and we [had] to move fast." It could not have escaped Dulles's and Eisenhower's notice that Powell had received a standing ovation on Capitol Hill upon his return from Bandung—or that Powell's take meshed with their own in-house analyses and with that of Carl Rowan, who had attended as a journalist with the blessing of Allen Dulles.[86]

Indeed, Foster Dulles was himself increasingly leaning in the same direction, and with an eye fixed upon the public dimension. At Geneva in late 1955, Dulles and British Foreign Minister Harold Macmillan discussed the idea of a "Bandung Conference in reverse." The meeting, to be organized by the colonial powers and the United States, would promote orderly, pro-Western decolonization and would thereby "catch the imagination of the world and take the initiative away from the Soviet Communists." Dulles and Macmillan agreed to explore this possibility. Dulles lobbied within the administration, winning the enthusiasm of the president himself.[87] As 1956 dawned, an "Anglo-American Bandung" was one medium through which the United States would put itself "on the right side of the anticolonial issue worldwide," although this would complicate relations with European allies. Dean Rusk at the Rockefeller Foundation, at Dulles's request, organized a study group that by April 1956 "was approaching a crystallization of ideas" about the Anglo-American Bandung.[88] But its British counterpart could not say the same. Given little evidence of British progress—and the onset of the Suez Crisis—the initiative was dropped soon afterward.

The administration took Bandung seriously from early on, enumerated its goals, and sketched a strategy for achieving them. That strategy moved in step with the administration's preferred dance: working behind the scenes via proxies, emphasizing psychological maneuver, and orchestrating low-cost, light-touch operations to advance US interests. Moreover, follow-up in the region would be logistically easier, as the USIA's Regional Production Center at Manila had reached new heights of productivity.[89] The broader stock-taking that Bandung engendered was not evident in equal measure in all parts of the administration. It was, however, very present in the USIA. Given the agency's attention to American standing, and to foreign opinion on the specific subjects of colonialism and race, this is unsurprising. The USIA had known for some time that Asian and African nationalism, and global racial dynamics, outranked the Cold War in the eyes of most on those continents. The Eisenhower team thought Bandung a victory in part because of the implicit allusion to the "red colonialism" trope in the conference communiqué, and indeed, in lawyerly terms it was one. But until American policy caught up with this rhetorical flourish, the latter could not count for much. Even if it were somehow believed by the Afro-Asian masses, which it simply was not, it was essentially a "tu quoque" defense. As such it would be more likely to confirm those of the neutralist-nonaligned persuasion, enunciated by Nehru at Bandung, in the belief that a pox on both Cold War houses was the best reply.

In between Bandung and the Suez crisis, as it began contemplating its reelection campaign, the Eisenhower administration had completed the retooling of the US information machinery. This had begun to produce results in terms of the efficiency and reach of operations. As Eisenhower adviser T. S. Repplier, who had spent six months evaluating the program around the globe, told the president in August 1955, "we [are] about past the learning period in our propaganda," although an attractive pro-capitalism trope was still needed.[90] Repplier and the agency suggested "People's Capitalism," which would become the centerpiece of a USIA campaign in subsequent months. As had its predecessor "red colonialism," the phrase sought to redefine the terms and rearrange the intellectual terrain in favorable ways. It would use the overhauled, expanded information machinery to show the world what the Western way could do for them, not just warn them about what the communist way would do to them.

But if the retooling had made such ambitions possible, the conceptual side of American outreach seemed more in flux than ever. US public diplomacy thus simultaneously hit a stride just as it began revisiting its own assumptions. Crises in Iran, British Guiana, and Guatemala had shown Washington that turmoil could come to the borders of the Cold War empires—but that it could be addressed with covert actions, including a healthy dose of public diplomacy. In Guatemala, emphasis on "the common democratic heritage and interdependence" and on the "true purpose of the Communist offensive" was in line with the intervention as a microcosm of the superpower conflict.[91] Stirrings in Bandung, however, suggested that more than just the Cold War was in play in large parts of the globe. Moreover, as the failure of one construct—red colonialism—to catch on became clear, another—Free World—seemed increasingly incomplete. The Eisenhower team did not coin that term, but during their first term they used it more or less as their predecessor had: to denote a largely undifferentiated group of nations outside the communist sphere. This mass contained gradations within it and had front lines: Berlin and the Iron Curtain from the late 1940s, the 38th parallel from 1950 onward. But a more nuanced map was emerging. It posed all at once an ideological, geostrategic, and public diplomacy challenge, and it prompted a deeper reassessment of the Free World. That reassessment unfolded slowly, but it brought forth inklings that race, colonialism, neutralism, and development were intertwining in increasingly important ways.

At just the moment, then, that the USIA had infused greater nuance into its operations by adopting a country-specific filter through which central themes would be screened, members of the Eisenhower administration were inching toward an inclusive conceptual framework pooling diverse regions. From its early days, administration officials had recognized the potential for coherent, continent-wide groupings. One astute analyst, two years before Bandung, had foreseen the possibility that anticommunism, but more likely neutralism, could serve as "a framework of hope for the Asians as Asians." This framework would not need to be pro-American to serve US interests. It would suffice if it proved to be "a political force which will weaken Communism. . . . Nehru's neutralism from time to time annoys us [but] he understands the Asian mind and aspirations much better than we do."[92] Bandung suggested that this notion might apply beyond Asia. An Eisenhower administration analysis, which sounds like it could have been written for one of the Bandung attendees but which actually assessed Guatemala on the eve of the coup, concurred:

> This typical underdeveloped country is now undergoing the social revolution that typifies underdeveloped countries generally in our time. That revolution is an expression of the impulse to achieve equality of status (a) for individuals and groups within the national society, and (b) for the nation-state within the international community. Social reform and nationalism are its two principal manifestations. We see the same revolution at various stages of development in Asia and Africa.[93]

If not yet a new bloc in the Cold War sense—these were "underdeveloped countries [within] the free world" and not yet a separate entity—it was nonetheless compelling enough to redirect US public diplomacy resources toward the Global South. As Osgood notes, the USIA "in mid-decade reduced its spending on European programs and concentrated [on] Asia, the Middle East, Africa, and Latin America." This included, for example, the USIA's establishment of "one-man sub-posts . . . in each of the two British [African] territories which are approaching self-government. . . . The purpose is to enlarge U.S. contact and influence with the Africans in these territories who are assuming political responsibility and leadership."[94]

Eight months after Bandung, Khrushchev led a Soviet delegation on a tour of South Asia, confirming that the bipolar battle for the conference's hearts and minds had been fully joined. The Soviets were warmly received, and their "economic offensive" rattled Washington, not least for its public diplomacy dimensions. The tour proved the impotence of the charge of red colonialism—here, after all, were its avatars in the flesh being welcomed by the world's leading anticolonialists. The charge itself, in retrospect, was a ham-handed, though telling, use of language. If Guatemala revealed "the continued predisposition [abroad] to believe in U.S. imperialism," it simultaneously confirmed the toxicity of that term in world discourse. Bandung redoubled the confirmation; in historian Dipesh Chakrabaty's phrase, the conference "brought into the imagination of [the UN] system a shared anti-imperial ethic."[95] This could not help but nudge the Eisenhower administration toward a ju-jitsu-style embrace of the term "colonialism" in their attempt to reach colonial audiences. Washington saw communism as imperial–colonial expansionism and used that language with Asian and African audiences in hopes that it would resonate. Those audiences were unpersuaded. They knew colonialism in its recent and ongoing western-European manifestations, and as colonialists the ushanka-wearing Soviets did not strike them as being in the same league as pith-helmeted Brits. Eisenhower's team and Afro-Asian nationalists agreed that the term "colonialism" was loaded, but they differed on just who truly met the definition. The argument over its meaning would proceed within a public diplomacy architecture expanded to encompass the tropical reaches of an increasingly nuanced and complicated Free World whose voices were noticeably multiplying.

Figure 1 Signaling the superpowers' growing attention to the Global South, Soviet leaders Nikita Khrushchev and Nikolai Bulganin (pictured here without their main host, Indian Premier Jawaharlal Nehru, but with local host Uttar Pradesh Governor Kanialal Maneklal Munshi) made a highly publicized goodwill visit to India in late 1955. (USIA Photo Archives, NARA)

Figure 2 Middle Eastern and South Asian USIA employees meet with Vice President Richard Nixon during a study and training tour of the United States. The use of such local talent corresponded with greater field-post flexibility in shaping output, and both reflected the Eisenhower administration's increased attention to the Global South. (USIA Photo Archives, NARA)

Figure 3 United Nations Day celebration in Seoul, Korea, in October 1950. US public diplomacy highlighted the event, and the United Nations in general, in its output in Asia. (USIA Photo Archives, NARA)

Figure 4 First US Congressman of Asian descent Rep. Dalipsingh Saund, interviewed by the VOA for broadcast in India. The USIA made frequent use of such diasporan figures in programming to their regions of origin. (USIA Photo Archives, NARA)

Figure 5 A triumphant Nasser greets the public at a train stop en route to Cairo, in the wake of his radio broadcast announcing Egypt's seizure of the Suez Canal. (USIA Photo Archives, NARA)

Figure 6 Nasser addressing the public—in person from the balcony, and across the region via Radio Cairo—during the Suez Crisis. (USIA Photo Archives, NARA)

Figure 7 Nasser addresses what the USIA called "the biggest single throng in Egyptian history" at Republic Square, to announce the merger with Syria that created the United Arab Republic. (USIA Photo Archives, NARA)

Figure 8 Ghanaian Justice Minister Ako Adjei records at the Voice of America's New York studios during a visit to the United States. As a veteran of the Gold Coast Broadcasting Service and as (like Nkrumah) an alumnus of Pennsylvania HBCU Lincoln University, Adjei well grasped the importance both of media and of the broader Black Atlantic to Africa's freedom struggle. (USIA Photo Archives, NARA)

Figure 9 A USIS Country Public Affairs Officer shows his camera to Kenyan attendees in front of the USIS stand at a 1957 agricultural fair in Nairobi. (USIA Photo Archives, NARA)

Figure 10 Renowned African American singer Marian Anderson being filmed for USIA media output while visiting a village outside Saigon during a goodwill tour of Southeast Asia. (USIA Photo Archives, NARA)

Figure 11 The HBCU-educated Premier of Eastern Nigeria, Nnamdi Azikiwe, spoke at a 1959 NAACP rally in New York City, spotlighting the transatlantic connections and mutual sympathies of the black freedom struggle. Left to right: New York City Mayor Robert Wagner, Congressman Adam Clayton Powell, UN official Dr. Ralph Bunche, Azikiwe, and Jackie Robinson. (USIA Photo Archives, NARA)

Figure 12 Small teams, often of only two members as the team pictured here in Cambodia, of American and local USIS field personnel took mobile units into the countryside to distribute various kinds of audiovisual media to remote populations. (USIA Photo Archives, NARA)

Figure 13 Unidentified African USIS employees arrive in Washington for training. (USIA Photo Archives, NARA)

Figure 14 A USIS field officer records Angoni dancers in Nyasaland, for inclusion in VOA programming and in the USIA serial film magazine *Today*, the latter of which regularly reached an African audience of thirty million. (USIA Photo Archives, NARA)

Figure 15 USIS official W. Clinton Powell presents a battery-powered radio to Paramount Chief Telewoyan of Voinjama District, Liberia. Such radios were given out all over the Global South, often accompanied by a questionnaire for self-reporting on village listening habits. (USIA Photo Archives, NARA)

Figure 16 Kennedy's point man on Africa, Assistant Secretary of State for African Affairs G. Mennen "Soapy" Williams, chats with Nigerian Federal Minister of Education Aja Nwachuku at a USIS library reception in Lagos. (USIA Photo Archives, NARA)

Figure 17 A shipment of American TV sets delivered to Guatemala for an Alliance for Progress (AFP) educational television project. A US Embassy Public Affairs Officer (dark suit, lower right) helps unload the TVs, which will also carry USIA programming promoting the AFP. (USIA Photo Archives, NARA)

Figure 18 The volume of communist propaganda in Latin America, such as these pamphlets captured in Buenos Aires, could at times and at particular sites dwarf the USIA's output on behalf of the AFP. (USIA Photo Archives, NARA)

Figure 19 An image used in USIA print output in Africa during the early 1960s, with the superimposed text of the Declaration of Independence connecting the United States and Africa, asserting a shared fight against colonialism and for freedom. (USIA Photo Archives, NARA)

Figure 20 An American official presents USIS pamphlets (perhaps containing a version of the image in Figure 19) to Governor of Northern Nigeria Sir Kashim Ibrahim for distribution through his regional government. (USIA Photo Archives, NARA)

Figure 21 Julius Nyerere makes his first public address as Chief Minister of the Tanganyika Government in 1960. The USIA used this kind of positive, uplifting photo in its materials addressing the arrival of independence in that Year of Africa as a counterpoint to the chaos in Congo. (USIA Photo Archives, NARA)

Figure 22 A still image taken from a TV broadcast of cheering crowds at the celebrations in Ghana of the fifth anniversary of independence. (USIA Photo Archives, NARA)

Figure 23 Fidel Castro addresses the Tri-Continental Conference that he had convened in Havana. After an earlier abortive attempt, the 1966 Solidarity Conference of the Peoples of Asia, Africa, and Latin America presented the fullest iteration of the Third World project to date. (USIA Photo Archives, NARA)

A "New Babel of Voices"

Cacophony and Community in the Decolonizing World

> The President said that rather than slow down the independence
> movement, he would like to be on the side of the natives for once.
> —discussion at 375th NSC Meeting, August 7, 1958

Violence in Vietnam and Algeria ensured that extra-European tumult would
accompany Eisenhower's re-election campaign in 1956. But few foresaw just
how dramatically the world situation would begin to change by his reinaugu-
ration. The new phase of the Cold War that began that year did share important traits with the preceding one. Among these was the fact that Vietnam and
Algeria were bloody, catastrophic outliers; outside Europe, the superpower
standoff in far more places took the shape of a media war rather than a military
one. A signal development of the new phase was how new actors confirmed
this dynamic by energetically engaging in large-scale public diplomacy. In the
process, they began to self-consciously play a role that they had begun script-
ing at Bandung.

The quickening tumult of 1956 and its aftermath underlined for these
actors, as it did for the second Eisenhower administration, the vital importance of information operations. The administration's public diplomacy campaigns in Europe—such as the USIA exhibits at the 1958 Brussels Worlds Fair
or the 1959 "kitchen debate" in Moscow—are among its best-known efforts.[1]
However, the later 1950s are equally notable for Eisenhower's expansion of
public diplomacy activities in Asia, Africa, and the Middle East. There US outreach encountered a set of challenges around the issues of race, empire, development, and decolonization—all of which were in intense and volatile flux as
they intersected with the dynamics of the Cold War. At a time when the image
of the United States in many minds worldwide was inseparable from Jim Crow
and from Washington's European-imperial allies, the cresting of these issues
put US public diplomacy understandably and unavoidably on the defensive.

A series of events—from Bandung to the Suez Crisis to the independence of Ghana—delineates the global race revolution of the postwar era, and together they highlight the challenges that race, empire, and decolonization posed for US Cold War outreach in areas outside of—but still or recently ruled by—Europe.[2] The USIA's infrastructure reached a kind of maturation point even as it reached its largest scope to date outside the European continent. The particular challenges of public diplomacy in these areas brought a number of realizations and innovations in its practice: its limitations as a means of damage control; the need to identify and target distinct sectors of foreign mass and especially elite opinion, and to play the "long game" with each; and the difficulty of competing in an increasingly crowded arena. But Washington was far from alone in this. The key events of the race revolution, especially Suez and Ghanaian independence, helped to prompt parties East and West—*and* North and South—to undertake or expand information operations. By the end of the 1950s, newly independent voices in India, Egypt, Ghana, and elsewhere had joined the global battle for hearts and minds, launching campaigns of their own. In addition to validating the strategic importance of public diplomacy, these campaigns also nurtured the coalescing of the Third World as an imagined community on the postwar landscape, as these countries' contributions to global dialogues increasingly united in rejecting the Cold War that Washington and Moscow were so insistently trying to introduce.

Spinning Sandstorms: Suez, Nasser, and the Media Front

The Suez Crisis was still distant on the horizon as the Eisenhower administration sorted through what C. D. Jackson called the "kaleidoscope of 1955," among whose most visible shards were the lessons of Bandung.[3] Although that conference was not the christening ceremony of neutralism-nonalignment it is often remembered to be, Bandung did nonetheless help to put the persuasion on Washington's radar screen. That persuasion was not yet synonymous with Afro-Asian bloc unity, which US officials had also worried about prior to the conference. The neutralism that most concerned the Eisenhower administration was not purely or even primarily a Global south problem but a European one. Nehru was the public face of the persuasion to most of the world, but Tito was not far behind—and if Europe proved susceptible to the malady, the United States might find itself at risk of losing the larger Cold War through a faltering of will on the West's front lines.

Among the other lessons of Bandung the Eisenhower administration gleaned was that whether or not neutralism would spread in Asia and Africa, the new nations there would increasingly assert a global role. The USIA thus made it a priority to target opinion-making sectors in sensitive decolonizing areas. Regarding "the Near East, South Asia, and African areas . . . the entire area is 'hot' and [our] greatest 'effort increase' [must be] in this direction."[4] The effort was prompted in part by the realization that the Soviets were serious about doing the same. Specifying the Middle East, Latin America, and South Asia—the last of which Khrushchev had finished touring just weeks before— an NSC discussion came to consensus that "the underdeveloped countries are a major target of the new Soviet economic and political tactics."[5] More ominously, these tactics seemed to be working.[6]

Partly owing to these trends, Washington faced "enormous propaganda problems" in 1955.[7] How to address these—and indeed the precise nature of the challenge that the new nations presented—remained murky. Whether and what kind of "neutralism" would take hold beyond those like India already committed to it; whether, assuming it did, this would constitute a significant, viable bloc in world politics; and whether this bloc would be wholly "Afro-Asian" in composition were open questions. No less a world leader than Egyptian premier Gamal Abdel Nasser, who had attended the conference, averred that he did "not consider that a Third Bloc has emerged from [Bandung], nor was this the objective. As for Egypt's neutralism, it is a neutralism of cooperation, not isolation."[8]

Moreover, where the new nations' aspirations converged with elements of psychology and demography, the United States might miss an historic opportunity. US Ambassador to the United Nations Henry Cabot Lodge pressed Eisenhower in the summer of 1956 for a "New Anticolonial Statement By You": "As a nation we are not appealing to young people [abroad because of] our apparent sympathy with the colonial powers." An anticolonial statement, accompanied by a USUN resolution, "which should appeal not only to the Latin Americans but to all the Bandung nations which voted against 'colonialism in all its forms' " was urgently needed. Even this might not be enough to turn the psychological factor to American advantage, given its inextricable connection to economic arrangements widely resented in "underdeveloped areas." Here, including in Nasser's Egypt, the "revolution of rising expectations" was one of the "great revolutionary forces" reshaping relations—and working against the US-sponsored status quo.[9]

The 1956 Suez Crisis brought these questions and issues to a head. While the episode has been well covered elsewhere, as with Bandung Suez's public diplomacy aspects tend to be overshadowed.[10] When the crisis exploded, American analysts were not entirely surprised. Earlier that year, the NSC had noted that the Middle East had become a wellspring: "The entire African continent is being affected by the trends of nationalism and neutralism that have originated in the Mideast and Far East," so much so that in US public diplomacy "a major feature of the work in all media has been the minimizing of Nasser" as part of the broader US initiative—Project Omega—to isolate Nasser and thereby neutralize the "propaganda problems derive[d] from the alarming emotional drive of Arab nationalism" that he spearheaded.[11] The lack of independent media in the region complicated efforts, since it left US officials all but unable to conduct "gray" operations. Any organ of note was state-controlled, leaving US fingerprints on media output visible to Mideast regimes, which gave at best "half-hearted cooperation."[12] This was true even in places like Egypt where the US had built media infrastructure for the regime. Indeed, one of the ironies and unintended consequences of the Suez episode was that Nasser eventually used US-furnished money, personnel, and equipment to build the media platforms from which he launched his campaigns against the West.[13] This presaged a pattern replicated by many of Nasser's peers by the end of the decade, as they used Global North assistance of various kinds to build media networks through which to conduct their own public diplomacy. But few could match his stature, or the power of his wildly popular broadcasts, especially after Suez.[14]

The combination of a floodtide of "emotional" nationalism, an inability to go gray, and a charismatic opponent equipped with Western-built media tools gave Suez a unique and revealing character compared to other Global South public diplomacy episodes. It had, for example, little American "spy" component to speak of, compared to the interventions in Guatemala and Iran. It also involved third parties—Britain, France, and Israel—whose roles gave the United States the chance, for once, to avoid being the bad guy it had become in Arab eyes, in the wake of its humiliating retraction of the Aswan Dam aid offer.[15] Its timing showed that even though Washington was increasingly sensitive to the need to treat the non-European world delicately, it was still overly Cold War-centric in doing so. In the Middle East, this amounted to a kind of tone-deafness that American officials were sometimes aware of but could rarely overcome. As a 1953 intelligence estimate put it, "the Arabs do not feel immediately threatened by the Soviet Union or recognize [a] stake in the East–West struggle," but were, rather, more preoccupied by Israel and European imperialism.[16] Finally, the crisis encompassed a unique mix of private and public diplomacy from the outset, as the United States used both in-theater media and venues like the UN to make its case to Arab and non-European peoples.

The crisis began on July 26, 1956 with Nasser's announcement to an ecstatic crowd at Manshiya Square that he would nationalize the Suez Canal. The Cairo throng thus learned of the move at the same time Washington and

London did, and indeed at the same moment his troops heard over Radio Cairo the code word—"Ferdinand de Lesseps"—to proceed with the seizure. The public nature of the initiative was itself a lesson. Nasser's speech included a "roasting" of the United States, as Nasser charged Washington with "punishing Egypt because it refused to side with the military blocs." He did so in "the Arabic of the streets, addressed directly to the people . . . playing on the responses of the crowd, touching their emotions."[17] The performance underlined to all players the role of Arab mass public opinion and Nasser's mastery of it.

Arab public opinion was wildly in favor of Nasser and Egypt, opposed to Anglo-French entreaties, and at first seemingly agnostic regarding the United States. In the early weeks of the crisis USIA guidance emphasized the importance of an international solution, the worrisome nature of Cairo's behavior, the need to avoid personal attacks on Nasser, and the need to avoid any linkage of the crisis to US aid, the Aswan project, or other sensitive waterways such as the Panama Canal. But American officials worried that the US image was entirely hostage to the whims of the Nasser regime, as precious little outreach to the Arab masses did not filter first through it. Worse still, US public diplomacy—having essentially deferred this front to Nasser's radio presence—had actively neglected its own wireless outreach to those masses. There was a "lack of facilities and signals" in the area because "for several years previous . . . the American diplomatic missions and USIS posts generally had been apathetic toward radio."[18] This greatly hampered the US ability to influence the narrative on the proverbial "Arab Street." By the end of the month, Egyptians held a growing belief that Washington was secretly on the side of Britain and France and would join them "in an effort to gain the downfall of [Nasser], or the international control of the Canal, by economic means."[19]

As tensions rose in the first weeks of October, the United States sought to be the highly visible arbiter of the standoff, although there was little evidence that this stance was gaining Washington any advantage in the all-important public dimension. The impasse between Nasser and the British and French, however, combined with the Soviet blocking of Western-sponsored moves at the UN, prevented any diplomatic progress. When the conflict became a military one with the Anglo-French-Israeli invasion of October 29, that dimension became central. At ground zero of the crisis and in the belligerent capitals, the public factor might now include the need to mobilize beyond the smallish intervention force. Within and beyond the military theater, the Suez crisis became a resonant symbol and subject in the information operations of all parties.

Nasser continued to use radio to stoke Egyptian passions and to undergird his claim to lead a Pan-Arab movement. For their part, the Soviets undertook "a massive propaganda campaign in the Middle East," prominently including radio. US analysts reported that "Moscow radio comment on Suez went up from 1% to 24% of Soviet broadcast time, more than twice the amount usually given to major international developments." The Soviets' purpose was two-fold: "In making these propaganda moves, the Soviet Union is undoubtedly motivated by a desire to emphasize its solidarity with Egypt during the current crisis. It is also concerned with distracting attention from [Hungary]."[20] The Hungarian intervention, in which Soviet tanks streamed into Budapest to crush a swelling national protest against communist oppression, had begun the week before the Suez invasion. It would have at any time been a media priority for Moscow. But the fact that it coincided with Suez should not obscure the landmark features of the Soviet propaganda offensive surrounding the Mideast crisis. The intensity of the campaign left US public diplomacy scrambling to keep up day to day.

As US and European diplomats thrust and parried behind closed doors, the American public diplomacy team tried to counter both Nasser's and Moscow's PR moves. Like its Russian counterpart, VOA increased its number of broadcast hours, from 1.5 to 14.5 hours per day. It sought to defuse false stories, sometimes successfully, as in India where a USIS officer convinced an editor to pull a piece falsely claiming that Eisenhower had advocated the use of force.[21] At the moment that the crisis had become a military one in late October, the USIA, scholar Brent Geary writes, "launched an aggressive program to distance the United States from [the invaders] and to illustrate America's role in supporting Egypt in the UN."[22] To the great frustration of American officials, the United States seemed to be playing catch-up. The crisis had a greater potential upside for the Americans than did most crises of the Eisenhower era. The operation had no hint of CIA fingerprints, and as Eisenhower said in a different context, it would be nice "to be on the side of the natives for once" as, on balance and in principle, American sympathies were with the invaded. But because its alliances were with the invaders, Washington found itself losing the spin war as the crisis deepened in November.

To address this, the OCB established the Ad Hoc Committee on Mideast Information (AHMEC). At its first meeting, AHMEC discussed the relevance of reporting the Soviet invasion of Hungary in Arab countries, the use of material on Soviet minorities and religious intolerance, the US record in the UN Security Council, and the use of Radio Baghdad, all as "steps to divide Nasser from other Arab states"—a quiet continuation of Project Omega.[23] Hungary particularly weighed on the deliberations. It was tailor-made for the kind of messages the United States wanted to send regarding the communist threat, but it was far from clear that those messages would resonate outside Europe. In addition, if the use of Hungary came across as mere opportunism—being used to distract Mideastern audiences from crises of higher concern to them—this too would cancel out the benefits of pushing the issue.

The solution lay in a variation on the Bandung strategy of using proxies, though in this case ones that were not allies. Rather, countries that were identifiably "free agents" such as India and Indonesia but that registered opposition to the Hungary invasion would be used in USIA materials to get Washington's point across. Their particular stance had the added virtue of harmonizing with US calls for a military stand-down and a nonmilitary solution to Suez; AHMEC "agreed that the denunciation by the Prime Ministers of India, Indonesia, Burma, and Ceylon of the Soviet attack against Hungary might be useful, inasmuch as it deplored the use of Soviet troops in Hungary and called for an end to big-power military intervention in small countries." This approach and message dovetailed nicely with events once the fighting wound down. In late November, as the first UNEF troops arrived and Britain began withdrawing its forces, the USIA issued to the field its "Information Guidance on Troop Withdrawal," which stressed that these troop movements were only initial steps and that "our primary aim is to reopen [the] Canal and pipelines."[24]

If the Egyptian crowds—chanting "li-yahya Nasser" ("long live Nasser") in Port Said as the Europeans left—were paying any attention to such subtleties in message or messenger, it was difficult to tell from Washington. Moreover, an AHMEC roundup at the end of November noted that information guidance to all posts had ultimately led to output that stressed fundamentally Cold War concerns: a return to NATO solidarity after the Anglo/Franco–American row and a spotlight on Soviet efforts to create a military foothold in Syria. The roundup did note some opportunities and fault lines within the Middle East. The serendipitously timed visit of Nasser's erstwhile neutralist comrade Nehru to the United States was one; interestingly, the USIA debated how best to use the visit "to put limits on public discussion." Nehru as an outside party to the Suez dispute might be able to contribute to a solution, a prospect roundly boosted in the Indian press. The agency elected to err on the side of heavy coverage: "The genuine cordiality of Americans toward a prominent Asian leader was made clear in all-media [sic] reporting" of the visit, even though analysts worried that doing so might ultimately feed the forces the United States hoped to contain.[25]

However, as historian Salim Yaqub has shown, looming large among the forces that the Americans hoped to contain was Nasserist Pan-Arab nationalism. Its emotional power was deployed in Egyptian pamphlets and films on the "Port Said atrocities" and war devastation.[26] US public diplomats also noted the irony that British and French outreach in the Mideast echoed some of Nasser's, and the Soviets', charges: "Nasser had [said he] expected the U.S. would take over French and British interests in the Near East," and once Anglo-French forces had begun leaving, "charges [were] being made by some British and

French that the U.S. seeks to grab Mideastern oil, and to supplant them in that area. France's clandestine 'Voice of the Arabs' network began claiming that the U.S. would be taking France's place as early as August 1957. It was pointed out that this line also is a Communist line." Among the difficulties in countering the charge—which was, in certain objective outlines, true—was the American presupposition that "the Arabs also are considered to be particularly susceptible to publicity of discussions of 'plots.' "[27]

All parties, Washington included, wrestled with the "timing, content and emphasis of information treatment of Nasser," who personified and championed that Pan-Arab nationalism.[28] Whereas the French used their clandestine radio assets, the British deployed their own proxies, especially Nuri Said of Iraq, which ended up backfiring. One consequence of Suez was that whereas Nasser's anti-Said propaganda had heretofore drawn a "generally adverse reaction" on the Iraqi street, Nasser had now transcended this tension, in part because "the Arab racial feeling tends to be ascendant over nationality," and in part because Nasser "was 'the little fellow attacked by big bullies who came out victorious.' "[29] This changed landscape may have been one reason why AHMEC had largely given up on winning over the Arab masses, concentrating instead on the middle and upper echelons of society, including in Egypt. USIS-Cairo reported that regular contact with the regime meant that "it appears that the U.S. point of view is getting across to the top level," and that despite its apparent lack of success with the Egyptian street, "that USIS-Cairo may be in its most favorable position since 1948."[30]

"Most favorable" was a relative term, given the dizzying array of countervailing voices on the Mideast ground. AHMEC noted as the withdrawal of British and French troops neared completion that "an apparent reduction in Soviet information activities" was being replaced by stepped-up campaigns by Iraq, India, and China, in addition to Nasser's Egypt. Cairo's "propaganda efforts [were] bent upon obtaining the Arab world's concentration on the 'enemies' of Egypt: Baghdad Pact, Iraq, Britain. Propaganda against Said has been [so] effective [that] Iraq has found it necessary to jam Damascus radio." American guidance was, in effect, to keep a low peaceful profile, cultivating regime contacts where possible and otherwise seeking to have Iraq play the role of proxy, not unlike the Philippines at Bandung. Posts were directed to be optimistic in their output regarding the Arab-Israeli clash, to emphasize the reduction of the flow of arms into the area, and to emphasize support for the UN, all this in Mideast and Asian capitals where the psychological atmosphere was "like wartime."[31]

Although the final withdrawal of European troops on December 23 ended the highest-stakes phase of the crisis, the continuing public diplomacy traffic by various players highlighted the flux of the postcombat moment. Within the region, Nasser's determination to keep the initiative and press his advantage

was manifest. The Soviets sought to expand their influence; communism was
an all but impossible sell in most parts of the Arab world, but the extension of
military ties with certain Arab regimes such as Syria was not an unrealistic
goal. The Eisenhower administration was equally determined to prevent either
the Soviets or Nasser from taking advantage of the post-Suez flux. In January
1957 the president announced the Eisenhower Doctrine, which would offer a
valuable lesson in the delicacy of public diplomacy on a stage as crowded as the
Middle East now was.

Beyond the need to affirm a regional strategy via the doctrine, Washington
gleaned other post-Suez lessons as well, including for its public diplomacy.
The first of these came with the doctrine itself, which declared an American
commitment, military if necessary, to prevent communism from encroach-
ing into the Middle East—and left undeclared the American objective of, in
Yaqub's phrase, "containing Arab nationalism." Also left uncertain, as historian Osamah Khalil notes, were the precise borders of the region in question.
As with the larger Third World taking shape, the geographical construct was
amorphous and evolving in a swirl of American strategic interests, British influence, and Arab assertion.[32] In remarks a few weeks before his speech to
Congress laying out the doctrine aimed at this blurry region, Eisenhower used
the phrase "fill the vacuum" in explaining its rationale. Mideast media reacted
fiercely. The USIA was quickly directed to stress "developing area strengths to
fill any power deficits and the term 'vacuum' will not be used except to refute
the charge."[33] Output was to be crafted carefully, guided by creative vague-
ness, totemic invocation of the UN, and tempered expectations for settling the
Arab-Israeli dispute. But "vacuum" more or less accurately reflected American
thinking about the Cold War Middle East, and could not be redeemed by
better-crafted rhetoric about it. As Yaqub writes, by the time of Eisenhower's
formal announcement, "the damage had been done." Proof came from Nasser's
lieutenant Anwar Sadat, who declared on January 9 on Radio Cairo that the
doctrine was "worse than . . . British imperialism."[34]

In addition to the need to choose language carefully, another post-Suez
lesson was the urgent need to use radio, more and better. "Possibly the most
significant result of the Mideast crises," reported the USIA, "was the sudden
recognition of the value of radio in the area. . . . As recently as late 1955, the
Agency had considered terminating broadcasts to Turkey. It is possible that
these attitudes have been largely responsible for the lack of facilities and
signals which would be of tremendous value at this time."[35] The Arab world
held only two million radios, a small percentage of the global total—but that
number had been essentially zero in 1950 when the VOA began its first meager
broadcasts in Arabic, and such growth was expected to continue. The messages those radios carried were worrisome even when the heat of the crisis

dissipated. The Soviets could be expected, analysts said, to continue the campaign they had begun at the crisis's peak. Moscow was making "a serious effort to assert Soviet influence as champion of anticolonial world" and in particular "to reap propaganda advantage by posing as champions of Arabs," with output "keyed to the subjects of Arab nationalism, independence, [and] anticolonialism . . . ultimately pinning responsibility for the crisis on the U.S."[36]

USIA officers bet that the proper deployment of the Eisenhower Doctrine could counter if not fully neutralize much of this Soviet effort. But they realized that the Soviet campaign was not the only factor. Analysts found general approval of the doctrine everywhere "with the significant exception of the 'uncommitted states' and the Middle East itself"—that is, everywhere except in the ostensible target regions. Indeed, "the press in most neutralist nations has attacked" it, even as their governments remained tactically and tactfully silent.[37] There was evidence of interest among Egyptians in the doctrine, potentially counterbalancing the manifest hostility of Nasser's government to it. USIS-Cairo reported that its Information Centers in Egypt had received 48,000 requests for the transcript of the Eisenhower Doctrine speech; "a vast number of well informed Egyptians hope that the [doctrine] will result in a turning point that will keep Egypt from increasing its dependency upon the Soviet bloc."[38] If the United States could avoid giving offense to national pride in its outreach regarding security and aid—and if it could avoid giving "the impression that we are sliding back to a cozy comradeship with Britain"—then post-Suez output centered on the doctrine might succeed in keeping communism and Arab nationalism at bay in the Middle East. The effort to do so, scholar James Vaughan observes, "proved to be one of the biggest single-issue campaigns that [USIA] had yet undertaken."[39]

As 1957 unfolded, this appeared increasingly to be a losing bet. As the Voice of the Arabs blasted away at Eisenhower and his doctrine over the spring and summer, it inadvertently echoed communist propaganda in the region, with which it shared the goal of eliminating Western influence.[40] By year's end, a confidential internal assessment found that American public diplomacy in the Middle East had been spectacularly unsuccessful. Its inability to meet logistical challenges—VOA's long-desired new and more powerful transmitter for the region remained out of reach, and state-run publications agreed to place only very little USIA material—doomed it to drowning in the torrents of Nasser's and other Arab media output.[41]

The longer shot was whether or not deploying the doctrine could do any better against the other forces, arguably more potent than communism, then in play—above all, Nasserite Pan-Arabism. Nasser himself continued to require careful handling. The USIA directed its posts to minimize attacks on the Egyptian leader, underplaying the reportage of independent media from

back home, and leaving no USIA fingerprints on materials critical of him—
though the indirect channel (critical materials unattributed to US sources and
furnished to non-US outlets) could still be tried when opportunity arose.[42]
However, as the public diplomacy ramifications of Suez began taking shape,
it became clear that Nasser was but one face of a larger phenomenon: the ability of nonsuperpower actors to seize the microphone. Nasser himself recognized this. As he put it to American scholar Daniel Lerner, "radio has changed
everything ... we live in a new world."[43] An assessment of "USIA Information
Problems in 1957" described that world:

> There have emerged on the world stage eloquent spokesmen for areas
> of public opinion heretofore inarticulate, or largely disregarded at the
> international level. Many nations, only a few years ago the colonial
> subjects of European Great Powers, now play significant roles in the
> crystallization of world opinion and in the determination of policies
> having worldwide effects . . . In other regions, as in Egypt and . . . the
> Arab world, supercharged nationalism has become a dangerous threat
> to orderly progress.[44]

Not only to orderly progress, the writer might have continued, but to American
interests and prestige as well. The goodwill that the Eisenhower administration felt it had won in the Suez crisis had all but vanished into the impassioned
currents of Nasserism. But to the extent this risk was real, it was not only because of the Egyptian premier's personality and program but also shortcomings in Washington's understanding of, and policies toward, areas in transition
away from European rule.

The Eisenhower administration had drawn a very large strategic lesson
from the Suez crisis, leading ultimately to the doctrine. But its grasp of the crisis's larger public diplomacy lesson remained weak. Its outlines could be dis-
cerned at Bandung and grew sharper at Suez. During the crisis, the shadow of
Bandung played an outsized role in communist output—suggestive of the ways
that side understood the issues in play. In its Suez output, the Soviets made a
show of calling on the Bandung nations to resolve the crisis, in contrast to the
Great Powers roster that made up the Suez Canal Users Association. Beyond
the contrast, as American analysts assessed the move, "it is the more unusual
in view of fact that the USSR was not a member of the Bandung Conference,
and the Asian countries have shown a disinclination to invite [them] to a
future conference. . . . The call for 'Bandung' action was apparently calculated
to strengthen that possibility and in any case to give added weight to Soviet
sponsorship of Asian and African independence, 'neutrality,' and solidarity."[45]

China played similar chords, showing "unusual" interest in Mideast affairs and "us[ing] extensively [the] theme of Western imperialism" in their output.[46] Eisenhower's team believed that its Suez diplomacy had sufficed to turn the Crisis to US advantage. Lodge thought that Suez was exactly the "Anti-Colonial Statement" he had pressed for, and he reported from the UN better evidence of public diplomacy impact than could usually be found: the "enthusiastic reactions from Afro-Asian nations about your policy here in the Near East crisis. . . . You have given us a position of moral *authority* which in turn has created a degree of *respect* which transcends the mere counting of noses."[47] But whatever goodwill Washington's Suez diplomacy had won proved short-lived, as the Eisenhower administration sabotaged itself during the followup: a tin-eared doctrine that to many minds outside Europe simply missed the point, and the ham-handed handling of aid programs that came across as at best paternalism or at worst bribery.[48]

The administration understood that the policy had to be right in order to get public diplomacy wins, even as they overestimated the payoff of their Suez stance among non-European hearts and minds.[49] Meanwhile, Eisenhower's public diplomats drew different implications for their subsequent tactics and strategy. One, signaled by the agency's largely ceding the field of mass opinion to Nasser, was the importance of targeting the elites of emerging nations. Another, as a review of 1957 operations put it, was "the perennial information problem of colonialism." While the "Agency continued to emphasize . . . U.S. intentions to view sympathetically the legitimate aspirations of colonial people for independence [and] economic and social betterment," it had to counter "the aggressive posture of the Soviets and Red Chinese as the only sincere friends of people seeking independence," charging that Washington "was insincere because [it] was unwilling to offend its 'colonialist' partners in NATO."[50] Relatedly, the phenomenon of neutralism was not going anywhere, and US outreach would have to adjust accordingly. "The uncommitted areas," read one analysis of the February 1957 Cairo communiqué on "positive neutrality," "fall generally into an Asian-Arab-African regional context, 'the Three A's of Neutralism' [whose] roster . . . reads like the majority roll-call of the so-called Bandung Powers." US policymakers agreed that "international communism is seeking to penetrate these racially conscious and nationalistic neutrals, using race consciousness and nationalism as weapons against the West," and as a consequence, "our propaganda should be more subtle in the uncommitted countries [and] be ever sedulous to recognize the supreme sensitivity of the new states as to their sovereignty." Of equal importance to their sensitivity was their potential solidarity in opposition to the Cold War powers as well. As Eisenhower remarked at the news of Nasser's seizure of the Canal, any wrong move might willy-nilly "array the world from Dakar to the Philippine Islands against us."[51]

However, perhaps most notable was a trend among those same new states, a trend that gained size and momentum after Suez: that American, Soviet, Chinese, and European voices were not the only ones in play. As newly independent nations, and their newly ensconced leaders, gained control of their own affairs, they too moved into the global PR arena. The field, that is, was getting crowded. In practice, as in Egypt's case, many of the new voices seconded Moscow's message: "With the close Soviet alignment of Egypt the Communist world gained a significant source of propaganda to African nations. Cairo added to its Arabic and Swahili broadcasts programs in Amharic, Somali, and Hausa, stressing the themes of anticolonialism and neutralism, and exploiting Islamic ties to win support for Egyptian claims to the leadership of African nationalism." But if these echoed communist output, they did so in languages, and more importantly with a credibility, that neither Cold War power could match.[52] Moreover, they advanced themes—anticolonialism, Pan-Arabism, Afro-Arab-Asian solidarity, neutralism-nonalignment, and economic autonomy—that resonated far more deeply with audiences, within and beyond the Sahara, asserting themselves increasingly in world affairs.

Speaking of Freedom: Ghana, Race, and the "New Babel"

These developments soon converged again at the western end of the African continent, albeit in less violently dramatic fashion than Suez. The British colony of the Gold Coast was scheduled to become the independent nation of Ghana on March 6, 1957. It would achieve that status smoothly, through mostly peaceful and cooperative collaboration with the metropole. It was the first in sub-Saharan Africa to do so, launching the second wave of postwar decolonization. The leader of Ghana's struggle, Kwame Nkrumah, was, along with Nehru and Nasser, part of the holy trinity in the crusade against empire. As in Egypt, the story in Ghana revolved around a single man who took up the mantle not only of national independence but of pan-national freedom. For Nasser the cause was Pan-Arabism; for Nkrumah, Pan-Africanism. Both cases saw the spectacle of a vividly national representative around whom the local struggle revolved, but who also assumed the role of spokesman for larger causes as well.

In addition, Nkrumah—as one of the best-known Africans on the world stage—by his presence and his rhetoric brought the issue of race to the forefront. Although the civil rights movement was still in its relatively early stages, the rise of African independence at the same time that African Americans were fighting for equality meant that a figure like Nkrumah could personify the intertwining of the struggles, in ways that W.E.B. DuBois, Marcus Garvey, and others around the Black Atlantic had long averred. The planned attendance at the Accra ceremonies of an honor roll of African American luminaries, including Martin Luther King, A. Philip Randolph, Ralph Bunche, and Adam Clayton Powell Jr., further confirmed the point.[53] For Washington, Nkrumah and Ghanaian independence would thus pose a public diplomacy challenge. For one, it helped to put American racial practices under intense scrutiny, increasing the pressure for domestic reform. It also meant that US outreach to nonwhite areas had to work that much harder to win over public opinion, thanks to doubts about American claims that the United States would treat nonwhite foreign nationals with equality and dignity. Regarding Ghana specifically, US public diplomats from time to time found unexpected wind at their backs, in that local media was both more active and more sympathetic than in many locales. In the summer before independence, for example, the Gold Coast Broadcasting System (GCBS) did a radio series on Gold Coasters in America, focusing especially on students enrolled in American universities, most of whom had followed in Nkrumah's footsteps by attending historically black institutions of higher education (HBCUs). USIA officials determined that this "offer[ed] an excellent opportunity to point up . . . America's friendship for the Gold Coast and its interest in its political and economic progress; [and] the progress being made by American Negroes," and all this through "native" voices, to boot.[54] However, this was an exception; the rule was that America's racial record made information-outreach in nonwhite, emerging nations like Ghana an uphill climb.

American public diplomats foresaw these challenges as they began preparations for the Ghanaian independence ceremonies. As the first of its kind in sub-Saharan Africa, the colony's "approaching independence [made] the USIS program [there] increasingly important." Existing programs—including "not only the usual activities" of a library, press output, exchange of persons, and film but also two officials deployed to the field in the northern section of the colony—were "realistic and appropriate" but would need to be augmented and in top form given the stakes. "The U.S. Information Program . . . presents a real challenge to the staff, first to operate in the transition period of colony to independent status, and second to operate in the beginning of a vast 'awakening' of a primitive people (estimates vary from 5–10% literacy for the country as a whole)."[55]

This language—"primitive" here, elsewhere "native," or "[men] in loincloth in the jungle"—in this and many other USIA documents illustrate how lacking in self-awareness many American officials of the time were. Yet racism and condescension in their phrasing obscures a persistent feature of their work on the eve of African independence: their greater awareness than many Americans then had of the way that race damaged the US image among non-white peoples, and the need to respect these sensitivities both in their messaging and, ultimately, in policy. As Ambassador Lodge had noticed at the United Nations, where he was reminded daily of the damage and the need, American public diplomats living among their nonwhite audiences in the field frequently held more enlightened attitudes about race than their compatriots back home, their often painful and dated language notwithstanding.[56]

The US Consulate in the Gold Coast planned to sponsor an "appropriate cultural presentation" at the celebration, possibly adding African dates to a USIA-organized tour of musical performances already planned for Europe.[57] This aligned with planning by the USIS post at Accra, which de-emphasized the political and explicitly racial aspects of US media outreach surrounding the celebrations in favor of "soft," culture-focused activities. A message from Eisenhower alongside a prerecorded musical salute by the African American opera singer Lillian Evanti, all broadcast on VOA locally and worldwide, topped the list; next came a "Year of Independence" photo calendar mixing images of the United States and Ghana. A stop on the tour of the traveling "People's Capitalism" exhibition was also scheduled to coincide with the ceremonies.[58]

As a midyear report to the NSC would later put it, "the drive of African territories for independence confronted [USIA] with significantly enlarged opportunities and responsibilities," and Ghana was the first of these. "Improving the quality of African programming [and] materials tailored specifically to African target audiences . . . was a major Agency task during 1957. Five major African posts . . . provide[d] footage for a USIS-produced African newsreel. . . . Shown in leading theaters throughout Africa this reel portrays US interest in Africa and seeks to build a bridge between Africa and the United States." The USIA "also sent a cameraman to film ICA [International Cooperation Administration] projects, and did radio shows on the accomplishments of Negro Americans and on African visitors [to the US]. All USIS efforts in Africa during 1957 were made in the face of Soviet and Satellite intensification of the pressures upon African countries, particularly in the independent nations and those approaching this status."[59]

The centerpiece of US outreach would be the Eisenhower administration's deployment of Vice President Richard Nixon to lead the the US delegation to the Ghana ceremonies. This would outrank the Evanti performance or filmed output in prestige and visibility, and would—so the agency, and Eisenhower, hoped—bestow America's blessing on the transfer of power in Africa. Sending Nixon to lead the delegation would demonstrate that the

United States "recognized . . . the singular importance of Ghana's independence." In early January, Dulles had emphasized to Nixon that the matter engaged both strategic and public diplomacy concerns. As he put it, "Africa . . . was the coming continent and we were anxious to do all we could."[60] The historic nature and strategic opportunity of the visit were hard to overstate. Nixon was the first American vice president to tour Africa and was slated to visit Morocco, Liberia, Uganda, Ethiopia, Sudan, Libya, and Tunisia after the Ghanaian ceremonies. As the representative of an Republican administration at a time when the GOP could still trade on being the Party of Lincoln, Nixon's presence would at least suggest sympathy to an African audience. The Nixon visit, the USIA later reported, thus "provided an opportunity to exploit substantially through all media US intentions to view sympathetically the legitimate aspirations of colonial people for independence and where possible to aid those who have gained independence in their progress toward economic and social betterment." The high profile of the visit could be traced in the propaganda response it elicited. Soviet radio networks, one field report noted, were "blast[ing] Nixon's African Tour as Bid for Expanded Influence and Bases."[61]

The visit itself went as smoothly as could as be hoped. To the surprise of those who doubted Nixon's PR talents, the vice president acquitted himself well. Nixon underlined the often-overlooked American connection to the education of African leaders such as Ghanaian intellectual James Aggrey, lauding his role and memory and presenting an "Eisenhower Fellowship" to the college he founded at Achimota.[62] Even Ghanians who had never heard of Aggrey (or, for that matter, of Eisenhower) appreciated Nixon's "acknowledgment [of] the importance of the 'common man,'" as expressed in his impromptu remarks to crowds gathered along his motorcade route. There and in more formal settings, Nixon paid due and repeated, though in some ways understated, respect to the momentousness of Ghana's achievement of independence, flattering his hosts and praising their achievement as the product of peaceable cooperation with the exiting British landlord. He did so in his brief remarks at the formal independence ceremony itself, and in subsequent appearances, including a press conference at which his "statement on colonialism was excellent and was widely appreciated," and in his prepared statement upon departure: "In a very real sense, the eyes of all nations and peoples are focused on the new state of Ghana . . . we have rejoiced with Ghana in its newly acquired independence. . . . These are indeed momentous events in the history of the entire Free World." This was as close as Nixon got to referring to the Cold War in his public remarks, a discretion that seemed to please his hosts; the GCBS, for example, broadcast this departure statement twice. If in the end the press coverage in Ghana was less than it might have been, due to Nixon's being overshadowed by the presence of the Duchess of

Kent, the embassy's survey reported home that the media campaign was nonetheless every bit the public diplomacy hit that the Eisenhower administration and the USIA had hoped for.[63]

Although the USIA counted Nixon's "subtle" visit a public diplomacy success, US information officers lived in more or less permanent fear that excessive subtlety would impede their effectiveness. The Ghana case was no exception, and field officials worried afterward that they had underplayed their hand. The Consul in Accra thought that Nkrumah had "showed special favoritism to the communist delegations," while USIS-Accra wondered if their efforts had fallen short not only of the communists' but also those of non-aligned voices.[64] But this, if true, was a risk inherent in the American design, since by the late 1950s the USIA leadership had sought to make subtlety the default setting when it came to racial and colonial issues. They had good reason to do so, given the agency's operating assumption that colonialism would remain "the perennial information problem" as decolonization spread—and the future assured more such dilemmas as anticolonial conflicts in Cyprus, Algeria, Indonesia, and elsewhere all mounted.[65] In addition, race relations—irretrievably interwoven as they were with most such colonial conflicts—promised yet more attention to race practices back home. Given these dynamics, the subtle approach as practiced at the Ghana independence ceremonies and afterward was the least risky option.

American race relations were not a new challenge for the USIA, of course, but they gained greater salience in the latter 1950s as the drives for African American civil rights and African decolonization rose in tandem. For US public diplomats race did not cut in only one direction, and they sought ways to use American assets such as HBCUs and jazz musicians. Both were deployed in Ghana output. Along with longer-running projects such as *The Negro in American Life* and the monthly newsreel series *Today* (produced for exclusive African distribution), the impact of such testaments could be strong. After a jazz band toured Africa—vouching for America's racial bona fides all the while—the embassy in Addis Ababa reported that an Ethiopian official "told [an embassy] staff member that he had now revised his opinion of the status of Negroes in the U.S. He said he would not have believed these facts had not the American Negro told him himself."[66] Historian Brenda Plummer confirms that "the feel-good performances of Louis Armstrong and other artists . . . helped to mute foreigners' perceptions of the [racial] conflicts occurring in the United States." No less a figure than the Francophone revolutionary Frantz Fanon, observes historian Frank Gerits, later opined that the jazz tour, African American diplomatic personnel, the Voice of America, and other non-African cultural activities had a large enough impact to have impeded the cause of African unity.[67]

The September 1957 civil rights showdown over public school desegregation in Little Rock changed the conversation. Its timing just six months after
Ghanaian independence fed the sense of a global quickening on racial issues.
As a public diplomacy matter, it had the makings of a potential disaster. The
crisis and its ramifications for the US image abroad threatened to undo the
progress USIA felt it had made at and since the ceremonies at Accra, via followup such as its coverage of the first civil rights act in eight decades. The crisis
gripped the world's attention for much of September.[68] Soviet propagandists
had a field day, attacking "race terror" in the American South. Dulles "said this
situation was ruining our foreign policy. The effect of this in Asia and Africa
will be worse for us than Hungary was for the Russians." Lodge reported from
the UN that "[here] I can see clearly the harm that [Little Rock is] doing. . . .
More than two-thirds of the world is non-white and the reactions of [their]
representatives is easy to see."[69]

The USIA showed a keen awareness of this dynamic in Africa and the
broader nonwhite world, and of the importance of countering it "particularly
when it seemed patent the Little Rock situation could arise again."[70] The figure
of Nkrumah made Ghana a locus for such efforts. Cary Fraser argues that the
Crisis "forced a departure from the administration's studied indifference"
to world opinion of American race relations, as Eisenhower's analysts noted
the growing assertiveness of African and other voices.[71] US public diplomats
sought to turn this confluence from liability to asset. The agency in Africa "addressed an audience increasingly preoccupied with creating for the continent
an independent voice in world affairs . . . which speaks for 'the distinctive
African personality.'" Thus "USIS activities were tailored to convince African
leaders [and] peoples . . . that the U.S. recognizes and supports Africa's emergence as a constructive force. The convening of the first conference of independent African states in Ghana [the April 1958 Conference of Independent
African States (CIAS)] provided a fine opportunity for displaying U.S. interest in the effort to define a common sphere of interest."

Indeed, in a harbinger of the fast-spreading public diplomacy competition in, for, and by Africa, the CIAS prompted a frenzy of media activity by
the USIA and other actors in anticipation of Nkrumah's All-African Peoples
Conference (AAPC) in December 1958 in Accra. As Gerits writes, "the success of [CIAS], and particularly Nkrumah's ability to act as an independent
actor, took the West by surprise."[72] In response, and as part of the public diplomacy embrace of African independence and unity, the USIS produced a
newsreel of the Accra meeting and screened it in over one hundred African
theaters. This exemplified USIA efforts "tailored to convince African leaders, specifically, and peoples generally, that the U.S. recognizes and supports
Africa's emergence as a constructive force."[73]

The emergence of such "common spheres" was a delicate and still very inchoate matter. Yet the answering of the HBCU-educated Nkrumah's call to "African Peoples" to come together at Accra—an act independent of but at the least goaded by "the use Nasser and Khrushchev were making" of US race troubles—suggested that something notable was beginning to take shape. Along with Sputnik, Little Rock dealt a severe blow to US media outreach, and it formed a point of stark contrast and sentimental connection with Africa's progress toward independence. Within the Eisenhower administration, this gradually crystallized the conclusion that the unity asserted at Bandung might be taking recognizable form. If not quite a race-based collective, there was nonetheless threaded through the rhetoric of figures like Nkrumah the nucleus of a new grouping that drew upon commonalities of racial and colonial experience. Ghana and Little Rock had put both Africa and race at the forefront of world attention in 1957 and had made clear that despite superpower interest, these were not exclusively or even primarily East–West issues. Rather they touched upon the concerns of the Global South at a time when media technology made it possible for that region to join the conversation.

In the wake of Suez, Ghana, and Little Rock, US officials noticed an explosion of media competition in—and by—the non-European world. By 1958 the critical mass was undeniable and had begun to produce a cacophony—both in and about Ghana, as well as in neighboring Africa, and by a wide range of actors. A 1960 USIA report put it this way: "African countries have entered the field of international broadcasting with extensive plans for future activity although few of them are now on the air. International broadcasting capability is becoming one of the major elements of national prestige and almost a prerequisite for 'real' independence." In 1958, only two African countries—Egypt and Morocco—were engaged in external broadcasting. By 1960 three others—Tunisia, Ghana, Sudan—would begin operations, and by the end of 1961, seven more were expected to do so.[74]

The phenomenon was not entirely new, but its growth spurt had begun to change the landscape. Nasser's Radio Cairo had blazed the trail, proving to Nehru, Nkrumah, and others that such media was a force-multiplier for new states. Sovereignty was a prerequisite for launching external networks, although many of the new states were able to overlay their output onto pre-independence diasporan circuits abroad. As the number of actors proliferated in the wake of the new states' arrival, though, it could prove difficult for any given one of them to get a message through in radio, film, and print. The USIS post in Accra called it "the new babel of voices" on the African airwaves: "In keeping with the increased tempo of the drive for independence now engulfing Africa and with Ghana's rise to leadership of that drive . . . Ghana's new role is attracting international attention. Other governments are increasing their bid for radio time, press space, etc." This "psychological atmosphere ... has complicated the role of USIS," as Ghana is "leaning over backwards to prove her neutrality on East–West issues" in a media field crowded by teams from "the United Arab Republic (UAR), Britain, Israel, Germany, India, and the U.S.S.R." The difficulty, though, was also due to policy decisions by the new states: "The government radio stations in independent African countries are devoting larger amounts of time to news and [material on] their own countries and the rest of Africa. International news, particularly the more controversial issues in the Cold War, is being sharply curtailed."[75] By 1960, some "outside" programming could get through to the expanding African audience—imports of radios had risen fifty percent in just five years—whether via proprietary networks or those of the new states. That year, "[non-African] countries with programs purposely tailored for Africa include[d] the colonial powers, the Communist bloc, Israel, India, and the UAR. Communist programming— initiated in 1958—totals more than 61 hours weekly."[76]

For the USIA, this dictated a low-key, adaptive strategy: "It would be fool-hardy to pit the resources of USIS-Ghana against the flow of history in this country ... Rather [we must exert] a steady pressure [over time] to convince those who need convincing that [our] policies ... will advance their legiti-mate aspirations for freedom, progress, and peace."[77] US public diplomats had learned that the tone of their programming needed to be subtle. Keeping the Cold War in the foreground, it turned out, often backfired. In Nigeria, for ex-ample, "USIS has been criticized, in all sincerity, for seeming to export a psy-chopathic American fear of Communists behind every bush. . . . Nigerians are determined not to be dragged into a Cold War which they consider exclusively a big-power, East–West concern." Ghanaian Foreign Minister Ako Adjei con-curred. He warned Washington that "U.S. programs [in Ghana] will be less effective if they appear to be motivated by 'Cold War' considerations."[78] By the close of the decade, the emphasis was on support of "native" goals and local needs, on neutralizing the effects of Jim Crow, and on generalized cultural sympathies rather than on the East–West conflict.

Even so, as one new nation after another found common ground with its neighbors in rejecting the Cold War, the challenge to the USIA was a steep one. The external media output of Ghana, Egypt, and other emerging nations offered various blends of "'non-alignment,' 'positive neutralism,' anticolonial-ism, and 'Pan-Africanism.'"[79] Moreover, they opportunistically and enthusi-astically seized upon Cold War issues, such as the 1959 French atomic bomb test in the Sahara, which fueled their themes.[80] African, Asian, and Mideastern audiences were thus confronted with a rapid rise in the number of media op-tions catering to them, including home-grown ones. But the diversity of views carried by this proliferation of outlets could obscure the fact that they often came to the same core conclusions about world affairs.

Above all these centered on the desire to be independent not just from Europe but, in a sense, from the Cold War itself—and to explore the possibilities for solidarity built on that desire. Although in practice any such sentiment was as much myth as reality, references to the "Bandung Spirit" could be found in the rhetoric of many Global South actors. For example, a roundup of press reactions to Nixon's Ghana trip found the Ethiopian government reaffirming its close ties to "the Bandung powers"; the Egyptian press claimed that Nixon sought to "break up the Afro-Asian grouping"; Radio Peiping detected the Bandung Spirit afoot in Africa.[81] Within two years of Ghana's independence, both Accra and Washington identified a distinct Afro-Asian bloc at the UN, with which Nkrumah's Ghana was "emotionally linked." An increasing convergence of message could be detected within the media cacophony: Egyptian, Indian, Ghanaian, Soviet/East Bloc, and Chinese programming were all expected to highlight "Afro-Asian solidarity themes."[82]

In one sense, this convergence was an unintended consequence of US policy. The USIA, one study reported, had along with ICA and State, "endeavored over the past years to assist many nations in the development of their mass media, [so] that there would be a greater flow of information into and out of those countries." This assistance took a variety of forms in both infrastructure and content. It allowed Washington to corner a number of niche markets. In some developing countries' media, the USIS was supplying ten thousand words per day of print output and thus "[had] become a de facto AP/UPI." It was expected that the distribution of media tools would also facilitate the emergence of "native" voices.[83] The prospect of their convergence had been more predictable (if equally unintended), even if it only caught US notice intermittently and impressionistically. Post-Bandung, and especially post-Suez, "solidarity" among these voices was often simply assumed to have communist roots. A clear example was the 1958 Afro-Asian Solidarity Conference in Cairo, in which US analysts saw "the Communist tactics of using the Bandung spirit and prestige for its own ends." In the hothouse moment between Bandung and Accra, to the extent US officials perceived an "Afro-Asian community of interest," they assumed it was inspired, and sure to be exploited, by communists.[84]

By the end of the decade, however, the reflexive linking of that "community of interest" with the Bloc had waned. USIA skeptics of this view realized that although communist rhetoric might mesh with Afro-Asian discourse, the two were not the same—and the latter was an organic and perhaps unstoppable phenomenon in its own right. The proliferation of newly independent voices manifested a determination to chart an autonomous and coherent course internationally.[85] It was, in a sense, the moment when the members of the Global

South had begun finding each other and finding their own voice. Preexisting circuits of connection dating back decades, across diasporas and through metropolitan capitals, could engage each other laterally in the media ether of the ex-imperial world. As Fanon wrote in 1959, "Having a radio meant paying one's taxes to the nation, buying the right of entry into the struggle of an assembled people . . . After having imposed the national voice upon that of the dominator, the radio welcomes broadcasts from all the corners of the world [which] link the fellah to an immense tyranny destroying wave."[86] An American analysis came to similar conclusions: the present was "a time of great awakening of the human spirit," as "the ex-colonial areas like Egypt [were] marked by a highly-emotional national consciousness," giving them "an influence on international developments difficult to foresee even a few years ago."[87]

It was dawning on Washington that this coalescence was not a communist creation but a collectively self-made one. USIA officials anticipated a twofold continuation toward a tripolar world: a "lessening of the bipolar aspect of world affairs," and the "rise of other forces and blocs with intensified nationalism in less-developed areas."[88] As C. D. Jackson described the new generation of African leaders: "Some of these men—unfortunately too few—are Western oriented. Some [of them] see an axis stretching from themselves to Cairo and Nasser. Some see an even longer axis, to Moscow. Some are playing *all 3 sides* of the street."[89] The fact that a Cold Warrior as hardcore as Jackson could now perceive a third side is telling, suggesting that one had begun taking recognizable shape on Washington's mental horizons. Jackson had taken some time to reach this conclusion, having argued just the year before that US policy could accommodate the "nationalist revolution" connecting "the Middle East . . . Asia, Africa, and Latin America" but that all of these belonged under "our effective leadership in the Free World *as a whole*." Nasser had protested Dulles's use of the latter coinage at the dawn of the Eisenhower years.[90] Now, at their dusk, the construct was becoming baldly untenable, as something altogether different was taking shape in the rhetorical self-conception of the Global South, and being broadcast far and wide.

US public diplomacy under Eisenhower had expanded and adjusted commensurately with the evolving map of the Cold War world. It had shifted in tone from aggressive bombast to subtler persuasion, partly in deference to the larger audience it recognized outside Europe—one which thanks to Jim Crow had good reason to doubt American rhetoric of freedom. Its scope had enlarged considerably. NSC-6013 noted that the kitchen debate was only the most famous instance of US outreach: "The U.S. government devoted more attention to overseas public opinion during the past year than during any other twelve-month period in its history. The president made goodwill trips to twenty-one countries," including in Asia, the Middle East, Africa, and Latin America, while "USIA [operated] in eighty-six countries." But even this was hardly enough to keep up: "It must be recognized, however, that the Sino-Soviet bloc stepped up its information and cultural activities even more energetically than we did."[91]

If the Moscow kitchen debate—a belated rebuttal to the Sputnik shock two years earlier—suggested that the ground zero of public diplomacy, as of the Cold War, remained in Europe, the broader global landscape had nonetheless changed radically by the late 1950s. The Eisenhower administration had started its tenure raising the non-European world higher on the public diplomacy priority list. If Bandung, Suez, and Accra had confirmed the wisdom of this move along the way, the September 1961 founding of the Non-Aligned Movement (NAM) would soon make it look positively prophetic. As decolonization reached its zenith, some in the USIA saw this as an advantage: "There is a trend toward a multipolar world which is on our side." However, if the Eisenhower administration in its last days was starting to grasp the contours of the poles taking shape, it was yet unclear what would ultimately define the one jelling in the Global South. Whether the putatively race-neutral NAM and its rejection of the Cold War dichotomy; or the Bandung spirit and its solidarity carrying the nonwhite world to a postcolonial destiny; or that spirit's subsets, the "Pans" in Nkrumah's African and Nasser's Arab regions; or the "revolution of rising expectations" and the faith that development and modernization could meet them would form its core remained to be seen.[92]

Moreover, although NSC-6013 did not give it the prominence that the USIA's own correspondence did, that defining conversation would take place in the public diplomacy of Global South parties, which had expanded at speeds comparable to that of the superpowers. The definitional convergence of this grouping—one neither East nor West but rather determined to chart its own perhaps collective path—formed an audience different in key ways. It was larger, poorer, and farther-flung; it was culturally non-European and wildly diverse; it was in the midst of an incipient but unmistakable political awakening; and as far as information operations were concerned, it was composed arguably more of elites than of the masses. It also held different priorities. The new nations' leadership could make tactical use of the Cold War competition, but on the whole they feared it more than they identified with it, and they had other interests and needs more urgent than the supposedly enormous stakes of the East–West clash. In policy as well as in public diplomacy, such missed connections could cascade.[93]

Above all, in ways that neither Washington nor Moscow had anticipated before Suez and Ghana, the convergent grouping was not only audience, but actor too. As their voices joined and found themselves groping toward some conclusions in common, they drove the continuing evolution of this Third World that Sauvy had christened just a few years earlier. Washington, grasping the limits of the concept of an undifferentiated Free World, was by 1960 coming to agree. In this sense, as the global race revolution threaded ever more the issues of race, identity, citizenship, and sovereignty into and through Cold War geopolitics, it served to begin pulling the conflict's lenses off of American eyes. The Eisenhower team further perceived that the diverse new grouping might grow larger still. The deliberations of the President's Committee on Information Activities Abroad (the Sprague Committee) that spring noted the "major problem [of] the progressive revolution among the underdeveloped nations ... few [of] which are 'out of the woods' and the list of foreseeable emerging problems was as long as the list of countries." This major problem, the Committee heard, had "particular reference to emerging new countries but [we should] not overlook older ones as are found, for example, in Latin America where the problem is almost identical."[94]

"Mucha Alianza, Poco Progreso"

The Alliance for Progress and the Development of the Third World

[Cuba is] on the side of those peoples that wish to be free, not only politically—for it is very easy to acquire a flag [and] a color on the map—but also economically free, for there . . . can be no political independence unless there is economic independence.
—Fidel Castro at the United Nations, September 1960

In a revolutionary world, economic colonialism is as dead as political colonialism.
—Kennedy advisor Peter Nehemkis, March 1961

For all the emphasis on change that Kennedy's election purportedly represented, it is easy to overstate his differences with his predecessor. The continuities in his diplomacy are at least as striking in retrospect. In key areas such as a focus on the non-European world and the integration of public diplomacy into foreign policymaking, the New Frontier continued the policy vectors of the later Eisenhower administration.[1] In elevating Latin America to the top of the priority list, and in applying modernization theory to policy toward those areas, however, his administration added some newer elements, and the combination nicely encapsulated the early-1960s US approach to the Cold War in the Global South. In this moment it also harmonized with many of the preexisting dynamics of Latin America's own Cold War as it was being waged by elite and radical factions across the hemisphere.[2]

Kennedy shared Eisenhower's conviction about the importance of public diplomacy, and it was perhaps fitting that the first modern "celebrity" president would name the first celebrity to head USIA and that his Cuban nemeses would be the biggest celebrity revolutionaries of the Cold War. The rise of Fidel Castro, building upon a wave of anti-Americanism in the hemisphere, gave the plight of the Global South a potentially threatening and acutely local aspect. If the war for hearts and minds had become truly worldwide over the previous five years, and the failure of the impoverished nations to feed stomachs and souls was nearing crisis proportions, Castro showed that the two could converge on the US doorstep. Though Kennedy and Castro offered polar-opposite prescriptions, both agreed broadly on the diagnosis: that the poorer, rapidly overpopulating nations were in a race against time and for development—and were now a key Cold War battleground. Any prescription would therefore have to capture the imagination of the peoples in question. Washington feared it was losing that battle, as Castro's revolution seemed to hold the greater appeal than did American social scientists in the fight for what Kennedy himself called "the most dangerous area of the world."[3]

The Alliance for Progress (AFP) was the Kennedy administration's central answer to this challenge and its signature initiative in Latin America. Conceived as a new beginning in inter-American relations, as a model of cooperative development aid, and as a pro-Western vaccine against Castroism, the Alliance was inseparable from—indeed was all but meaningless without—its public diplomacy dimension.[4] That dimension was in some ways more successful than the policy itself—and thereby inadvertently bears some responsibility for the policy's failure. The AFP's design required mass public buy-in to succeed. The Alliance encapsulates some of the most important aspects of the Kennedy administration's public diplomacy: the expansion and revamping of US information machinery and its integration into policymaking; the attention and priority given to Latin America and the Global South; and the elevation of "modernization" expertise. Its accomplishment amounted to the triumph of style over substance—that is, of public diplomacy over the policy that it was meant to support. The career of the AFP, moreover, left a broader legacy still by contributing to the further coalescence of a shared North and South definition of the Third World and to its expansion to include Latin America.

"We Lag Behind": Murrow, the Southward Turn, and the *Alianza*

Kennedy and his predecessor agreed with the Sprague Committee's assessment that the USIA had suffered from chronic organizational confusion: "The principal information agency has been renamed six times, reorganized four times, and until recently has been subjected to great year-to-year variations in its appropriations, much to the disadvantage of long-term programs [and] effective planning."[5] JFK's team sought to resolve this chaos once and for all and to instill the agency with their most hallowed quality: "vigor." Revealing his interest in the matter, Kennedy approached journalist Edward R. Murrow soon after Election Day about heading the USIA and appointed him during his first week in office. Murrow brought prestige, credibility, enthusiasm, and charisma beyond all his predecessors combined. He agreed with Kennedy on "the crying need to improve public understanding of the U.S. abroad." The president established a direct and open USIA line to the Oval Office, giving the agency his very visible blessing.[6] Murrow took advantage of this confidence to implement their shared vision, and he set about revamping operations. Among other reforms, this produced a streamlined feedback channel between field posts and their DC headquarters, and a seat at the policy table. As he reported two months into his tenure, "USIA is, for the first time, being heard on the consequences of policy *before* policy is made." A report later that year found that this went some distance toward solving "the successive failures" that had previously bedeviled US public diplomacy.[7]

This integration occurred alongside the rapid expansion of USIA activities begun in the Eisenhower years. Speaking to his former colleagues at the National Press Club, Murrow reported that USIA was opening around a dozen new posts annually worldwide and would soon be operating in more than one hundred countries. Its purview encompassed "seven principal media—radio, TV, movies, press, book publishing, exhibits and the arts, and personal contact." The activity in any one of these areas matched that of a large multinational media corporation: radio broadcasts in thirty-five languages; 40,000 to 50,000 words of copy distributed among five areas of the world; films that reached a weekly global audience of 150 million; and 50 million books published (in fifty languages) annually. As a former television journalist, Murrow was well positioned to appreciate the fast-growing importance of that medium to public diplomacy. His agency counted 160 million viewers worldwide, a number bound to rise, as did the pace of USIA's television operations alongside it.[8]

The lion's share of this expanded activity targeted the non-European world. Eisenhower and Kennedy both agreed with the Sprague Committee that this expansion should continue.[9] Kennedy had argued since his 1957 Algeria speech that decolonizing areas were the next key battleground of the Cold War, and that the United States had to manage its European alliances accordingly. Latin America at that time was not yet part of this battleground; the speech included references to Asia, Africa, the Mideast, and the "uncommitted world," but none to the western hemisphere.[10] International events during 1960 affirmed the importance of this new battleground, as did the vastly expanded communist bloc and "native" media output in the emerging nations. The challenge was all the more acute given what the Kennedy team saw as the communist lead in the contested areas. As ambassador Chester Bowles put it to Murrow, "in the sphere of giving of ourselves to the peoples of the underdeveloped world we have perhaps done least. . . . In achieving a sense of identification of our cause with that of the indigenous peoples, we lag behind."[11]

This suggested a dual failing, on both the definitional and informational fronts, and the outlines of a solution for a battleground that Washington had come to think of as larger than just the decolonizing world. The new states in Asia and Africa had been born into a shared matrix of poverty and deprivation that could catch fire, especially if ignited by agents-provocateurs. But Castro's revolution had shown that such a scenario was neither hypothetical nor limited to the Old World. The geographical area of concern was defined not primarily by its recent colonial status, or by its Afro-Asian-ness, or by its adherence to nonalignment, but above all by its poverty. In the Sprague Committee's words: "We are facing a revolt of the have-nots, particularly in Asia, Africa, and Latin America."[12] While the emphasis on economics did not vitiate the other defining qualities of the non-European world, it did signify the expansion of the area on Washington's mental map. Kennedy demonstrated the centrality of the enlarged area to his own thinking in his 25 May 1961 address to Congress, a speech usually remembered as the "Moon Shot" speech: "The great battleground . . . is the *whole southern half of the globe*— Asia, Latin America, Africa and the Middle East—the lands of the rising peoples. Their revolution is the greatest in human history." Moreover, the struggle for their allegiance "has highlighted the role of our Information Agency," for which JFK pleaded to Congress for additional funding, especially for Latin America where bloc radio output was triple that of the United States: "China alone does more . . . broadcasting in our own hemisphere than we do [and] powerful propaganda broadcasts from Havana are heard throughout Latin America, encouraging new revolutions."[13]

For JFK's public diplomats, a change in terminology accompanied this geographical expansion. Murrow described this in a mid-1961 memo to Sorensen. He had directed the USIA "to drop from our lexicon the words 'underdeveloped [or] undeveloped countries,' 'backward countries' [and] 'emerging countries'"; these would replaced by "'developing countries' and 'modernizing countries.'"[14] The latter terms would accommodate Global South sensitivities while capturing the main thrust of US policy toward the region: "modernization as ideology."[15] The premise held that the non-European world was fundamentally defined by its poverty, marking an "earlier" stage of civilization. Modernization offered a formula more or less universally accessible and in line with American strengths. Accordingly, it ranked high on the list of themes Murrow directed his troops to promote.[16] Kennedy did his part, calling for a concerted Western effort to guide a "decade of development," a trope that quickly spread in USIA output.

The amended public diplomacy lexicon was, in part, an indirect response to Castro. The Cuban Revolution showed that despite having won its decolonization more than a century earlier and having spent the intervening decades nurturing a continental-cultural identity as "Latin America" apart from the rest of the Global South, the region shared enough of the decolonizing world's problems that it too could become part of the geopolitical Cold War stakes.[17] Many Latin Americans wondered if Washington got the message. As late as two weeks before his inauguration, a task force had warned Kennedy that "substantial Latin American apprehension exists that the incoming Administration, while justifiably upgrading Asia and Africa, may continue to leave Latin America a step-child. We think [your] Administration promptly on inauguration should emphasize its vivid interest in Latin America."[18] Part of the solution was to show that US estimation of the high Cold War stakes in the Global South included Latin America, making the region part of the Afro-Asian narrative by defining their shared conditions—and US solutions for them—in such a way as to neutralize Castro.

However, another part of the solution was to put Latin America not just in Washington's spotlight, but the world's as well. Since 1945 the United States had considered Latin America to be, by and large, the least worrisome front of the Cold War—exceptional episodes like the 1954 Guatemala coup notwithstanding. That view changed during the late Eisenhower administration, whose default setting for Latin America had been "trade not aid." Latin Americans thus enviously watched the Marshall Plan pay off in Europe, while US business dominated their own economic lives. They did so, as US analysts would later detect, while undergoing a pair of mutually reinforcing revolutions—that of "rising expectations" and that in mass communications media. These had widened, diversified, and radicalized Latin American public opinion such that it now sought "fundamental structural changes [in] the social order."[19] The Eisenhower team barely sensed this nexus of simmering resentment until it boiled over during Nixon's 1958 visit to South America. The episode rattled Washington, and six months later when Castro triumphed in Cuba, the administration's response produced a variety of new policies for security and aid in the hemisphere. These, including a prototype of the Alliance for Progress, were bequeathed to the incoming administration. Already predisposed to view the non-European world as the new Cold War battleground, Kennedy put Latin America at its center, and resolved that no more hemispheric dominoes would fall.[20]

The Alliance for Progress would be the paramount weapon—though by no means the only one—deployed in this battle. The AFP was a prime example of modernization theory, but that aspect was no less central than the program's other qualities.[21] The Alliance had made an appearance in JFK's campaign rhetoric, where it was tentatively named. Once coined, it took clearer shape at a Harvard meeting in December 1960.[22] Even before it had gotten much further than this brainstorm stage, the notion achieved circulation in Latin America when Kennedy included the phrase in his inaugural address. The US Ambassador in Buenos Aires reported that the usually "standoffish and difficult" Argentine press had paid the new president lavish attention: it was "an altogether extraordinary reception" thanks in large part to Kennedy's "remarks on 'a new alliance for progress.' "[23] In a speech Americans remember more for "pay any price, bear any burden," the slogan resonated in its target region before there was a program to back it up.

This suggests the public diplomacy value of the Alliance in outreach to the hemisphere. Among the awakenings of the late-Eisenhower administration regarding Latin America had been that despite a long head start, US public diplomacy had fallen behind the bloc there.[24] The Sprague Committee had sounded the alarm, finding "an urgent need for substantially increased efforts in the critical areas of Latin America and Africa." Catching up with the bloc was only part of the task. Just as important:

> In the face of the sweeping social, economic, and political revolution now underway [we must] identify ourselves with forces of progress toward stable and democratic institutions, and disengage ourselves from the outmoded and resented aspects of the status quo and the colonial past ... [Our outreach must] expose and counter ... the multifaceted Sino-Soviet offensive against the orderly development of these areas, [and] provide effective support through information means to US development programs.[25]

Done right, the Alliance for Progress—whatever its longer-term payoff in terms of actually abetting Latin American development—could accomplish all these public diplomacy tasks at once. Castro, one official wrote the president on February 27, had peaked, and his popularity paled next that to JFK: "Your prestige continues high [while] Latin American disavowal of Castro, but not of his social reform, leaves a psychological vacuum which we believe can be filled with vigorous leadership and a practical social development program geared to the middle and lower classes." The moment was right to seize Castro's thunder. The February 27 memo urged JFK to "take the initiative" by giving life to the slogan of an "Alliance for Progress."[26]

With careful planning, the USIA agreed, "an enormous amount of enthusiasm can be generated around this program [but] the timing and spacing of the propaganda push ... are most important." A presidential speech would be the ideal launch, but the content and tone of its "premiere" would have to

be carefully managed. The ghost of the Marshall Plan hovered over the planning. The fear—prescient in key respects—was equally of overpromising dol-
lars and overpromising results: "We may create 'great expectations' impossible
to fulfill, with inevitable Latin American disillusionment." This could be as-
suaged by highlighting particular aspects of the program. The "'AFP' should
be clearly identified as [an] umbrella [for extant aid programs like] Peace
Corps, Food For Peace, [and] ICA." In addition, "the JFK speech should hit
hardest at the social rather than the economic development aspects of program [and it] should emphasize strongly [its] mutual aspects." To reinforce
these, "Bolivar's idea of Inter-American unity should be emphasized." In any
case, the risk of overpromising had to be run. Rallying the publics of Latin
America, not just its regimes, was crucial. As ambassador Lincoln Gordon
noted, the Alliance "must energize the great reservoir of human talent in Latin
America."[27] The JFK speech would roll out the campaign to do so. It would be
disseminated throughout the hemisphere, via two hundred Latin American
radio stations that were slated to carry the translated speech live. Follow-up included comprehensive press coverage alongside a TV and film blitz, pamphlets
and cartoon booklets, and binational center exhibits. Combined, these would
hit all sectors of mass public opinion. The NSC ordered "State, USIA and CIA
[to] pull out all the stops on an information program built around the Kennedy
speech [and] the aid message. . . . The 'Alliance for Progress' must become as
well-known as the 'Monroe Doctrine' and the 'Good Neighbor Policy.'"[28]

At a White House gathering of the Latin American diplomatic corps on
March 13, 1961, Kennedy announced his successor to the Good Neighbor.
Taking his public diplomats' advice, he proclaimed in Bostonian Spanish the
"Alianza Para Progreso." The cooperative effort would pool hemispheric resources, including an unspecified amount from the United States, to support
Latin American social reform and economic development. This would raise
living standards, counteract Castroism, and show the way forward for the
non-European world: "The unfulfilled task [of the western hemisphere] is to
demonstrate to the entire world that man's unsatisfied aspiration for economic
progress and social justice can best be achieved by free men working within
the framework of democratic institutions."[29] The immediate reception in the
room was electric, and the USIA filed daily reports of its crackling through the
networks of the hemisphere. In a followup interview on VOA, Costa Rica's José
Figueres Ferrer praised it "as the first time in history the U.S. has responded
to the call of Bolivar in [his own] language." In print, USIA reported "on the
extraordinarily fine press play given to the President's speech. Mostly it has
been lead-story, page-one treatment."[30] Such reactions gratified Washington.
The "press coverage was extraordinarily extensive" and replete "with glowing
phrases in almost all quarters . . . the tone of the speech [was] hailed as a new

departure." This allowed the USIA to create a coverage feedback loop, as the speech's glowing reception was turned into a news item in its own right, allowing the agency to keep "the story current [via] fast media."[31]

A week later the dividends were still rolling in and validated virtually every item of the USIA's prespeech advice. The agency reported that "overall reception [is] typified [by] one commenter who hailed it as the greatest contribution to Pan-Americanism in a hundred years. The most frequently applauded aspects [are] its sympathetic understanding of aspirations and problems of Latin American people [and its] call for active Latin American participation." The rollout was a triumph. The agency concluded that Latin American "comment has been so overwhelmingly favorable that the few dissenting voices have been drowned in a tidal wave of enthusiasm and hope." Two weeks later, Argentine President Arturo Frondizi wrote Kennedy to express the same and avow that the Alliance's success was a foregone conclusion: "I already consider AFP as a reality that is on the march."[32] Followup of this type set a tone for related activities, such as Kennedy's upcoming address to the OAS Council, Latin American coverage of which seemed to confirm that the Alliance rollout had helped to create a favorable climate for US initiatives in Latin America. Expecting the dividends to continue, on April 17 USIA reported that a one-hour VOA documentary on the Alliance for Progress had been distributed to all twenty-one posts in the hemisphere for immediate broadcast.[33]

The tape reels were just arriving on post when their rebuttal began unfolding at the Bay of Pigs. The CIA-orchestrated invasion of Cuba, meant to spark a general uprising but doomed to end in fiasco, was another inheritance from the prior administration. Its juxtaposition with the Alliance is less well-recognized, but very revealing. At first blush, the invasion—a singularity of operational incompetence, ideological malevolence, and reflexive interventionism—would seem to undercut the themes that the USIA had used the AFP to advance. Worse still, the invasion came as a complete and unpleasant surprise to the USIA. Unlike the conception stages of the Alliance, Murrow and the agency were far out of the Bay of Pigs loop.[34] But they reacted quickly, springing into action while the invasion was still underway. "On Cuba," Murrow recounted to his former colleagues, "we had no choice but to be truthful and complete." This meant expanding Spanish-language radio broadcasts to Latin America from one to nineteen hours per day during and after the crisis. The coverage was deliberately unpropaganda-like in tone. Murrow "mention[ed] with some pride. . . . There were Latins relaying our broadcasts who said 'you are too honest, you will be misunderstood.' "[35] In PR terms, keeping the spin to this minimum was a risky move. It was, however, in line with Murrow's general approach and with his boss's acceptance of responsibility for the fiasco.

In part thanks to this approach to the crisis—and to the hemispheric good feelings stoked by AFP—the USIA concluded, perhaps overly optimistically, that the Bay of Pigs did the United States less damage, and Castro less good, than one might have expected. "Followup inquiry," ran one assessment a week later, "made it evident that . . . the Cuba landings apparently *did not increase favorable opinion of the Castro regime*."[36] This regional reaction was more or less unique. Most comment worldwide correctly assumed American support for the insurgent invaders and found that the episode damaged US prestige while enhancing Castro's. But mainstream Latin public opinion appeared to USIA analysts to be rallying behind Washington against Castro—for which analysts credited the AFP. They cited the April 22 joint declaration by Frondizi and Brazilian President Jânio Quadros as "contribut[ing] to a better psychological climate for the U.S." in that it "condemned alien infiltration of the western hemisphere" and rallied " 'support [for] JFK's AFP.' " The South Americans were echoing Kennedy's April 20 speech accepting responsibility for the crisis, and in which he too affirmed that the Alliance, not the Bay of Pigs, would be the blueprint for US relations with the hemisphere. The speech "had a powerful impact in Latin America. [It got] prominent play in every important paper, and has elicited many [approving] commentaries . . . implying that Latin America should rally behind the U.S. president." Another analysis two weeks after the Bay of Pigs concurred that the Alliance had helped to blunt its impact.[37]

In retrospect, this is perhaps less surprising than much of the scholarship would have it. Though the Bay of Pigs fiasco is seen as a decidedly low point in Cold War inter-American relations, it took place on a intellectual and media landscape in Latin America that was, despite some wariness, on balance hopeful about the Kennedy administration—sentiments that the AFP at this early stage could easily fuel. As a mid-1961 survey of Latin American public opinion put it, "Castro has *not* captured these symbols of social revolution, for only small minorities say that [his] revolution presents a good example for their own country."[38] This was not for lack of effort on Fidel's part. Like many of his contemporaries in the decolonizing world, Castro marked Cuban "independence" by launching overseas radio and news wire services, adding a Cuban voice to the rapidly expanding bloc offerings in the hemisphere.[39] Through his overseas information services, notably *Prensa Latina* and radio, Castro sought to inject a radical perspective into Latin American media. But these efforts, as often as not, faltered as Fidel moved closer to the bloc's embrace.[40]

However, even as USIA analysts found that the media landscape on balance favored the United States, they knew that their outreach efforts in no way guaranteed victory. A study of Latin American opinion found it "startling to face the long list of Latin American grievances against us," noting "the theory than Pan-Americanism means 'Pan' for the North and only Americanism for the South."[41] The scale and sophistication of their campaign worried US public diplomats pondering the longer term. The Task Force on Latin America warned that the "Communist-bloc program [was] operating on a scale approximately seven times the current U.S. effort . . . They are [so] effective in targeting the narrow stratum of political/intellectual types [that in a few years they can] virtually take over the functioning of the country." The Policy Planning Staff (PPS) urged countering this by leveraging JFK's Alliance momentum to capture "the revolutionary and nationalistic forces to which Communism is appealing by associating the U.S. with [Latin American] desires for higher living standards, more social justice, and a sense of independent national pride." According to the USIA's research, stealing Castro's thunder in this way remained a realistic aspiration. PPS went on to call for increased outreach centered on the AFP, as the Alliance's organizational meeting at Punta del Este, Uruguay, drew near.[42]

The conference was the biggest of the follow-up opportunities envisioned in the original AFP rollout back in March. But JFK's public diplomats were wary. In their eyes, Punta del Este had to engender excitement—but not too much. This was one reason the hugely popular Kennedy declined to attend; he feared his presence would overemphasize either the Cold War angle or his own celebrity.[43] On the surface, the meeting's personnel and purpose—economic ministers building interstate administrative machinery—would be intrinsically dull. However, excitement was already at such a high level that Latin American audiences were primed for expectations to rise unreasonably higher. Recounting his tour of the hemisphere, Kennedy advisor and US ambassador to the UN Adlai Stevenson in June had "encountered a unanimous and intense interest in the Alliance for Progress program. The president's address [left] a profound impression in Latin America, the most favorable since FDR's Good Neighbor policy" and thus raised hopes for Punta del Este—despite the fact that there was no real agreement on what would constitute a successful conference.[44]

USIA lamented as much in its information guidance on the eve of the meeting. "Because the overall objectives are so challenging," it advised, "great care is needed to keep in focus . . . what may be expected of the present meeting," which was, after all, technocratic in nature. Output should underline that no funds would be disbursed there, nor would "spectacular country or regional projects" be announced. Rather, "in preparation for the meeting we have emphasized *national* plans and programs rather than some sort of single hemisphere-wide" one. The final item on the USIA guidance agenda revealed the agency's dilemma at Punta del Este and after: "The main objective here is to develop ways and means of informing the public and enlisting their support of the national plans and programs. *The success of the whole enterprise depends*

heavily upon the sustained interest of and support by the people."[45] The people
and their leaders alike were interested, moreover, in a subject about which the
Kennedy administration wanted to remain vague: the amount and schedule
of the US financial contribution. Indeed, the "single overriding preoccupation
of all is extent of U.S. commitment." Nor was this the only delicate topic. The
stagecraft had to be managed in such a way as to finesse intrahemispheric rivalries and neutralize, to the extent possible, the wildcard presence of Cuba's
delegate Che Guevara.[46]

As the August meeting opened Che threatened to be a thorn in the US side,
denouncing the "Alliance for Exploitation." The US team reported that in the
meeting's early stages, "Guevara so far has not done well," alienating most of
the Latin American delegations. But this did not prevent him from having a
larger public impact: "Unfortunately press is playing him up." This, indeed,
was likely his stratagem all along—playing a public diplomacy game of his
own. In his attacks on the Alliance, "he made little substantive impression on
delegates. However, he was aiming over their heads at people of Latin America,
and we cannot from here estimate how successful he was in this effort."[47]

Che the revolutionary might seem a mismatch in the popular battle of images
when contrasted with the gray-suited Treasury Secretary Douglas Dillon leading the US delegation. Yet by most accounts Dillon won that battle. His surprise announcement of a billion-dollar-plus US commitment was "received by
[a] large audience with prolonged applause" and became the centerpiece of US
public diplomacy at and after Punta del Este. Postmeeting assessments found
that whatever Che's success, Washington's had been considerable. "The close
of the conference," reported Dillon, "was a remarkable show of solidarity on
the part of all except Cuba and Bolivia. Final result is, I think, everything we
could have hoped for and the Alliance for Progress has now been fully and
successfully launched." The USIA found the same: "Few events in recent years
have caught [this degree of] attention [from] Latin American leaders, editori-
alists, and commentators. . . . The high degree of expectation [was] tempered
with skepticism based on past U.S. failure to make firm commitments and on
awareness that the [Alliance] depends in large measure on the temper of the
U.S. Congress." The policy and public diplomacy challenges of Punta del Este
thus intertwined. The former was to negotiate the technocratic agenda—to
cooperate without getting coopted. In historian Jeff Taffet's phrase, "the US
could not dominate the program, but at same time, it *had* to dominate the
program." The challenge was to direct the stagecraft accordingly—striking
the balance between stoking and tempering popular sentiment, and with a
proper note of mutual partnership accomplished via the invocation of former
Brazilian President Juscelino Kubitschek's Operation Pan-America and the
1960 Inter-American Conference at Bogotá. The effort succeeded well enough

that afterward even "the leftist Venezuelan *Ultimas Noticias* [pointed out that] 'the first front on which the U.S. needs to win the Cold War is Latin America, for obvious strategic reasons, and in Punta del Este we must point out, objectively, that they have hit a political home run.' "48

USIA was determined to keep scoring: "It is essential to maintain the momentum gained in Punta del Este . . . to continue to publicize and explain [its] Declaration and Charter [and] draw attention to actions that various nations [including the United States] are taking to realize the great potential in the AFP."49 Output would reinforce the Alliance's basic themes as well as Washington's specific recent moves in support of it: inter-American cooperation *and* individual country initiative; government activity *and* private citizen engagement; reforms to drive both social progress *and* economic development; savvy long-term planning; strong but reasonable expectations of success; and Washington's honoring of its financial commitment. The Alliance's rebuttal of Che would remain for the most part implicit. The USIA strategy accentuated the positives of the AFP rather than the negatives of the Cuban communist regime.50

In keeping with the cooperative thrust of Punta del Este, the OAS was slated to take over AFP public diplomacy over the next few years. The relevant USIA programming would at that time be folded into OAS operations, though the agency would retain responsibility for highlighting the specific US contributions to the Alliance.51 In the meantime, the USIA continued to flood the Latin American media landscape in support of it. A 10,000-word print file was sent daily to all hemisphere posts, with heavy emphasis on the Alliance. This resulted in more than a hundred stand-alone news stories, many of which could then in turn generate future coverage. The agency called this "cross-play technique" a way "to take advantage of such developments as the endorsement of the AFP by [Peru's] APRA, particularly convincing to liberal elements in Latin America." The hit ratio of these barrages seemed quite high. USIS posts estimated that "local press usage ranged from forty to seventy percent of all Agency materials distributed, and that radio/TV usage was much higher." USIS-LaPaz reported that "hardly a day goes by in which some USIS items do not make the frontpage."52

Beyond the press, the USIA distributed millions of pamphlets, posters, leaflets, and cartoon booklets with such titles as "Diez Pasos Hacia la Prosperidad de las Americas." The agency also subsidized a special edition of the OAS magazine *Américas* "devoted exclusively to Punta del Este and other aspects of the Alliance for Progress."53 The agency was also working on "a 'before and after' photo-story series which will show a locale in Latin America before Alliance aid was given, and a year or two afterward when results are visible." Film production and distribution expanded too, giving wide reach to AFP-centered USIA films such as *United in Progress*. As the year closed, US public diplomacy on the AFP had achieved a breadth and efficiency unmatched in most other parts of the globe. When Kennedy visited Latin America in December, his trip became the subject of a short documentary *JFK's Good Neighborly Trip*. The finished film was on its way to western-hemisphere posts even before the president had returned to DC.[54]

Through 1962, US information operations in Latin America sustained a steady focus on the Alliance for Progress. There was reason to believe the outreach was succeeding: "Response to [the AFP] was most favorable throughout the area except in Cuba." An unidentified official proposed that Kennedy coin a slogan in a "happy anniversary" speech to the Alliance: "This second year of [the AFP] could be called 'the year of the great awakening.'" That awakening could be detected in various corners of Latin America. In urban Brazil, "a USIA study [found] that, after a slow start, the Alliance 'has captured the imagination of most Brazilian opinion-forming groups.'" Public awareness of the AFP had risen from 4 percent to 31 percent.[55] Reports from Peru and the Dominican Republic seconded the notion, and in the latter case demonstrated that public diplomacy outreach was having its effect, as an unprompted general survey question that did not mention the Alliance for Progress elicited spontaneous references to it. But the awakening fell short of universal. As *Life* magazine reported, "On the Alliance for Progress's first birthday this week . . . Latin Americans are saying, '*mucha alianza, poco progreso*.'" If public awareness was not yet as high as the Kennedy team might have hoped—Murrow reported to JFK that "most Mexicans asked to identify the Alliance for Progress answer: '*Qué es eso?* [what is that?]'"—nonetheless the Alliance seemed to be measurably progressing in the public mind.[56]

However, by summer 1962, some observers worried that the outreach was succeeding better than the policy and that eventually the latter's shortcomings would catch up with the spin. More worrisome still, to the extent that US public diplomacy successfully spread the word, it seemed to be conveying the wrong messages. This, along with the disparity between policy and publicity, slowed the momentum of Kennedy's Latin American initiative. A joint State-USIA-AID assessment observed "a growing tendency to criticize [AFP] for failure to produce tangible and conspicuous results quickly enough, and to label the Alliance as a 'U.S. aid program for Latin America'. . . . On every appropriate occasion [we must] set the record of the Alliance straight [and] identify it correctly as a hemispheric cooperation program." However, rebuttal could be a delicate task: "For us to seem over-sensitive to criticism of the Alliance is also to confirm the growing conception that [it] is a U.S. program for which we are primarily responsible." Secretary of State Dean Rusk concluded that in seeking to resolve the policy–publicity disparity, "how we and citizens of [Latin America] feel about the Alliance may 'turn out to be the most difficult part of all. . . . We are dedicating ourselves to a decade of impatience.'"[57]

Good Neighbors in Progress? Spreading the Word, Sharing the Burden

The impatience of which Rusk had spoken had begun setting in well before Washington realized it. In Bolivia, for example, "the [information] program for the [AFP] went through several stages . . . [it] started as all-out effort, evoking tremendous interest and enthusiasm . . . followed by impatience as to when [the Alliance] would get off the ground." The post explained this by "follow[ing] the line 'Rome wasn't built in a day,'" only to find themselves stopped short when Washington rejected a much-anticipated AID loan for construction at the La Paz airport. This led to "increased criticism about U.S. policy and cynicism about the AFP."[58] A report from Brazil found that despite smooth USIA operations supporting the Alliance, success in reach did not mean success in reception: "Alliance accomplishments to date have not lived up to the 'rising expectations' stimulated in the minds of many Brazilians by the widespread AFP publicity . . . [henceforth] our publicity should be played in a low key." Continuing as before risked not only disappointment but backfire. Brazil was in this sense something of a microcosm of the region. As USIA analysts noted, the Alliance benefitted from "a vast amount of publicity mainly self-generated because of the power of the ideals which inspire its concept. With such a beginning, the job of maintaining a favorable image over the long pull becomes herculean. [Thus] for the near future, the public affairs job [entails] fewer high-lever generalities and a steady stream of low-key specifics on progress."[59]

This, however, risked disconnecting the Alliance from the bigger picture. Already some US observers detected an "ideological gap" hampering the project: "To many Latin American eyes [AFP is] simply a money-lending operation [and is] increasingly seen . . . as a U.S. policy." As such it was disconnected from its Latin American environments, origins, or needs: "The biggest psychological obstacle AFP is facing is that it has not been wedded to Latin American nationalism [which is] the single most powerful psychological force now operating [there]." A May 23 memo agreed that the Alliance was losing the larger ideological battle: the Alliance "remains a shadowy idea. It badly needs . . . clarification of [its] basic *ideology* and a stepped-up *psychological campaign* to sell it." This "stepped-up information effort" should emphasize whole-hemispheric rather than bilateral cooperation, regional projects, the joint belief that *"economic development must be accompanied by social progress,"* the key role of Latin self-help, and vitally the *"participation of all groups in each country."*[60] In a sense, US public diplomats were getting a clearer sense of the challenge before them. They had been congratulating themselves on getting the word out efficiently and widely, only to discover it wasn't being heard in the right way, by the right people, and in the right context.

Progress reports in mid-1962 confirmed the misgivings. At most sites, in-
vestigators found "considerable disarray" in the policy and information machinery. In many of these countries, the Alliance was well on its way to being
a disappointment in terms of actual results. The disappointment would be all
the more acute in light of the public diplomacy side of the ledger. Expectations
were "high and even unreasonable" across the Americas—"and as yet grossly
unmatched by performance." While the outreach had "heightened appreciation that the U.S. is no longer neglectful" of Latin American needs, this was
"coupled with a great increase in expectations of [further] U.S. assistance" and
with inversely low expectations of their own governments. It was dawning on
public diplomats that the Alliance, because of the cooperative ideal enshrined
at Punta del Este, entailed specific and unique challenges to their work:

> Past publicity about U.S. foreign aid ... has [sought] primarily to
> foster friendly attitudes toward the U.S. This appears to continue to
> be the prime objective. [But] a much more important purpose to our
> publicity efforts exists. ... Presidential statements have emphasized
> the need for self-help, local responsibility, and [Latin American] ini-
> tiative. ... [But] none of the country teams appear to know how to
> translate these generalities into effective information activities that
> create indigenous pressures to foster the desired local initiative and
> responsibility.[61]

Exacerbating this "translation" problem was the fact that Latin American governments were not yet pulling their public diplomacy weight. The development
of indigenous information organs, like so much else of the Alliance still a work-
in-progress, would assist with translation as well as awaken Latin Americans
to their own commitments. "The U.S. has inadequate knowledge," concluded
the inspectors, "about what meaning is given to Alliance words, symbols, and
projects by various elements of the Latin American public. We use such general terms as 'national planning,' 'land reform,' and 'peaceful social revolution'
but we do not know [the reactions to these] among various important groups."
The USIA concluded, in sum, that it had to find the language to convey the
core values of the Alliance to Latin publics, to identify target groups within
those publics, to motivate its partner governments, and to refute the reflexive
conclusion that the "AFP basically means U.S. aid."[62]

The middle two tasks had highest priority. The State Department's intelligence bureau (INR) had encouraged smarter niche-targeting as early as
January 1962. While it was increasingly a central feature of US outreach in the
Global South, it was only once the midyear misgivings coalesced that the USIA
supplemented its mass output approach with narrower, group-based appeals

in Latin America. Kennedy's Labor and Commerce Departments established advisory committees to spread the Alliance word via their Latin counterparts. Students were another target, as were intellectuals, via cultural diplomacy, exchanges, and print patronage. Attention to the niches would remain central as partner governments and the OAS assumed increased information responsibilities. The OAS proposed to form "in each country [a] committee composed of a cross-section of national life . . . giving [the Alliance] thousands of effective new advocates." By year's end this would be a component of "a public information program in support of the Alliance," for the establishment of which the newly formed US Agency for International Development (AID) gave a grant to OAS.[63]

The initiative would join a crowded media landscape. During 1962, the number of bloc film showings and radio hours broadcast in Latin America rose sharply. This programming carried as its major themes "a) national liberation in all its ramifications, the most important of which in 1962 was the discrediting of [the Alliance]; b) Cuba as symbol of revolution; c) peace and coexistence; [and] d) Soviet scientific achievements." Attesting to its high profile, the Alliance was equally the center of both US and bloc output, the latter blasting it "as a project of U.S. imperialism." In some cases this meant actual physical assaults as US and bloc public diplomats crossed paths and on occasion threw punches.[64] Though infrequent, such confrontations were part of the uphill battle that US outreach faced: "In comparison with the total effort exerted by Communists (economic, social, political) our USIS program is inadequate to the need." Some US analysts worried that the bloc, in this crowded field, was standing out—that its volume and effectiveness were helping it to win the day: "The Communists attempted with some success to align themselves with the forces of nationalism throughout the area [through] promotion of the idea that the basic problem of Latin America was exploitation by the United States."[65]

Other American analysts were less convinced. Their skepticism came to the ironic conclusion that communism's outreach in the hemisphere was in fact being undercut by its homegrown avatar. A USIA survey of urban Latin American opinion in summer 1962 found that "disapproval extends beyond Castro personally to almost all [the] policies of his government . . . He has not succeeded in exporting his revolution as a model [and indeed] predominant sentiment in all three cities was that the Castro regime was a danger to other Latin American nations." Although there were grounds for worry that the communists' public diplomacy was winning more hearts and minds than Washington's was—it had better aligned itself with nationalism, and "there still existed a real attraction for revolutionary solutions to the problems of backwardness"—the agency found that Castro was losing a portion of those that his side had apparently gained.[66]

This conclusion found further confirmation in the Cuban Missile Crisis. As it had during the Bay of Pigs, the USIA mobilized all its resources for the crisis, covering developments in real time, and making it the centerpiece of output not just in Latin America but worldwide. Given the intense global interest, such "promotional" effort was almost unnecessary. The agency did, however, foreground the US position in the standoff—and given earlier soundings of Latin opinion, little spin was needed to align it with that of the hemisphere. Kennedy's "quarantine" speech marked a critical moment when "[hemisphere] comment ... gave unqualified support to the president's strong stand [to which] all media gave ... heavy and prominent play."[67] This support remained strong through the end of the crisis and found, to Washington's gratification, that Castro's reputation had sunk even further in its wake. "[Latin American] comment makes clear it is obvious that Castro was a puppet and that as a symbol of revolution [his] position has been seriously weakened." It is hard in retrospect to ascertain how much of this was the result of successful prodding by USIA, given Latin America's intense interest and preexisting positions. But the US Advisory Commission on Information gave great credit to the agency. The Commission ranked the Crisis as one of the three major Cold War public diplomacy clashes to date and lauded the "USIA [being] properly used. ... The U.S. position was presented to world rapidly, authoritatively, and effectively."[68]

However, the commission emphasized that although the missile crisis was over, the larger hemispheric one—and the Cuban threat within it—was not. "An area-wide revolution is exploding. The desire to reduce illiteracy, poverty, disease ... has gained momentum [and is] being exploited by Communist forces reinforced from their base in Cuba." This, reaffirmed the USACI, "call[s] for a continuous and expanded USIS effort" centered as before on the Alliance as the main anti-Castro weapon.[69] If Fidel had been a proximate cause of the AFP's launch and a hovering influence on its design, he himself seemed less worrisome as public diplomats thought about ways to make their post-missile crisis case. But the larger contest was as worrisome as ever, especially as it became increasingly obvious that the Alliance's internal flaws were at least as big a threat to its public diplomacy success as were any external factors.

Throughout 1963, the USIA continued churning out voluminous media output in support of the Alliance for Progress.[70] As during the previous year, there was both reason to believe they were succeeding in spreading the word and reason to worry how that word was being received. A midyear survey showed a glass half-full. A comprehensive study of public opinion in seven Latin American countries confirmed that the "revolution of rising expectations" had taken hold but radicalism had not, and surmised that was at least partly thanks to the Alliance for Progress, awareness of which "has now reached majority proportions in the urban population of four of [the] countries" and which was viewed much more positively than previous "inadequate" US aid programs. The study concluded that "the image of the Alliance . . . is highly favorable. The [vast] majority of those who know of [it] approve of it [and] contrary to current widespread assumption, there appears to be very little popular disillusionment with [it]."[71]

However, the chronic concern over transmission of the Alliance's ideological values persisted. A despatch early in the year recounted the variety of local-level outreach aimed at "democratic self-help." The post urged "provid[ing] greater emphasis [on] democratic processes and institutions [in] a way calculated to [convey] the ideological factors underlying the Alliance for Progress, i.e. the importance of self-help in achieving the dignity of the individual under a free society."[72] Another embedded value—hemispheric cooperation—also continued to trouble public diplomats. In a discussion of plans to capitalize on the second anniversary of the Punta del Este conference, such as the issuance of an AFP postage stamp by the United States and eight other countries, officials noted the "U.S. desire [to] avoid contributing to the idea still prevalent in other member states that the Alliance for Progress is a U.S. aid program rather than the multilateral effort put forth in the [Punta del Este] Charter."[73]

Kennedy's information-operations team identified an opportunity to convey these themes at the upcoming meeting of the UN Economic and Social Council (ECOSOC) meeting in São Paulo. USIA guidance for the meeting directed posts to stress that the Alliance was "a multilateral effort [whose] success depends primarily on its nineteen Latin American members. It is not a U.S. aid program [although we are] meeting [our Charter] aid obligations." At the meeting, "we want coverage to show that the Alliance for Progress has made a good beginning—but only a beginning."[74] The conference itself gratified Washington, exceeding expectations on both the policy and information fronts. Afterward, State informed its hemisphere posts that "the São Paulo meetings can be considered to have been most successful, not just because of the specific actions taken, but more importantly, because after two years of existence the Alliance for Progress has enlisted the support and the open commitment of responsible Latin American governments." Most gratifying to the Kennedy administration was that expectations of "a strong Latin American initiative for the creation of a Committee to provide a more multilateral character to the Alliance . . . were fully verified."[75]

This was true for the public diplomacy aspect of this multilateral effort as it was getting off the ground. ECOSOC provided not only a media opportunity in its own right but also a chance to assess what the conference report called "dissemination." The report details the ways in which USIA during the previous year had shared the burden of that task, assigned to the OAS General Secretariat. Using Alliance for Progress funds disbursed by AID, the

OAS organized national information committees and coordinated activities among them and hemisphere-wide organizations. Employing the niche-target approach, the body convened "seminars and working groups [of] representatives of public opinion in American countries." These included "democratic political leaders, labor representatives, university personnel, legislators, writers, journalists, scientists, and publicity and information experts."[76]

In addition, the OAS created the Special AFP Information Team, whose portfolio included production and distribution of 26,500 copies of the Alliance's weekly newsletter, the maintenance of relations with both the press and the government in each member state, and the pursuit of new ways for both to promote the Alliance for Progress. The team expanded and internationalized the Alliance's broadcast media footprint, working with the Pan-American Union's radio division to produce programming for national markets, and researching AFP projects from the country in question to be rediffused there and selectively elsewhere in the Americas.[77] Below the airwaves, the team also used this research to design "retail" efforts, such as public lectures, binational center exhibits, a variety of niche fora, and a series of popular seminars to discuss the national development plans concocted under the aegis of the Alliance. This would simultaneously help to raise the AFP's profile via a multilateral effort that thus both embodied and transmitted the theme of "cooperation."

Notwithstanding US optimism over São Paolo and the multilateral breadth of the Alliance's messaging, worries lingered. Kubitschek and Colombian President Alberto Lleras, for example, registered their concern that the AFP was falling victim to a chicken-and-egg conundrum: the Alliance needed political and "spiritual" support from peoples to complete its individual projects and accomplish its objectives, but until it completed its individual projects and accomplished its objectives, it could not elicit such support, no matter how comprehensive the media outreach was. Although it had reached new heights in dissemination and market research, something was amiss; the outreach alone wasn't to blame but it wasn't blameless either. The USIA recorded the Kubitschek and Lleras position, quoting their language that carried echoes of Havana:

> [They say that AFP is failing because of] a lack of *political will*. [They contend] the AFP is, and must be, carried out as a *political operation*, as a vast and magnetic political enterprise, as a movement whose heart is the spirit of the people. Imbuing the Allliance with this mystique is no mere matter of PR. All this can become a useless, routine task, as long as two basic conditions are not met: there must be evidence of Alliance accomplishments, that is, consciousness of the changing environment [and of] the principles, ideology, and spiritual significance of the Alliance.[78]

If not a "mere matter of PR," public relations was nonetheless the indispens-
able vehicle for achieving the exalted purpose Kubitschek and Lleras desired.
Nor were they outliers; by all available contemporary accounts, they represented public opinion accurately. At the OAS's niche workshops across Latin
America, participants agreed that "before [the Charter] can be carried out,
there must be a deep-seated revolutionary consciousness in the people."[79]

This position recalled earlier US concerns that the Alliance might ultimately fail if its publicity proved unable to convey on an adequate scale the
right themes, in the right way, and to the right sectors of the Latin American
public. But it was in a way more ominous. If "awareness had reached majority proportions" in June 1963, so too had incomplete understanding. Was
the Alliance faltering due to flaws inherent in the policy, or was it faltering
because the public diplomacy had produced insufficient buy-in and thus had
contributed to the AFP's stall? Historians have identified shortcomings in the
design and execution of the Alliance for Progress, some of which were evident
at the time. But its public diplomacy dimension was in some respects the sine
qua non. The Alliance required popular support, "ownership" by the masses,
if it was to achieve its goal of transforming Latin American society. Popular
support could only be had by effective, multilateral public diplomacy that
appeared not to be forthcoming. This, in turn, might doom whatever future
prospects the Alliance for Progress still had in September 1963, when Deputy
Assistant Secretary of State for Inter-American Affairs Richard Goodwin estimated to JFK that it was "operating at about one-half effectiveness."[80]

Soon thereafter, the US profile in Latin America got an unexpected boost
from an undesired tragedy. A week after the final ECOSOC gavel fell at São
Paolo, Kennedy was assassinated. The USIA reported that most coverage
around the hemisphere referenced the AFP: "Latin America reacted to [the]
news with consternation followed by expressions of grief and mourning for
the founder of the Alliance for Progress." A follow-up analysis found the
same: "Latin American affinity with the United States became more pronounced under the leadership of the Kennedy administration . . . [and now]
their immediate concern is the Alliance." Another survey noted that this was
in line with worldwide reactions to the assassination, as the various areas
foregrounded their "own preoccupations and predicaments"—and in Latin
America, "it was the Alliance for Progress."[81] New President Lyndon Baines
Johnson reassured Latin Americans that his administration would continue
the Alliance, and a subsequent roundup of Latin opinion found "growing confidence" that he would. But even had Johnson been as invested in the AFP as
JFK had been, there was little chance he would match his predecessor's inspirational martyrdom, nor be as automatically and lastingly associated with
JFK's signature initiative.[82] Even had Kennedy lived, the subsequent course

of the Alliance for Progress suggests that his charisma would not have been enough to save a project whose flaws—including the gap between its publicity, its ideals, and its accomplishments—would become steadily more pronounced until its quiet death at decade's end.

The Alliance for Progress represented the confluence of key elements of Kennedy's foreign policy: a new focus on the non-European world with special attention to Latin America; modernization-driven development as a cure to these areas' ills and as an anticommunist vaccine; and a revamped public diplomacy to transmit both. In Washington, the reorganization had put the USIA Director at the president's right hand, so that "[USIA's] role [in foreign policy] formation . . . has been greatly strengthened. No longer is USIA handed a policy and told to make the best of it."[83] In the field, the agency had implemented the president's geopolitical focus, having "increasingly emphasized operations in Africa and Latin America, and because of these priorities has had to curtail somewhat operations in Western Europe." By some measures, all this had succeeded in selling the Alliance. A 1964 study of Latin American opinion found "a favorable disposition toward the gradualist reforms embodied in the [AFP] . . . the preponderance of opinion in *all* classes is pro-American, pro-Alliance [and] anti-communist and anti-Castro." Another report six months later drew similar conclusions, but warned: "In many countries, general awareness still lags . . . [the] Alliance is broadly approved and increasingly well-known . . . [But] while support of the AFP is good, understanding of it is not so good on several counts."[84]

Even so, Alliance-driven public diplomacy can plausibly claim to have scored a few particular diplomatic successes. It made JFK the most popular US president in Latin America in decades, his reputation forever linked to but far exceeding that of the Alliance. It bolstered preexisting Latin public opinion regarding the United States and communism, and it aided in crisis management during episodes like the Bay of Pigs and the Cuban Missile Crisis. But in retrospect, it ultimately offset these gains by inadvertently helping to kill its host. As an October 1964 report put it:

> Initial expectations of an enthusiastic mass awareness and support of the Alliance were perhaps unrealistic, and the let-down led to a contrasting pessimism. Vocal opposition from extremes Left and Right were mistakenly assumed to extend more broadly in the population [and all this] began to have a cumulative effect. They reinforced each other . . . pessimistic judgments by Latin Americans were picked up in the U.S. press and became the norm—even while awareness of the Alliance, which had started slowly, was steadily increasing. [Lleras]

lamented that "the program is fascinating, and the surprising thing is that it fails to fascinate. . . . [The Argentine Foreign Minister agreed] that the Alliance had failed to capture the popular imagination."[85]

Alliance-driven public diplomacy succeeded by some metrics better than its subject. From a standing start, it disseminated word in support of the AFP across a hemisphere in the full range of contemporary media. By the time of Kennedy's death, this dissemination had succeeded in purely "reach" terms to such a degree that the Alliance was synonymous with the president. But this reach was wider than it was deep—broad awareness did not generate true "alliance"—and thus the AFP-driven public diplomacy failed in its most important task. Its success was fleeting, as it proved unable to correct lingering misconceptions or—most crucially—to convert the enthusiasm derived from the program's embedded ideals into a lasting buy-in by the Latin American public. As the gap between the outreach and what historian Stephen Rabe calls "a notable policy failure of the 1960s, superseded only by the U.S. debacle in Vietnam," became progressively clearer, all crumbled.[86]

However, at Kennedy's death, the ultimate failure of the Alliance later in the decade was as yet unknown. In that moment, thanks to the public diplomats plugging it on every continent, the program took on an importance beyond the western hemisphere. By design, the Alliance for Progress was to showcase modernization-driven development done right, Western-style and gradual. Its implication was that Latin America had more in common with decolonizing areas than first appeared—namely, "postimperial" poverty. This suggested a unity of interest that had a stake in the East–West split but was more fundamentally drawn along North–South lines. As Bowles had argued to the national security team in the first year of the Kennedy administration:

> One of our difficulties [with Latin America] has been that we have continued to think in European terms. We considered that world stability depended on European stability. When we finally realized that Europe was no longer the place where all policy decisions were made, we adapted ourselves to the new look in Asia and Africa, but we continued to take Latin America for granted. We can no longer do that, for a real revolution has come to this area.[87]

The follow-on notion that the "real revolution" was in its essentials the same one as in Asia and Africa represented a kind of unspoken and remarkable agreement among the United States, the Soviet Union, Castro, and Latin America that the world was divided along economic lines—not ideological, not racial-ethnic, not religious or cultural ones—first and foremost.[88]

Just after JFK's May 1961 allusion to the "the whole southern half of the globe," USIA reported that Castro "abandon[ed] plans for a 'Conference of Underdeveloped Nations of Africa, Asia, and Latin America' for lack of response."[89] This failure was notable, though temporary; Castro would later successfully convene the Tricontinental Conference of African, Asian, and Latin American Peoples in Havana, in January 1966. But it is less significant than the tacit agreement between him and JFK on the terms of international debate. In a sense this accord undercut the hemispheric unity that the Alliance for Progress was trying to establish—by implicitly agreeing that Latin America had more in common with Asia and Africa than it did by being geographically accidental neighbors with the *yanqui* colossus. Nor were JFK and Castro the only actors to avow this insight. In what became known as his "Wars of National Liberation" speech in 1961, Khrushchev confirmed that "Africa, Asia, *and Latin America* are now the most important centers of revolutionary struggle."[90] Moreover, as part of the quickening Global South conversation, the crosscurrents of public diplomacy carried the notion along. Arab outreach to Latin America, for example, had during these years been emphasizing "a kind of community of poverty" between the two regions. Historian Jeffrey Byrne notes that the Algerian National Liberation Front (FLN) actively nourished Cuban–Algerian ties via a "shared African connection," imitating Castro's tactics and declaring the Latin revolutionaries to be kindred spirits. As one Algerian diplomat put it, "their combat is our own."[91] For his part, Castro rarely missed a chance to agree, stressing the "colonial" affinity animating their struggles: "On the map we were in a different color from that of the United States [but] in reality, Cuba was a colony."[92]

If the Alliance for Progress had "failed to capture the popular imagination," then, trans-South commonality grounded in imperialized poverty nonetheless did catalyze both Old and New World imaginations, sending them off in further unforeseen directions, especially what proponents and detractors alike would come to call *tercermundismo* ("Third Worldism").[93] It was fitting that Latin America helped to cultivate the emerging conclusions, since it was after all the Argentine Raúl Prebisch who in 1950 had first coined the term "underdeveloped countries" not long before Sauvy coined his famous phrase.[94] The notion of a fundamental commonality of interest among diverse areas of the Global South was taking root. The Kennedy administration, for its part, was becoming ever more convinced of it. In the administration's last year, historian and presidential advisor Arthur Schlesinger emphasized this again to a Venezuelan audience: "If we succeed here [via the AFP], we set an inspiring example for two-thirds of our world. . . . The basic choice confronting Latin America is therefore between the democratic revolution and the communist revolution. . . . The people of Asia have become vividly aware in recent months that they confront the same choice."[95] A survey the following year of public opinion in LDCs—less-developed countries—included for the first time ever Argentina, Brazil, Mexico, and Venezuela alongside Asian and African nations. Just as American analysts were expanding the "southern half of the globe" to include Latin America, another suggestion appeared that they were right to do so. In the third year of Alliance public diplomacy blanketing Latin America in promotion of hemispheric unity, the USIA found that "as a result of preoccupation with domestic problems, an existing nationalism and a trend for non-alignment on East–West issues . . . a nascent neutralism appears to be developing."[96]

6

True Colors

*Nonalignment, Race, and the Proliferation of Public
Diplomacy in the Formation of the Third World*

One need only recall the heady wine of our own independence in
1776 to appreciate the new intoxication of Africa.
—Edward R. Murrow, speech to National Press Club, May 24, 1961

The "nascent neutralism" Washington suspected in Latin America had already
achieved a kind of critical mass elsewhere in the Global South. By 1961, variations
on the term—soon refined into "nonalignment"—could be heard from a range
of voices worldwide.[1] Although the nuances often differed, a number of common
themes connected them. One was economic development for the world's have-
nots, a point on which there was wide agreement among the world's haves as well.
A second common element was an active rejection of the Cold War as an apocalyptic threat to peace, paired with assertion of the nonaligned countries' constructive role in defusing this menace. A third element was an internally diverse
one: the avowal of quasi-mystical identities grounded in racialized people-hood
and shared colonial suffering—in the Afro-Asian-Arab "Bandung spirit"—on
which solidarity and progress could be built. The various groupings that connected the three elements were allied against the world schema created by imperialism and the Cold War—and if not actively opposed to such alignments, then at
least avowedly apart from them. All three served as bases for a powerfully desired
unity on the part of the newly emerged and relatively powerless.

The ranks of this rough grouping were growing in the early 1960s. The cresting second wave of postwar decolonization brought dozens of new sovereign
members into the world community, literally and figuratively changing the
complexion of international institutions and affairs. The sheer growth in this
global flag count affected each of the three core elements in various ways. But
perhaps its largest impact was on the content and parameters of the global conversation about them. As the UN roll call grew, it enlarged the battlefield for

hearts and minds by increasing the size of its audience, and more importantly the number of its speakers. American and Soviet public diplomats were, by the early 1960s, far from alone in seeking ways to direct world discussion to their respective advantage. So too did the proliferating actors in JFK's "southern half of the globe," who took public diplomacy seriously, launching or expanding their own campaigns meant to pursue local, national, and collective interests via the media ether, and to redefine the terms of the "global Cold War."

This chapter examines the public diplomacy of the Kennedy administration and its counterparts regarding the interplay of the three elements around which a Third World continued to concretize in the early 1960s. That moment offers a kind of inflection point as they converged on the events this chapter analyzes: the Nonaligned Movement (NAM) Conference in Belgrade, the Congo Crisis, and the black freedom movement in sub-Saharan African and the US South. The USIA sought to engage the three elements as they coursed through the still inchoate but evidently expanding grouping. The battle was acute for Washington given the Cold War crises of 1961–1962, the administration's focus on the Global South, and the freedom struggle around the Black Atlantic. But it was, as well, an intensely multilateral battle. It marks the point at which a recognizable Third World began taking shape, as luminaries from Khrushchev and Kennan to Nkrumah and Castro acknowledged. The question was which of the three elements would principally define it: poverty and underdevelopment, Cold War nonalignment, or "Afro-Asianist" racial and anticolonial solidarity? Kennedy's team leaned toward the first. It oriented US information operations accordingly and avoided the worst-case public diplomacy outcomes that might have sprung from any of the three. But Washington could not be sure which direction the increasingly vocal Third World project would ultimately go. Whether a development-first vision, or Nehruvian nonalignment, or a racial identity potentially touching the US home front, would triumph was unclear. By 1963, however, it was unquestionably clear that the emergent entity presented something different, recognizable, and seemingly permanent on the international landscape.

"What Might Come Out of This Bag of Eels": The United Nations, Nonalignment, and the Belgrade Conference

The Kennedy team joined a national security community in Washington that had spent the last few years brainstorming the impact of the changing international landscape. As a mid-1960 USIA study of Africa put it, "in the 1960s—Africa's 'Decade of Destiny'—the region's problems, impatience, ambitions, and embryonic world-view are likely to be both puzzling and challenging to the rest of the world."[2] Most puzzling in US eyes was the non-European world's simultaneous obsession with colonialism and lack of interest in the Cold War. Just after JFK's election, the USIA mulled over its failure to turn the obsession to Western advantage by branding Soviet foreign policy as "colonialism":

> To Africans, colonialism is an aspect of Western society [that] still affects them . . . involving: white rule over black or yellow races, intimately connected with [capitalism]. . . . In desiring to project Africa as an independent force [they] maintain a cautious reserve about . . . "Cold War" issues which they believe do not concern them and can only serve to realign them with their colonial masters. . . . Africans tend to reject Western charges of Soviet colonialism . . . propagated by nations who are present or former colonial powers and therefore not competent judges.[3]

A USIA study titled "The Foreign Image of American Power" found likewise: "[Arabs and] Africans . . . are overwhelmingly concerned with independence, socio-economic development, and the preservation of 'positive neutralism.' By comparison they have a tangential interest in the Cold War."[4] This was of a somewhat different flavor than elsewhere in the non-European world, but was not of an entirely different cuisine. In South Asia, India and most of her neighbors displayed "a strong desire not to become involved in the Cold War conflict [through] alignment with either side. Their paramount concern in world affairs is [that] conflicts between East and West [be] reduced and disarmament achieved so that greater resources can be allocated to the fight against poverty, disease, and ignorance." These countries shared Africa's antipathy toward white supremacist colonialism and its reticence to apply the term to the East bloc.[5]

Although Washington figured that "for most of the new nations, neutralism is probably the best we can expect," the Kennedy team "doubt[ed] the coalescence of a neutralist bloc into a strong 'third force.'" But the conclusion that nonetheless "neutralism is a fact of national and international life to which the West must adjust" had implications for JFK's USIA overhaul.[6] The appointment of Murrow and the expansion of USIA infrastructure were the most visible aspects of the revamp, but it also touched the more abstract aspects of agency dealings with the welter of issues swirling through the non-European world. Greater sophistication in audience research; supplementing mass outreach with a "niche" approach targeting present and future leaders; sensitivity to the language used in the Global South; exercises in damage control there, above all regarding the civil rights movement; and the tighter meshing of public diplomacy with policymaking all reflected the administration's attention to nonalignment and related currents.

Murrow resolved to expand and refine the USIA's research capabilities and to deploy the results overseas, without giving "the impression abroad or at home that U.S. foreign policy is determined on a 'popularity' basis." The rethinking of the terminology of US output underlaid, in one way or another, this and all other aspects of the agency overhaul. In his first weeks in the job, Murrow recommended that American officials avoid the terms "East" and "West."[7] While he did not go so far as to label the remainder, the advice foreshadowed his order some months later regarding "underdeveloped" in agency output. The targets of this revised rhetoric, moreover, would be more finely grained. Murrow had no intention of abandoning mass communications. But—here implementing conclusions first drafted during the Eisenhower years—the agency would seek out niche-sectors of the neither-East-nor-West societies:

> The diffusion of effort and output that [had] characterized USIA is ended . . . no longer does USIA scatter its fire indiscriminately to all segments of all populations. "Targeting," always an ideal, is now a reality. Audiences are carefully selected—together with the techniques of reaching them and the contents of the message—to achieve maximum influence leading to political action.[8]

The USIA now deployed both "shotgun" and "rifle." In the southern hemisphere, the USIA decided to prioritize the new states' proverbial movers and shakers. The masses' generally lower literacy, along with the "legacy" hierarchies of local authority, together formed relatively small circles of opinion-making. These were both more powerful than their Global North counterparts vis-à-vis their mass publics and more interested in external affairs. Thus in advance of Tanzanian independence, for example, "priority USIS audiences [were] members of the National Assembly including European and Asian legislators, TANU political leaders, labor officials, student/youth groups, teachers, and editors." The USIA found this to be true with minor variation in African, South Asian, and Arab states alike, and diversified and targeted its research and rhetoric accordingly.[9]

Both niche and mass audiences were receptive to the theme of nonalignment, which along with its attendant issues of race, decolonization, and Cold War would be repeatedly in the spotlight through JFK's first year in office. A sequence of such moments leading up to the September 1961 founding conference of the Non-Aligned Movement in Belgrade, Yugoslavia, challenged American public diplomats, as the USIA sought to shape the narrative on the nexus of Global South issues and US policy toward them. The first of these moments on the timeline, the Congo Crisis, highlighted the evolving role of the United Nations, left the USIA scrambling to keep up, and drew together nonalignment and its avatars into the makings of a Third World grouping.

All parties could see in the Congo Crisis a postwar moment of truth. The UN intervention there underscored the institution's potential role in colonial transitions, in Global South diplomacy, and in North–South relations. It furnished a catalyst for Afro-Asian unity in defense of a Congo victimized by the West and its UN puppet—and an anvil on which Third World solidarity could be forged. This was how it appeared to Khrushchev, who took to the UN General Assembly's podium to blast the institution and its Secretary General Dag Hammarskjöld. The Soviet premier proposed to create a "troika," replacing the office of Secretary General with a triumvirate of representatives from East, West, and Afro-Asia. Khrushchev hoped that the troika reform would render the UN incapable of another Congo operation and would appeal to the nonaligned by institutionalizing their presence. The proposal thus signaled, at minimum, superpower acknowledgment of a third bona fide cohort.

However, those leaders—the erstwhile champions of Global South solidarity—instead saw the troika as a danger to something they prized even more highly: the UN itself, which in Nkrumah's words held "the responsibility of keeping the Cold War out [of] Africa."[10] The USIA found the ostensible beneficiaries resistant to Khrushchev's charm, as the pro-troika Soviet propaganda offensive found few takers. The Sprague Committee had written that "in the underdeveloped and emerging countries, public opinion and mass media follow UN developments with special intensity," which would in theory bolster support for the troika. But opinion in the Global South objected to the evisceration of the Secretary General and by extension the UN itself. While masses and leaders alike envisioned a greater role for the nonaligned countries, almost all wanted to achieve it through the existing, rather than a radically reformed, UN. The USIA found that India in particular resisted the formalization of a "neutral bloc or third force" that would curtail each individual country's full independence.[11] In the Arab countries, state media indicated some openness to UN structural reform but mainly sought to preserve a neutralist stance that "provides them the opportunity to exploit this [East–West] rivalry to Arab advantage." Aspects of the proposal were endorsed by Nkrumah and Guinea's Sekou Touré, and discussions lingered over the next year. However, "ultimately," write historians Aleksandr Fursenko and Timothy Naftali, "none of the Soviet Union's Third World allies [except Guinea] supported" the troika.[12]

If the Congo Crisis had failed to elicit Global South support for a reformed UN, it did highlight the ways the Cold War could infect a colonial transition—and the limitations created by the UN's reticence to confront the issue.[13] This reticence was no longer tenable as the General Assembly's ranks grew and changed so rapidly. Even without the troika reforms, as historian Arne Westad writes, "the UN as an anticolonial battlefield was in itself a problem for the United States, which attempted to keep the focus of world condemnation on the Communist states. . . . The advent of new, independent Third World states began already in 1960 to change the role of the UN into a more diverse forum, less susceptible to American influence than before."[14] Indeed, the cresting of decolonization had led to this. As British Prime Minister Harold Macmillan's "winds of change" blew through Africa—adding seventeen new flags to the UN—they fanned impatience with the redoubts of white colonialism that remained, and with the failure of the UN to aid in their struggle. The failure was all the more acute given the success of Algeria's revolutionaries in leveraging the international arena to turn around the fortunes of what had seemed a lost cause.[15] By the fall of 1960, the Congo was the UN's most pressing matter, but the newer members of the body had already begun pushing beyond it for an institutional statement on decolonization.

The passage of UN Resolution 1514 avowing that "the process of [colonial] liberation is irresistible and irreversible" signaled the centrality of nonalignment, decolonization, and Cold War in the international assembly—and the critical mass of the Global South in its ranks. USIA analysts reported, as the General Assembly session opened, that "the South Asian press has emphasized that [it] will probably prove to be the most important [session in its] history and has stressed the crucial role to be played by the Afro-Asian nations." The Sprague Committee, concluding its deliberations amidst General Assembly debates over the resolution, detected the Global South's heightened interest in the body and urged Washington to "take a more active and effective interest in the psychological and information aspects of our participation in the UN."[16] However, because of the US government's low enthusiasm for resolution 1514 and eventual abstention on the vote, the USIA underplayed the episode. Output instead focused—when the subject came up—on America's historic sympathy for self-determination and on US agreement that a troika-less UN should facilitate it. Despite the understatement, by the time the resolution passed in December 1960, superpower interest in the Global South was visibly higher. US support for the UN Congo operation, though endorsed by the major Afro-Asian leadership, dismayed many African nationalists. On the other side, Khrushchev's January 1961 endorsement of "wars of national liberation" touched off Soviet media campaigns in the Global South "pledg[ing] moral and material support for [such] righteous violence," and declaring that "next to the emergence of socialist states in the world, the breakup of the colonial holdings was the most important development of our era."[17] Heightened superpower interest in the Global South could worry—or, at times, entice—the latter's avatars and feed the rise of nonalignment as a form of self-protection grounded in the anticolonial sentiment of Resolution 1514.

The major nonaligned powers behind the diplomatic triumph of 1514 saw it as part of a larger conversation. Nehru's coinage of the term "nonalignment" in May 1950 fueled that conversation, which had already begun thanks to Indian and Yugoslavian foreign policy. It continued at Brioni in July 1956 among Nehru, Nasser, and Tito—and before that at Bandung, plus Sukarno and minus Tito. The UN–Congo Crisis gave it a renewed fillip and helped prompt the three elder statesmen of nonalignment to begin organizing the Non-Aligned Conference to be held in Belgrade, and each of the three had his own domestic and regional reasons for championing nonalignment. Each could legitimately claim to represent his own country's feelings on the matter. While these differed in national and regional particulars, they meshed sufficiently across borders to constitute a transnational persuasion imperfectly defined but sincerely held.[18] In the sense that it sought to prevent the entry of the Cold War into the Global South, nonalignment might be thought of as the Third World's containment doctrine.

The Kennedy administration debated how to approach the prospective Belgrade meeting. As historian Robert Rakove shows, there was broad internal agreement on the importance of the nonaligned nations and on the need for good bilateral relations with each as, in effect, an unspoken strategy of divide-and-conquer. This offered a way to pre-empt the least desirable outcome from the administration's perspective: the formation of a bloc.[19] But there were internal disputes over the best way to engage collective moments like Belgrade that could not be addressed via JFK's preferred bilateral-interpersonal approach and that were inseparable from their public diplomacy dimension. The main internal dispute pitted the "engagement" faction led by presidential advisor Robert Komer against the "downplay" faction led by Secretary of State Dean Rusk. The former argued that the United States should insert itself into the Belgrade proceedings, in hopes of explaining American actions, signaling a sympathetic understanding of neutralism, and in the process defanging anti-Western sentiment. The Rusk camp believed that any such insertion would be seen as unwanted meddling and could offer an easy target for the angrier voices in attendance.

Uncertainty as to what exactly the conference held in store compounded the indecision. The uncertainty owed in part to the haphazard nature of its origins, born as it was of internal rivalries among the nonaligned trinity of Nehru, Tito, and Nasser. As late as a month before the meeting, US analysts surmised that their Soviet counterparts were "undoubtedly . . . as uncertain as we are as to what might come out of this bag of eels." This was understandable given that the preparations were "a shambles" and the organizers unhappy and working at cross-purposes. "Prospects for the conference," only weeks away, "do not seem highly promising at the moment. Nothing is firmly known (at least by us) about the agenda or even about the participants."[20] Cold War events threatened to rewrite the agenda in any case. The Berlin Crisis, the fight over nuclear testing, and the still-unresolved troika question were sure to influence the proceedings, especially given Nehru's resolve that nonalignment affirm its role in the Cold War independent of issues touching upon race and decolonization. Notwithstanding Nehru, "anticolonialism will be the unifying emotion and there is not much we can do about that."

Between the internal dispute and the external uncertainties, the Kennedy team chose a hands-off policy in regards to Belgrade. The USIA conducted itself accordingly, keeping virtually silent until the eve of the conclave. This discretion was also the better part of avoiding an uphill battle: "Unfortunate American press stories ... that the U.S. government had decided on a propaganda campaign to influence ... neutralist leaders" made a hands-off stance wise.[21] To the extent the United States might influence the proceedings, it would have to rely on friendly journalists and intellectuals and on US Ambassador George F. Kennan. In several key respects, this meant replaying the Bandung public diplomacy approach at Belgrade. An inability to speak from the main conference stage, a focus on Cold War priorities over race and decolonization, uncertainty about the agenda and course of the conference, loose coordination with London, and the use of proxies and journalists all reprised Washington's predicament at Bandung. Going a step further, unlike in 1955, the administration planned no public statement on the upcoming gathering.

However, a confluence of crises in the weeks before Belgrade altered the calculation. The USIA had made the Berlin Crisis a focus of its worldwide output, and it found varying levels of interest in national and regional presses, corresponding less with USIA coverage than with local positions on nonalignment and the Cold War.[22] In August, the Berlin standoff reached new heights as construction of the Wall began. The crisis brought in its train the unresolved matters of "two Germanys" and nuclear testing. Outside of Europe, strains on the Diem government in South Vietnam—like the continuing Congo Crisis, another site where anticolonial struggles could morph into Cold War theaters—along with the conflicts in Algeria and Tunisia outraged nonaligned leaders. In both its public diplomacy in Belgrade-attending nations and in private discussions with friendly-nation attendees who could serve as American proxies, the administration sought to connect these crises to Berlin by framing that contest as a crisis of self-determination.[23]

The White House worried that these developments might induce the Belgrade Conference to intervene in the Cold War crises—especially

Berlin—on the wrong side, and might fuse with the strong anticolonial feeling among attendees sufficiently to revive the troika proposal. On top of this,
Khrushchev and Mao had ended their silence and issued messages to the conference. Washington thus reversed course and drafted a presidential message.
Some officials wondered if the case for silence still persisted: a message "might
be seen as 'unwarranted interference' [and a] clumsy last-minute attempt to
offset Khrushchev."[24] But the Kennedy team concluded that the critical mass of
crises plus the Khrushchev statement made the pros of a presidential message
outweigh the cons. Presidential advisor Ted Sorensen and Deputy Assistant
Secretary of State Carl Rowan led the team that drafted the statement. The
text avoided reference to the Cold War crises in favor of broad assertions of
America's historic interest in anticolonial self-determination. It expressed the
hope that the assembly would contribute to resolving world crises through the
United Nations. Advance word of the message was sent to major European
allies: "While maintaining [our] 'hands off' policy with respect to the Belgrade
Conference it was deemed desirable make a public statement of this type in the
interest of encouraging moderate and constructive Belgrade resolutions." The
USIS was directed to "make appropriate dissemination" to foreign publics.[25]

Most of the assembled governments expressed appreciation for Kennedy's
message. Its reception was aided by a Soviet diplomatic blunder on the eve
of the conference, one that altered the landscape for the USIA. On August
30—the day that Kennedy's salute to the conference went out over the wire—
Khrushchev announced the Soviet resumption of nuclear testing. Whether or
not he did so to send a message to those assembled, they took it as one and
said so in blistering fashion at the podium. Khrushchev's move was not strictly
speaking a public diplomacy initiative, aimed as it was at leaders instead of
publics; there is no evidence to suggest that he made this move to persuade
the average Ghanaian, Indian, or Egyptian citizen of the Soviet position. But it
became public diplomacy material thanks to the responses of those countries'
leaders. Given the outsized role they played in shaping coverage in their often
state-controlled media back home, it amounted to a grievous Soviet misfire
that, Washington hoped, would minimize any damage Belgrade might do. As
Kennan wrote midway through the conference, "there appears increasing likelihood that on several important issues the sense of the conference will be less
damaging to U.S. interests than the more pessimistic forecast anticipated."[26]

As the meeting proceeded, the acrimony on-site was palpable. Divisions
among the trinity surfaced in their interactions and found their way into the
resolutions. These divisions, US analysts found, were reflected in the major
Belgrade speeches, which could be grouped into three categories: "leaning
West, middle of the road, and pro-Soviet," with the middle group larger than
the other two combined.[27] Given this, the USIA debated whether or not to

chime in. The agency lamented the lack of resolutions on Cold War matters and the failure of the trope of self-determination for Berlin. But it noted that "Colonialism was hit hard [in the resolutions] as expected but without language as extreme as the public speeches." Except for Cuba's "relative success [in] achieving recognition of its demands" and Nkrumah's proximity to the Soviet line, "the speeches and resolutions emerged in about the form anticipated." American officials decided that an official statement "would [be] counterproductive." Though some felt this "line [was] much too soft" and were unhappy with the diplomatic outcome of Belgrade, the USIA concluded it best to let the conference's disharmony, its virtual abstention on Cold War issues, and its fixation on colonialism speak for themselves, unspun.[28]

US public diplomacy thus returned to a hands-off stance. Information officers tracked reception of the conference, surveying a battlefield they had ceded. They found a number of actors seeking to use Belgrade and Berlin to make a larger point. Before the conclave, Nasser's media abroad had emphasized "the positive role neutral nations must play in lessening East–West tensions, [building] the Berlin crisis to a fever pitch just prior to [Belgrade], then emphasiz[ing] the contribution the conference had made to the lessening of . . . tensions." In South Asia, the meeting was declared "a qualified success by commentators of participating nations." An early USIA report found that "comment from participating [Mideast and South Asian] countries . . . rationalized the end results . . . by emphasizing the potential contribution of [their] special appeals [and] their particular local interests and delegations." But beyond exercises in self-flattery were charges that might stick: "Not unexpectedly, Sino-Soviet comment emphasized the 'anti-imperialism' posture of the Conference and ignored its less favorable aspects." Since anticolonialism had been one of few points of consensus, this might resonate. Unfortunately for Moscow, though, the nuclear testing announcement would find at least equal purchase in African media, which "devoted wide play to Belgrade. . . . [Attendees'] shock over Soviet nuclear test resumption has heightened fears of world conflict. . . . Nkrumah's shock at the conference was widely disseminated. . . . Radio Accra stated Belgrade 'assumed a new importance' thanks to the Soviet action, and 'emphasized the [need] for a voice of reason and caution . . . in world councils.'"[29]

The final draft of the USIA report reaffirmed the original findings. It found "heavy news and editorial coverage [and] general satisfaction with the outcome of the conference" among participating nations; that most of these nations' media coverage was influenced above all by their internal and intraregional dynamics; and that these reflected fundamental, organic disagreement over the meaning of Belgrade and the substance of nonalignment. Citing examples from the South Asian press, the report found Belgrade coverage to have showed

> "realism in placing first things first" and ... expressed "satisfaction that such issues as Algeria, Bizerte, Angola, and apartheid" had "taken second place" although it emphasized that this "does not imply any slackening of the pressure against the colonial powers." ... Other [Indian] comment stressed that the Conference must not degenerate into a "pro-Western propaganda show" and must not encourage the formation of a third bloc ... The anti-Western, pro-communist [Pakistani] *Observer* [said Belgrade] "is at best an assembly of nations that have only a common label of neutralism." ... A [Ceylonese] broadcast said the Conference had "no common interests [nor] a common program to put forward."[30]

This division could be a source of relief to Washington, insofar as it reassured that another bloc, let alone one legitimized in a troika, was unlikely to take shape. But it was also a source of genuine confusion over how to approach the post-Belgrade collective. Given the fractious assembly and its participants' mixed messages, such confusion was all but unavoidable. While, for example, as Rakove writes, Nehru's speech "emphasize[d] questions of war and peace over those of colonialism and poverty [and thus] proved the most satisfying to U.S. observers, and most disappointing to their Communist counterparts ... Nehru [was] nearly alone in [this] emphasis ... which was submerged in a torrent of anticolonial rhetoric from the other attendees."[31]

At the highest levels of the administration, there was less worry about lasting damage from this rhetoric. Though dismayed that Belgrade was what Rakove calls "a setback to [their] hopes," the Kennedy team wagered that the president's personal diplomacy with individual leaders would secure US interests.[32] However, for those in USIA reading the post-Belgrade tea leaves, there was an inescapable uncertainty over which trends would dominate amid the post-conference grouping. The hands-off approach to Belgrade was duly conveyed through the USIA, whose coverage was notable for its reserve. The exception—the well-received JFK message—reinforced the subtlety. This strategy seemed to have produced, at worst, a PR tie for the United States. But where the newly minted Belgrade movement, by turns determined and diffuse, would go was unclear. Its public diplomacy challenge was accordingly confused—or, at the least, left US officials unsure whether hands-off would meet it as well again in the future.

Africa, the Congo Crisis, and the New Communications Frontier

If the founding of its movement meant that, as Rakove writes, "nonalignment [was] a more inclusive uniting principle than Afro-Asian identity," it was nonetheless far from certain at the time that it would eclipse that identity, or the competing theme of poverty and underdevelopment. Certainly given Belgrade's relative inattention—amid the "torrent of anti-colonial rhetoric"— to the Cold War issues that nonalignment existed to address, Nehru's position could not be presumed to have won. Race and anticolonialism preoccupied the Belgrade parties as much or more. Contemporary observers like African American economist and AID official Robert S. Browne said the same:

> The tremendous bloc of newly independent [and] neutral nations are primarily concerned about one issue—the assertion of the equality of the white and the non-white races. In comparison . . . all other issues such as communism, space travel, economic development, even a third world war, shrink to insignificance.[33]

Belgrade's fractiousness suggested that nonalignment as a political persuasion, driven as it was by a Cold War that was manifestly more important to North than South, had its limits. The movement could on paper appeal to anyone. But it could be eclipsed just as easily by the impassioned calls to racial and anticolonial solidarity either of the "Pan" variety within regions, or beyond them across what Prashad calls "the Darker Nations."[34]

Browne noted that to many, especially in Africa, race and anticolonialism were the far more pressing concern and the more unifying factor. Reporting on Belgrade, for example, the Indian press had "referred to the displeasure of African countries over Nehru's playing down colonialism, [in a] 'whispering campaign that India was playing a Western game' [by] focusing attention on disarmament to the exclusion of colonialism.'"[35] This did not indicate deep dissent from nonalignment; Nkrumah referred frequently to "positive neutralism" as the correct, necessary, and indeed distinctly African stance for new independent nations on the continent. The USIA nevertheless found that Africans—especially the masses but often the elites as well—consistently ranked race and anticolonialism as higher priorities:

> Africans felt themselves removed from the Cold War and thus tried to insulate Africa from its effects by remaining non-aligned. . . . [Their] react[ions] to external issues . . . were colored by an intense bias

against Western colonialism and imperialism—which they saw in such issues as Cuba, Congo, Bizerte, Angola. . . . Africans regard independence as only the first step in the rejuvenation of their people. . . . They deeply resent the racial implications of colonialism [and its] partitioning of the African continent.[36]

Such sentiment predated nonalignment and the Cold War by decades. If inchoate and contested, the will to Pan-African solidarity and the sense of a Pan-African destiny were nonetheless strong and long-running, as a Black Atlantic response to the European "scramble" for empire. They had found expression since 1900 in the writings of W.E.B. DuBois, had spread markedly in interwar diasporan circles, and were now championed by offspring of empire like Nkrumah and Léopold Senghor.[37] The USIA found that these visions had persisted. Négritude, for example, found its way onto the agency's radar screen in the months after Belgrade. Analysts assessed that although it had originally been a literary movement it "appears to be broad enough to [also] provide a basis for some of the more militant nationalistic political trends current today in West Africa," and along with kindred sentiments reinforced Pan-Africanism in potentially significant ways.[38]

The worldwide visibility of any such race-inflected issues, given the American domestic situation and the Kennedy administration's interest in cultivating US–Africa relations, made USIA attention to them imperative.[39] While Kenyan labor leader Tom Mboya reflected that the Kennedy years were "the beginning of a completely new era," African reactions at the time ranged from "high enthusiasm to 'wait and see.'"[40] Striking the right tone in US public diplomacy amid what all parties felt was a moment of destiny included some difficulties—and assets—unique to Africa. US objectives included supporting peaceful steps toward political, economic, and cultural progress; nurturing a free press; presenting a friendly United States itself making racial progress; and countering communist propaganda. The assets were few, but not inconsequential. One was the US-educated African nationalist cohort, including leaders like Nkrumah and Nnamdi "Zik" Azikiwe. In some cases, as in Zik's Nigeria, this enabled the USIS to place more material in the local press than any other foreign information service. The USIA also had by now a sizable infrastructure in place. It had opened one new post per month in Africa in the last year, for a total of more than thirty. Logistical obstacles limited film access outside these mostly urban posts, but USIA did succeed in screening the serial film magazine *Today* before an African audience that regularly topped thirty million people.[41] Radio ownership was low, but rising fast. Finally, the United States' reputation in Africa was—surprisingly, given Jim Crow—as far as most USIA analysts could tell, actually pretty good.[42]

The Congo Crisis unleashed a maelstrom of racial, anticolonial, and Cold War dynamics that would test this reputation mightily. Simmering since mid-1960, the crisis was the chaotic exception to a generally peaceful "Year of Africa" as independence was won. The Congo's traumatic decolonization began when Belgium departed pell-mell. Within a week of Independence Day on June 30, the mutiny of the army against its white officers left the central government unable to enforce order. The mutiny metastasized, as rival regional and ethnic factions fought for mastery against each other and against the central government headed by Patrice Lumumba, with 100,000 Belgian settlers caught in the middle. Amidst the violence, Belgium deployed troops to protect the settlers and to secure the mining areas. The newborn state's sovereignty was thus assaulted from within and without, as European intervention dovetailed with intra-African civil war, and breakaway regions such as the mineral-rich Katanga seceded. Lumumba appealed to the UN to reverse the secessions, evict the Belgian forces, and restore the national government and borders. Hammarskjöld agreed. But disagreement over the terms of the UN mandate left Lumumba frustrated, and he appealed to Washington and Moscow for military help in restoring Kinshasa's writ over Katanga and three other breakaway regions. Eisenhower demurred. The Soviets sent aid, prompting CIA help to Congo's Secretary of National Defense Joseph Mobutu, who seized power in a coup and placed Lumumba under house arrest. Days before JFK's inauguration, Mobutu sent Lumumba to Elisabethville, where Katangese gendarmes murdered him as Belgian officers watched.

The first phases of the Congo Crisis between mid-1960 and early 1961 thus brought together a number of issues—UN power, Cold War proxies, African nation-state-hood, and the struggles for decolonization and racial justice as white rule in Africa ended.[43] Any of these by itself would have required careful handling by the USIA. Together, they created a huge challenge for the agency and threatened that the multifaceted Global South grouping might morph into one organized around race and anticolonialism rather than around nonalignment. The organic links and budding tensions between the two were obvious to observers North and South. A retrospective analysis by the post-independence Algerian diplomatic service, for example, found that "the interaction between the two movements is so deep that we can say that Non-Alignment is the adopted child of Afro-Asianism."[44] US observers tended to be more skeptical, but remained wary of their potential during the Congo Crisis and after.

The Eisenhower team realized the outsized importance of the crisis and passed along its findings to Kennedy's team. Though the Congo was only one of seventeen new African nations that year—and the only one whose transition went so badly awry—it took on an importance well beyond its fractured borders. As the USIA reported shortly after JFK's inauguration:

> The Congo crisis ... has had a great impact on African opinion throughout the continent. ... Many Africans were legitimately concerned lest the inability of the Congolese to govern themselves should impede the colonial liberation movement and the African's quest for world recognition of his dignity and capacity. In the wake of political de-colonization, individual Ghanaians and Nigerians, for example, became more "Africa-conscious" and shifted their interest to the still-dependent areas of Africa—Algeria, the British multi-racial areas, and the Portuguese territories—[seen] as the lingering vestiges of the colonial era.[45]

The Year of Africa had left a significant part of the continent still under white metropolitan or settler rule. The conviction that the winds of change had yet to reach these areas—but that they eventually would—deepened in the Congo Crisis. This new atmosphere affected the public diplomats' work. The report continued: "Africanizing governments, [feeling] popular pressure, stepped up the process of 'Africanization' of ... [media] content [as] African opinion more stridently insisted that Africa must be allowed to manage or mismanage its own affairs. ... Africans tended to attach a racial connotation to the Congo and some Western observers felt [a rise in] anti-white, as distinct from anti-European, sentiment."[46]

During the second half of 1960, communist output goaded this sentiment. The desperate Lumumba and the Congo's agony spurred an expanded outreach in Africa across all media, attacking "Belgian and American 'neo-colonialist' efforts [and] 'puppet governments'" while giving "propaganda support to the Lumumba and Gizenga regimes which were said to represent 'authentic African nationalism,'" and blasting "UN operations [as] a cover for 'NATO-backed Western imperialism.'" The crisis gave a sharp edge to Moscow's "prodigious efforts to identify the Soviet Union as the patron saint of anti-colonialism [whose] major theme ... was the charge of 'imperialist machinations' and Western unwillingness to give up its colonial holdings." It found expression in various fora, including demonstrations against Belgium, its allies, and the United Nations. One such demonstration saw attacks on the Belgian embassy in Belgrade just months before the meeting there. Coverage of the protests, and denunciation of imperialist and UN intrigues, led bloc media output, which doubled in the wake of Lumumba's death.[47] Mao's output was even more radical: "The murder of Lumumba evoked a massive [Chinese] propaganda campaign ... which sought to fix blame for his death on the U.S. and on Hammarskjöld, [and to argue] that revolutionary violence alone would lead to liberation in the Congo and elsewhere in Africa."[48]

The Kennedy administration feared that this campaign was working and scrambled for an effective response. Rusk, concurring with a USIA review of the matter, asked Murrow to emphasize US support for the UN and for humanitarian relief in the Congo, since "preliminary consideration of possible countermoves . . . indicates that it would not be desirable for the U.S. to undertake an all-out campaign of denial" regarding Lumumba's death. The safer bet was to assert the multilateral interest rather than an American one and to use restraint rather than bombast. In this Washington was in step with the nonaligned, as discussions at Belgrade would affirm the view of the Congo as a test of the UN. The USIA accordingly promoted the theme of a "strong effective UN [and] one specific application of this theme now would be to stress: 'the best way to keep the Cold War out of Africa is to keep the UN in.'" For the moment, even a subdued, sympathetic, and multilateralist approach was an uphill climb. Touré wrote a scathing letter to Kennedy about the "unspeakable crime" of Lumumba's murder and its damage to US engagement with African nationalism.[49] In Nigeria, the perceived American role in the crisis damaged the "largely favorable . . . general public image" of the United States, to the extent that "the windows of a new USIS center in Lagos were smashed." In addition, the formerly friendly Nigerian press "has erected an 'iron curtain' around its own views of Congo which USIS has been unable to penetrate. There has been an almost complete blackout of news which might portray U.S. actions in the Congo situation in favorable light."[50]

Congo—"the great question mark," as JFK's point man on Africa, G. Mennen "Soapy" Williams, reported a year into the crisis—thus held importance beyond its internal agonies. Lumumba did too. A USIA study of the "Lumumba symbol in Africa" found the "'hero-martyr' invoked at every opportunity. Safely removed from the political scene, [he] is now glorified by African 'radical' nationalists as the symbol of African aspirations. . . . Few African leaders can now afford to denounce Lumumba or *not* to espouse certain of the goals associated with him." This climate made it hard for the USIA's subtle message of multilateralism to be heard. Washington lacked a comparably powerful figure to be the face of its African policy, one able to match the loudest African voices. At the March 1961 All-African Peoples' Conference in Cairo, "impassioned denunciations of 'the imperialists' murder of [Lumumba were] added to every speech," as were "anti-UN and anti-U.S. outbursts [and] also some anti-white overtones." After his death, "statements by his widow condemning imperialists for the murder [were] published and broadcast periodically from Cairo, Moscow, and Stanleyville radio." Guinea's delegate to the UN proclaimed that "'Guinea could well be Congo, and Congo, Africa.'"[51]

Nkrumah's African Bureau exalted Lumumba as the personification of "the 'nationalist unifier, the courageous, uncorrupted, anticolonial nation-builder.'" The two men had forged a strong personal bond. In a September 1960 letter, Nkrumah had written him that "in this struggle, Ghana and the Congo are one," and after his death, he spoke with bitter passion about the loss of his comrade. Nkrumah felt that Lumumba was, like himself, a living symbol of Pan-Africanism—"a movement" US officials in 1959 judged as "embodying racial, cultural, and regional solidarity." He made Accra into its information headquarters, reinforcing its status as what historian Jeffrey Ahlman names "perhaps the most vibrant anticolonial hotspot on the continent."[52] Contemporaries saw great potential in the movement. As scholar Rupert Emerson put it:

> The realist is likely . . . to dismiss Pan-Africanism as an idle and romantic dream. . . . Events may well prove him to be correct, but in the interim the devotion to Pan-Africanism is both widespread and charged with emotion. Nkrumah is far from being alone in his repeated insistence that independence . . . takes on its full meaning only if all of Africa is free and if African unity is achieved.[53]

The Kennedy team, for its part, took it seriously. Early in the administration, for example, Rusk urged the president to reply publicly to a communiqué of the Pan-African Freedom Movement of East and Central Africa "as PAFMECA generally represents the authentic voice of African political movements which are either in power, or can reasonably aspire to it in a short time."[54] Nkrumah, for whom historian Frank Gerits says the Congo Crisis was a "wakeup call that signaled more Pan-African activism was needed," had long promoted the persuasion, which now struck chords across the continent and beyond. Tanzanian Premier Julius Nyerere argued that "African nationalism is meaningless, is dangerous, is anachronistic if it is not at the same time pan-Africanism." A USIA study of public opinion in British East Africa confirmed "an attraction" to it, while it elicited thinly veiled hostility from Western officials such as Ralph Bunche and Hammarskjöld, the latter of whom called it an "African Hitler-Mussolini Drive."[55]

At the February 1962 PAFMECA meeting in Addis Ababa, Lumumba was repeatedly invoked. Nkrumah boasted of training propagandists for the continuing struggles for African nationalism and unity, and against apartheid. His African Bureau, according to a USIA study, "masterminds the activities of more than a hundred agents throughout Africa."[56] These activities included distribution of the print edition of *Voice of Africa*—"a monthly hate sheet"— along with other audiovisual media. Virtually all of them presented Lumumba as the personification—and victim—of a continent-wide struggle whose only legitimate endpoint was Pan-African solidarity and sovereignty. Chinese and Soviet output opportunistically fused support for both to its themes before and after the murder, while Accra, the USIA found, simply assumed longstanding Western hostility to both. The power of such calls to brotherhood fired racial passions and drew not just on the Lumumba story but on anger at apartheid, which along with the Congo was "the major catalyst for increased anti-white sentiment" on the continent.[57]

In the wake of Belgrade, Nkrumah could deploy his Pan-African gospel and the martyred Lumumba as its fallen messiah, in an effort to secure a stake in the leadership of the nascent nonaligned movement—if not as its head, then as a partner who could deliver its African constituency.[58] But it held other implications for the USIA, because of its racial dimension—and because of Nkrumah's standing in Black America. His 1958 tour of the United States had been a triumph. He had reconnected with Martin Luther King, visited the White House, and spoken at Howard University. At an NAACP dinner in his honor, Executive Secretary Roy Wilkins declared that Nkrumah's Ghana was the "embodiment of world-wide aspiration toward the ideals of human freedom to which we have so long been dedicated."[59] His profile meant that the USIA in Africa could use the tour to good effect, as part of the uphill battle for African hearts and minds. However, Nkrumah's ability to command attention on both sides of the Black Atlantic, and the sensitivity of the American racial situation, meant that his Pan-Africanism required special finesse. The agency found in late 1961 that these efforts appeared to be paying off: "American prestige [had] noticeably recovered" in Africa, even in regards to the Congo Crisis.[60] But it could never be taken for granted that this would last any longer than the next Dixieland confrontation if Jim Crow was not adequately pre-empted. US public diplomacy in Africa thus devised a two-pronged approach: using African issues to counter Nkrumahian Pan-Africanism in the short and medium term, while attempting to turn weakness into strength over the longer term by spinning the civil rights movement.

Civil Rights at Home and Abroad, Amid Cacophony and Coalescence

Racial segregation was, on its face, the biggest obstacle US public diplomats faced—not just in Africa but across the world. Few other subjects so stained the image of the "land of the free" as did Jim Crow.[61] In pro-West Ivory Coast, for example, the still-predominant French press played up every single story of racial discrimination. In Nigeria, the USIS had little trouble placing materials on American racial progress, perhaps out of local curiosity; Nigerians "resent[ed] the 'second-class citizenship' of many American Negroes and believe the United

States should have taken a firmer and earlier stand against apartheid and for African 'liberation.' [They are] asking such questions as: 'is the U.S. the kind of nation we want to tie up with permanently?" But while African resentment of Jim Crow makes intuitive sense in retrospect, it can be overstated. USIA researchers found in British East Africa, for example, that opinion of the United States included a "rather surprising point[:] Only a minority criticizes America for race discrimination" and pluralities of all groups saw improvement in US race relations.[62]

Such surprises recurred in the USIA's research, often reflecting local particularities, but it did little to change the baseline: the United States was always on the defensive when it came to race. "African misconceptions of U.S. race relations," found a wide-ranging 1962 study, formed "the most critical barrier to [Africans'] correct understanding of the United States." Another study surmised that "the underlying resentment . . . which the 'colored' peoples have had in their relations with 'whites' feeds upon U.S. racial incidents"—a sentiment which "may well be a much stronger force in shaping their response to the West over the long-haul than current media concern with a specific incident."[63] There was obvious truth to this. As Bowles had put it to Murrow early on, the "Negro sees all of black Africa in the process of getting self-rule, for which it may or may not be ready, while he is widely denied the right to drink a cup of coffee." Both men knew this was true in reverse as well. Independent Africans looked across the Atlantic with dismay, and "extensive publicity on anti-Negro feeling in the United States" ensured they knew of the travails African Americans faced.[64]

They knew of these things, and Murrow knew furthermore that the heat of repeated "incidents" could harden those generalized feelings into something permanent. The USIA sought to counteract such an outcome via both message and messenger, for example recruiting African Americans so that black faces abroad could contextualize, if not offset, the beating of black faces back home.[65] But the main rhetorical thrust was to present Jim Crow violence as an embarrassing anomaly opposed by white and black Americans of goodwill. When the Freedom Rides exploded, one post reported that African editorial comment was "surprisingly light but increasingly bitter."[66] The USIA, resigned to the reality, saw a spin opportunity:

> Despite progress there will continue to be race incidents [so] we must try to put it in perspective [and] show that the picture is not one of whites against Negroes . . . but of the vast majority of whites and Negroes striving together for progress. . . . USIA is emphasizing [this] with things such as photos of Freedom Riders.[67]

Spinning such episodes as the summer 1961 violence endured by the Freedom Riders—which one USIA Assistant Director said could well receive more coverage in Africa than in the United States, and which a Pakistani paper said had "out-Little Rock'd Little Rock"—was a tall order. Failing could do damage for years, especially in the face of bloc output saying that the Freedom Riders violence "'proved' the hypocrisy of American aid offers to Africa."[68] The USIA strategy in reply was, in effect, a calculated gamble: acknowledge and admit the stain of segregation; explain the federal and other structural obstacles to removing it; pivot to the progress manifest in such "growing pains"; and identify JFK overseas with civil rights progress in keeping with his focus on the Global South.

Done properly, this could offer the platform for just the kind of themes Murrow's USIA wanted to push in the non-European world. In any case, ignoring the subject or denying its evils were equally impossible. African and indeed world curiosity was strong. After the Freedom Rides, the agency spotlighted stateside visits of African diplomats, despite the risk of backfire when the visitors encountered racism.[69] These instances were widely enough known to prompt retaliation, as when "students in Dakar forced a visiting U.S. delegation, [set to be housed] on university premises, to seek other facilities." African students in the United States, on the other hand, became examples of the openness USIA wanted to convey. Mboya convinced the Kennedy administration to bring thousands to America for higher education in the "Kenya Airlift," a story emphasized in agency output across the continent.[70] Highlighting such retail friendliness to Africa and acknowledging slow progress toward equality guided a US information approach aimed at bolstering the moderate sectors of African opinion against interwoven radical, Pan-African, and bloc critiques. It was, in a sense, an attempt at a "soft" Pan-Africanism stressing Black–Atlantic connections to America, as an alternative to Nkrumah's harder version.

By late 1962, when James Meredith's attempt to attend the University of Mississippi triggered violent racist resistance—bringing Jim Crow again to the fore—this strategy appeared to be working reasonably well. The Mississippi episode, though soon overshadowed by the Cuban Missile Crisis, redounded to Kennedy's reputational benefit as the USIA underlined Washington's "resolute insistence . . . in enforcing" Meredith's rights, winning praise in the African and world press. A review found that the "strongest expressions of criticism [were] from Africa, the Near East, and South Asia. Rarely, however, was comment wholly critical. . . . Noteworthy is that some [often-critical] African sources . . . have not in this case launched attacks but have instead praised the federal action." While this could not be definitively attributed to the USIA's handiwork, there was reason to believe that the spin doctors were achieving their goal of steering foreign public opinion away from a hostile stance:

> There is no evidence that adverse racial incidents have caused any
> nation to align itself against us, even in Africa, but they are an added

and explosive burden to carry in a world where "white nations" are
in a minority. . . . Opinion surveys, beginning in 1955, have generally
shown that people overseas, while in the main friendly to the United
States, are both aware and critical of . . . discrimination against
Negroes here. There is also some evidence of recognition of improvement in American race relations.[71]

More than a few Pan-Africanist and nonaligned leaders had their own domestic reasons for this recognition and for counseling patience when it came to
intrasocietal ethnic tensions. During the Little Rock crisis, Nehru reminded
South Asians that caste and violence were not unique to the United States,
while Nyerere, "to maintain harmonious cooperation among the races and
tribes which constitute his country, has also sought to promote recognition
of the progress of the Negro American," as did Mboya and other nationalists.
However, the study ended on a cautionary note, affirming that "racial prejudice and discrimination continue to constitute the 'most disliked' character-
istic of the white American as stereotyped in [foreign] public opinion," and
warned that "adverse racial incidents, which are widely reported and pictured,
sustain and accentuate the concept formed many years ago."

Any success in pre-empting African anger at Jim Crow was always hostage
to the next incident. While a January 1963 study worried that the USIA was
on balance underachieving in Africa due to the erroneous application of outreach techniques designed for Europe and to still inadequate output on US
race relations given the "great interest in Africa about the life and progress of
the American Negro," the greater worry was the next explosion. This arrived
in Birmingham just a few months later. The violence there was unspinnable,
and the reaction in Africa was furious. Touring Africa again, Soapy Williams
reported hearing it directly from Kenyan Prime Minister Jomo Kenyatta: "The
people of Kenya deplore the continuing oppression of Negroes in the Southern
United States which belies U.S. claim to true democracy. We express solidarity with American Negro freedom fighters." These sentiments were echoed in
heavy press coverage replete with "inflammatory headlines [such as] 'Riots
Flare in US South—Infants sent to Jail' [and] 'Prisons packed as Southern
Negroes fight Segregation,'" and film of the violence broadcast on KBC.[72]

In reply, the USIA placed a message from Williams in the local press, emphasizing civil rights progress, and "suppl[ied] additional materials in all
media to handle other aspects of Birmingham problems since the Kenyatta
message has rekindled interest in the flare-up . . . thus adding to unfortunate
impressions already widely held." The reaction was by no means limited to
Kenya—"Ghanaian comment," another media survey found, was "especially
critical and caustic"—but it was more limited than might be suspected in

hindsight. Those two countries had their own incentives—for Kenyatta, an election campaign and imminent independence in a settler-dominated Kenya, and for Nkrumah, his on-again off-again anti-American campaign—for their public expressions of outrage. Elsewhere, in the "large volume of comment and reporting on Birmingham ... potential critical comment in other countries of Africa has not materialized to any degree. [Rather, there has been] surprisingly moderate and balanced reporting."[73]

As with the Alliance for Progress and with Ole Miss, JFK's direct intervention, as far as USIA could discern, had made a decisive difference. If it did not quite turn the Birmingham crisis into a positive asset, the president's speeches on the matter redirected the narrative along channels that US public diplomats had spent the last few years digging. While many voices in the African press chided Kennedy for taking so long to get involved, all praised him for finally doing so—even Nkrumah's *Voice of Africa*, "normally sharply critical of the U.S., grudgingly termed [it] 'forthright, sober, and constructive.'" In short, the world media reaction was positive: "Strong endorsement of the president's speeches was almost universal [as was] optimism ... about the eventual solution of the race problem in the U.S."[74]

Birmingham reconfirmed an old truth: that public diplomacy's effectiveness could not far outrun policy. However, it also affirmed the value of long-term media battlespace preparation. The steady stream of features emphasizing progress on race by Americans of goodwill, American interest in African affairs, the challenges of the federal system, and the cultivation of African nationalist and media contacts helped to blunt the impact of the worst incidents. This approach also set the stage for eventual presidential insertion into the story. When it came, concluded one survey of USIA and consular personnel, "the most effective force for the U.S. in Africa on civil rights is action by JFK and the federal government." This, they continued, should be emphasized but not oversold: "They felt the need for increased flow of background material and guidance, [and] felt USIA output should be very candid, not overly optimistic, should avoid giving a misleading impression, [and] should be increased."[75]

This last point was of capital importance, given the salience of the issue to US outreach to Africa and beyond and the expanding, intensifying international discourse on Black Atlantic freedom. The racial justice this subject entailed exerted a gravity on the unresolved membership and meaning of the post-Belgrade Global South. As that conversation proceeded, racially driven themes were a staple of public diplomacy by virtually all parties. Japanese propaganda in Asia, for example, stressed "racial kinship," and in reply outreach aimed at Japan by its neighbors "invoked similarity of complexion and hair ... as a reason for establishing greater cooperation." *Time* reported that Chinese public relations in Latin America highlighted "that the [Latin American] republics and the 'People's Democracy' share colored skin."[76] Mao's outreach in Africa, meanwhile, "[sought] to exploit the emotions of peoples on such subjects as nationalism, Pan-Africanism, anti-colonialism, and racialism. Displaying unrelenting skepticism of the peaceful transition from colonialism . . . Peking [argued] that its own example of revolution was more relevant [than that] of the far more mature and *essentially European* Soviet Union." A followup report concurred: "The Chinese stress[ed] the[ir] former colonial status [and] their nonwhite and non-European origins, and their common problems with Africa."[77] US analysts often doubted the extent and staying power of nonwhite racial solidarity. But in the context of Pan-African and Black-Atlantic dialogues, civil rights unrest, and the broader dynamics of race across the Global South, they could not dismiss it as a potentially major obstacle to managing the US image abroad.

The largest such obstacles, however, were the longstanding one of US policy itself—and the newer, arguably bigger one: intense public diplomacy competition that fed "misconceptions" about it. In April 1958, Radio Moscow had begun direct radio transmissions to Africa. They were soon joined by Radio Peking. Both were latecomers, as was the United States, to an arena historically dominated by the BBC but recently marked by the entry of Radio Cairo. Nasser had long been deft in his use of radio, but in the late 1950s he deployed other instruments southward: film, print, and cultural, political, and religious contacts. While his main target was the Arab world, "independent or soon-to-be independent areas of East and West Africa, was the second target. . . . Egypt promised support for . . . African liberation movements and excoriated imperialism, colonialism, and 'racialism."[78] In most respects, this reinforced bloc themes. It differed in the emphasis on Afro-Asian solidarity, on nonalignment, and on Egypt's leadership of both: "UAR objectives . . . are to accelerate the decline of Western power and expand Egyptian influence [via] the tactical appeals of Arab nationalism, African nationalism, and Pan-Islam."[79]

The bloc sought to catch up, substantially ramping up its own African outreach, and assisting the new states' efforts to build communications infrastructure.[80] Czechoslovakia and Poland assisted Guinea with the construction of a radio station, while East Germany set up a journalism school in the country, and sold Accra a printing plant at a discount. These facilities exceeded either country's internal media needs, and it was expected that much of their output would be aimed externally—possibly at the direction of Moscow's new press agency, *Novosti*, "which is expected to emphasize underdeveloped countries in its operations."[81] Those countries, though, had plans of their own. Nasser was not the only non-European actor to move aggressively in the African public diplomacy arena. The Algerian FLN, inspired by the reach and power of Nasser's broadcasts, by 1961 had built a radio network of sixty-plus transmission stations reaching all of Algeria proper and beyond it from Guinea to Mali.[82] Nkrumah had a Nasser-sized media presence in mind as well. His *Voice of Africa* began broadcasting in June 1961, and the USIA "expected [it] to be audible throughout the continent [and to] expound . . . Pan-African liberation and political unification." The radio service shared a name not only with a print publication (one of fifteen Accra produced) but also with Nasser's new programming launched the next month. The competing *Voices* illustrated the battle for leadership of African nationalism and the importance its combatants placed on media. The multilateral African Peoples Conference in March had called for an African radio network; Nasser and Nkrumah then each acted unilaterally to establish his own country as its base.[83]

The crowded field posed a challenge in and of itself. But the challenge to the USIA—which wondered whether its rapid expansion in "Africa represent[ed] too little too late"—could be acute if, in time of crisis, the disparate voices agreed enough to join forces.[84] The multiplying voices found common ground in directing the conversation to the themes—anticolonialism, independence, Pan-Africanism, civil rights, nonalignment, antiracism, and poverty and underdevelopment—for which their audiences hungered more every day. While European and bloc output to Africa had peaked in 1960–1961, the spread of homegrown Afro-Asian-Arab media continued apace. USIA Radio Director Henry Loomis had noted on a 1959 tour:

> In the bush of Tanganyika . . . a young African [told] me in good English that he listened to the following radio stations: BBC, Nairobi, Dar-es-Salaam, VOA, Moscow, Salisbury, Leopoldville, Brazzaville, Cairo, and Peking. He was unhappy because he could not get Ghana [he did not mention Delhi or Karachi]. Programs are being "Africanized," by Africans, for Africans, about Africa . . . While each country is concerned about the broadcasts of others, most are very eager to share their experience with their neighbors and become the leader of emerging Africa. In Dakar I was told that external broadcasts took precedence over internal [ones].[85]

The trend continued over the next four years, by which time the young Tanzanian would indeed have been able to hear the signature of Radio Ghana. By that time, as well, another half-dozen African networks could be heard in Dar-es-Salaam, where could also be found print and film public diplomacy by powers both North and South.

Among both strident and subdued voices, patterns emerged. One was a determination to avoid the Cold War. In most areas, this harmonized with the various strains of nonalignment. But in Africa, this also meshed with the

inclination toward Pan-Africanism: "Educated Africans were almost completely preoccupied with local and regional problems: [building] nation-
hood [and] exploring means to achieve greater security in regional unity.
They sought to serve African interests by projecting their collective influence
on the world stage [but] felt themselves removed from the Cold War [which
they] wanted to keep ... out of Africa." Similar strains could be detected in
South Asia, Latin America, and the Arab world.[86] A survey of opinion in India,
Panama, the Dominican Republic, Ghana, the Philippines, and Brazil—all
now sharing the category of "underdeveloped"—found that "to them [the
Cold War] is a faraway problem. [These] findings lend strong support to the
view of those in USIA who have been saying that we face a difficult task in
getting the underdeveloped countries [to] perceive the Communist danger as
affecting *them*, rather than just a 'battle between two giants' that they want to
stay out of."[87]

However, for Africans in particular, it was as much a matter of avoiding the Cold War as it was of pressing the case that race and anticolonialism were simply more important. "For most Africans," a 1962 study found,
"colonialism—past, present and potential—and not the Cold War [which
was seen] as a contest between rich and powerful nations [of] the non-colored
world ... was the primary international conflict."[88] Attesting to the appeal
of Pan-African solutions to it, the 1963 founding of the Organization of
African Unity (OAU) showed that whatever misgivings about Nkrumahism
divided the "Monrovia" and "Casablanca" camps, there was broad agreement about the proper meaning and endpoint of the shared struggle. A hint
of agreement could be found abroad too, given the coincidental timing of
OAU—just one week after the release of Martin Luther King's "Letter from
a Birmingham Jail." Such racialized dynamics thus ran beyond Africa. They
were cause for doubt about long-term commitments to the land of Jim Crow
and were cause for curiosity about the bonds, persistently invoked, among
nonwhite peoples.

Still another recurring motif in non-European information activities—this
one echoed in US output to a greater extent than the other themes—was poverty and underdevelopment with modernization as the cure. Even before the
Congo Crisis, the USIA found Nkrumah's African Bureau "alert[ing] Africans
to a 'new colonialism'" by which "the colonial (and by extension all Western)
powers" would vitiate independence by controlling the new states' economic
life. For US public diplomats this meant proceeding cautiously: in material on
US "interest ... in Ghana's economic life and development, it is of overriding
importance that the 'no strings attached' concept be kept ever in mind." But
such subtlety could be lost in the informational crosscurrents of Nkrumah's
and his peers' networks, which reached far beyond Africa.[89]

The Global South convergence of conclusions did not mask their differences of opinion. India's definition of nonalignment was more activist than was many of its erstwhile partners', as well as more purist in its insistence that nonaligned countries, by definition, could not constitute a bloc. The Arab world's internal solidarity was shot through with rivalries, but was nonetheless far more cohesive than its tenuous external bonds with the Afro-Asian grouping. For Africa, US analysts found that "neutralism and non-alignment—often used interchangeably—were the catchwords of Africa's external relations. In a very real sense, Africans demonstrated anew the difficulty ex-colonial nations have had in adopting a recipe for neutralism since they cannot agree on its ingredients." Ethno-racial solidarity seemed at least as likely to produce "Pan-blocs" within a Global South grouping as to produce a broadly shared non-white coalition across it, especially as leaders like Nasser and Nkrumah used their regions as political bases in the competition to lead a prospective such bloc.[90] Poverty and the desire for modernization were perhaps the strongest and most widely held potential rallying points, but even these could founder on the unequal distribution of natural resources, and on the greater likelihood of economic competition than complementarity among Global South nations.

However, if the coalescence of these issues coursing through the world dialogue in 1963 was uneasy and uncertain, their presence and potential were unmistakable. At a minimum, their constant promulgation and dissection in the public diplomacy of all parties ensured they would remain on the global stage. In its broadest survey to date, "The Developing Countries: A Miscellany of Values, Concerns, Desires," the USIA perceived this broader, changing map:

> [This] map [suggests] that in addition to the familiar East–West division . . . there is a "North–South" division that is perhaps equally—if not actually more—significant. . . . A line thru the Rio Grande, the Mediterranean and the boundary between the Soviet Union and China would divide the world rather cleanly into a more-advanced and a less-advanced group of countries. Naturally there are exceptions [but] perhaps [we can rather] speak of "the underdeveloped tropics" than of "the underdeveloped South."[91]

If the boundaries of this imagined community were uncertain, its importance on the crowded battlefield for hearts and minds was not. By 1964, the USIA had expanded its infrastructure and activities in Africa and Latin America at the expense of those in Western Europe. This was in part because in the latter, "normal communications with the U.S. are full and open"; some internal critics even asked whether the agency should continue to operate there at all. No such debate was entertained for the non-European world.[92]

The Kennedy administration's public diplomacy in Africa succeeded well enough, as it had also done in Latin America, in fusing JFK's charisma with his agenda of better relations with the developing world that his assassination elicited sorrow and worry there. USIA output on the assassination emphasized both the pain of America's loss and the continuity in its governance as Johnson took office. Reports from the field found that media reception keyed the news to issues of local interest, and "in Africa it was the fate of the civil rights movement. . . . Some slippage of the U.S. image is noted in Algeria, Ghana, Nigeria, and Congo," perhaps in part because African coverage "show[ed] heavy emphasis on the racist theme. The contention is that the president was shot because of his civil rights stand." In most respects, this was a triumph of spin over substance, as JFK was neither as committed nor as effective in these areas as such analyses suggested. But to the extent that he had begun changing the underlying policies, and given that Kennedy deployed his rhetoric to great effect, the USIA had excellent material to work with. By the summer of 1963 it seemed on balance to be working, though perhaps more effectively at elevating JFK's personal image than America's national one.[93]

Jim Crow posed a threat to the latter in the Global South. Despite embarrassments, such as the boycott of the US embassy at Accra's July 4 celebrations by some visiting white and black Americans, USIA studies continued into the mid-1960s to find evidence of African esteem for the United States and of African belief that US race relations were improving.[94] At a minimum, Kennedy-era public diplomacy on race and nonalignment worked passably well as damage control. Thanks in part to Soviet missteps and to JFK's personal diplomacy with nonaligned leaders, Washington weathered the Belgrade meeting without much visible damage and even saw that event put the troika proposal publicly to rest. On the race–anticolonial nexus, the USIA minimized the blow of the Congo Crisis and the fallout from Jim Crow violence. On poverty, the highlighting of modernization telegraphed American agreement on this central challenge defining the Global South. US public diplomats of the early 1960s detected but could not dominate these crosscurrents. The USIA crafted its outreach to balance subtlety, sympathy, and New Frontier charisma, and to convey to non-European actors that whether or not they were interested in the Cold War, the Cold War was interested in them.

Yet even this limited success carried a long-term risk and an unintended consequence. An approach built on subtle persuasion risked being swamped by media competition, as new voices joined the fray on the non-European ground. Still, it was better than the alternatives—provided that USIA was identifying the questions and crosscurrents correctly. This was by no means guaranteed. While US public diplomacy, especially its research tools, became more sophisticated during the Kennedy years, these too could be hampered by

Cold War-induced blind spots. These blind spots slowed the American realization that the crosscurrents—a swirl of "contradictory forces" including among others Pan-Arabism, Pan-Africanism, nationalism, Négritude, and neocolonialism, and flowing through print, radio, and visual media to and from newly independent countries—were abundant.[95] These intellectual tides were also producing an unexpected result. What had been called at various times the Bandung nations, the under- or less-developed countries, and the Afro-Asian peoples, were by 1963 the Nonaligned Movement, one label that stuck. The convergence of these defining issues, as they connected Belgrade to the Congo to Birmingham, in the explosion of Global South public diplomacy first practiced by Nasser and Nkrumah and subsequently by a dozen more, meant that it would not be the only label to do so. So too, in one of the more momentous unintended consequences of Cold War history, would the term "Third World" and its accompanying imagined community. As the cacophonous conversation expanded it not only drowned out the prospect of Global North voices having the final say in shaping the narrative of world affairs, but also thereby nurtured an evolving definition of the Third World project. This project could incorporate more than even an expansively understood nonaligned bloc to include also modernization-development and nonwhite solidarity—and now seemed to be in the ascendant.

Conclusion

Murrow's Wager

The "Third World" has been more of a politician's phrase than a political reality, but it symbolizes the rise of important forces that present propagandists as well as diplomats with a set of [vastly different] targets, objectives, and strategic problems [as] African and Arab nationalisms have demonstrated a capacity for independent action that exploits the rivalry and anxiety of the Great Powers.
—Leo Bogart, *Premises for Propaganda*, 1976

So universal has Cold War rhetoric been that it has been a force in dividing the world. At first we thought of the political world as divided into two parts [but] soon the unaligned nations began to think of themselves as a force, and the concept of the Third World was born.
—Martin Medhurst, *Cold War Rhetoric*, 1997

With apologies to Blaise Pascal, American Cold War public diplomacy operated on a premise that might be called Murrow's Wager. The USIA conducted its operations in the absence of conclusive proof that they were having any effect, but in the belief that they were and that they thus may as well continue their work. Its missionaries evangelized far and wide, and looked for signs that their gospel was taking hold. Absent a public profession of faith from their individual or collective audiences, they lacked incontrovertible proof that they were if not converting souls, then at least successfully winning hearts and minds. They and their employers in Washington held fast to the conviction that their public diplomacy efforts were helping the United States to win the Cold War.

Yet their greatest impact was one they neither intended nor predicted. By carrying the Cold War into the non-European world, the superpowers' public diplomats prompted a reaction from their counterparts in newly independent states, helping to catalyze a collective identity among impoverished, imperialized areas. Drawing upon long-running indigenous critiques of empire, capitalism, and white supremacy, leaders of the new nations composed the philosophical nucleus of nonalignment, underdevelopment, race consciousness, and anticolonialism at the core of the Third World project. They expressed it to the wider world and to each other in public diplomacy media outreach of their own. The rhetoric of the newly independent, race-conscious, nonaligned, and impoverished Third World ended up changing the terms of the Cold War.

Although the Third World project proved a disappointment to its proponents, it is easy in retrospect to overlook the senses of urgency, possibility, and indeed of destiny that animated its evolution. Because the project's solidarity in practice and its record of tangible accomplishment fell so far short of its at times revolutionary rhetoric, it is easy to miss its vital role as both product and producer of Cold War history—and its place on an even longer timeline. While it is important not to romanticize the Third World project, it should nonetheless be appreciated for what it represented in its time. The sense of epochal transformation occasioned by decolonization—an historical moment at which, for the first time in recorded history and virtually overnight, human civilization renounced the practice of territorial imperial expansion and rule—was profound. It raised questions about the nature, dynamics, and inheritances of empire, of domination, of sovereignty, of self-rule. Even as it took as given the norm of the nation-state, it imagined other possibilities—other borders, polities, and unities that encompassed and expressed "peoples" beyond that construct. The timing of this transition amidst the Cold War raised its stakes and, in some places, twisted its fate. But the superpower conflict did not eclipse the constituent parts of the Third World nucleus. On the contrary, the conflict brought them into sharp relief, broadening their definitions and expanding the ranks of their adherents to include long-decolonized Latin America. The Third World project was the site—geographical, intellectual, spiritual—where two great twentieth-century stories, the Cold War and decolonization-cum-race revolution, met. Public diplomacy, first by the superpowers and then by the Third World actors themselves, brokered their convergence. To miss the significance of the rise of the Third World project is to write Global South agency out of postwar history—and to miss the catalytic role that public diplomacy played in spurring it to reflection, discussion, and action.

The Third World project continued, and arguably peaked, over the dozen or so years after 1963. The end of the Kennedy years nonetheless marks a useful bookend as regards US public diplomacy activities in the Global South. Such activities continued, and indeed in some ways intensified, as the Third World became a primary arena of the Cold War. But the end of the second wave of decolonization, the transition to the Johnson administration, and above all the Vietnam War demarcate a new chapter in US public diplomacy history. Johnson maintained the funding and access arrangements his predecessor had given the USIA, under the leadership of its first African American director

Carl Rowan, but the Texan was not the true believer that JFK had been. He did, however, oversee a profound though ultimately temporary change in the USIA's role, thanks to his Americanization of the war in Vietnam. That conflict popularized the phrase "winning hearts and minds," in pursuit of which the Johnson administration reorganized the US public diplomacy machinery, hiving off parts of USIA to create the Joint United States Public Affairs Office (JUSPAO) in-theater. The initiative blurred lines between white-gray-black propaganda, and between information and intelligence activities, in ways rarely seen since pre-USIA days. It thus resuscitated some of the soul-searching of those early years of postwar public diplomacy. Nor did it help matters that the war itself proved a near-impossible sell in the Third World. Despite its putative proof of the US commitment to anticommunist self-rule in the Global South, the American intervention looked like warmed-over imperialism to many audiences there. Vietnam put the United States on the defensive like virtually nothing else, save perhaps Jim Crow violence, during the Cold War. The war so battered the American image that it stands in retrospect as a watershed in US public diplomacy, dealing a blow—especially in the non-European world—from which the United States never fully recovered.

The American discovery of that wider postwar non-European world came haltingly and unevenly—but it came organically, growing out of the intrinsic logic of Washington's strategy for waging the Cold War. Armed conflict in Southeast Asia had signaled that the postwar crisis was not confined to Europe, but even after the Truman Doctrine theoretically incorporated such distant corners into the twilight struggle, Washington saw them primarily for their relevance to the task of reconstructing Europe. The failure to mobilize fully US public diplomacy in theaters from Latin America to South Asia is puzzling in retrospect, as their peoples had been brought in principle into a global contest that Washington had declared—but then neglected to explain to them. The Korean War brought proof that the contest was indeed underway. Its violence prompted a flood of outreach to various and far-flung populations, some of whose hearts and minds were now on the front lines. The Korean theater and its environs broadened the geographical scope of American public diplomacy and precipitated the first differentiations within it—a forerunner to the niche-targeting that would mark US outreach in the Third World. On the whole, Truman-era US public diplomacy outside Europe started late, focused incompletely and inaccurately, and never achieved liftoff. Its organizational chaos reflected a genuine philosophical and thus geographical confusion about the breadth and depth of the Cold War outside Europe and about the need to win the allegiances of peoples there. But the Truman years ended with an increasing awareness of them and the conviction that they must be won.

Eisenhower took office already firmly convinced, and thanks to the coincidence of his inauguration and Stalin's death within six weeks of each other, the timing was propitious for the vast expansion of the contest for hearts and minds into the non-European world. He charged his newly founded USIA— given a respected though not quite peer status within the administration— with the task and with instructions to jettison bombast in favor of persuasiveness in its programming. In places like Guatemala, US public diplomacy acted as a companion to seedier activities undertaken in the crusade against communism. But even divorced from such intrigues, the Eisenhower administration sought to use it creatively to win over public opinion in the Global South. At Bandung and Suez, the USIA settled on a light-touch strategy that deployed proxies—witting or not—to inject US interests and a positive US image into the narrative. In Ghana, an in-person soft-touch campaign of subtle support de-emphasized the Cold War. It also underlined American friendship for African peoples, though the latter point was soon undercut by the Little Rock Crisis that in many Global South eyes connected across the Black Atlantic. Although the Eisenhower administration tended to tune its foreign policy to Cold War considerations over those of race and decolonization, it increasingly recognized the mid-1950s watershed in global race relations. Among the brightest indicators was the USIA's realization that its task had become harder thanks to the new Babel in the tropics: a highly competitive global media war for the hearts and minds—and including the voices—of the Third World, a still amorphous concept that would soon make the leap from French to English usage.

The concept, if not yet the term, guided the new Kennedy administration's foreign policy thinking as well as its public diplomacy. In most respects the new team consummated the trends of its predecessor in that arena. It elevated the USIA in the hierarchy, launched foreign policy initiatives to improve the American image, and prioritized the "southern half of the globe" where it expanded the US public diplomacy infrastructure. Yet it did so in a media maelstrom that at times made it hard for particular USIA campaigns to reach their desired audiences. Those that did owed their success in part to JFK's celebrity and in part to initiatives like the Peace Corps and the Kenya Airlift that embodied a new chapter in US relations with the Global South. In part, though, the USIA found that these gained the most traction when they harmonized with the Third World's own analysis of global affairs. At Belgrade, the agency employed the tried-and-true proxy strategy to convey acceptance, if not approval, of the various strains of nonalignment. It did so in part by continuing to emphasize US support for the UN, a central piece of its outreach on the Congo Crisis as well. This had the added advantage of de-emphasizing the Pan-African-inflected currents coursing through the latter, in favor of conveying sympathy—and in hopes that African opinion would return the favor as the violence of Jim Crow and apartheid continued to crest.

However, if Congo represented the most acute crisis of sub-Saharan decolonization, for Washington it was Latin America that Castro had rendered "the most dangerous area in the world." The signature Kennedy initiative there, the Alliance for Progress, depended on mass and elite buy-in, to be facilitated by public diplomacy. American outreach conveyed sympathy for the suffering caused by poverty and underdevelopment, and promoted modernization under the AFP model—driven by both popular participation and elite support—as the cure. In doing so, it validated the position that economics, more than nonalignment or racial–anticolonial solidarity, ranked as the defining common feature of the Global South. USIA output joined the public diplomacy cacophony about all three elements as that conversation continued hashing out the Third World project, whose fluidity was demonstrated by, among other things, fusing post-Castro Latin America to the freshly decolonized lands of Africa and Asia as its constituent parts.

This book only begins to explore these Third World public diplomacy responses to USIA activities. It tracks USIA awareness of those responses and sketches how the Third World concept looked to Washington as it rose and evolved in Global South public diplomacy but—being a Washington-centric account drawn from US archives—does not delve into their backstories. Studies focused on particular non-European areas and drawing on archival sources there are necessary to flesh out the story more fully. However, a number of conclusions can be gleaned from these episodes, beyond the overarching, unintended consequence of the Third World's emergence. A major feature of the story is gradualism. The US and Soviet "discovery" of the non-European world took time, and it happened when it did in part as a consequence of both superpowers deciding they needed to make their Cold War cases there. Their claims to universality and modernity did not equate overnight to active trumpeting of those claims far afield in the Global South. It took events both there and in the Global North to push Washington and Moscow into full-scale public diplomacy in those areas. Once they did, it spurred the process of identifying their stake in the Cold War.

That process, including the currents that would eventually shape the Third World project, was in important respects already underway. The interwar nationalist movements launched amid expatriate communities in the metropoles were vital precursors, as the "Wilsonian moment" suggested their struggles were not solely single-nationalist in nature. Their consciousness of, and connections among, each other sketched the intellectual prototype of the anticolonialist agenda. Vijay Prashad credits this convergence, especially at the 1927 Brussels meeting of Anti-Imperialists, with launching the Third World project. Nico Slate affirms that its currents of nonwhite racial solidarity were themselves long-running by the time of the Cold War that frequently eclipsed them: "Decades of efforts to construct a colored world survived in reduced form in new notions of a Third World," which were "constructed in tension with the American and Soviet blocs."[1] Yet in the historical moment, the power of these currents seemed both unpredictable and potentially strong. As a USIA analyst noted in a 1962 study of Pan-Africanism, Jean-Paul Sartre's preface to Léopold Senghor's anthology of African poetry "compared Négritude to an African Eurydice, recaptured from the power of Pluto by the song of Orpheus" and it animated black anticolonialism, which was embedded in "Négritude . . . in principle since its inception." Pan-Africanism, similarly, reached back decades, percolating through the Third World project from its earliest phases. The Cold War added nonalignment and underdevelopment to the project—as one 1967 analysis had it, "what 'Third World' originally was, then, is clear; it was the *nonaligned world* [and it] was also a world of *poor countries*"—but beyond this it launched the project's decisive consummation.[2] The Cold War alone did not create the Third World in the non-European lands that it gradually discovered. The agency and vision of Nehru, Nasser, Nkrumah, and their compatriots were ultimately decisive in that creation. But it takes nothing away from their efforts to note that the superpower conflict inadvertently invigorated the conversation and attempted to set the post-1945 parameters of world affairs within which they worked. The collective entity they built over time was in opposition to those two poles, which were remagnetized daily in Third World media thanks to the USIA and its Soviet counterparts.

The gradual spread of this outreach to encompass the non-European world was just one such evolution—from dim awareness of the non-European world to belief in its centrality, and consequently from a narrow European focus to a worldwide scope in its activities—in the story. Others saw US public diplomacy trace a progression from organizational chaos to order, from operational improvisation to sophistication, and from an emphasis on mass outreach to one that targeted niche sectors as well. The USIA machinery became more finely tuned as its output became more finely grained, and it expanded in both physical and philosophical terms. It wrestled with challenges it never quite resolved, not least of which was the competition. But there were others, including some that bordered on the ironic, that grew out of the interplay of US Cold War image management with the ripostes it elicited from the Global South.

As the USIA became more aware of the issues animating Third World conversation, it sought language that could fuse those issues with the Cold War in resonant ways. The 1961 Berlin crisis that culminated in the building of the Wall, for example, was pitched in recently decolonized African countries as a battle over "self-determination." In a similar vein, for the better part of the 1950s US public diplomats charged the Soviets and Chinese with "red colonialism." Some of the largest USIA campaigns of that decade, "Atoms for Peace" and "People's Capitalism," were not exclusively targeted at the Global South but did seek to frame the American nuclear and socioeconomic stances, respectively, in ways that tempered the menace audiences there might otherwise sense. In virtually every case, even when a particular campaign seemed to improve the American image on the margins, there was little evidence that the tropes were having the desired effect of persuading Third World audiences that these Cold War topics were "their" issues in the same way that, say, race relations or colonialism viscerally were. It bears noting that the Soviets' tropes fared little better. Reviewing the communist public diplomacy of the Congo Crisis, for example, the USIA found that having failed "to gain African acceptance of the view that the Bloc is the vanguard of the 'colonial liberation movement' in Africa, Moscow attempted to pose as the 'protective shield' holding the West at bay and thus making Africa's successful anti-colonial revolution possible."[3]

The failure of the superpower tropes is instructive. Part of the explanation for both Cold War sides surely lies in the "permanent problem" of public diplomacy: the gap between word and deed. The repression of racial and ethnic minorities by both East and West, for example, discredited their claims to championing social equality. Armed interventions and nuclear weapons buildup by both superpowers undercut their stated commitment to peace. Moreover, neither side missed many opportunities to highlight the other's inconsistencies, ensuring that specific instances of the gap between spin and policy would be widely known among Global South peoples. Even when the distance between policy and public relations was relatively short, such peoples were often skeptical of the wisdom of superpower policies. Soviet and American conduct could come across as destructive, stupid, misguided, or simply wrong—and for the most part only tangentially connected to their own struggles. But awareness of the gap—constantly reinforced by each side against the other, and increasingly over time by indigenous Third World media output—made selling Cold War tropes there a long shot at best. The permanent problem could no more be solved there than in Global North theaters of public diplomacy.

The impossibility of solving it was all but guaranteed by that proliferation of voices, which also rendered more difficult the "permanent question" of public diplomacy: whether or not it was achieving its desired results. But the proliferation itself offers an answer of sorts. Given the difficulty, then as now, of demonstrating the effectiveness of public diplomacy, anything more than a tentative verdict cannot be tendered. However, the energy with which new Third World nations jumped into the public diplomacy arena suggest that they believed it sufficiently effective to be worth pursuing—and even if its effectiveness could not be proved, its importance was accepted as given. Engaging in external outreach signified arrival on regional and world stages; it manifested independence, generated prestige, and extended influence in ways that little else could; and above all, everyone was doing it. It enabled push-back against Cold War tropes and provided a platform for debate about the way forward for the exploited South. The new players did little by way of audience research or other empirical means of answering the permanent question. They flatly assumed that the answer was yes. Leaders like Nehru, Nasser, and Nkrumah understood outreach as not just worthwhile in its own right but also as a tool for asserting independence, spreading influence, and building coalitions, and proceeded accordingly.

Washington too assumed an affirmative answer and decided to err on the side of belief that US public diplomacy was successful in serving American strategic interests. Some in Congress disagreed strongly enough that even under supportive presidents, the USIA could find its budget cut in a given year. But the basic Washington consensus was that public diplomacy—which was relatively cheap—was worth the investment. In most cases its provable effects fell short of its proponents' hopes; its most common success was not widespread "conversion" but damage control. However, especially given its low cost, this rarely led to any serious questioning of its utility—and the proliferation of Third World public diplomacy attests that this consensus was shared far beyond Washington. Indeed, in this sense it was not just Murrow's Wager but also Nkrumah's, Nehru's, Nasser's, and virtually all of their peers', since they all proceeded with the public diplomacy enterprise even in the absence of unimpeachable proof that it was working.

The case studies included in this book point to the messages and techniques that the USIA thought most effective in producing at least marginal tactical and strategic results. In the Third World, to an arguably greater extent than in First or Second, US public diplomacy often seemed to work best when it did least and to be more successful over the long run than the short one.[4] Bombast backfired. Persuasion gave better odds, if pursued via a light touch, behind-the-scenes orchestration of messaging via proxies. These, preferably, were "native" voices with a credibility that American representatives found hard to acquire. Such voices also helped to reach differentiated niche-sectors as well as mass ones, and the tandem targeting of both became a near-constant trait of US outreach in the Third World. Opinion of the United States across both niche and mass sectors could sour overnight due to difficult subjects like Jim Crow. But the USIA found that presenting the long view of such topics could aid efforts at damage control in moments of crisis. So too could a commitment, explicitly foregrounded under Murrow though still more elusive ideal than practical reality, to journalistic impartiality. Finally, the act of taking the American message to the Third World confirmed for the USIA that listening was as important as talking.[5] Though definitive proof of effectiveness remained elusive, listening aided the crafting of subsequent US messages, and revealed the contours of the Third World's own contributions to the global conversation.

The multipolarity of that conversation had become clear by the end of the Kennedy years, as was its potentially transformative impact on the Cold War. That conflict was itself evolving beyond its bipolar origins in those very years, thanks to the Sino–Soviet split and to Global South decolonization. The explosion of external media outreach in the global battle for hearts and minds accelerated, and in key respects redirected, that evolution. It did so by bridging the two processes of the postwar era—decolonization and the Cold War—to produce two overlapping maps: one containing nearly two hundred nation-states, the other revealing three worlds. The latter map had its genesis in the injection of Cold War public diplomacy into the non-European world, whose inhabitants were on the whole far more likely to encounter a USIA pamphlet than a US Marine. The injection provoked a response in kind. At the podium in Belgrade in 1961, nonaligned leaders took positions—broadcast back home and among their neighbors via their own South–South public diplomacy—whose import George Kennan recognized:

> There is a certain irony to the fact that just as East–West differences reach the point of maximum intensity and dangerousness, twenty-four nations should assemble to document, in effect, their lack of confidence in both of the causes for which the Soviet and Western camps conceive themselves . . . to be acting. While the main reasons for this detachment are probably geographic, we must also recognize the failure of both Soviet and Westen sides to identify themselves effectively with the feelings of [the] *third world.*[6]

It was fitting that the father of containment would be the first US official to use the term "Third World," in a sense that Sauvy or Sartre would recognize, in American diplomatic correspondence. The entity was an indirect riposte to Kennedy and Johnson advisor Walt Rostow's notion of a "community of free nations" encompassing the pro-West members of both North and South. It was not fanciful to imagine that an American construct of this sort might find its way onto the world's mental map. After all, US public diplomacy had, however inadvertently, validated key components of the idea of a grouping that included diverse parts of the Global South. But the consequent creation—a Third World grounded in a collective identity among imperialized areas who rejected the constraints of the Cold War—was the fruit of the global conversation among actors at Bandung, Belgrade, and beyond. They responded to the war for their hearts and minds by adding their voices to it. The resulting cacophony revealed mutual interest in, if not agreement on, the defining qualities of the Third World project: nonalignment, underdevelopment, and antiracist anticolonialism. The media storm also revealed fissures in the project, as the limits of solidarity among its principals became clear. By the 1960s, nonalignment and Afro-Asianism had become vehicles of competition among rival member nations seeking to lead the Third World project.

Yet the very existence of this project—arguably among the most important consequences of US public diplomacy, and certainly an unintended one—changed the terms of the postwar debate. As Jeffrey Byrne observes, the rise of Third Worldism seemed in its moment rich with possibility and latent with destiny: "Hopelessly ambitious perhaps, but in an era of European integration, small bands of rebels defeating entire armies, and dogs in space . . . Third Worldism had at least one foot on the ground."[7] It had, moreover, its sights on the stars. Westad sums it up thusly: "The Third World was the future of the world, as the Third Estate had been the future of France in 1789. It was powerful, plentiful, and proud."[8]

The Third World project did not emerge Athena-like full-grown from the Cold War. It developed over time as a part of the Global South's response to—and very unintended consequence of—the Global North's attempt to implant the Cold War in diverse imperialized areas pursuing an often-wrenching decolonization. The superpower conflict forced choices and carved channels that had the effect of fusing the diverse intellectual and geographic parts of the Global South together, by persuading their peoples of their common interest in seeking to transcend rather than join the Cold War. In joining the media competition about the meaning of that global conflict for the postimperial non-European world—becoming not just listeners but speakers, not just media consumers but media producers—and in offering their own analyses and prescriptions in their own voices, the Third World created itself.

NOTES

Introduction

1. Odd Arne Westad, *The Global Cold War*.
2. John Lewis Gaddis, *The Long Peace*.
3. Minkah Makalani, *In the Cause of Freedom*, 43; James T. Campbell, "'A Last Great Crusade for Humanity,'" in Bruce J. Schulman, ed., *Making the American Century*, 71–91; Pankaj Mishra, *From the Ruins of Empire*; Leslie James, *George Padmore and Decolonization from Below*; Michael Collins, *Empire, Nationalism, and the Postcolonial World*; Cemil Aydin, *The Politics of Anti-Westernism in Asia*; Alan McPherson, *Yankee No!*.
4. Erez Manela, *The Wilsonian Moment*; Vijay Prashad, *The Darker Nations*.
5. Louis Lansana Beavogui, "Africa Speaks to the United Nations," 319.
6. See, e.g., Nicholas Cull, *The Cold War and the United States Information Agency*; Kenneth Osgood, *Total Cold War*; Osgood and Brian Etheridge, eds., *The United States and Public Diplomacy*; Laura Belmonte, *Selling the American Way*; Walter Hixson, *Parting the Curtain*; Justin Hart, *Empire of Ideas*.
7. See Steven Casey and Jonathan Wright, eds., *Mental Maps in the Early Cold War Era, 1945–68*; and Aiyaz Husain, *Mapping the End of Empire*. In some areas, Washington held a preexisting "mental map" into which the Cold War at first fit uneasily. See for example Matthew Jacobs, *Imagining the Middle East*.
8. Alfred Sauvy, "Trois mondes, Une planète," 14. For insightful explorations of the term, see Arturo Escobar, *Encountering Development*; and Martin W. Lewis and Karen E. Wigen, *The Myth of Continents*.
9. It took longer for the term to catch on in English; as late as 1972, the term was not included in William Safire's *The New Language of Politics*. Leslie Wolf-Philips, "Why 'Third World'?," 1312. A smattering of earlier mentions of the term can be found; for example, Eisenhower's Special Assistant Eric Johnston used it in the *Washington Post* as part of his efforts to promote the Mutual Security Act ("'Third World' is New Arena for the Other Two," July 6, 1958; and "The 'Third World,'" January 29, 1959), and it surfaced again in a discussion of Cuba policy but did not make a strong distinction between "third world countries [and] Bloc countries." Document #536, *FRUS 1958–1960 Vol. VI: Cuba* (https://history.state.gov/historicaldocuments/frus1958-60v06/d536#fn1). David Engerman notes that "Soviet writings typically avoided [the term], preferring "developing countries" (*razvivaiushchiesia strany*), "the East," (*vostok*), or "economically underdeveloped countries" (*ekonomicheski slaborazvitye strany*). Engerman, "The Second World's Third World," 183 fn1.
10. US Embassy-Belgrade to State, September 5, 1961, 396.1-BE/9-161, Box 732, Dept. of State Records, Central Decimal File (CDF) 1960-63, Record Group (RG) 59, US National Archives, College Park, Maryland (NARA).

11. The phrase "non-European world" is meant geographically to denote the lands outside Europe. It does not suggest the absence of a lingering European imprint in places where, for example, cricket is played or baguettes are baked. "Global South" too is used somewhat anachronistically and is meant primarily geographically. Hints of the phrase can be found in the contemporary records but its best-known modern usage dates to after the period in this study.

12. The alternating use of the terms "political," "psychological," and soon "information" warfare is especially instructive. See Osgood, *Total Cold War*, 7–9, on the evolution of this terminology in the 1950s. On the extent to which the terms represented clashing bureaucratic responsibilities, see Gregory Mitrovich, *Undermining the Kremlin*, 59. Only in the 1960s would "public diplomacy" come into wide use, although Cull notes that the term was around long before the 1965 coinage of its present sense. Cull, "'Public Diplomacy' Before Gullion."

13. Heonik Kwon, *The Other Cold War*, 148.

14. Cull defines "cultural diplomacy" as one of public diplomacy's "five core components: . . . the dissemination of cultural practices as a mechanism to promote the interests of the actor, [such as] an international tour by a prominent musician." Cull, *Cold War and the United States Information Agency*, xv. Penny Von Eschen, *Satchmo Blows Up the World*. For further discussion of the term, see Richard Arndt, *The First Resort of Kings*, xvi–xix.

15. Quoted in Hart, *Empire of Ideas*, 10.

16. See Victoria DeGrazia, *Irresistible Empire*; Reinhold Wagnleiter and Elaine Tyler May, eds., *"Here, There, and Everywhere": The Foreign Politics of American Popular Culture*; and Rob Kroes, *If You've Seen One, You've Seen The Mall*.

17. Cull, *Cold War and United States Information Agency*, xvii.

18. For the "raft," see n6. Regarding the "overlooked" global South, outstanding work like Osgood's and Cull's discusses USIA activities there, but scholars are just now beginning to treat specific sites in depth; see dissertations by Frank Gerits and Hannah Higgin.

19. Westad, *Global Cold War*; Prashad, *Darker Nations*; Melvyn Leffler, *For the Soul of Mankind*; Manela, *Wilsonian Moment*; Matthew Connelly, *A Diplomatic Revolution*; Ryan Irwin, *Gordian Knot*; Robert Rakove, *Kennedy, Johnson, and the Nonaligned World*; Jeffrey James Byrne, *Mecca of Revolution*. On the link between print-capitalism and modern nationalism, see Benedict Anderson's seminal work *Imagined Communities*.

Chapter 1

1. Steven Casey, *Selling the Korean War*.

2. Mitrovich, *Undermining the Kremlin*, 2.

3. The legacy of the OIAA was in some ways more significant than the other bodies now conjoined, even if this would not be fully manifest until the founding of the USIA. According to Hart, its "importance [was] as a model for what [State] decided to do in the postwar period: integrate economics, culture, and information into a comprehensive worldwide strategy for public diplomacy." Hart, *Empire of Ideas*, 37. On the newborn CIA, see NSC-4A, December 17, 1947, Document #253, *Foreign Relations of the United States (FRUS) 1945–50: Emergence of the Intelligence Establishment*.

4. Cull, *Cold War and the United States Information Agency*, 22–25. The information machinery under Truman underwent a name change with each bureaucratic reorganization; see Cull, *Cold War and United States Information Agency*, chapter 1; Belmonte, *Selling the American Way*, chapter 1; and Hart, *Empire of Ideas*, 117. On the OIAA, see Darlene Sadlier, *Americans All*.

5. Within mere weeks of V-E Day, for example, the Soviet Union began an Arabic-language wire service. Cull, *Cold War and United States Information Agency*, 29.

6. Moseley to Lovett, October 15, 1947, Document #242, *FRUS 1945–50: Emergence of the Intelligence Establishment*.

7. Roger Trask, "The Impact of the Cold War on United States–Latin American Relations, 1945–1949," 283–311. More recently see the clashing analyses in Hal Brands, *Latin America's Cold War*, and Stephen Rabe, *The Killing Zone*. See also Aaron Moulton on the

ways in which Latin regimes were fighting their own regional cold war well before the superpower conflict. Aaron Coy Moulton, "Guatemalan Exiles, Caribbean Basin Dictators, Operation PBFORTUNE, and the Transnational Counter-Revolution Against the Guatemalan Revolution, 1944–1952."

8. Hart, *Empire of Ideas*, 3.
9. For an example of the centers' effectiveness, see US Consulate-Concepcion to State, December 27, 1946, 711.25/12-2746, Box 3276, CDF 1945-49, RG 59, NARA.
10. Frank Ninkovich, *Diplomacy of Ideas*, 30–31, 34.
11. Rockefeller quoted in Ninkovich, *Diplomacy of Ideas*, 36; Ninkovich, *Diplomacy of Ideas*, 119–120. See also Max Paul Friedman, *Nazis and Good Neighbors*.
12. Leslie Bethell and Ian Roxborough, eds., *Latin America Between the Second World War and the Cold War*, x.
13. Ninkovich, *Diplomacy of Ideas*, 31, 63–64. On niche-targeting, see chapters 5 and 6. This offers another example of the way in which Latin America provided a sort of testing ground for US public diplomacy in the Global South, and presaged its evolution there.
14. US Embassy-Montevideo to State, March 11, 1947, 711.00/3-147, CDF, RG 59, NARA. One article in the series asserted that "the Monroe Doctrine is a cloak for colonialism and imperialism . . . [whose] results [were interventions in] Santo Domingo and Haiti."
15. US Embassy-Rio de Janeiro to State, April 1, 1947, 711.32/4-147; Shorthand notes of Speech by Brazilian Foreign Minister Raul Fernandes, undated, Box 3277, CDF 1945-49, RG 59; US Embassy-Santiago to Truman, April 30, 1947, folder "Chile #1," Box 150, PSF—Subject Files, Papers of Harry S. Truman, Harry S. Truman Library, Independence, Missouri (hereafter HSTL); US Embassy-Rio to State, April 28, 1947, 711.32/4-2847; Memorandum of Conversation, May 21, 1947, 711.32/5-2147, Box 3277, CDF 1945-49, RG 59, NARA. This meshed with the "propaganda themes" that US intelligence recommended for the region, which was seen as deeply, latently anticommunist. However, what little outreach was conducted in-country around the Truman Doctrine and the Rio Pact made little use of this perceived latency. Report, "Soviet Objectives in Latin America," April 10, 1947, folder "ORE 1947: 15–39," Box 214, PSF—Intelligence Files, Papers of Harry S. Truman, HSTL.
16. US Embassy-Rio to State, April 28, 1947. A possible exception to this pattern was the production of a pamphlet, "To Protect the Peace," though it is unclear from the photo archives record when and whether this was distributed in Spanish and Portuguese in Latin America, or in English in the United States, or both. Photo #52-1742, RG 306-PS-A Personalities: Keogh to Nelson, USIA Photo Archives, NARA.
17. Weekly Review, State Department, July 2, 1947, folder "1947: Speech and Conference Notes/Memoranda," Box 18, Truman Admin. Papers: Speech File, George Elsey Papers, HSTL. Truman to Woodward, July 18, 1947, "State Department Correspondence, 1948-49, #1," Box 39, White House Central File (WHCF), Papers of Harry S. Truman, HSTL. On the two "camps" in the Latin American press, examples of the first could be found in for example the communist weekly *Justicia*, which called the conference "the disgraceful realization of an imperialistic enslavement of" Latin America. US Embassy-Montevideo to State, July 22, 1947, 711.00/7-2247; US Embassy-Montevideo to State, August 11, 1947, 711.00/8-1147; US Embassy-San Jose to State, August 25, 1947, 711.00/8-2547, Box 3146, CDF 1945-1949. In the second camp, see US Embassy-Santiago to State, June 25, 1947, 825.00/6-2547; and US Embassy-Santiago to State, September 12, 1947, 825.00/9-1247, Box 5353, CDF 1945-49, RG 59, NARA.
18. Latin American commenters concluded this too. See the editorial sent to Washington in US Embassy-Panama to State, September 15, 1947, 711.00/9-1547, Box 3146, CDF 1945-49, RG 59, NARA.
19. US Embassy-Rio to State, October 21, 1947, 711.32/1-2147, Box 3277, CDF 1945–49, RG 59, NARA.
20. "Hillenkoetter as DCI" (Section Introduction), *FRUS 1945–50: Emergence of the Intelligence Establishment*, 751–52; see also Memorandum of Conversation, Hillenkoetter et al., April 16, 1948, Document #136, in ibid.

21. Beaulac to State, April 23, 1948, *FRUS 1948*, vol. 9, 58. A retrospective assessment in 1952 judged that the Brazilian communists were ahead of the curve in this respect, using targeted campaigns at demographic niches—like the barracks-pamphlets noted above— to greater effect than the default US strategy of working through mass media. "Brazil" (Country Paper), April 22, 1952, folder: "USIA Country Papers 1952—Latin America and Near East," Box 5, Records of International Information Administration (State Department), RG 59, NARA.

22. Hart, *Empire of Ideas*, 129.

23. As Sarah Ellen Graham notes, American outreach frequently fell short of its goals in India, due in no small part to the fact that "strategy outweighed idealism in shaping the inten- tions behind U.S. propaganda [during the war]." Graham, "American Propaganda, the Anglo-American Alliance, and the 'Delicate Question' of Indian Self-Determination," 225. See also Graham, "Engaging India: Public Diplomacy and Indo-American Relations to 1957," Paper #10, Perspectives on Public Diplomacy, University of Southern California Center on Public Diplomacy, 2012.

24. For an outstanding recent account of partition, see Yasmin Khan, *The Great Partition*. On postwar US–South Asian relations, see Robert McMahon, *The Cold War on the Periphery*, 39–44; Andrew Rotter, *Comrades at Odds*; Husain, *Mapping*; and Paul McGarr, *The Cold War in South Asia*.

25. "Illuminatingly, in September 1947 . . . South Asia was ranked [by the CIA] at the bottom of the US' list of regional priorities, below Western Europe, the Middle East, and Southeast Asia." McGarr, *Cold War in South Asia*, 40.

26. Merrell to State, February 14, 1947, *FRUS 1947*, vol. 3, 142.

27. Block to Secretary of State/OIC, April 18, 1946, "Department of State Information Programs (IP's)—1946—Monthly Reports—India," Box 8, Papers of Charles Hulten, HSTL.

28. Memorandum of Conversation, Hickerson et al., February 20, 1947, *FRUS 1947*, vol. 3, 143–144; Near Eastern Affairs to Secretary, February 24, 1947, 711.45/2-2447, Box 3314, CDF 1945-49, RG 59, NARA; Acting SecState to US Embassy-London, April, 4, 1947, *FRUS 1947*, vol. 3, 151.

29. Ogburn to Vincent, June 9, 1947, 711.45/6-947, Box 3314, CDF 1945-49, RG 59, NARA. Though India would later be a main target of Moscow's secret operations in the Third World, at this time it was still "regarded as an imperialist puppet." Christopher Andrews, *The World Was Going Our Way*, 312.

30. See McMahon, *Periphery*, 87–88; Brenda Gayle Plummer, *Rising Wind*, 221–222; Mary Dudziak, *Cold War Civil Rights*, 33–34, 58–60.

31. US Embassy-New Delhi to Acheson, May 23, 1947, 711.45/5-2347, Box 3314, CDF 1945- 49, RG 59, NARA.

32. US Consulate-Bombay to State, June 18, 1947, 711.00/6-1847, Box 3145; US Consulate- Bombay to State, August 1, 1947, 711.45/8-147; US Consulate-Bombay to State, August 8, 1947, 711.45/8-847, Box 3314, CDF 1945-49, RG 59, NARA. A War Department in- telligence roundup of global reactions found this take to be one of three generally: "The Communist line accuses the United States of imperialism that will undermine the United Nations. The moderate, middle-of-the-road groups are generally apprehensive and express fear of what may result. The right-wingers are jubilant." Cited in Denise M. Bostdorff, *Proclaiming the Truman Doctrine*, 135.

33. G. H. Jansen, *Non-Alignment and the Afro-Asian States*, 18; Itty Abraham, "From Bandung to NAM," 195–219, and Tanvi Madan, "With an Eye to the East," especially chapter 2. On the "mutual affinity," see Nico Slate, *Colored Cosmopolitanism*.

34. US Consulate-Bombay to State, December 12, 1947, 711.45/12-1247, Box 3314, CDF 1945–49, RG 59, NA.

35. State Department Report, December 5, 1947, "State Information Programs—1947- Stereotyped Concepts of US," Box 9, Hulten Papers, HSTL.

36. Dudziak, *Cold War Civil Rights*, 26–27. She notes further that from an early stage, American officials confirmed "the increasing tendency of the Soviet Union to exploit American racial problems" (38).

37. Scholars like Nico Slate, Penny Von Eschen, Jim Meriwether, Tim Borstelmann, and Brenda Plummer confirm that this attention was neither confined to newly independent peoples abroad, nor strictly one-way. Plummer, *Rising Wind*; Von Eschen, *Race Against Empire*; Jim Meriwether, *Proudly We Can Be Africans*; Tim Borstelmann, *The Cold War and the Color Line*; Slate, *Colored Cosmopolitanism*; Matthew Connelly, "Taking Off the Cold War Lens," 739–769.

38. NSC-4, December 17, 1947, Document #252, *FRUS 1945–50: Emergence of the Intelligence Establishment*. In June, NSC-10/2 outlined the ways in which the United States was to join the battle. "The Inauguration of Political Warfare," Policy Planning Staff, May 4, 1948, Document #269; NSC-10/2, June 18, 1948, Document #292, *FRUS 1945–50: Emergence of the Intelligence Establishment*. NSC-10/2 led to the creation of the Office of Policy Coordination, which signaled the point at which "psychological warfare [was] fully ensconced in the Truman administration's Cold War repertoire." Mitrovich, *Undermining*, 22. He also notes the key role played by Kennan in the "ensconcing"—which may shed light on the low priority given to areas outside Europe in such operations, given Kennan's ranking of Eurasia atop US strategy.

39. See Cull, *Cold War and United States Information Agency*, 39–41; Belmonte, *Selling the American Way*, 32–33; and Hart, *Empire of Ideas*, 132–137.

40. In this the Act echoed NSC-4, which had put it this way: "The present world situation requires the immediate strengthening and coordination of all foreign information measures of the US Government designed to influence attitudes in foreign countries in a direction favorable to the attainment of its objectives and to counteract effects of anti-US propaganda." NSC 4, December 17, 1947, Document #252, *FRUS 1945–50: Emergence of the Intelligence Establishment*.

41. Cull, *Cold War and United States Information Agency*, 38–39. See also Shawn Parry-Giles, *The Rhetorical Presidency, Propaganda, and the Cold War, 1945–1955*.

42. Henderson, *United States Information Agency*, 41. On Marshall Plan public diplomacy, see Regina Longo, "Marshall Plan Films in Italy, 1948–1955."

43. Hixson, *Parting the Curtain*, 15.

44. Prashad, *Darker Nations*, 62.

45. It also, as Sheyda Jahanbani points out, redefined the very term "poverty": "When Harry Truman commenced his inaugural address on the frosty morning of January 20, 1949, poverty was largely taken to mean an economic condition that could befall any unlucky soul. Less than an hour later, the word "poverty" conveyed more than just misfortune; it was the condition that resulted from an absence or inadequacy of development [among those who] existed outside of the scope of modernity. In addition, unlike [the biblical] notion of poverty . . . underdevelopment was an ailment for which there was a known cure." "'A Different Kind of People,'" 149.

46. Woodward to Stone, November 17, 1947, "Information Program to Counteract Anti-U.S. Propaganda, 1947–52," Box 4, State Department Office of Public Affairs—Subject Files (MLR1530), RG 59, NARA.

47. USIE-Egypt to State, September 25, 1947, "1949—Egypt INP," Box 198, State Records Relating to Intl. Information Activities 1938-53, Lot Files (Lot 53D84) (MLR1559), RG 59; "OIC Program in Far East Area," author unidentified, June 3, 1947, "Summary of International Information," Hulten Papers, HSTL.

48. "Stereotypes of Americans," author unidentified, February 5, 1947; "Need and Effectiveness of OIC Program, Near East and African Division," author unidentified, June 3, 1947, "Summary of International Information," Box 9, Hulten Papers, HSTL. According to this report, even ready-made instances as US food aid to India did not produce the hoped-for positive public relations, because US officials were too busy countering communist charges to go on offense, and lacked an equivalent "megaphone" that could trumpet the US side. USIE-Egypt to State, September 25, 1947.

49. Hardy to Daniels, November 19, 1950, "Point Four #3," Box 1, Benjamin Hardy Papers, HSTL.

50. Hardy to Russell, November 23, 1948, "Point Four #1," Box 1, Hardy Papers, HSTL. Hardy would go on to oversee the first stages of this campaign, serving as the TCA's chief

public diplomat before dying (along with TCA Director Henry Bennett) in a 1951 plane crash in Iran.

51. (Cited in) Salant to Truman, December 20, 1948, "Point Four File," Box 2, Walter Salant Papers, HSTL; Truman Speech on 10th Anniv. of Point Four, undated, "General—April 1959—10th Anniv. Point Four," Box 730, Post-Presidential Files, Truman Papers, HSTL. On the spread of "New Deal" DNA, see David Ekbladh, *The Great American Mission.*

52. Russell to Kostching, December 22, 1948, "Truman Inaugural Speech," Box 2; Memorandum, Clifford, January 11, 1949, "Point Four #1," Box 1, Hardy Papers.

53. Truman Inaugural Address, January 20, 1949, www.trumanlibrary.org/whistlestop/ 50yr_archive/inagural20jan1949.htm. The other members of the quartet were support for the United Nations and international agencies, for continued world economic recovery, and for "freedom-loving nations against the dangers of aggression."

54. Shepherd-Jones to Russell, February 1, 1949, "Point Four #1," Box 1, Hardy Papers.

55. Hardy to Russell, February 17, 1949, "Point Four #1," Box 1, Hardy Papers.

56. Draft, "Notes for a Section of a Paper Entitled 'The Position of the United States in World Affairs 1950-51,' undated, "Guidance: General 1949-50," Box 115, State Records Relating to Intl. Information Activities 1938-53, Lot Files (Lot 53D48) (MLR1559), RG 59, NARA.

57. Jones to Russell, February 8, 1949, "Point Four #2," Box 1, Hardy Papers. After the Inaugural, an interdepartment committee titled it the "Program For World Economic Progress Through Cooperative Technical Assistance," to be promoted as "Point Four" for short, overseas and domestically. Russell to Hardy, January 28, 1949, "Point Four #1," Box 1, Hardy Papers.

58. Truman to Congress, June 24, 1949, "Point Four, 1 of 3," Box 20, SMOF: David Lloyd Files, Truman Papers, HSTL.

59. Pamphlet, "Helping People Help Themselves," Public Affairs Institute, undated [1950], "Point Four, 2 of 3," Box 20, Lloyd Files.

60. "The United States and the Underdeveloped Areas," George McGhee, *Department of State Bulletin,* June 26, 1950; Booklet, *The Point Four Program,* December 1949, "Foreign Relations—Point Four, Pamphlets & Misc.," Box 62, Elsey Papers, HSTL. McGhee emphasized that the United States was not trying to force anyone into a bloc, and noted the need to rebut charges of American racism in many of these areas.

61. Memorandum, Advisory Committee on Technical Assistance, July 27, 1949, "Point Four, 1 of 3," Box 20, Lloyd Files; Memorandum, "Requirements of the Point Four Program," author unidentified, May 13, 1949, "Point Four File," Box 2, Salant Papers.

62. Memorandum, Advisory Committee on Technical Assistance, July 27, 1949. Countries such as Iran, India, and Ethiopia thus received the bulk of Point Four aid. See Amanda McVety, *Enlightened Aid.*

63. Memorandum, Advisory Committee on Technical Assistance, July 27, 1949.

64. Memorandum, Lloyd, December 3, 1949, "Point Four, 2 of 3," Box 20, Lloyd Files; Claxton to Hayes, June 9, 1949, "Point Four—General 1949," Box 4, State Dept. Lot Files—Studies on Foreign Aid 1945-59 (Lot 59D265) (MLR1537B), RG 59, NARA.

65. Russell to Lehrbas, May 13, 1949, "Overseas Information 1946-52 #1," Box 6, State— PA—Director's Subject Files 1944-52 (MLR1530), RG 59; Booklet, "Point Four," State Department (PA), January 1950, "Point Four," John Ohly Papers, HSTL; Speech, Salant to ADA, January 18, 1950, "International Relations 1950," Box 2, Salant Papers.

66. Acheson to Truman, attached to Claxton to McFall, December 28, 1949, "Point Four— General 1949," Box 4, State Dept. Lot Files—Studies on Foreign Aid 1945-59 (Lot 59D265) (MLR1537B), RG 59, NARA. Acheson pointed out that "almost ... every American Embassy and Consulate abroad has received inquiries about Point Four." Speech, Hayes to American Society of Civil Engineers, November 3, 1949, "Point Four, 1 of 3," Box 20, Lloyd Files.

67. Resolution S. 243, US Senate, March 22, 1950, "Point Four, 2 of 3," Box 20, Lloyd Files; Acheson to SFRC, March 10, 1950, "Point Four—General 1950," Box 4, State Dept. Lot Files—Studies on Foreign Aid 1945-59 (Lot 59D265) (MLR1537B), RG 59, NARA.

68. Report, "Measures to Implement Pres. Truman's 'Point Four,'" September 12, 1949, "Foreign Relations—Point Four—Correspondence," Box 61, Elsey Papers. In a May 1950 discussion, a participant noted that "the peoples of India . . . are fed up with talk about things like Point Four . . . they are tired of words and no deeds." Memorandum of Conversation, Information Policy Committee, May 15, 1950, "Near East and Africa—Info. Programs 1947-51," Box 6, State—PA—Director's Subject Files 1944-52 (MLR1530), RG 59, NARA.

69. Memorandum, Gardiner to Jones et al., May 31, 1950, "Point Four—African Institutes," Box 7, State Department Lot Files—NEA—Subject Files Related to Economic Affairs 1947-51 (Lot 55D643), RG 59; "Opinion in Various Parts of the World on Point Four and Related U.S. Assistance Programs," INR, January 12, 1951, "Foreign Opinion Reports," Box 4; US Embassy-Cairo to State, August 22, 1951, "Restricted #1," Box 16, TCA Program Information & Reports Staff—Office of Program Information: Records Relating to Public Opinion of Point Four (hereafter TCA—Public Opinion of Point Four), RG 469, NARA.

70. Harris to Phillips, January 20, 1951, "Point Four," Box 45, State Records Relating to Intl. Information Activities 1938-53, Lot Files (Lot 52D365) (MLR1559); Anderson to Hardy, November 29, 1951, "Point Four," Box 110, State Records Relating to Intl. Information Activities 1938-53, Lot Files (Lot 53D48), RG 59, NARA. That division of labor would, for example, prevent public diplomacy funds from paying for manuals on chicken-coop construction.

71. "Report of Field Trip to Near East," Howe, November 2, 1951, "Near East—General," Box 1, State Department Lot Files—NEA—Subject Files Related to Economic Affairs 1947-51 (Lot 55D643), RG 59, NARA. On the turf war, "[Welles] says if point IV sets up its own information facilities, he will volunteer a 50% cut in his staff because so much of his work is point IV type."

72. That film tour also included *The UN Aids Korea*, which the audience "applauded," but the "disease" and "louse" offerings were reportedly the most popular. "IMP Summary of USIE Reports," USIE, November 27, 1950, "51–100.25 IMP (#1)," Box 102, State Records Relating to Intl. Information Activities 1938-53, Lot Files (Lot 53D126) (MLR1559), RG 59, NARA.

73. Draft Notes, "The Position of the United States in World Affairs 1950-51," undated. Memorandum, NSC, August 9, 1951, "Reports: Senior NSC Staff Meetings: Point Four," Box 173, PSF: Subject File—NSC File, Truman Papers, HSTL.

74. Grondahl to Evans, March 31, 1951, "Point Four," Box 110, State Records Relating to Intl. Information Activities 1938-53, Lot Files (Lot 53D48), RG 59; Brown to Iverson, August 1, 1952, "Area Development," Box 3, IIAA Program Staff—Subject Files 1952-54, RG 469, NARA.

75. Memorandum, "Effectiveness," Vardaman to Fisk, January 17, 1951, "Evidence of Effectiveness," Box 199, State Records Relating to Intl. Information Activities 1938-53, Lot Files (Lot 53D84) (MLR1559), RG 59, NARA. At the same time, USIE declared itself effective at narrower targeting: *"Our target groups are properly selected: The target groups are being persuaded,"* on the evidence of incidents like the mobile-unit distribution in Israel of an antituberculosis film, the day after which saw inoculation centers so crowded that extra police were required. In sum, USIE found itself *"an effective instrument in the psychological offensive"* [emphasis in original].

76. "IMP Summary of USIE Reports," USIE, November 27, 1950; Transcript, "Gradacion de la Entrevista por Radio Nacional Transmitida el 14 Febrero 1951," "Bennett (#2)," Box 2; US Embassy-Asuncion to State, March 5, 1951; US Embassy-Bogotá to State, March 31, 1952, "Restricted #2," Box 16, TCA—Public Opinion of Point Four, RG 469, NARA.

77. US Embassy-San Jose to State, June 13, 1952; US Embassy-San Salvador to State, July 1, 1952, "Restricted #1," Box 16, TCA—Public Opinion of Point Four, RG 469, NARA; "Opinion on Point Four," INR, January 12, 1951. INR also noted that "communists and other confirmed critics of the United States have denounced the program as imperialism in a new guise."

78. Memorandum of Conversation, Information Policy Committee, May 15, 1950; "Opinion on Point Four," INR, January 12, 1951.

79. "Opinion on Point Four," INR, January 12, 1951. A campaign to counter the "snake-oil" trend, centered on the Gray Report and a PR tour by US Ambassador Henderson, renewed Indian interest in Point Four but soon led to disillusionment. US Embassy-New Delhi to State, August 17, 1952, "Restricted #1," Box 16, TCA—Public Opinion of Point Four, RG 469, NARA.
80. "Opinion on Point Four," INR, January 12, 1951.
81. Ruehbausen to Lloyd, February 21, 1951, "Rockefeller Report," Box 5, Lloyd Files. A report later that year grouped the same areas under a premonitory title: "Point Four Pioneers: Reports from a New Frontier," State Department, October 1951, "Foreign Relations—Point Four Pamphlets & Misc.," Box 62, Elsey Papers.
82. Notes, PA Information Programming Committee for Near East, South Asia, Africa," March 20, 1951, "Near East and Africa—Info. Programs 1947-51," Box 6, State—PA— Director's Subject Files 1944-52 (MLR1530), RG 59, NARA; "Report to PAO Conf." (Mtg. Notes), IIA Committee on Content, December 18, 1951, "IIA 1951-52 #2," Box 5, Howland Sargeant Papers, HSTL.
83. "Point Four Pioneers: Reports from a New Frontier," State Department, October 1951; "Years of Change," IIAA film, 1951, (ARC11972) (Local ID 59.178), Moving Images, RG 59, NARA.
84. US Embassy-Cairo to State, March 28, 1951, 511.74/3-2851, "Restricted #1," Box 16, Box 16, TCA—Public Opinion of Point Four, RG 469, NARA; Report on USIE, INP, January 25, 1952, "USIE Progress and Problems," Box 110, State Records Relating to Intl. Information Activities 1938-53, Lot Files (Lot 53D48) (MLR1559), RG 59, NARA.
85. "Danger in the Arab East," A. T. Steele, *New York Herald Tribune*, July 20, 1952, in "Middle East 1952," Box 7, TCA—Public Opinion of Point Four, RG 469, NARA.
86. "Point 4 Activities—Report for Week Ended 28 Sept. 1951," TCA, October 1, 1951, "Point Four—Weekly Reports," Box 14, TCA—Public Opinion of Point Four, RG 469, NARA.
87. US Consulate-Calcutta to State, February 13, 1952 and February 28, 1952, "Restricted #3"; US Embassy-Addis Ababa to State, July 22, 1952; US Embassy-Beirut to State, May 17, 1952, "Restricted #1," Box 16 TCA—Public Opinion of Point Four, RG 469, NARA.
88. "Danger in the Arab East," July 20, 1952. An item dated June 8, 1952 in the *Spokane Spokesman-Review*, echoed this finding. Citing a *Readers' Digest* essay by Stephen Penrose titled "The Arabs Don't Love Us Any More," the editorial lamented that "the Arabs' bitterness has not been modified by other policies designed to win their friendship, including Point Four."
89. "Remarks by Secretary Acheson," April 9, 1952, www.trumanlibrary.org/whistlestop/ study_collections/pointfourprogram/documents/index.php?pagenumber=3&docum entdate=1952-04-09&documentid=10-4. Truman, not Acheson, was slated to give the speech, but the steel crisis intervened.
90. Draft speech, author unidentified, April 8, 1952, "4/8/52: Point Four Read by Acheson"; Bell to Ayers, April 11, 1952, Box 201, PSF: Subject File—NSC File, Truman Papers.
91. Elsey to Lloyd, April 9, 1952, "Foreign Relations—Point Four (Conf.)," Box 61, Elsey Papers. It bears noting, though, that the bloc lines were still at least a little blurry. A 1952 program overview, for example, included Greece in the "underdeveloped" category. Report, "A Theme for the President's Point Four Speech," William Korns (PSB), attached to Allen to Neustadt, March 17, 1952, "Point Four Conf., April 1952," Box 20, Lloyd Files.
92. Clipping, *Economist*, August 22, 1953, in "1953 Point Four/TCA #3," Box 10, Stanley Andrews Papers, HSTL.
93. "Statement by the President," September 8, 1950, "Point Four #1 of 3," Box 20, Lloyd Files.
94. "Opinion on Point Four," INR, January 12, 1951; Jones to Stephens, May 23, 1951, "Guidances, General 1951," Box 115, State Records Relating to Intl. Information Activities 1938-53, Lot Files (Lot 53D48) (MLR1559), RG 59, NARA.
95. Marc Selverstone, *Constructing the Monolith*.

Chapter 2

1. Hart, *Empire of Ideas*, 145.
2. Recent scholarship—Mitrovich, *Undermining the* Kremlin, and Osgood, *Total Cold War*, among others—has shown, however, that it is easy to overstate the "rollback" qualities of NSC-68, given the aggressiveness of its antecedents.

3. Steven Casey, "Selling NSC-68," 660.

4. NSC-68, April 7, 1950, *FRUS 1950*, Vol. I: National Security Affairs, 245, 251–256.

5. Belmonte, *Selling the American Way*, 39–40; see also Casey, "Selling NSC-68," and Casey, "White House Publicity Operations During the Korean War, June 1950–June 1951," 691–717, on Truman's troubles in crafting a domestic message about the war. The propaganda deluge was both Soviet and Chinese. As Chen Jian notes, during "spring 1950, Chinese propaganda continuously [blasted] America's 'military encirclement and economic blockade' of China [and] 'U.S. imperialist ambition of aggression.'" Chen Jian, *China's Road to the Korean War*, 120.

6. David Krugler, *The Voice of America and the Domestic Propaganda Battles, 1945–53*, 110. As Shawn Parry-Giles puts it, "Truman explained [that] the Campaign of Truth sought to empower those enslaved by communism to gain their own freedom against the despotic forces." Parry-Giles, *Rhetorical Presidency*, 77.

7. Arndt, *First Resort of Kings*, 255. On USIS promotion of the campaign, see Henderson, *United States Information Agency*, 45.

8. Kwon, *Other Cold War*, 16.

9. Ethridge to Truman, July 14, 1950, OF 20r: USACI, Box 167, WHCF: OF, Papers of Harry S. Truman; Branscomb to Truman, July 20, 1950, OF 20s: Campaign of Truth, Box 167, WHCF: OF, Papers of Harry S. Truman, HSTL. For Benton, it was bitter proof of the inadequacy of previous American public diplomacy; Laura Belmonte notes that Benton testified to Congress that "the fighting in Korea ... demonstrated the tragic failure of the United States 'to project the idea of democracy to the world.'" Belmonte, *Selling the American Way*, 43; Krugler, *Voice of America*, 117.

10. "The Communists had the upper hand in the propaganda war in Asia ... [their] propaganda offensive was, if anything, more formidable in Asia than in Europe ... [and] reached a far larger audience ... than did the Americans." William Stueck, *The Korean War*, 80. Soviet radio programming during the first months of the war more than doubled the US output. Belmonte, *Selling the American Way*, 43.

11. US Embassy-Tokyo to State, May 15, 1950, 511.94a/5-1550, Box 2537, CDF 1950-54, RG 59, NARA.

12. US Embassy-Manila to State, August 1, 1950, 511.96/8-150, Box 2542, CDF 1950-54, RG 59, NARA. Note: both primary and secondary sources use the terms Regional Production Center (RPC) and Regional Service Center (RSC) more or less interchangeably; this book follows suit.

13. Barrett to Rooney, July 27, 1950, 511.00/7-2750, Box 2237; Muccio to Rusk, May 25, 1950, 611.95b/5-2550, Box 2888, CDF 1950-54, RG 59, NARA. Krugler, *Voice of America*, 100–101.

14. Dyke to Sargeant, November 6, 1950, folder "Correspondence: Deputy Assistant Secretary for Public Affairs, 1947–50," Box 4, Papers of Howland Sargeant, HSTL. See also Steven Casey, "Wilfred Burchett and the UN Command's Media Relations During the Korean War, 1951–52," 821–845; and Mark Jacobson, "Minds then Hearts."

15. *IIA Newsletter*, August 1951, Box 1, Records of Dept. of State—IIA—Newsletters (MLR P-231), RG 59, NARA.

16. *IIA Newsletter*, August 1951; Orr to Connors, July 13, 1950, 511.94a/7-2650, Box 2537, CDF 1950-54, RG 59, NARA. As Henderson observes, this could provide complementarity as well as confusion: the military "had complete charge of psywar so far as combat and enemy areas were concerned, but USIS personnel continued to operate among civilians, in many instances working jointly [with] the military and sometimes providing useful facilities otherwise unavailable to [them]." Henderson, *United States Information Agency*, 63.

17. *IIA Newsletter*, August 1951; State to Far East Posts, July 26, 1950, 511.00/7-2650, Box 2237, CDF 1950-54, RG 59, NARA.

18. Article, *Washington News*, July 13, 1950, folder "Foreign Relations—VOA," Box 65, Elsey Papers, HSTL.

19. Report, NYU Research Center on Human Relations, July 1951, "VOA 1951—China, Broadcasts to during Cold War and Korean War Periods," Box 16, Hulten Papers, HSTL; Krugler, *Voice of America*, 118.

20. The document was NSC-4—as Cull notes, "a major milestone in the development of U.S. propaganda." Cull, *Cold War and United States Information Agency*, 39. See also Osgood, *Total Cold War*, 36–37, and Mitrovich, *Undermining the Kremlin*, 17.

21. Memorandum of Conversation, Dyke, Sargeant, et al., November 29, 1950, folder "Correspondence: Deputy Assistant Secretary for Public Affairs, 1947–50," Box 4, Papers of Howland Sargeant, HSTL. See also NYU Report, July 1951, and the USIS pamphlet "United Action in Korea," whose cover featured the UN flag, with no US marking to be found. Pamphlet, undated, folder: "Pamphlets—Postwar Propaganda—English #1," Box 26, Hulten Papers, HSTL.

22. Cull, *Cold War and United States Information Agency*, 55–56.

23. Lewis to Chartrand, July 25, 1950, "IMP—General 1949–50," Box 199, Lot 53D84 (MLR 1559): Records Relating to International Information Activities 1938-53, Lot Files, General Records of Dept. of State; Jones to Edwards, November 7, 1950, "IMP—Film Reviews 1949–50," Box 199, Lot 53D84 (MLR 1559): International Information Activities 1938-53, RG 59, NARA.

24. State to Far Eastern posts, June 27, 1950, 511.00/6-2750; US Embassy-Manila to State, July 31, 1950, 511.96/7-3150, Box 2237, CDF 195-1954, RG 59, NARA.

25. Gullion to State, June 27, 1950, 795.00/6-2750, *FRUS* 1950, Vol. VII: Korea, 193; State to All Posts, June 29, 1950, 795.00/6-2950, *FRUS* 1950, Vol. VII: Korea, 232.

26. Madan notes that Nehru played a "recurring role" in Korean War diplomacy, especially between the United States and China. Madan, "With an Eye to the East," 58. This led to recurring—though selective—US use of Indian diplomatic initiatives in regional output.

27. State to Far Eastern Posts, June 29, 1950, 511.00/6-2950; State to Far Eastern Posts, June 30, 1950, 511.00/6-3050, Box 2237; Jessup to Rusk, July 21, 1950, 611.94a/7-2150, Box 2882, CDF 1950-54, RG 59, NARA; VOA Broadcast Schedule and Transcript, July 9, 1950, Box 5, VOA Daily Broadcast Reports and Script Translations, RG 306, NARA.

28. Krugler, *Voice of America*, 218; Etheridge to Truman et al., July 14, 1950, 511.00/7-1450; State to Certain Posts, July 19, 1950, 511.00/7-1950, Box 2237, CDF 1950-54, RG 59, NARA.

29. State to Far East Posts, July 26, 1950; State to Certain Posts (Far East Annex), August 10, 1950, 511.00/8-1050, Box 2238, CDF 195-54, RG 59, NARA. The line of response to these attacks varied according to region. In the western hemisphere, public diplomats were guided to "continue stressing the heroic conduct of US Negro troops in Korea to counteract . . . 'white versus colored' propaganda on the Korean conflict." A variation aimed at Europe and Asia three weeks later instructed that the "race rivalry" theme was a "serious continuing problem [because it gave the impression that Westerners are ranged against Asians]." State to Western Hemisphere Posts, August 26, 1950, 511.00/8-2650; State to Certain Posts, September 14, 1950, 511.00/9-1450, Box 2238, CDF 1950-54, RG 59, NARA.

30. State to Certain Posts, August 17, 1950, 511.00/8-1750; State to Certain Posts (Far East Annex), September 7, 1950, 511.00/9-750; Barrett to Acheson, September 23, 1950, 511.00/9-2350, Box 2238, CDF 1950–54, RG 59, NA.

31. State to Certain Posts (Far East Annex), September 21, 1950, 511.00/9-2150, Box 2238; State to Certain Posts, September 28, 1950, 511.00/9-2850; State to Certain Posts, October 5, 1950, 511.00/10-550; State to Certain Posts, October 7, 1950, 511.00/10-750, Box 2238, CDF 1950-54, RG 59, NARA.

32. State to Certain Posts (Far East Annex), October 12, 1950, 511.00/10-1250; State to Certain Posts (Far East Annex), October 19, 1950, 511.00/10-1950; State to Certain Posts, October 19, 1950, 511.00/10-1950; State to Certain Posts (Far East Annex), October 25, 1950, 511.00/10-2550, Box 2238, CDF 1950-54, RG 59, NARA.

33. State to Certain Posts (Far East Annex), October 26, 1950, 511.00/10-2650, Box 2238; US Embassy-Manila to State, December 18, 1950, 511.96/12-1850, Box 2542, CDF 1950-54, RG 59. In anticipation that battlefield success would continue across the 38th parallel, the guidance now included the assertion that that line "has no further legal validity and no practical value." "Weekly Information Memorandum," Dept. of State, October 7, 1950, "Information Memoranda," Box 4, State Department Public Affairs Office: Subject Files

1944-52 [MLR1530], RG 59; US Embassy-Manila to State, October 19, 1950, 511.96/10-1950; US Embassy-Manila to State, October 9, 1950, 511.96/10-950, Box 2542, CDF 1950-54, RG 59, NARA.

34. State to Certain Posts (Far East Annex), November 2, 1950, 511.00/11-250, Box 2238; Stephens to Barrett, November 8, 1950, 611.95b/11-850, Box 2888, CDF 1950-1954, RG 59, NARA.

35. Krugler, *Voice of America*, 125; Leaflets, Far East Command/Psywar Branch, undated, "Psywar, #1," Box 207, Papers of Harry S Truman: Korean War File: Frank Lowe File, HSTL.

36. Ogburn to Connors, November 8, 1950, folder: "Political & Psychological Warfare," Box 11a, Lot File 64D563: Records of Policy Planning Staff 1947–1953, Lot Files, RG 59. This was delicate elsewhere too. Across the world, the US Consulate in the colony of British Guiana reported that the pamphlet *The Korean Crisis* elicited great local interest and newspaper commentary—including the freighted language of "independence" and "self-government." US Consulate-Georgetown to State Department, August 25, 1950, "British Guiana," Box 158, Lot 53D89 (MLR 1559): International Information Activities 1938-53, RG 59, NARA.

37. State to Certain Posts (Far East Annex), November 16, 1950, 511.00/11-1650, Box 2238; State to Certain Posts (Far East Annex), November 22, 1950, 511.00/11-2250, Box 2239; State to Certain Posts (Far East Annex), December 8, 1950, 511.00/12-850, Box 2239, CDF 1950-54, RG 59, NARA.

38. State to Certain Posts, November 29, 1950, 511.00/11-2950; State to Certain Officers, November 28, 1950, 511.00/11-2850, Box 2239, CDF 1950-54, RG 59, NARA.

39. State to Certain Posts (Far East Annex), November 24, 1950, 511.00/11-2450, Box 2239, CDF 195-54, RG 59, NARA; Report, NYU Research Center on Human Relations, July 1951, "VOA 1951—Broadcasts to Korea," Box 16, Hulten Papers, HSTL; State to Certain Officers, December 6, 1950, 511.00/12-650, Box 2239, CDF 1950–54, RG 59, NARA.

40. State to Certain Posts (Far East Annex), December 1, 1950, 511.00/12-150, Box 2239, CDF 1950-54, RG 59, NARA. The semiannual report to Congress on the USIE Program, did, however, include expanded sections on areas outside Europe. Moore to DeLong, November 21, 1950, 511.00/11-2150, Box 2239, CDF 1950-54, RG 59, NARA.

41. State to Certain Posts (Far East Annex), December 1, 1950; State to Certain Officers, December 5, 1950, 511.00/12-550; State to Certain Posts (Far East Annex), December 15, 1950, 511.00/12-1550, Box 2239, CDF 1950-54, RG 59, NARA.

42. Benton to Acheson, December 14, 1950, 511.00/12-1450, Box 2239, CDF 1950-54, RG 59, NARA. In this Benton was echoing the frustrations felt by others in his sector, who felt that the lack of progress on the military front was matched on the psychological/public diplomacy one. McFall to Rusk and Barrett, January 16, 1951, 611.95b/1-1651, Box 2888, CDF 1950-54, RG 59, NARA.

43. Cull notes that the Korean "crisis underlined the need for an effective information effort." Cull, *Cold War and United States Information Agency*, 62.

44. Barrett to Rooney, July 27, 1950; Moore to DeLong, November 21, 1950; Annex #5 to NSC-68/3, December 8, 1950, *FRUS 1950*, Vol. I: National Security Affairs, 452; McGhee to Warren, August 11, 1951, *FRUS 1951*, Vol. VI Part 2: Korea and China, 2170.

45. Scammon to Nitze, September 13, 1950, folder: "Political & Psychological Warfare," Box 11a, Lot File 64D563: Records of PPS 1947-1953, Lot Files, RG 59, NARA; US Embassy-Manila to State, December 10, 1950, 511.96/12-1050; US Embassy-Manila to State, December 14, 1950, 511.96/12-1450, Box 2542, CDF 1950-54, RG 59, NARA; Benton to Acheson, December 14, 1950.

46. US Embassy-Manila to State, December 26, 1950, 511.96/12-2650, Box 2542; US Embassy-Taipei to State, November 29, 1950, 511.94a/11-2950, Box 2537, CDF 1950-54, RG 59, NARA; Memorandum of Conversation, Dyke et al., December 5, 1950, folder: "Special Projects—Korea," Box 1, (IFI/D) Spec Projs Files 1949-53, Lot 66D487, Miscellaneous Lot Files, RG 59, NARA; Savage to Nitze, December 7, 1950, folder: "Political & Psychological Warfare," Box 11a, Lot File 64D563: Records of Policy Planning Staff 1947-1953, Lot Files, RG 59; US Embassy-Manila to State, December 20,

1950, 511.96/12-2050, Box 2542, CDF 1950-54, RG 59, NARA; Rankin to Dept. Asst. Secy. for Far Eastern Affairs, December 20, 1950, *FRUS 1950*, Vol. VI Part 1: Korea and China, 607.

47. Osgood, *Total Cold War,* 43.

48. Hooker to Nitze, March 27, 1951, folder "1951–53 [#1]," Box 11a, Lot File 64D563: Records of Policy Planning Staff 1947-1953, Lot Files, RG 59, NARA.

49. "Psychological Operations 1945–51," Edward Lilly, February 4, 1952, "091.412 File #2, Field and Role of Psychological Strategy in Cold War Planning, #2," Box 15, Papers of HST—SMOF: PSB Files, HSTL. Most scholars concur with Mitrovich: "The PSB not only failed to offer the necessary coordination [among agencies], it exacerbated the problem. The debate over the extent of the PSB's mandate set back psywar development nearly a year." Mitrovich, *Undermining the Kremlin,* 184. See also Krugler, *Voice of America,* 153; Sarah-Jane Corke, "Bridging the Gap: Containment, Covert Action, and the Search for the Elusive Missing Link in American Cold War Policy, 1948–53," *Journal of Strategic Studies* 20:4 (December 1997): 45–65, cited in Chris Tudda, *The Truth is Our Weapon,* 79.

50. *IIA Newsletter,* August 1951.

51. *IIA Newsletter,* June 1951, Box 1, Records of Dept. of State—IIA—Newsletters (MLR P-231), RG 59, NARA. The in-print languages were "Burmese, Bicolano, Chinese, Cebuano, English, French, Hiligaynon, Indonesian, Ilongo, Ilocano, Korean, Malaysian, Tagalog, Thai, Tamil, Visayan, Vietnamese, and Pampango."

52. Ibid.

53. Morgan to Browne, March 4, 1952, "091.412 File #2, Field and Role of Psychological Strategy in Cold War Planning, #2," Box 15, Papers of HST—SMOF: PSB Files, HSTL.

54. Referenced in Memorandum of Conversation, PSB (Weaver, Allen, et al.), May 6, 1952, "091—Korea," Box 8, Papers of HST—SMOF: PSB Files, HSTL.

55. Sherman to Browne, May 5, 1952, "091—Korea," Box 8, Papers of HST—SMOF: PSB Files, HSTL.

56. "Questionnaire on Key Words in American and Free World Propaganda," attached to State Department to Certain Diplomatic and Consular Officers, March 20, 1952, "Intelligence Reports (on the Orientation of the Foreign Press)," Box 6, TCA Program Information and Reports Staff: Office of Program Information: Records Relating to Public Opinion of the Point Four Program, RG 469, NARA. As Belmonte observes, "the fact that U.S. officials were still searching for the proper words seven years after World War II speaks volumes about the information program in the Truman era." Belmonte, *Selling the American Way,* 48.

57. "Report to PAO Conference" (Meeting Notes), Committee on Content, December 18, 1951, "IIA 1951-52, #2," Box 5, Papers of Howland Sargeant, HSTL. All emphasis in original.

58. Bell to Ayers, April 11, 1952, Box 201, PSF: Subject File—NSC File, Truman Papers.

59. *USA News Review,* May 26, 1952, "English," Box 1, Records of the State Department: IIA— "USA News Review" (MLR P-232), RG 59, NARA.

60. *USA News Review,* October 23, 1952, "English," Box 1, Records of the State Department: IIA—"USA News Review" (MLR P-232), RG 59, NARA; Stueck, *Korean War,* 303.

61. Kathryn Weathersby, "Deceiving the Deceivers," 177. See also Casey, "Wilfred Burchett"; Chen Jian, *Mao's China and the Cold War,* 107–112; William Stueck, *Rethinking the Korean War,* 160–178.

62. Stueck, *Korean War,* 424–25, fn21.

63. Memorandum of Conversation, Johnson and Tomlinson, March 3, 1952, 695.0026/3-352, *FRUS 1952-54,* Vol. XV, Part 1: Korea, Document #51; Acheson to Truman, March 11, 1952, 795.00/3-1152 *FRUS 1952-54,* Vol. XV, Part 1: Korea, Document #54; Memorandum of Discussion at State-JCS Meeting, March 19, 1952, *FRUS 1952-54,* Vol. XV, Part 1: Korea, Document #64. For their part, the PRC leadership believed the attacks were having the desired effect. See Shu Guang Zhang, *Mao's Military Romanticism.*

64. Notes of 9:30 Meeting, Sargeant et al., March 12, 1952, "IIA 1951–52, #2," Box 5, Papers of Howland Sargeant, HSTL.

65. As Stueck writes, "the POW issue had replaced . . . bacteriological warfare as the number one item on the Communist propaganda agenda" and had become the major "stumbling block" to peace. JCS to CINC-Far East, June 5, 1952 (795.00/6-2852), #168, *FRUS* 1952-54 Vol. XV, cited in Stueck, *Korean War*, 426, fn56. But the germ-atrocity accusations lingered around Asia. A July 1952 summary of Pakistani press comment recorded "one editorial on germ warfare that appeared in *DAWN* which stated that 'the need remains for truth to be discovered . . . mere accusation and denials lead nowhere.'" US Embassy-Karachi to State, July 16, 1952, "Restricted #2," Box 16, Records Relating to Public Opinion of the Point Four Program, RG 469, NARA.

66. Stueck, *Korean War*, 244. See also 258–65. Charles Young shows the extent to which Washington's handling of the POW issue lengthened the war. Charles Young, *Name, Rank, and Serial Number.*

67. *China Pictorial* (English-language PRC magazine), March 1961, "Pamphlets—Postwar Propaganda—English #2," Box 26, Hulten Papers, HSTL.

68. *2nd Review of Operations,* USIA, January–June 1954, "Pamphlets #1," Box 27, Hulten Papers, HSTL.

69. *VOA Radio News,* January 21, 1953, "Report on Korea"; *VOA Radio News,* May 15, 1953, "Faithful Wife"; *VOA Radio News,* October 20, 1952, "Korea: UN Series," Box 2; *VOA Radio News,* March 1952, "Battle Without Armor," Box 3, Records of the State Department: IIA—"VOA Radio News" (MLR P-229), RG 59, NARA. The last of these was adapted from an NBC series about "Peter Holborne, who . . . during the Puritan Revolution in England, fought and died for freedom of religion . . . [and whose] stubborn fight for freedom is similar to the one now being waged by Koreans under Communist domination. Not only the rebellion against the invasion of human rights, but the devotion to family and the unity of husband and wife in a common cause are qualities Koreans will recognize as part of their own way of life."

70. *VOA Radio News,* February 27, 1952, "Filipinos In Korea," Box 3, Records of the State Department: IIA—"VOA Radio News" (MLR P-229), RG 59, NARA.

71. Madan, "With an Eye to the East," 84, 90.

72. *IIA Newsletter,* June 1951.

73. The ambassador further asserted that this collaboration had London's blessing: Fraser writes that "according to [Charles] Malik, Britain in 1950–51 had encouraged the Arab, African, and Asian states to work together to moderate US policy, as the latter was perceived to be extreme." Cary Fraser, "An American Dilemma: Race and Realpolitik in the American Response to the Bandung Conference, 1955," in Brenda Gayle Plummer, ed., *Window on Freedom,* 129.

74. As Hart puts it, the war forced "public diplomats to reconceive their mission . . . Greater attention to the non-Western world would be paired with an increasingly rigid Cold War framework, posing even tougher choices . . . . [The] PSB's . . . many analyses [reveal] the growing alarm within the Truman administration about America's image outside Europe." Hart, *Empire of Ideas,* 154, 165.

75. Krugler, *Voice of America,* 139.

76. Report, "Problems of U.S. Policy Regarding Colonial Areas," Policy Planning Staff [PPS], October 2, 1952, folder: "Colonialism," Box 8, PPS 1947–1953, RG 59, NARA. US records used the term "Arab-Asian" more often than "Afro-Asian" or "Arab-Afro-Asian" at this stage, and more or less interchangeably.

77. *FRUS 1952–54:* Vol. II Pt. 1, National Security Affairs, NSC Key Date book, as transmitted August 5, 1952, 178–179, cited in Cull, *Cold War and United States Information Agency,* 75 fn201.

78. Scammon to Nitze, September 13, 1950.

79. Cull, *Cold War and United States Information Agency,* 65.

80. Evans to Hutchins, August 29, 1951, and Harris to Lacy, May 14, 1952, folder "Information Centers 1952–53," Box 1, Office of Administration 1952-55, RG 306, NARA; Report, Field Operations Branch, July 31, 1952, folder "NSC-68—Annex V Optimum Program FY53," IIA (IFI/D) Subject Files 1951-53, Box 4, Lot 66D487, Miscellaneous Lot Files, RG 59, NARA. For examples of the "tracking" of various media deployed locally, see

individual country reports in Box 1, IIA—Subject Files of the Administrator 1952-53, RG 59, NARA.

81. Excerpt from "Report on International Information Administration—1952," IIA Administrator to Secretary of State, December 31, 1952, folder "Report on IIA 1952," Box 3, IIA—Subject Files of the Administrator 1952-53, RG 59, NARA.

Chapter 3

1. As Cull memorably puts it, the 1947 exclusion of information activities from the new-born NSC "echoed down the decades like Original Sin." Cull, *Cold War and United States Information Agency*, 38.

2. Robert L. Johnson, "Report on Operations of IIA," July 29, 1953, folder: "International Information Service #1," Box 21, Eisenhower Papers as President—Whitman File (hereafter Whitman File)—Admin. Series, Eisenhower Library, Abilene, Kansas (hereafter DDEL).

3. "Review of Mideast, South Asia, and Africa Programs for NSC-135," NSC, December 15, 1952, Box 58, Lot 62D385, State Department Lot Files—Misc. Lot Files: Subject Files Relating to National Security Policy 1950-57, RG 59, NARA.

4. "Report: Part 7 [of NSC-5430]," USIA, August 12, 1954, folder "OCB 040.USIA (#5)," Box 20, WHO-NSC Staff: Papers 1948-1961, OCB Central File Series, DDEL. In a revealing request showing the power of the term and the delicacy of the balancing act, State asked USIA to use the term "imperialism" instead of "colonialism" in Latin American output. Memorandum, "5th Meeting," OCB, September 29, 1954, folder "OCB 091.4 Latin America (file #2)(6), Box 72, WHO-NSC Staff: Papers 1948-1961, OCB Central File Series, DDEL. Regarding the term "Free World," a study for the USIA explained that "to provide one uniform fashion of referring to the U.S., the Western powers, the UN, OAS and the like [including European colonies], the term Free World . . . was adopted for use here." Report S-8-53, "Themes to Be Stressed in USIA Materials," American University Bureau of Social Science Research, October 1953, Box 1, USIA Office of Research—Special Reports 1953-63, RG 306, NARA.

5. "Note by Executive Secretary—Reappraisal of U.S. Objectives and Strategy for National Security," NSC (Lay), September 16, 1952, folder "NSC-135 (#1)," Box 58, Lot 62D385, State Department Lot Files—Misc. Lot Files: Subject Files Relating to National Security Policy 1950-57, RG 59, NARA.

6. The PCIIA (Jackson) Committee that Eisenhower appointed at the outset of his presidency should not be confused with the President's Committee on Information Activities Abroad (PCIAA), or Sprague Committee, which Eisenhower appointed at the end of his tenure.

7. Jackson Committee Report, June 30, 1953, *FRUS* 1952-54—National Security Affairs, Vol. 2 Part 2, 1795-1899; "Material Furnished [to] Jackson Committee on Overt Information and Propaganda by IIA," February 1953, folder "Data for Jackson Committee," Box 1, IIA—Deputy Director for Field Programs (IFI/D) Subject Files 1951-53, Gen. Records of State Department, RG 59; Browne to Morgan, March 5, 1953, "PSB 334 PCIIA (2)," Box 22, PSB Central File Series, WHO, DDEL. For background on the reorganization, see Memorandum, Stokes, June 10, 1953, folder "Projects 1954," Box 3, Office of Admin. 1952-55; and Report S-1-53, "Intelligence Requirements of IIA," Box 1, Records of USIA, RG 306, NARA.

8. "USIA First Report to Congress," December 1953, folder "USIA #2," Box 37, Whitman File; Cover note to "Rockefeller Committee Report," Washburn, undated, folder "Rockefeller Committee Report," PCIIA (Jackson Committee) Records, 1950-53, Box 15, DDEL. Among the "related agencies" were the TCA, the MSA, and the State Department.

9. William Benton Oral History, Butler Library, Columbia University, 166.

10. Cull, *Cold War and United States Information Agency*, 97–98. The creation of the Office of Research and Intelligence was the last of the three to occur, in late 1954.

11. Eisenhower to Conant, July 20, 1953, folder "Eisenhower Correspondence 1953 (#2)," Box 50, C. D. Jackson Papers (hereafter CDJP), DDEL. On the McCarthy assault on US public diplomacy, see Cull, *Cold War and United States Information Agency*, 85–94; Belmonte, *Selling the American Way*, 51–57; Osgood, *Total Cold War*, 55–56; Memorandum of

Conversation—discussion of NSC-165, NSC, October 22, 1953, *FRUS* 1952-54—
National Security Affairs, Vol. 2 Part 2, 1750.

12. Osgood, *Total Cold War*, 64–66. It was equally a dress rehearsal for the enlistment of business and private entities into the cause. Eight months later, for example, Ike's "Atoms For Peace" address at the UN deployed US business to spread the word: "Over three hundred thousand copies of [it] in ten languages were distributed by 263 U.S. business firms . . . overseas." NSC-5407 Part 7: "Information Program," March 1, 1954, folder "NSC-5407 (#6)," Box 4, WHO-OSANSA: Records 1952-61, NSC Series- Status of Projects Subseries, DDEL.

13. Press release, Hagerty, July 8, 1953, folder "PCIIA 1953," Box 72, Lot 64D563, State Department General Records—Records of PPS 1947-53, Subject Files, RG 59, NARA.

14. Richard Boyd, *Broadcasting in the Arab World*, 25–27; Report S-15-53, "International Broadcasting of All Nations," December 31, 1953, Box 2, Office of Research—Special Reports, USIA Records, RG 306, NARA. This represented a near threefold increase in a half-decade. See also "USIA IBS VOA World Handbook," February 24, 1953, Box 1, State Dept. Records, IIA—Office of Admin. Subject Files 1952-53, RG 59, NARA.

15. See for example Report S-38-53, "Comparative Study of the Audience for Mass Media in Three Latin American Capitals," International Public Opinion Research (for USIA), October 1953, Box 3, USIA Records—Office of Research, Special Reports 1953-63, RG 306, NARA.

16. Memorandum, author unclear (White?), October 12, 1953, folder "S-42-53," Box 4, USIA Records—Office of Research, Special Reports 1953-63, RG 306, NARA.

17. Memorandum, "USIA Strategic Principles," undated, author unidentified, folder "OCB 040.USIA (#5)," Box 20, WHO-NSC Staff: Papers 1948-1961, OCB Central File Series, DDEL.

18. Washburn to Jackson, May 18, 1953, folder "Misc. File Material #2," Box 12, Jackson Committee Records, DDEL.

19. NSC-153/1, NSC, June 10, 1953, *FRUS* 1952–54: National Security Affairs, Vol. 2 Pt. 1, 384; The Bandung Conference occasioned the greatest such insights to date, but similar smaller ones could be found earlier. See for example the PSB report, "Exploratory Study to Identify Problems [in] Africa," April 13, 1953, folder "PSB091.4 Africa," Box 14, PSB Central File Series, WHO-NSC Staff: Papers 1948-61, DDEL.

20. Report—Jackson Committee Interview of Mann et al., March 6, 1953, folder "Misc. File Material (1)," Box 12, Jackson Committee Records, DDEL.

21. Memorandum, Posner to Berding, May 20, 1954, folder "OCB 040.USIA (#2)," Box 20, WHO-NSC Staff: Papers 1948-1961, OCB Central File Series, DDEL. "Visiting Good Neighbors—Pre-release Film Evaluation," Rept. S-29-53, March 5, 1954, Box 8, Office of Research—Special Reports, USIA Records, RG 306, NARA; "USIA First Report to Congress," December 1953; NSC-5407 Part 7: "Information Program," March 1, 1954.

22. Memorandum of Conversation, Schoenfeld et al., April 1, 1953, folder "Misc. PCIIA Reading Material," Box 13, Jackson Committee Records, DDEL. With Árbenz's eviction of several US officials in mind, there was consensus on the need to go gray: "The greatest problem . . . is our insistence on conducting our [political warfare] under the full glare of publicity . . . [We should instead use] an unorthodox way whereby materials are filtered into the target rather than broadcast overtly with attribution."

23. "IIA: USIE Semi-Annual Evaluation Report," US Embassy-Guatemala to State Department, January 9, 1953, 511.14/1-953, Box 2288, CDF 1950-54, RG 59, NARA.

24. NSC Minutes, July 30, 1953, *FRUS* 1952-54—Natl. Security Affairs, Vol. 2 Part 1, 438; "USIS Country Plan," US Embassy-Guatemala to State Department, June 1, 1953, 511.14/6-153, CDF 1950-54, Box 2288, RG 59, NARA.

25. Max Paul Friedman, "Fracas in Caracas," 669–689; Friedman, *Rethinking Anti-Americanism*, 129–152.

26. Mexico and Argentina abstained, but *Time* magazine called the vote a "diplomatic triumph" and a "warning to despots." "Success at Caracas," *Time*, March 22, 1954. Nor were these three the only actors to push back; Friedman argues that "what actually happened at Caracas was a multinational effort to persuade the United States not to intervene in

Guatemala." Max Paul Friedman, "Anti-Americanism and U.S. Foreign Relations," 507; Friedman, "Fracas in Caracas."

27. "Report on Actions Taken by the United States Information Agency in the Guatemalan Situation," USIA, July 27, 1954, document #280, *FRUS 1952-54*—Vol. IV: American Republics, 432; "Report: Part 7 [of NSC-5430]," August 12, 1954.

28. NSC-5407 Part 7: "Information Program," March 1, 1954. The document also notes that "special techniques are being used and resources reallocated to meet developing situations in certain areas. In Guatemala, unattributed materials are regularly fed into the independent press." The USIA anticipated a 56 percent increase in funding devoted to Latin America—the largest increase for any theater, though still (at less than 10 percent) the smallest outlay of any USIA target areas.

29. "Report: Part 7 [of NSC-5430]," August 12, 1954. "Immaturity and irresponsibility" is from OCB, "Recommendations for Dealing with Certain Basic Psychological Problems Confronting the U.S. at Caracas," March 17, 1954, Box 71, Latin America (2), OCB Central File Series, NSC Staff Papers, DDEL, cited in Friedman, "Anti-Americanism," 507, fn37.

30. Memoranda, Halle to Bowie, May 28, 1954; and Halle to Bowie, May 26, 1954, folder "Guatemala," Box 79, Lot 65D101, Records of PPS 1954, State Dept. Lot Files, RG 59, NARA. In the West Indies, for example, the one-two punch of the British Guiana intervention and Caracas gave Jamaican Chief Minister Alexander Bustamante impetus to secure a ban on communist activity—which, conveniently, formed the spine of the opposition to his government.

31. Memoranda, Halle to Bowie, May 28, 1954.

32. US Embassy-Panama to State, June 3, 1954, 611.14/6-354, Box 2748, CDF 1950-54, RG 59, NARA.

33. "Report: Part 7 [of NSC-5430]," August 12, 1954.

34. US Embassy-Guatemala to State, June 8, 1954, attached to US Embassy-Guatemala to State, May 24, 1954, 611.14/5-2454, Box 2748, CDF 1950-54, RG 59, NARA; Memorandum, "3rd Meeting of Working Group on Latin America," OCB, June 18, 1954, folder "OCB 091.4 Latin America (file #1)(7), Box 72, WHO—NSC Staff: Papers 1948-1961, OCB Central File Series, DDEL; "Report on Actions Taken by [USIA] in the Guatemalan Situation," July 27, 1954.

35. Memorandum, "4th Meeting of Working Group on Latin America," OCB, June 25, 1954, folder "OCB 091.4 Latin America (file #1)(8), Box 72, WHO—NSC Staff: Papers 1948-1961, OCB Central File Series, DDEL.

36. "Report on Actions Taken by [USIA] in the Guatemalan Situation," July 27, 1954.

37. "205th Meeting of NSC, July 1, 1954," Box 5, Whitman File (NSC Series), DDEL.

38. Report S-48-54, "Worldwide Reaction to the Guatemalan Revolution," USIA-ORI, September 2, 1954, Box 9, USIA Office of Research—Special Reports 1953-63, RG 306; Memorandum, Halle to Bowie, June 23, 1954, folder "Guatemala," Box 79, Lot 65D101, Records of PPS 1954, State Dept. Lot Files, RG 59, NARA.

39. "Report on Actions Taken by [USIA] in the Guatemalan Situation," July 27, 1954.

40. Osgood, *Total Cold War*, 147–148.

41. Memorandum, "Special Report on the Implementation of NSC-144/1," July 8, 1954, folder "OCB 091.4 Latin America (file #2)(1)," Box 72, WHO—NSC Staff: Papers 1948-1961, OCB Central File Series, DDEL; Memorandum, Clark to Holland, July 21, 1954, 511.14/7-2154, Box 2288, CDF 195-54, RG 59, NARA.

42. State Department to US Embassy-Guatemala, July 2, 1954, 611.14/7-254, Box 2748, CDF 1950-54, RG 59, NARA.

43. "Worldwide Reaction to the Guatemalan Revolution," September 1954.

44. "Report on Actions Taken by [USIA] in the Guatemalan Situation," July 27, 1954.

45. "USIA Fifth Report to Congress," December 1955, folder "USIA #2," Box 37, Whitman File, DDEL; "Progress Report on NSC 5432/1," OCB, December 27, 1954; and "Special Report on the Implementation of NSC-144/1," July 8, 1954, folder "OCB 091.4 Latin America (file #2)(1)," Box 72, WHO-NSC Staff: Papers 1948-1961, OCB Central File Series, DDEL.

46. Friedman, "Anti-Americanism and U.S. Foreign Relations," 508.

47. Memorandum, "4th Meeting of Working Group on Latin America," June 25, 1954.

48. The Latin American press, on the whole, remained skeptical. "Progress Report on NSC 5432/1," December 27, 1954; "NSC-5525 Part 6—The USIA Program," USIA, August 11, 1955, folder "NSC-5525 (#6)," Box 6, WHO-OSANSA: Records 1952-61, NSC Series- Status of Projects Subseries, DDEL. Public diplomacy activities within the United States were forbidden, but the home front was on Dulles's mind after the coup. He urged C. D. Jackson—who loved the idea—to find "someone with an 'Uncle Tom's Cabin' or Ida Tarbell touch ... to write something on the Guatemala affair." Memorandum of Telephone Conversation, Dulles and Jackson, July 3, 1954, folder "Tel. Memoranda July–Aug. 1954 (#5)," Box 2, Tel. Cons. Series, John Foster Dulles Papers 1951-59 (hereafter JFDP), DDEL.

49. Report S-27-54, "Study of USIA Operating Assumptions" Vol. 1, Institute for Communications Research (for USIA), December 1954, Box 7, Office of Research—Special Reports 1953-63, USIA Records, RG 306, NARA.

50. Report S-27-54, "Study of USIA Operating Assumptions" Vol. 2.

51. Ibid., emphasis in original. Regarding the racist condescension, it bears mention that their language notwithstanding, in-country public diplomats often displayed greater sensitivity to racial dynamics than most of their contemporary colleagues back home.

52. As Dulles put it to the president in another context, "the theme of nationalism [can be] most rewarding but this has to be played carefully because of the Communist use of this theme in North Africa and other colonial areas." Memorandum, Dulles to Eisenhower, November 10, 1954, folder "USIA #2," Box 37, Admin. Series—Whitman File, DDEL.

53. Nehru and Sukarno, along with the rest of the "Colombo Powers"—former colonies of Burma, Ceylon, India, Indonesia, and Pakistan—organized the meeting for a combination of ideological and parochial reasons. See George McTurnan Kahin, *The Asian-African Conference*, 2–3. Contemporary works on Bandung include Richard Wright, *The Color Curtain*; Carlos Romulo, *The Meaning of Bandung*; G. H. Jansen, *Non-Alignment and the Afro-Asian States*. On the Bandung spirit in the arts and letters of the Black Atlantic, see John J. Munro, "The Anticolonial Front."

54. Cary Fraser, "An American Dilemma: Race and Realpolitik in the American Response to the Bandung Conference, 1955," in Plummer, ed., *Window on Freedom*, 115. Other scholars, including Brands and Borstelmann, who focus on US diplomacy and race relations have treated Bandung at various length. See Jason Parker, "Cold War II," 867–892; Matthew Jones, "A 'Segregated' Asia?," 841–868; Von Eschen, *Race Against Empire*, 167–173; Plummer, *Rising Wind*, 247–256; Lauren, *Power and Prejudice*, 209. Nicholas Tarling has examined the place of the Conference in London's foreign policy: Tarling, "'Ah-Ah,'" 74–112. Christopher Lee examines the conference's impact in a wider setting, in Lee, ed., *Making a World After Empire*, as do See Seng Tan and Amitav Acharya, eds., *Bandung Revisited*.

55. Borstelmann, *The Cold War and the Color Line*, 93.

56. The "Five Principles," codified in an April 1954 agreement between India and China, were mutual respect for territorial integrity and sovereignty, mutual nonaggression, mutual noninterference in internal affairs, equality and cooperation, and peaceful coexistence.

57. Robert McMahon, *The Limits of Empire*, 84.

58. Speech, Nehru, concluding session of Afro-Asian Conference at Bandung, April 24, 1955, in *Nehru and Africa*, 20; Lee, "Introduction," *Making a World*, 15. For a recent example of this view, see James Sidaway: "Bandung resonated across the world, and a promising Third Worldist Afro-Asian imaginary was articulated." Sidaway, *Imagined Regional Communities*, 113. Robert Vitalis reminds us, though, that myths tend to outrun the facts of the meeting as it actually unfolded. Vitalis, "The Midnight Ride of Kwame Nkrumah and Other Fables of Bandung," 261–288.

59. Memorandum of Telephone Call, Dulles and Robertson, December 31, 1954, folder "Tel. Conversations—Gen. Nov.–Dec. 1954," Box 3, Telephone Calls Series, JFDP; Memorandum of meeting, Eisenhower and Judd, June 25, 1954, folder "Whitman Diary June 1954 #1," Box 2, Whitman Diary Series—Whitman File, DDEL.

60. Dulles to Certain Diplomatic and Consular Offices, December 31, 1954, *FRUS 1952–54* Vol. XII: East Asia and Pacific, Part 1, 1084–85.

61. Notes of Discussion, January 5, 1955, folder "230th Meeting of NSC, January 5, 1955," Box 6, NSC Series—Whitman File, DDEL; Memorandum of Conversation, April 9, 1955, *FRUS 1955–57* Vol. XXI, 82; Dwight D. Eisenhower, *The White House Years: Mandate for Change, 1953–56*, 480, 482.

62. The State Department chaired the Working Group, which included a half-dozen agencies including Defense, the CIA, and the USIA. Memorandum, Staats to OCB, January 11, 1955, folder "OCB 092.3 [International Affairs—Conferences & Boards] (9) January 1954–April 1955," Box 85, OCB Central File Series, WHO-NSC Staff Papers 1948-1961, DDEL.

63. Report "Attachment B," OCB Staff, no date given, attached to Memorandum, Staats to OCB, January 11, 1955.

64. Report "Attachment A," "Reactions," January 10, 1955; Report S-27-54, "Study of USIA Operating Assumptions," Vol. 1. On Japan and Bandung, see Kweku Ampiah, *The Political and Moral Imperatives of the Bandung Conference.*

65. Memorandum, "Exposing the Nature of the Afro-Asian Conference," McNair to OCB, January 21, 1955, folder "OCB 092.3 (9)," Box 85, OCB Central File Series, WHO-NSC, DDEL.

66. OCB 337 Minutes, OCB, January 31, 1955, folder "OCB 092.3 (9)," Box 85, OCB Central File Series, WHO-NSC, DDEL.

67. Memorandum, Landon to OCB, February 7, 1955, folder "OCB 092.3 (10)," Box 85, OCB Central File Series, WHO-NSC, DDEL.

68. Ibid. The proxies would "expose the difference between [Chou's] words of 'peaceful coexistence' and the deeds of aggression" and comment on nuclear-arms tests and on Formosa.

69. Telegram, Dulles to Eisenhower, February 26, 1955, folder "Dulles February 1955 (1)," Box 4, Dulles-Herter Series—Whitman File, DDEL; Minutes of USACI meeting, March 30, 1955, folder "U.S. Advisory Commission on Information—Minutes," Box 1, Gen. Records of USACI, USIA Records, RG 306, NARA.

70. Andrew Rotter, *Comrades at Odds*, 170–171.

71. Letter, Lodge to Knowland, March 15, 1955, folder "Lodge, Henry Cabot 1955 (4)," Box 24, Admin. Series—Whitman File, DDEL.

72. Extract, OCB 337 Minutes, April 1, 1955; Attached to Memorandum, Staats to Villard, March 28, 1955, folder "OCB 092.3 (10)," Box 85, OCB Central File Series, WHO-NSC, DDEL.

73. Memorandum, Staats to Villard, March 28, 1955, folder "OCB 092.3 (10)," Box 85, OCB Central File Series, WHO-NSC, DDEL. In some cases, American public diplomats briefed delegations before the latter departed for Indonesia. Cull, *Cold War and United States Information Agency*, 126.

74. Memorandum, Dulles to Adams, March 31, 1955, folder "White House Correspondence—General 1955 (4)," Box 3, White House Memoranda Series, JFDP, DDEL.

75. Memorandum, Rockefeller to Adams, April 6, 1955, folder "116-FF Asia-Africa Conference," Box 592, OF 116-FF, White House Central File (WHCF), DDEL [Emphasis in original].

76. Memorandum of Telephone Call, Dulles and Hagerty, April 11, 1955, Tel. Calls Gen. Series, JFDP, folder "Tel. Calls—Gen. March 7–Aug. 29, 1955 (3)," Box 10, DDEL. Adam Clayton Powell would confirm this when he met with Dulles and Eisenhower after Bandung.

77. Quotes from Eisenhower-Dulles meeting, in Press Release, Dulles (via Hagerty), April 17, 1955, folder "JFD April 1955 (1)," Box 5, Dulles-Herter Series, Whitman File, DDEL.

78. Report, INR No. 6903, "Results of the Bandung Conference: A Preliminary Analysis," April 27, 1955, attached to Memorandum, Staats to OCB, May 12, 1955, folder "OCB 092.3 [file #2] (2) April–November 1955," Box 86, OCB Central File Series, WHO-NSC, DDEL.

79. Minutes, Cabinet Meeting, April 29, 1955, folder "Cabinet Meeting of April 29, 1955," Box 5, Cabinet Series—Whitman File, DDEL.

80. Minutes, Cabinet Meeting, April 29, 1955; "For Chou and Nehru, A Rude Awakening: Friends of the West Speak Up," *Life*, May 2, 1955, 29.

81. Minutes, Cabinet Meeting, April 29, 1955. Observers such as Dulles's friend Freddie Mayer perceived the same: "I believe we should seriously consider capitalizing on, to our future as well as our present advantage, the surprising independence, wisdom, and courage of many of the Bandung conferees." Mayer to Dulles, April 23, 1955, folder "Re: Bandung Afro-Asian Conference 1955," Box 89, John Foster Dulles Papers, Seeley Mudd Library, Princeton, N.J.

82. Report, CA-7532, "Preliminary Evaluation of Results of Asian-African Conference," May 2, 1955, attached to Memorandum, Staats to OCB, May 12, 1955, folder "OCB 092.3 (2)," Box 86, OCB Central File Series; Memorandum, "Post-Bandung Thoughts," CIA to OCB, May 11, 1955, folder "Bandung (4)," Box 2, Planning Coordination Group Series (PCG), WHO-NSC, DDEL.

83. Memorandum, Staats to OCB, May 12, 1955. Among these ramifications was that the administration's plan had worked: "the careful planning and effective briefing of our friends by the Department and Embassies, and . . . the skillful maneuvers of the pro-Western delegations." See also Memorandum of Conversation, Eisenhower and Muir, May 25, 1955, folder "Whitman Diary May 1955 #2," Box 5, Whitman Diary—Whitman File, DDEL.

84. Augusto Espiritu, "'To Carry Water on Both Shoulders,'" 180. Romulo quote cited in Espiritu from Mohamed Abdel Khalek Hassouna, *The First Asian-African Conference*, 74–75, in Espiritu, 189, fn31.

85. Report IM-65-55, June 2, 1955, USIA, folder "USIA 1954-60 #3," Box 18, WHO-OSANSA: Records 1952-61, NSC Series- Briefing Notes Subseries, DDEL.

86. Letter, Jackson to Jessup, October 5, 1955, folder "Jessup, J.," Box 63, CDJP; Letter, Powell to Eisenhower, December 8, 1955, folder "Department of State November–December 1955," Box 70, Subject Series—WHCF (Confidential File), DDEL; Singh, *Black Is a Country*, 178; Fraser, "An American Dilemma," 124.

87. Memorandum of Conversation, Dulles and Macmillan, November 16, 1955; Memorandum of Conversation, Dulles and Lange, October 27, 1955, folder "Policy of Independence for Colonial Peoples," Box 7, Subject Series; Brands, *Specter*, 117–118; Memorandum, Dulles to Hoover, November 23, 1955, White House Memoranda Series, folder "White House Correspondence—General 1955 (1)" Box 3; Memorandum of Telephone Conversation, Dulles and Rusk, November 21, 1955, folder "Tel. Conversations—Gen. Sept. 1–Dec. 30, 1955 (3)," Box 4, Telephone Calls Series, JFDP, DDEL.

88. Other "right side" moves included revision of the Anglo-American Caribbean Commission (AACC) and renewed consideration of Alaskan and Hawaiian statehood (the quote specifically refers to the AACC revision). Memorandum, Hanes to McCardle, December 6, 1955, folder "Macomber—Hanes Chron. Dec. 1955 (3)," Box 9, Special Assistants Chronological Series; Memorandum of Conversation, Dulles and Rusk, April 6, 1956, folder "Policy of Independence for Colonial Peoples," Box 7, Subject Series, JFDP, DDEL.

89. USIA Inspectors' Report, May 23, 1955, folder "Far East—RPC May 1995," Box 3, USIA Inspection Staff Reports & Related Records 1954-62, USIA Records, RG 306, NARA.

90. Memorandum of Conversation, Eisenhower and Repplier, August 3, 1955, "Whitman Diary Aug. 1955 #5," Box 6, Whitman Diary—Whitman File, DDEL.

91. "USIA Fifth Report to Congress," December 1955.

92. Norberg to Browne, March 31, 1953, folder "PSB091.4 Africa," Box 14, PSB Central File Series, WHO-NSC Staff: Papers 1948-61, DDEL.

93. Halle to Bowie, May 28, 1954, "Guatemala," Box 79, Lot 65D101, Records of PPS, State Department Lot Files, RG 59, NARA.

94. Draft statement "Basic National Security Policy," NSC Planning Board, December 14, 1954, *FRUS* 1952–54 National Security Affairs, Vol. 2 Part 1, 810; Osgood, *Total Cold War*, 114; The two British-Africa colonies were Gold Coast and Nigeria. "NSC-5525 Part 6—The USIA Program," USIA, August 11, 1955.

95. "NSC-5611 Part II," USIA, undated, folder "NSC-5611 Pt. II (#3)," Box 7, WHO-OSANSA: Records 1952-61, NSC Series-Status of Projects Subseries, DDEL. See also McMahon, *The Limits of Empire*, 99; Dipesh Chakrabaty, "The Legacies of Bandung: Decolonization and the Politics of Culture," in Lee, ed., *Making a World*, 51.

Chapter 4

1. On Moscow, see Cull, *Cold War and United States Information Agency*, 162–169; Hixson, *Parting the Curtain*, 210–213; Belmonte, *Selling the American Way*, 87–88. On Brussels, see Belmonte, *Selling the American Way*, 134, and Michael Krenn, "'Unfinished Business,'" 591–612.

2. Jason Parker, "'Made-in-America Revolutions'?," 727–750.

3. Jackson to Luce, June 21, 1955, folder "C. D. Jackson 1955 #1," Box 22, Admin. Series—Whitman File, DDEL.

4. Memorandum, Phelps to Berg, January 30, 1956, folder "Country Requirements—Morocco/Egypt," Box 13, USIA-ORI—HQ Subject Files 1955-1970, USIA Records, RG 306, NARA. The document went on to propose that USIA "wrap up" six countries (Pakistan, Sudan, Egypt, India, Iran, Morocco) into one Mideast-Africa-Asia programming package, in which the "red colonialism" meme would be flogged. See also Lilly to Staats, January 17, 1956, folder "OCB 040.USIA (7)," Box 20, PSB Central File Series, WHO—NSC Staff: Papers 1948-61, DDEL.

5. Draft of NSC-5501, author unidentified (NSC), January 28, 1956, folder "NSC-5501, Basic National Security Policy," Box 60, Lot 62D385, State Dept. Misc. Lot Files—Subject Files Relating to National Security Policy 1950-57, RG 59, NARA.

6. See for example USIS-Egypt to USIA, September 23, 1955, folder "Africa (1)," Box 1, USIA Records—Foreign Service Despatches 1954-65 (Africa & Australia), RG 306, NARA.

7. Report, "NSC-5611 Part II, #3," undated, Box 7, NSC Series—Status of Projects Subseries, WHO-OSANSA: Records 1952-61, DDEL.

8. Report, "Evolution of Egyptian Neutralism," July 9, 1956, INR, "Egypt #2," Box 108, Lot 66D487, State Dept. Lot Files—Records of PPS 1954-56, RG 59, NARA.

9. Lodge to Eisenhower, June 26, 1956, folder "H.C. Lodge 1956 #1," Box 24, Admin. Series—Whitman File; "Source Book of Individual Papers," Rockefeller panel, November 1955, folder "Psychological Aspects of U.S. Strategy," Box 15, NSC Series—Briefing Notes Subseries, WHO-OSANSA: Records 1952-61, DDEL.

10. As William Roger Louis notes, it bookends the era of European imperialism, as in its wake the Europeans began scrambling *out* of Africa. Louis, *Ends of British Imperialism*. Exceptions to the "overshadow" are Tony Shaw, *Eden, Suez, and Mass Media*; James Vaughan, *The Failure of American and British Propaganda in the Arab Middle East, 1945–1957*, 206–229; Gary Rawnsley, "Overt and Covert," 497–522; and Brent Geary, "A Foundation of Sand."

11. "NSC-5611 Part II, #3," undated. On the isolation of Nasser via "Project Omega," see Salim Yaqub, *Containing Arab Nationalism*, 47.

12. Osgood, *Total Cold War*, 134.

13. Geary notes that both American and Egyptian sources attest to CIA and USIS resources being used in this way. Geary, "Foundation of Sand," 100–102, 115–116.

14. As James Brennan writes, "radio broadcasts from Cairo offered a powerful vision of an emerging Afro-Asian world that would assist . . . colonies to throw off the chains of Western colonialism." James R. Brennan, "Radio Cairo and the Decolonization of East Africa, 1953–64," in Lee, ed., *Making a World*, 174.

15. USIA Director Theodore Streibert later called this the greatest propaganda disaster of his tenure. Theodore Streibert Oral History (OH-153), DDEL.

16. Document #114, NIE (National Intelligence Estimate) 76, "Conditions and Trends in the Middle East Affecting U.S. Security," January 15, 1953, *FRUS 1952–54* Vol. IX Part 1: Near and Middle East, http://history.state.gov/historicaldocuments/frus1952-54v09p1/d114.

17. Keith Kyle, *Suez*, 132–133.

18. Minutes, Broadcast Advisory Committee, January 25, 1957, "Broadcast Advisory Committee 1953–55," Box 1, General Records of US Advisory Commission on Information, Records of USIA, RG 306, NARA.

19. State to Certain Posts, August 11, 1956, 511.00/8-1156, Box 2072, CDF 1955-1959, RG 59, NARA.

20. Report, November 13, 1956, "Current Developments Near East-South Asia-Africa, 1956," Box 2, Current Developments to Requestor Only Reports—USIA Office of Research, Records of USIA, RG 306, NARA.

21. Report, "7th Review of Operations," USIA, December 31, 1956, "USIA 1954–60 #3," Box 18, NSC Series—Briefing Notes Subseries, WHO-OSANSA Records 1952-1961, DDEL.

22. Geary, "Foundation of Sand," 160.

23. Memcon, AHMEC, November 14, 1956, folder "OCB 091.4—Middle East #4," Box 77, OCB Central File Series, WHO-NSC Staff: Papers 1948-61, DDEL.

24. Memcon, AHMEC, November 15, 1956, "OCB 091.4—Middle East #4"; Memcon, AHMEC, November 27, 1956, "OCB 091.4—Middle East #5," Box 77, OCB Central File Series, WHO-NSC Staff: Papers 1948-61, DDEL.

25. Memcon, AHMEC, November 30, 1956, "OCB 091.4—Middle East #5," Box 77, OCB Central File Series, WHO-NSC Staff: Papers 1948-61, DDEL; Report, "7th Review of Operations," USIA, December 31, 1956.

26. Memcon, AHMEC, December 17, 1956, "OCB 091.4—Middle East #5," Box 77, OCB Central File Series, WHO-NSC Staff: Papers 1948-61, DDEL.

27. Memcon, AHMEC, November 30, 1956.

28. Memcon, AHMEC, December 17, 1956.

29. Ibid.; Memcon, AHMEC, December 21, 1956.

30. Memcon, AHMEC, December 17, 1956.

31. Memcon, AHMEC, December 21, 1956.

32. Osamah Khalil, "The Crossroads of the World," 299–344.

33. Memcon, AHMEC, January 18, 1957, "OCB 091.4—Middle East #6," Box 77, OCB Central File Series, WHO-NSC Staff: Papers 1948-61, DDEL.

34. Instruction, State to Certain Posts, January 11, 1957, 511.00/1-1157, Box 2073, CDF 1955-59, RG 59; Yaqub, *Containing Arab Nationalism*, 83–84; BBC, *Summary of World Broadcasts: Near East*, January 9, 1957, cited in Geary, "Foundation of Sand," 181.

35. Minutes, Broadcast Advisory Committee, January 25, 1957.

36. Report, "Worldwide Distribution of Radio Sets," USIA, February 15, 1957, "P-9-57," Box 2, USIA Office of Research—Production Division Reports 1956-59, RG 306. The report estimated that there were 130 million radios in operation outside the United States, of which 120 million were in Eastern and Western Europe, East Asia, and Latin America; State to Certain Posts, November 20, 1956, 511.00/11-2056, Box 2072, CDF 1955–59, RG 59; Report, "Current Developments Near East-South Asia-Africa, 1957," USIA, March 4, 1957, Box 2, Records of USIA—Current Developments to Requestor Only Reports, RG 306. On "keyed" output, see Report, "Soviet Propaganda to Near East in Current Crisis," December 3, 1956, "P-158-56," Box 1, Office of Research—Production Division Reports—Records of USIA, RG 306, NARA.

37. Report, "World Reactions to Eisenhower's Middle East Policy Address," INR, January 28, 1957; "Reactions to Eisenhower Doctrine in Certain Countries of Near East, South Asia, and Africa," March 7, 1957, folder "Information Policy," Box 120, Lot 67D548, State Dept. Lot Files—Records of PPS 1957-61, RG 59, NARA.

38. Memorandum, Stephens to Toner, March 24, 1958, folder "USIA 1-350," Box 21, WHO-Staff Research Group Records 1956-61, DDEL. USIS-Cairo reported that the Arabic version of the USIA publication "What Is Communism?" got the biggest ad campaign and press run ever, and had such phenomenal success that a second run was rushed out.

39. Washburn to Staats, January 24, 1957, "OCB 091.4—Middle East #6," Box 77, OCB Central File Series, WHO-NSC Staff: Papers 1948-61, DDEL; Vaughan, *Failure of American and British Propaganda*, 233.

40. Report P-67-57, "Egypt's External Propaganda," August 1, 1957, Box 4, USIA Records—Office of Research, Production Division Reports 1956-59, USIA Records, RG 306, NARA.

41. "United States Psychological Warfare Program in the Middle East—Study and Recommendations for Improvement" [the "Moose Report"], December 12, 1957, folder "Near and Mid-East 1957," Box 154, Lot 67D548, State Dept. Lot Files—Records of PPS 1957-61, RG 59, NARA.

42. Instruction, State to Certain Posts, March 25, 1957, 511.00/3-2557; Instruction, State to Certain Posts, August 10, 1957, 511.00/8-1057, Box 2073, CDF 1955-59, RG 59, NARA.

43. Daniel Lerner, *The Passing of Traditional Society*, 214.

44. Report, "USIA Information Problems in 1957," USIA, undated, "USIA #7," Box 19, PCIAA (Sprague Committee) Records 1959-61, DDEL. The report went on: "Within these countries . . . there is evident a new sense of importance and self-assurance among the people . . . and an inclination on the part of their leaders to go constantly further in meeting popular demands . . . In [some places nationalism] has become a tool of irresponsible extremists, or it has been manipulated by Communists . . . In some places, nationalism has in effect made prisoners of its own leaders, who may well be appalled at the emotional vehemence of their supporters."

45. Report, November 13, 1956. The report also notes that the Soviet call came through its Muslim republics "in order to identify the USSR as an Asian power."

46. Memcon, AHMEC, January 18, 1957. Observers also noted "increased ChiCom Activity in the area" throughout and after the crisis. Memcon, AHMEC, December 21, 1956.

47. Lodge to Eisenhower, December 21, 1956, folder "H.C. Lodge 1956 #1," Box 24, Admin. Series—Whitman File, DDEL. See also "USIA Information Problems in 1957," undated, which noted: "the highly favorable response from many newly-independent and small nations . . . to U.S. leadership in the UN [on Suez]. This response unquestionably facilitated the task of gaining support for U.S. leadership on other questions such as Hungary."

48. "We have as yet been unable to obtain maximum results from U.S. aid programs to . . . Asian countries largely because the terms and administration of these programs have given rise to widespread belief that in some way U.S. economic assistance involves undesirable subservience on the part of recipients." "USIA Information Problems in 1957," undated.

49. Ibid. The administration took away one other public diplomacy lesson from these weeks—in Hungary. As Johanna Granville argues, US encouragement of the rebellion was only rhetorical; Hungarians found to their dismay that broadcasts of US moral support did not translate to any concrete aid. Granville, "'Caught With Jam on Our Fingers,'" 811–839.

50. Report for NSC-5720, USIA, undated, folder "NSC 5720 (#5)," Box 7, NSC Series—Status of Projects Subseries, WHO-OSANSA: Records 1952-61, DDEL.

51. Report, "U.S. Policy in the Uncommitted Areas," PPS (McClintock), March 12, 1957, folder "Neutralism," Box 123, Lot 67D548, State Dept. Lot Files—Records of PPS 1957-61, RG 59, NARA; Document #34, Memorandum of Conversation with [Eisenhower], July 31, 1956, *FRUS 1955–57* vol. XVI: Suez Crisis, http://history.state.gov/historical-documents/frus1955-57v16/d34.

52. Report for NSC-5720, undated. Within two years, Radio Cairo programming could be heard at all hours all across the Arab World in a half-dozen European languages as well as Hebrew, Turkish, Farsi, and Urdu. Lerner, *The Passing of Traditional Society*, 255.

53. Borstelmann, *Cold War and the Color Line*, 121. Brenda Plummer notes that "African leaders themselves skillfully played on black American sensibilities. No one did so as adroitly as Nkrumah, who knew American racial politics well." Plummer, *In Search of Power*, 50. For insights into the importance of Nkrumah in reorienting African American thinking, see Meriwether, *Proudly We Can Be Africans*, 150–180. In addition to these guests, fifty-six national delegations attended the Ghanaian ceremonies. Thompson, *Ghana's Foreign Policy*, 28.

54. Memorandum, "Interviews with Gold Coasters in America," US Consulate-Accra to USIA, July 25, 1956, "B—Program 1956," Box 1, Records of Foreign Service Posts—Ghana—General USIS Records 1951-58, RG 84, NARA. Upon independence, the GCBS changed its name to the Ghana Broadcasting Corporation (GBC).

55. "Inspection Report: USIS-Ghana," USIA, August 9, 1956, "Gold Coast 3/11/56," Box 4, Inspection Reports and Related Records 1954-62—Records of USIA, RG 306, NARA.

56. In addition, a small but growing number of USIA personnel were African American, potentially magnifying the impact of US messages abroad regarding race. This was in keeping with a gradually rising sensitivity to race matters in the State Department during these years. See Michael Krenn, *Black Diplomacy*.

57. US Consulate-Accra to State, December 26, 1956, 511.45k/12-26-56, Box 2141, CDF 1955-1959, RG 59, NARA.
58. Memorandum, "USIS Participation in Gold Coast Independence," US Consulate-Accra to USIA, November 21, 1956, "B—Program 1956," Box 1, Records of Foreign Service Posts—Ghana—General USIS Records 1951-58, RG 84, NARA.
59. Report, "NSC-5720 #5," no date. Post-Suez, the Soviets could leverage the large Egyptian media presence to supplement their own networks: "With the close Soviet alignment of Egypt the Communist world gained a significant source of propaganda to African nations."
60. Buchanan to Shanley, February 26, 1957, "Ghana (formerly Gold Coast) #8," Box 16, International Series—Eisenhower Diary, Whitman File, DDEL; Memorandum of Telephone Conversation, Dulles and Nixon, January 8, 1957, "Memoranda of Telephone Conversations—General—Jan.–Feb. 1957," Box 6, Tel. Conversations Series, John Foster Dulles Papers 1951-59, DDEL; Memorandum of Conversation, Dulles and Nixon, February 2, 1957, "VP Nixon #3," Box 6, Subject Series, Dulles Papers, DDEL.
61. Report, "NSC-5720 #5," no date; Report, USIA, March 4, 1957.
62. US Embassy-Accra to State Department, March 19, 1957, "B—Program 1957," Box 1, Records of Foreign Service Posts—Ghana—General USIS Records 1951-58, RG 84. On Aggrey and the US connection to black education abroad, see Parker, "'Made-in-America Revolutions.'"
63. US Embassy-Accra to State Department, March 19, 1957.
64. US Embassy-Accra to State, March 14, 1957, "350-Political-Ghana, Jan.–Jun. 1957," Box 1, Records of Foreign Service Posts—Ghana—Classified General Records 1956-58, RG 84; Report, "NSC-5611 Part II, #3," no date.
65. Report, "NSC-5720 #5," no date.
66. Ibid. See also Von Eschen, *Satchmo Blows Up the World*; and Belmonte, *Selling the American Way*. *Today* was initially distributed in theaters in Ghana, Nigeria, Sudan, and Liberia (and soon afterward in Morocco and Ethiopia), and in nontheater venues in South Africa, Kenya, Tunisia, French West Africa, and Southern Rhodesia. Memorandum, Stephens to Toner, January 1, 1958, folder "USIA 1-350," Box 21, WHO-Staff Research Group Records 1956-61, DDEL; "2nd Semi-Annual Report: President's Special International Program," author unidentified, June 30, 1957, "USIA 1954-60 #2," Box 18, NSC Series—Briefing Notes Subseries, WHO-OSANSA 1952-61, DDEL.
67. Plummer, *In Search of Power*, 111; see also Von Eschen, *Satchmo Blows Up the World*. Frantz Fanon, *Toward the African Revolution: Political Essays*, trans. Haakon Chevalier, 178, cited in Frank Gerits, "The Ideological Scramble for Africa," 133.
68. In Europe the press gave "heavy but balanced coverage" to Little Rock, while African newspapers, perhaps surprisingly, were somewhat more sparing. Memorandum, Stephens to Toner, September 13, 1957, folder "USIA 1-350," Box 21, WHO-Staff Research Group Records 1956-61; Loomis to Dearborn, November 22, 1957, "Image of America," Box 3, OCB Series—Subject Subseries, WHO-OSANSA Records 1952-61, DDEL; USIS-Leopoldville to USIA, September 14, 1957, and USIS-Salisbury to USIA, September 17, 1957, "Desegregation 1957," Box 11, ORI-HQ Subject Files 1955-70, RG 306, NARA. While some public diplomats felt that Ike's dispatch of troops helped to offset the negative public relations, it was difficult to tell whether this was anything more than a mere band-aid. Memorandum, Stephens to Toner, September 30, 1957, folder "USIA 1-350," Box 21, WHO-Staff Research Group Records 1956-61, DDEL. On the crisis, see Cary Fraser, "Crossing the Color Line in Little Rock," 233–264; Melinda Schwenk, "Reforming the Negative through History," 288–306; Borstelmann, *Cold War and the Color Line*, 102–104; Dudziak, *Cold War Civil Rights*, 115–151.
69. In a conversation with the Attorney General, Dulles alluded to a USIA report on "the use Nasser and Khrushchev were making of [the crisis]," though *FRUS* researchers did not find the report. Document #208, Telcon, Dulles and Brownell, September 24, 1957, in *FRUS 1955–57*, Vol. IX: Foreign economic policy; foreign information program, 613; Lodge to Eisenhower, September 25, 1957, "H.C. Lodge 1957–58 #3," Box 24, Whitman File—Admin. Series, DDEL. The deepening connections across the Afro-Asian world in

the wake of Bandung ensured that crises like Little Rock would continue to resonate. See for example Ali Bahr Aldin Ali-Dinar, "Contextual Analysis of Dress and Adornment in Al-Fashir, Sudan," Appendix 1, which notes the 1950s appearance of Sudanese tobe styles (traditional women's apparel) called "Asia and Africa" and "The Conference of Bandung." (I am warmly grateful to Marie Grace Brown for this reference.)

70. "NSC-5819 #5," Box 8, NSC Series—Status of Projects Subseries, WHO-OSANSA: Records 1952-61, DDEL.

71. Fraser, "Crossing the Color Line," 254–255.

72. Gerits, "Ideological Scramble for Africa," 132.

73. "NSC-5819 Part 6: The USIA Program," USIA, undated. Post-Little Rock, the USIA also redoubled efforts to develop African leadership and media networks friendly to the United States. Sprague to Eisenhower, July 26, 1960, "Africa 31 #1," Box 9; unidentified to Brown, March 31, 1960, "Staff Working Papers #2," Box 19, Sprague Committee Records 1959-61, DDEL.

74. Report, "Increases in Foreign Information Activities by Near East, South Asian, and African Countries," June 20, 1960, "Requestor Only Reports, Africa 1960," Box 2, Current Developments to Requestor Only Reports—USIA Office of Research, RG 306, NARA.

75. Report, "Inspection Report—USIS-Ghana," USIA, March 28, 1959, "Ghana," Box 4, Inspection Reports and Related Records 1954-62—Records of USIA, RG 306, NARA. The presence of so many new actors confirmed the US conclusion that despite Nkrumah's East–West balancing act, Ghana "is of strategic importance for the U.S. because of [its] leadership in the drive for independence sweeping Africa. Ghana has little military importance but psychologically wields regional influence." Report, "New Factors Affecting African Radio Content: Neutralism, Censorship, and Africanization," USIA Office of Research, September 2, 1959, "P-43-59," Box 7, Office of Research—Production Division Reports, Records of USIA, RG 306, NARA.

76. Report, "A Survey of Radios in Africa South of the Sahara," February 29, 1960, Office of Research—HQ Subject Files 1955-70, Records of USIA, RG 306, NARA. The hours of communist bloc programming in Africa, combined with the Mideast and South Asia, totaled 634 hours per week. Report, "Communist Propaganda Activities in Near East, South Asia, and Africa," April 15, 1960, "R-21-60," Box 1, Office of Research "R" Reports, Records of USIA, RG 306, NARA. This was the fruit of a successful, years-long bloc push to expand its media presence, which by 1958 had quadrupled its international broadcasts—one-fourth of which was aimed at the "Third World." Memorandum, Stephens to Toner, March 24, 1958, "USIA 1-350," Box 21, WHO-Staff Research Group Records 1956-61, DDEL.

77. USIS-Accra to USIA, February 2, 1960, "Africa (#3)," Box 1, Foreign Service Despatches 1954-65: Africa & Australia, USIA Office of Research, RG 306, NARA.

78. USIS-Lagos to USIA, June 26, 1959, "Africa (#2)," Box 1, Foreign Service Despatches 1954-65: Africa & Australia, USIA Office of Research, RG 306, NARA. The document notes that 75 percent of USIS programming is devoted to Objective #1: "to assist, in sympathetic partnership, in Nigeria's nonviolent evolution toward independence within the British Commonwealth because this offers a solution to the problems besetting emerging Africa"; Memorandum of Conversation, Adjei et al., October 5, 1959, "20.2 American Foreign Policy (GHA)," Box 1, Bureau of African Affairs-Office of West African Affairs, Country Files 1951-63 [Lot File: Africa], RG59, NARA.

79. Inspection Report, USIA Inspection Staff, March 28, 1959, "Ghana," Box 4, Inspection Reports and Records 1954-62—Records of USIA, RG 306, NARA. Interestingly, the USIA debated whether it should "agree" as regards Pan-Africanism, wondering in 1959 whether *Today* "should visually endorse Pan-African activity." Inspection Report, USIA Inspection Staff, April 17, 1959, "Nigeria," Box 7, Inspection Reports and Related Records 1954-62—Records of USIA, RG 306, NARA.

80. Plummer, *In Search of Power*, 73–77; Gerits, "Ideological Scramble for Africa," 183–185.

81. Report, "Nixon Trip to Africa," April 23, 1957, "S-3-57," Box 14, Office of Research—Special Reports 1953-63, Records of USIA, RG 306, NARA. On the Bandung spirit in African American culture, see Munro, "The Anticolonial Front."

82. Memorandum, Dulles to Eisenhower, July 19, 1958, "Ghana (formerly Gold Coast) #6," Box 16, International Series—Eisenhower Diary, Whitman File, DDEL; US Embassy-Accra to State, March 14, 1957, Memorandum of Conversation, Eisenhower, Nkrumah, Dulles, et al., July 24, 1958, "Ghana (formerly Gold Coast) #6," Box 16, International Series—Eisenhower Diary, Whitman File, DDEL; Memorandum, Halla to Gray, May 11, 1959, "New Independent Countries, U.S. Policy Toward, 1959," Box 14, NSC Series—Briefing Notes Subseries, WHO-OSANSA 1952-61, DDEL; Report, "Estimate of Situation in Africa in 1961," October 21, 1958, "S-17-58"; Report, "Estimate of Situation in the Near East and South Asia in 1961," October 21, 1958, "S-18-58," Box 15, Office of Research-Spec. Reports 1953-63, Records of USIA, RG 306, NARA.

83. Report, "Statement of Developments regarding Freedom of Information," author un-identified, no date, "International Flow of News #5," Box 4, Sprague Committee Records 1959-61, DDEL.

84. State to Certain Posts, November 25, 1957, 511.00/11-2557, Box 2073, CDF 1955-59, RG 59, NARA; Memorandum, Stephens to Toner, December 27, 1957, folder "USIA 1-350," Box 21, WHO-Staff Research Group Records 1956-61, DDEL.

85. USIS-Ghana to USIA, June 24, 1960, "Africa #2," Box 1, Foreign Service Despatches 1954-65—Africa & Australia, Records of USIA, RG 306, NARA.

86. Frantz Fanon, *A Dying Colonialism*, 97–98.

87. Report, "USIA Information Problems in 1957," USIA, undated.

88. Evans to Ellington, October 23, 1959, "USIA #1," Box 19, Sprague Cmte. Records, DDEL.

89. Emphasis added. C. D. Jackson, Speech to Paper Industry (New York), February 24, 1959, "C. D. Jackson 1958-59 #2," Box 22, Administration Series, Whitman File, DDEL.

90. Jackson to Dulles, August 7, 1958, CREST, NARA, cited in Geary, "Foundation of Sand," 251; on Nasser and "Free World," Mohammed Heikal, *The Cairo Documents*, 32, cited in Geary, "Foundation of Sand," 126.

91. "NSC-6013 Part 5: The USIA Program," Box 9, NSC Series—Status of Projects Subseries, WHO-OSANSA: Records 1952-61, DDEL. As the report noted, the VOA was ranked third in volume of international broadcasting (after the USSR and China), though the UAR had "actually moved ahead of VOA in [international broadcast] hours though not in areas covered."

92. Memorandum, Washburn to Sprague Committee, March 16, 1960, "Minutes #13," Box 27, Sprague Committee Records, DDEL.

93. As Adjei told his interlocutors, "the attitude of the U.S. toward Africa [is] 'adolescent' [and] the U.S. needs to make up its mind with respect to Africa, otherwise it is in danger of loosing [*sic*] the entire continent." Memorandum of Conversation, Adjei et al., October 5, 1959.

94. Minutes, Meeting of Sprague Committee, March 15, 1960, "Chron. File—Staff Members (#1)," Box 12, Sprague Committee (PCIAA) Records 1959-61, DDEL; Livingston to Gullion (Sprague Committee), February 29, 1960, "PCIAA," Box 131, Lot 67D548, State Dept. Lot Files—Records of PPS 1957-61, RG 59, NARA. See this document as well for a discussion of the conceptual limits of "free world."

Chapter 5

1. For a recent interpretation, see Bevan Sewell, *The U.S. and Latin America*. Stephen Rabe underlines the continuities of US policy through the two administrations, regarding for example the Alliance For Progress and the Bay of Pigs intervention. Rabe, *The Killing Zone*, 70, 87–88.

2. Brands, *Latin America's Cold War*; Greg Grandin and Gilbert Joseph, eds., *A Century of Revolution*; Gilbert Joseph and Daniela Spenser, eds., *In From the Cold*.

3. Stephen Rabe, *The Most Dangerous Area in the World*.

4. Even many of the best studies of the AFP, such as Rabe, *Most Dangerous Area in the World*, and Jeff Taffet, *Foreign Aid as Foreign Policy*, underplay the central importance of this dimension.

5. Report, "Conclusions and Recommendations of PCIAA," December 1960, "PCIAA 1960," Box 468, Papers of John F. Kennedy—Presidential Papers, National Security Files (NSF), John F. Kennedy Library, Boston, Massachusetts (hereafter JFKL).

6. Interview of Donald Wilson, Oral History Collection, JFKL; Bowles to Murrow, March 3, 1961, "Information Policy," Box 120, Lot 67D548, Records of PPS, State Department General Records, RG 59, NARA. His enthusiasm notwithstanding, the *New York Times* reported on January 28, 1961 that Murrow hesitated to take the job because of the 90 percent pay cut. On JFK's priority on the USIA and his trust in Murrow: "USIA . . . remains an independent agency, reporting directly to me. I have charged State with the responsibility of providing policy guidance to you and other agencies dealing in Foreign Affairs . . . I [JFK] consider you one of my principal advisors [on] psychological factors dealing foreign affairs." Attached to memo, Murrow to Bundy, March 10, 1961, "USIA, Gen. Jan.–June 1961," Box 290, NSF, JFKL.

7. Murrow speech to National Press Club, May 24, 1961, "USIA 1960–May 1961," Box 91, President's Office File—Papers of President Kennedy (hereafter POF), JFKL; Minutes, "5th Regional Operations Conference," USIA, October 16, 1961, "State Oct.–Dec. 1961," Box 88, POF, JFKL. Cater to Battle, November 9, 1961, 511.00/11-261, Box 1046, CDF 1960-63, RG 59, NARA.

8. Murrow speech to National Press Club, May 24, 1961. Regarding TV, as one analyst put it, thanks to technological advances and audience-critical-mass, "a dramatic breakthrough is at hand in dealing with the problem of communication with the masses of illiterate and uninformed peoples throughout the underdeveloped areas of the world." Cox to Bundy, March 9, 1961, "USIA Jan.–June 1961," Box 290, NSF, JFKL.

9. "Conclusions and Recommendations of PCIAA," December 1960, including attached letter, Eisenhower to Sprague, January 9, 1961. As Bowles later reflected: "A 'new world' in Latin America and Asia and Africa had developed, and we were not giving it thoughtful or adequate attention . . . I talked it out with the President, and I became convinced he was very serious about giving this 'new world' the attention it deserved." Interview of Chester Bowles, Oral History Collection, JFKL.

10. The closest JFK came to referring to Latin America was: "Whatever the history and lawbooks may say, we cannot evade the evidence of our own time especially we in the Americas whose own experiences furnish a model from which many of these new nations draw inspiration." See www.jfklink.com/speeches/jfk/congress/jfk020757_imperialism.html.

11. Bowles to Murrow, March 3, 1961.

12. The document went on to obliquely validate the importance of reaching foreign publics if their leaders could not be brought around: "We have to deal with the Lumumbas, the Castros, and the Sukarnos [as they are]. They are largely immune to persuasion." "Conclusions and Recommendations of PCIAA," December 1960.

13. Emphasis added. JFK Speech to Congress, May 25, 1961, http://www.jfklibrary.org/Research/Research-Aids/JFK-Speeches/United-States-Congress-Special-Message_19610525.aspx. "This new [funding] request is for additional radio and television to Latin America and Southeast Asia. These tools are particularly effective and essential in the cities and villages of those great continents as a means of reaching millions of uncertain peoples to tell them of our interest in their fight for freedom."

14. Murrow to Rostow, July 19, 1961, "USIA Gen. Jul.–Aug. 1961," Box 290, NSF (also found in *FRUS* at http://history.state.gov/historicaldocuments/frus1961-63v25/d127). Murrow elaborated: "When your shop has time, I would like to have an updated 'Guidance on Preferred Terminology' prepared which would propose possible words to be used as substitutes for such terms as 'East–West', 'Cold War', 'pro-West', 'pro-American country' and many others which are misleading, inaccurate, and not in our best interests. All new suggestions should be checked out for worldwide translatability." The response came a week later: Memorandum, "Useful Terminology," Bundy to NSC Staff, July 26, 1961, "FG 296—USIA Jan.–Jul. 1961," Box 184, White House Central Files—Subject File—Papers of Pres. Kennedy (hereafter WHCF), JFKL.

15. This might be called the Rostovian persuasion in US foreign policy. See Michael Latham, *Modernization as Ideology*. See also Nils Gilman, *Mandarins of the Future*; and David Ekbladh, *The Great American Mission*.

16. "Modernization of newly developing nations can best be achieved through democratic, pragmatic political and economic development consistent with the traditions, character and aspirations of a people." Murrow to USIA Heads and USIS Posts, July 24, 1961, Document #129, *FRUS 1961–63*, Vol. XXV, http://history.state.gov/historicaldocuments/frus1961-63v25/d129. As Latham notes, public outreach was a key feature, indeed a driver, of the modernization process: "The import of modern media . . . altered the psychology of traditional men and women, changing the way they perceived their relationship to their fellow citizens and creating opportunities for rapid political and economic transformations." Latham, *The Right Kind of Revolution*, 2–3.

17. As Bowles put it, "Castro deserves credit for waking us up on the subject of Latin America." Interview of Chester Bowles, JFKL. See also Speech (Caracas, Venezuela), "The Alliance For Progress: Prospects, Perils, and Potentialities," Arthur Schlesinger, May 11, 1963, "AFP Apr.–May 1963," Box WH-2, White House Files, Arthur Schlesinger Papers, JFKL. On the collective identity of "Latin America," Michel Gobat writes that it grew in significant part from the US provocations of the region in the mid-nineteenth century: "The rise of 'Latin America' was perhaps the most enduring outcome of one of the first anti-U.S. moments in world history." Michel Gobat, "The Invention of Latin America," 1347. See also Martin W. Lewis and Karen Wigen, *The Myth of Continents*.

18. Report from Task Force on Immediate Latin American Problems to President-elect Kennedy, January 4, 1961, Document #2, *FRUS 1961–63*, Vol. XII, http://history.state.gov/historicaldocuments/frus1961-63v12/d2.

19. Report R-4-61, "Role and Trend of Public Opinion in Latin America," January 31, 1961, Box 4, USIA Office of Research—"R" Reports 1960-63, RG 306, NARA.

20. As Rabe writes, "fighting and winning the Cold War in Latin America was JFK's paramount concern." Rabe, *Most Dangerous Area in the World*, 19.

21. Nor could it, as Thomas Field powerfully argues, be detached from the administration's affinity for military authoritarianism as the best available vehicle for modernization. Field, *From Development to Dictatorship*. Brad Simpson shows that this impulse was not confined to Latin America, in *Economists With Guns*.

22. Gordon to Goodwin, March 6, 1961, "AFP Jan–Dec. 1961," Box 290A, NSF (Depts. & Agencies), JFKL (also in *FRUS*: http://history.state.gov/historicaldocuments/frus1961-63v12/d5). Taffet confirms multiple sources of JFK's vision of the AFP, including its debt to Brazilian president Juscelino Kubitschek's Operation Pan America. For the campaign trail, see Goodwin to Kennedy, undated, "Goodwin, R.," Box 30, POF, JFKL; Memorandum, Schlesinger to unidentified, March 7, 1964, "AFP 1963—Memoranda," Box W-2, Schlesinger Papers, JFKL; Interview of Charles Halleck, Oral History Collection, JFKL; Nehemkis to Cerf, March 27, 1961, "AFP Jan.–Dec. 1961," Box 290A, NSF (Depts. & Agencies), JFKL; Speech, Jack Berhman, Foreign Policy Clearinghouse at Harvard University, December 19, 1960, "AFP, Origins of—Reports," Box 1, Papers of Jack Behrman, JFKL.

23. McKnight to Wilson, February 16, 1961, "Memoranda 1961–64," Box 1, USIA Papers (WHCF), JFKL. The Brazilians too expressed great hope in the new approach. Milam to McGovern, February 19, 1961, "AFP—Origs./Memoranda," Box W-2, Schlesinger Papers, JFKL.

24. Report R-13-60, "Communist Propaganda Activities in Latin America 1959," March 3, 1960, Box 1, USIA Office of Research—"R" Reports 1960-63, RG 306, NARA. The report found that the bloc had greatly increased its Latin American operations, and had gained acceptance of "certain aspects or features of Communism and its techniques." In a case of imitation-as-flattery, they had achieved this breakthrough in part through the opening of new binational centers—long a US staple—and also through an increase in radio output on par with wartime VOA activity.

25. Report, "Conclusions and Recommendations of PCIAA," December 1960.

26. "Item for Presidential Letter," author unidentified, February 27, 1961, "Requestor Only Reports—Latin America," Box 2, USIA Office of Research—Classified Research Reports, RG 306, NARA; R-4-61, "Role and Trend of Public Opinion in Latin America," January 31, 1961.

27. Wilson to Goodwin, March 6, 1961, "Mema. 1961-64 #1," USIA Papers (WHCF), JFKL.

28. R-4-61, "Role and Trend of Public Opinion in Latin America," January 31, 1961. The report noted that "significant public opinion, once exclusively old elite, now includes large sectors of the new elites as well as illiterate and semi-literate masses . . . The phenomenal development of mass opinion in Latin America in relation to elite opinion is clear." Document #9, Memorandum, "Programs and Actions to Implement Ten-Year Plan for the Americas," Smith, March 20, 1961, http://history.state.gov/historicaldocuments/frus1961-63v12/d9.

29. Cited in State to Certain Posts, July 15, 1961, 511.00/7-1561, Box 1045, CDF 1960-63, RG 59, NARA.

30. US Embassy-San Jose to State, March 14, 1961, 611.20/3-1461, Box 1290, CDF 1960-63, RG 59, NARA. Presidents Haedo (Uruguay), Ydigoras (Guatemala), and Lleras (Colombia) all did the same. Similar reports came in from around the hemisphere: McKnight to Wilson, March 14, 1961, "Memoranda 1961-64 #1," Box 1, USIA (WHCF), JFKL (Brazil); US Embassy-Caracas to State, March 15, 1961, 611.20/3-1561; US Embassy-Tegucigalpa to State, March 16, 1961, 611.20/3-1661; and US Embassy-Quito to State, March 16, 1961, 611.20/3-1661, Box 1290, CDF 1960-63, RG 59, NARA. Memorandum, "2nd Day Handling of President's Latin America Address," McKnight to Wilson, March 15, 1961, "Memoranda 1961–64 #1," Box 1, USIA (WHCF), JFKL.

31. Report S-7-61, "Reactions to Pres. Kennedy Address on Latin America," USIA-IRI, March 16, 1961, Box 20, USIA Office of Research—Special Reports 1953-63, RG 306, NARA; Memorandum, "3rd Day Handling of President's AFP Address," McKnight to Wilson, March 16, 1961, "Memoranda 1961–64 #1," Box 1, USIA (WHCF), JFKL.

32. Report R-11-61, "Reactions to Kennedy Address on Latin America," USIA-IRI, Box 4, USIA Office of Research—"R" Reports 1960-63, RG 306, NARA. The Frondizi quote is from Schlesinger to Berle, April 17, 1961, "AFP Gen. Material," Box W-1, Schlesinger Papers, JFKL. The Argentine continued: "I am certain this opinion is held by all the American governments."

33. Schlesinger to Berle, April 17, 1961; Loomis to Wilson, April 11, 1961, "Memoranda 1961–64 #1," Box 1, USIA (WHCF), JFKL.

34. Interview of Donald Wilson, Oral History Collection, JFKL; Cull, *Cold War and United States Information Agency*, 190–191.

35. Murrow speech to National Press Club, May 24, 1961.

36. Report S-14-61, "Public Opinion Impact of Cuban Landings: A Flash Survey," USIA-IRI, April 27, 1961, Box 20, USIA Office of Research—Special Reports 1953-63, RG 306, NARA.

37. Report S-14-61, USIA-IRI, April 27, 1961; Note, IRI to White House, May 4, 1961, "Requestor Only Reports, Latin America 1961–62," Box 2, USIA Office of Research—Classified Research Reports, RG 306, NARA.

38. Memorandum, "Opinions in Latin America," Stephens to Wilson and McKnight, August 2, 1961, "S-56-61," Box 21, USIA Office of Research—Special Reports 1953-63, RG 306, NARA.

39. Not only nearby; in 1960 Cuba notified the International Frequency Registration Board of its intent to broadcast daily fourteen hours to the full western hemisphere, Europe, and the Near East. Report R-29-61, "Communist Propaganda Activities in Latin America 1960," June 7, 1961; see also Report R-44-61, "Developments in Communist Bloc Broadcasting," USIA-IRI, August 25, 1961, Box 5, USIA Office of Research—"R" Reports 1960-63, RG 306, NARA.

40. It bears noting that this could have gone otherwise; as the USIS field office reported, "Until that time [that he became a communist ally], Castro had been a hero to virtually every segment of the Venezuelan people." USIS-Caracas to USIA, July 13, 1961, "Latin America #5," Box 5, Foreign Service Despatches—1954-65 Latin America, USIA Records, RG 306, NARA.

41. Booklet, "Inter-American Relations: What Latin Americans Think," attached to Barlow to ARA, June 9, 1961, 611.20/6-961, Box 1210, CDF 1960-63, RG 59, NARA.

42. Berle to Kennedy, July 7, 1961, 611.20/7-761, Box 1210, CDF 1960-63, RG 59; Policy Planning Staff to State, June 2, 1961, 611.20/6-261, Box 1210, CDF 1960-63, RG 59, NARA. Only secondarily, PPS argued, should US public diplomacy aim to "expose the Communist conspiracy centered in Cuba. The baseline "U.S. Policy Toward Latin America" reaffirmed this stance a month before Punta del Este, ranking "emphasis on the principle of self-help" as the #1 priority. "U.S. Policy," July 3, 1961, Document #15, *FRUS 1961–63* Vol. XII, http://history.state.gov/historicaldocuments/frus1961-63v12/d15.

43. Rabe, *Most Dangerous Area in the World*, 30. Lincoln Gordon later regretted Kennedy's not attending. Interview of Lincoln Gordon (#1), Oral History Collection, JFKL.

44. Stevenson speech to National Press Club, June 26, 1961, quoted in State to Certain Posts, July 15, 1961, 511.00/7-1561, Box 1045, CDF 1960-63, RG 59, NARA.

45. Emphasis added. State to Certain Posts, July 15, 1961. To accomplish this "main objective," the document relays that "a report has been prepared by a group of editors and opinion leaders from several Latin American republics" advising how to go about it.

46. State to Certain Posts, July 15, 1961, noted that "a major problem confronting [us] at the meeting will be Latin American interest in knowing the amount of US financial assistance over an extended period." See also Document #20, US Embassy-Montevideo to State Department, August 6, 1961, in *FRUS 1961–63*, Vol. XII, http://history.state.gov/historicaldocuments/frus1961-63v12/d20; US Embassy-Santiago to State, July 15, 1961, 611.25/7-1561, Box 1215, CDF 196-63, RG 59, NARA.

47. Document #20, August 6, 1961; US Embassy-Montevideo to State Department, August 9, 1961, Document #22, *FRUS 1961–63*, Vol. XII, http://history.state.gov/historicaldocuments/frus1961-63v12/d22.

48. Footnote #2 of Document #20, August 6, 1961; Rabe, *Most Dangerous Area in the World*, 30; Document #30, August 16, 1961, in *FRUS 1961–63*, Vol. XII, http://history.state.gov/historicaldocuments/frus1961-63v12/d30; Report R-47-61, "Latin American Commentary on the Punta del Este Conference," August 23, 1961, Box 5, USIA-IRI, USIA Office of Research—"R" Reports 1960-63, RG 306, NARA. The exception was the Cuban press, whose "tenor . . . can be summarized by references to the 'AFP' as the 'Alliance For Slavery' "; Taffet, *Foreign Aid as Foreign Policy*, 30–31.

49. State to All Posts, September 27, 1961, 511.00/9-2761, Box 1045, CDF 1960-63, RG 59, NARA.

50. State to All Posts, September 27, 1961. Che, for his part, blasted the Charter as an "attempt by the U.S. to solve hemispheric problems within a 'framework of U.S. imperialism.' "

51. McKnight to Murrow, November 27, 1961, "Memoranda 1961–64 #1," Box 1, USIA (WHCF), JFKL. "USIA's job since Punta del Este has been to maintain an effective level of information support for the AFP pending completion of the OAS publicity machinery."

52. Ibid.; "USIA Review of Operations," USIA, December 31, 1961, 511.00/5-262, Box 1046, CDF 1960-63, RG 59, NARA.

53. "USIA Review of Operations," December 31, 1961. Regarding comics, Robert Elder records that the agency "distributed over seven million cartoon books [in] Latin America during the first half of 1963 alone." Elder, *The Information Machine*, 8.

54. McKnight to Murrow, November 27, 1961; Office of Public Information to USIA Employees, October 28, 1963, "Memoranda 1961–64 #3," Box 2, USIA (WHCF), JFKL; "USIA Review of Operations," December 31, 1961. Illustrating the evolving media environment of the 1960s, more Colombians saw Kennedy in person than on TV. Report S-8-62, "Impact of President Kennedy's Visit Upon Attitudes Towards Alianza in Bogota," USIA-IRI, January 1962, Box 22, USIA Office of Research—Special Reports 1953-63, RG 306, NARA.

55. Report R-10-62, "Role and Trend of Public Opinion in Latin America 1961," USIA-IRI, February 16, 1962, Box 7, USIA Office of Research—"R" Reports 196-63, RG 306, NARA; "Suggested Points to be Included in Remarks to Alliance Group," attached to Speech, Kennedy to Brazilian Students, July 30, 1963, "Brazil," Box 46, POF, JFKL. Moscoso to Kennedy, May 11, 1962, "AFP Reports, May–Jul. 1962," Box 291, NSF, JFKL; Country

Assessment Report, USIS-Brazil to USIA, February 22, 1963, "Latin America #1," Box 5, Foreign Service Despatches—1954-65 Latin America, USIA Records, RG 306, NARA.

56. Dungan to Kennedy, June 6, 1962, "Dungan Jun–Dec. 1962," Box 62a, POF; JFKL; Memorandum ("Dominican Attitudes Toward U.S."), unidentified to Kennedy, undated, "S-45-62," Box 23, USIA Office of Research—Special Reports 1953-63, RG 306, NARA; Editorial, "For Alianza, A Warning," *Life* magazine, date not included, "Alliance For Progress," Box 95; Murrow to Kennedy, undated, "USIA Jan-Jun. 1962," Box 91, POF, JFKL.

57. State to Latin American Posts, May 4, 1962, "AFP May 1962," Box WH-2, Schlesinger Papers, JFKL. Rusk summed up: "That [decade of impatience] is the meaning of the Alliance."

58. USIS-Bolivia to USIA, January 26, 1962.

59. Interdepartmental Survey Group to Kennedy, November 3, 1962, "Brazil Nov.–Dec. 1962," Box 390, NSF, JFKL; Report, "Prospectus for Alianza Public Affairs Staff," undated, "AFP: Public Information," Box 2, James Bradshaw Papers, JFKL.

60. Emphasis in original. Rostow to Bundy, May 3, 1962, "AFP Apr.–Jun. 1962," Box 290A, NSF, JFKL. Rostow went on: "Nationalism . . . provides the emotions and slogans for political action through the ideological spectrum. It animates the military and the extreme Left. It dominates the universities and the labor unions. Unless AFP is able to ally itself with nationalism, to influence it in a constructive direction . . . [we] will be pouring money into a psychological void." Rice to Schlesinger, May 23, 1962, "AFP May 1962," Box WH-2, Schlesinger Papers, JFKL.

61. "Staff Report: Survey of AFP in Brazil, Argentina, Chile, Bolivia Jun.–Jul. 1962," Bureau of the Budget, July 1962, "AFP July 1962," Box 290A, NSF, JFKL. The report concluded: "In sum, our information policies and programs must be concerned with matters much more related to AFP objectives in each country than [with] publicity about American aid and American life, foreign policy, and democratic faith."

62. The despatch put it pithily: "Most political leaders identify the AFP exclusively with US aid. Very few of them understand . . . what Chile has obligated itself to do." US Embassy-Santiago to State, August 14, 1962, "Chile Jul–Oct. 1962," Box 20a, POF, JFKL; "Staff Report," Bureau of the Budget, July 1962. On terminology, one discussion included the observation that "recommendations have been made in D.C. that Brazil should concentrate on basic reforms, such as agricultural reform. D.C. forgets that these words do not have same meaning or value in Brazil. 'Reform' in the U.S. means one thing, but in Brazil it means Communism. When the AFP recommends agricultural reform, this in Brazil means aiding Communism. [It] means revolution." Memorandum of Conversation, Martin et al., August 29, 1962, 611.32/8-2962, Box 1218, CDF 1960-63, RG 59, NARA.

63. INR to State (ARA), January 19, 1962, "AFP Jun. 1961–Mar. 1962," WH-2, Schlesinger Papers; Brubeck to Bundy, June 28, 1962, "AFP Apr.–Jun. 1962," Box 290A, NSF, JFKL; Rostow to Bundy, May 3, 1962. One study observed that "the intellectual occupies a strategic position in Latin American life . . . He is, in a very real sense, the cultural voice and conscience throughtout the hemisphere." Latin American Policy Committee, May 24, 1962, "Cultural Aspects of AFP," Box 2, Bradshaw Papers, JFKL; "Report on First Year of AFP," OAS, October 26, 1962, "AFP Aug.–Dec. 1962," Box 290A; Moscoso to Kennedy, December 6, 1962, "AFP Reports Nov.–Dec. 1962," Box 291, NSF, JFKL.

64. Report R-123-63, "Selected Communist Propaganda Activities in Latin America 1962," USIA-IRI, June 28, 1963, Box 16, USIA Office of Research—"R" Reports 1960-63, RG 306, NARA; USIS-Bolivia to USIA, January 26, 1962. The latter notes that in certain areas of Bolivia, "the Communist [sic] have physically denied us access by stoning our representatives, or threatening to kill them."

65. "Inspection Report—USIS-Bolivia," USIA, May 4, 1962, "Bolivia," Box 1, USIA Inspection Staff—Inspection Reports and Related Records 1954-62, RG 306, NARA; Report R-123-63, June 28, 1963.

66. Report S-22-62, "Castro's Standing in Latin America," USIA-IRI, July 24, 1962, Box 22, USIA Office of Research—Special Reports 1953-63, RG 306, NARA; Report R-123-63, June 28, 1963.

67. Report R-118-62, "Overseas Reactions to Kennedy's Cuba Announcement," USIA-IRI, October 23, 1962, Box 11, USIA Office of Research—"R" Reports 1960-63, RG 306, NARA.

68. Report R-136-62, "Overseas Reactions to Kennedy's Cuba Announcement (#7)," Box 11, USIA Office of Research—"R" Reports 1960-63, RG 306; US Advisory Commission on Information (USACI) Report to Congress, January 1963, "511.00/7-362," Box 1046, CDF 1960-63, RG 59, NARA. The Commission went on to note that the USIA's Missile Crisis performance had "received national acclaim . . . NBC's *Monitor* program said 'The USIA has once again proved its worth in getting the American point of view across to people abroad.'" The other two "major strategic confrontations" were the 1948 Berlin blockade and the outbreak of the Korean War.

69. USACI Report to Congress, January 1963.

70. USIS Chiefs of Mission in Latin America ranked AFP the highest-priority "psychological objective" by far. Report IRS/AL-266-63, author unidentified, September 20, 1963, Box 1, USIA Office of Research—Classified Research Reports, RG 306, NARA.

71. Report R-110-63, "Economic and Political Climate of Opinion in Latin America and Attitudes Toward Alliance for Progress," USIA-IRI, June 1963, Box 16, USIA Office of Research—"R" Reports 1960-63, RG 306, NARA.

72. USIA to USIS Posts, February 18, 1963, "Telegrams in & out, 1963–64," Box 2, USIA (WHCF), JFKL.

73. Read to Bundy, August 9, 1963, and State to Latin American Posts, July 26, 1963, "AFP Jan.–Aug. 1963," Box 290A, NSF, JFKL.

74. Pauker to Clarke et al., October 25, 1963, "AFP 1963, Memoranda," Box W-2, Schlesinger Papers, JFKL (also Document #67, *FRUS* 1961–63 Vol. XII, http://history.state.gov/historicaldocuments/frus1961-63v12/d67). The USIA's Wilson replied: "USIA thinks this is an excellent job and one which will give us a good basis for our operations throughout Latin America during IA-ECOSOC." Wilson to Schlesinger, October 25, 1963, in ibid.

75. State to All Posts in the American Republics, December 10, 1963, Document #72, *FRUS 1961–63* Vol. XII, http://history.state.gov/historicaldocuments/frus1961-63v12/d72.

76. Report, "Alliance For Progress: Its Second Year," IA-ECOSOC (Pan-American Union/OAS), 1964, Box 4, Papers of Teodoro Moscoso, JFKL.

77. Despite television's rise, radio was the best bang-for-the-buck. As Schlesinger was told, "Even in the worse barriadas people have . . . radios." Symington to Schlesinger, March 15, 1963, Document #57, *FRUS 1961–63*, Vol. XII, http://history.state.gov/historicaldocuments/frus1961-63v12/d57.

78. Emphasis in original. "Alliance For Progress: Its Second Year," IA-ECOSOC, 1964.

79. Ibid.

80. In addition to Taffet and Rabe, see also Dustin Walcher, "Missionaries of Modernization"; and Cristobal Zuniga Espinoza, "The Struggle for Promoting Development"; Goodwin to Kennedy, September 10, 1963, Document #63, *FRUS 1961–63*, Vol. XII, http://history.state.gov/historicaldocuments/frus1961-63v12/d63.

81. Radio script, VOA to Latin American Desks, November 23, 1963, "VOA Extra Copy: Kennedy 11/23/63," Box 2, USIA Special Collections Branch—Records Relating to Coverage of JFK Assassination, RG 306; Briefing Item (#IRS/AL-343-63), author unidentified, December 5, 1963, "Latin America 1962–63," Box 1, USIA Office of Research—Classified Research Reports, RG 306; Report R-212-63, "Foreign Reactions to Presidential Succession," USIA-IRI, December 6, 1963, Box 18, USIA Office of Research—"R" Reports 1960-63, RG 306, NARA.

82. Report R-223-63, "Worldwide Reactions to First Month of Johnson Administration," USIA-IRI, December 24, 1963, Box 18, USIA Office of Research—"R" Reports 1960-63, RG 306, NARA; "Foreign Reactions to Presidential Succession," USIA-IRI, December 6, 1963. Kennedy and the AFP were tightly connected in western-hemisphere eyes: "The prestige and integrity of the Kennedy Administration are deeply committed to . . . make this program successful. Indeed many Latin Americans already refer to the program not as the 'Alliance For Progress' but as the 'Kennedy Plan.'" US Embassy-Mexico to Kennedy et al., October 20, 1961, "AFP 1961–62," Box WH-2, Schlesinger Papers, JFKL (*FRUS*

1961–63 Vol XII., Doc. #34, October 19, 1961, http://history.state.gov/historicaldocu-ments/frus1961-63v12/d34). Despite what Andrew Kirkendall identifies as some important continuities in the AFP during LBJ's first years as president, Kennedy's death could not help but pull the program away from center stage. Andrew J. Kirkendall, "Kennedy Men and the Fate of the Alliance For Progress in LBJ-Era Brazil and Chile," 745–772. See also Thomas Tunstall Allcock, "Becoming 'Mr. Latin America,'" 1017–1045.

83. Office of Public Information to USIA Employees, October 28, 1963.

84. Report R-50-64, "Economic and Political Climate of Opinion in Latin America and Attitudes Toward AFP," USIA-IRI, April 30, 1964, Box 2; Report R-148-64, "Public Attitudes in Latin America: Some Reassuring Perspectives," USIA-IRI, October 1964, Box 4, USIA Office of Research—"R" Reports 1960-63, RG 306, NARA.

85. Report R-148-64, USIA-IRI, October 1964.

86. Rabe, *Most Dangerous Area in the World*, 148.

87. Summary Minutes of Meeting, Interdepartmental Committee of Undersecretaries on Foreign Economic Policy, November 29, 1961, Document #35, *FRUS 1961–63*, Vol. XII, http://history.state.gov/historicaldocuments/frus1961-63v12/d35.

88. Indeed, as historian Daniel Immerwahr writes, foregrounding economic development and prioritizing modernization helped to unite not only the Third World but also to conjoin First and Second: "Once one uses modernization as a lens through which to observe postwar history, the East–West axis, which divided the warring superpowers, seems less prominent than the North–South one, which united them." Immerwahr, "Modernization and Development in U.S. Foreign Relations," *Passport* (September 2012), 23. See also his *Thinking Small*.

89. Report R-29-61, USIA-IRI, June 7, 1961. See also Eric Gettig, "'Trouble Ahead in Afro-Asia,'" 126–156.

90. Emphasis added. "Analysis of the Khrushchev Speech of January 6, 1961," Hearing of Senate Subcommittee on Internal Security, Senate Judiciary Committee, 87th Congress 1st Session, June 16, 1961, Washington (GPO, 1961), 35.

91. "Egyptian Propaganda Activities 1958," February 25, 1959; Rusk to Kennedy, November 28, 1961, "Africa Gen.—Nov. 1961," Box 2, NSF, JFKL; Byrne, *Mecca of Revolution*, 77–80.

92. "Castro at U.N. Asks 'Colonial' Revolt," September 27, 1960, in Castro Speech Database, http://lanic.utexas.edu/project/castro/db/1960/19600927.html.

93. Brands, *Latin America's Cold War*, 10.

94. Prebisch's foundational text, published in 1950 as part of his tenure directing the UN Economic Commission for Latin America (ECLAC), was *The Economic Development of Latin America and its Principal Problems*. See also Edgar Dosman, *The Life and Times of Raúl Prebisch, 1901–1986*, chapters 12–13.

95. Speech (Caracas, Venezuela), Arthur Schlesinger, May 11, 1963.

96. Report S-15-64, "The Developing Countries: A Miscellany of Values, Concerns, and Desires," USIA-IRI, undated, Box 1, USIA Office of Research—Spec. Repts 1964-82, RG 306, NARA.

Chapter 6

1. On the evolution of "neutralism" into "nonalignment," see Mark Lawrence, "The Rise and Fall of Nonalignment," in Robert McMahon (ed.), *The Cold War in the Third World*, 139–155; and Jason Parker, "Ideology, Race, and Nonalignment in U.S. Cold War Foreign Relations: or, How the Cold War Racialized Neutralism Without Neutralizing Race," in Scott Lucas and Bevan Sewell (eds.), *Challenging U.S. Foreign Policy*, 75–98.

2. Report R-31-4-60, "Communist Propaganda Activities in . . . Africa 1959," USIA-IRI, May 6, 1960, Box 1, USIA Office of Research—"R" Reports 1960-63, RG 306, NARA.

3. Report S-21-60, "Africa and the Question of Soviet Colonialism," USIA-IRI, December 8, 1960, Box 19, USIA Office of Research—Special Reports 1953-63, RG 306, NARA.

4. Report S-33-60, "The Foreign Image of American Power: Near East, South Asia, and Africa," USIA-IRI, undated, Box 19, USIA Office of Research—Spec. Repts 1953-63, RG 306, NARA.

5. Report R-6-61, "Role and Trend of Public Opinion in Africa 1960," USIA-IRI, January 30, 1961, Box 4, USIA Office of Research—"R" Reports 1960-63, RG 306, NARA.

6. In this, the Kennedy team agreed with its British counterparts. Report, "Comment on British Paper, 'Neutralism: The Role of Uncommitted Nations in the Cold War,'" Fuller, March 8, 1961; and Report, "Neutralism: Suggested U.S. Policy Toward Uncommitted Nations," PPS, May 29, 1961, in "Neutralism," Box 123, Records of PPS 1957-61 (Lot 67D548), RG 59, NARA.

7. Document #118, February 7, 1961; and Document #116, undated (both in *FRUS 1961–63* Vol. XXV, at http://history.state.gov/historicaldocuments/frus1961-63v25/d118 and http://history.state.gov/historicaldocuments/frus1961-63v25/d116). See also Wiebe to Murrow, July 10, 1961, "S-43-61," Box 21, USIA Office of Research—Special Reports 1964-82, RG 306; Sorensen to Murrow, March 7, 1961, "396.1-BE/9-1561," Box 733, CDF 1960-63, RG 59, NARA.

8. Speech, Murrow to P.R. Society of America, November 13, 1961.

9. "Country Plan," USIS-Dar es Salaam to USIA, August 31, 1961, "Africa #1," Box 1, USIA Office of Research—Foreign Service Despatches 1954-65: Africa & Australia, RG 306; Report R-6-61, USIA-IRI, January 30, 1961. One of the better-received forms of USIA outreach in non-Anglophone areas were English-language classes, offered to various societal strata but mainly to the upper tier. As Murrow proudly reported to the US Public Relations society, the classes were very popular in Africa: in Togo, forty out of fifty Members of Parliament were taking part. Speech, Murrow to P.R. Society of America, November 13, 1961.

10. Nkrumah, "Africa Speaks to the United Nations," 319.

11. Report S-19-60, "Reactions to U.N.," USIA-IRI, October 7, 1960, Box 16, USIA Office of Research—Special Reports 1953-97, RG 306, NARA.

12. Report R-5-61, "Role and Trend of Public Opinion in Arab States," USIA-ORI, January 30, 1961, Box 4, USIA Office of Research—Research Reports 1960-99, RG 306, NARA. Aleksandr Fursenko and Timothy Naftali, *Khrushchev's Cold War*, 318, fn120. See also Sergey Mazov, *A Distant Front in the Cold War*; and David Engerman, "The Second World's Third World," 183–211.

13. On this reticence, see Mark Mazower, *No Enchanted Palace*.

14. Westad, *Global Cold War*, 136. As historian Seth Center notes, at the UN, "energized by the decolonization movement, the developing world began to express its discontent and demand redress for global political, economic, racial, and social inequities." Center, "Supranational Public Diplomacy: The Evolution of the UN Department of Public Information and the Rise of Third World Advocacy," in Kenneth Osgood and Brian Etheridge, eds., *The United States and Public Diplomacy*, 137.

15. See Matthew Connelly, *A Diplomatic Revolution*; and Jeffrey Byrne, *Mecca of Revolution*.

16. Report S-19-60, "Reactions to U.N.," USIA-IRI, October 7, 1960; Report, "Conclusions and Recommendations of PCIAA," December 1960.

17. Report R-19-62, "Soviet Satellite Propaganda 1961," USIA-ORI, February 28, 1962, Box 7, USIA Office of Research—Research Reports 1960-99, RG 306, NARA.

18. Report S-38-60, "Aspects of Indian Attitudes Toward U.S. and Other Countries," USIA-IRI, undated, Box 16; White to Stephens, April 12, 1962, "S-12-62," Box 18, USIA Office of Research—Special Reports 1953-97; and Report R-5-61, "Role and Trend of Public Opinion in South Asia," USIA-ORI, January 30, 1961, Box 4, USIA Office of Research—Research Reports 1960-99, RG 306, NARA.

19. Robert Rakove, *Kennedy, Johnson, and the Nonaligned World*, 70–74.

20. Schlesinger to JFK, August 3, 1961, 396.1-BE/9-1561, Box 732, CDF 1960-63, RG 59, NARA. Moreover, the attendees list was in constant flux, as various actors calibrated their own interest in attending to the matrix of political objectives. See James Hershberg, "'High-Spirited Confusion,'" 373–388.

21. Hulick to Kohler, August 23, 1961, "Berlin Belgrade Conference 1961," Box 50, State Department Bureau of Public Affairs (Lot 62D370[I]), RG 59; Washington asked Kennan for updates, and to "give unattributed background briefings to selected American newsmen [to preempt] contentious reporting which would be offensive to conferees. If you

should learn of developments seriously adverse to U.S. interests your urgent recommendations re possible counter measures would be appreciated." State to US Embassy-Belgrade, August 30, 1961, 396.1-BE/8-161, Box 732, CDF 1960-63, RG 59, NARA.

22. Wilson to Kennedy, August 1, 1961, "USIA-Gen. Jul.-Aug. 1961," Box 290, NSF, JFKL.

23. Talbot to State (via Johnson), September 7, 1961, 396.1-BE/9-161, Box 732, CDF 1960-63, RG 59, NARA.

24. US Embassy-Belgrade to State, August 31, 1961, 396.1-BE/8-161, Box 732, CDF 1960-63, RG 59; Draft memorandum, "Pros and Cons of JFK Message to Belgrade," author unidentified, undated, "Berlin Belgrade Conference 1961," Box 50, State Department Bureau of Public Affairs (Lot 62D370[I]), RG 59, NARA.

25. State to All Posts, August 29, 1961, 396.1-BE/8-161, Box 732, CDF 1960-63, RG 59, NARA.

26. US Embassy-Belgrade to State, August 31, 1961. See also US Embassy-Rabat to State, September 1, 1961, 396.1-BE/9-161, Box 732, CDF 1960-63, RG 59; US Embassy-Belgrade to State, September 5, 1961, 396.1-BE/9-161, Box 732, CDF 1960-63, RG 59, NARA.

27. "Summary and Analysis of Major Belgrade Speeches," attached to Talbot to State (via Johnson), September 7, 1961.

28. "Counterproductive" seemed especially the case "in light of the tendency among participating nations to react to such criticism with vituperative propaganda against the United States"—a backlash that would outweigh any public diplomacy good that a statement might do. Ibid.; Nunley to Ball, September 8, 1961; and Talbot to State, September 9, 1961, 396.1-BE/9-161, Box 732, CDF 1960-63, RG 59, NARA.

29. Report R-13-62, "Public Opinion in Arab States 1961," and Report R-14-62, "Public Opinion in South Asia, 1961," USIA-IRI, February 16, 1962, Box 7, USIA Office of Research—Reports 1960-99; Report RN-26-61, "Initial Worldwide Reactions to Belgrade Conference," USIA-ORI, September 12, 1961, Box 4, USIA Office of Research—Notes, RG 306, NARA.

30. Report S-62-61, "Belgrade Conference," author unidentified (USIA-ORI), 1961, Box 18, USIA Office of Research—Special Reports 1953-97, RG 306, NARA.

31. Rakove, *Kennedy, Johnson, and the Nonaligned World*, 78–79.

32. On the setback, Washington did see one bright spot—the death of the troika proposal—and that London "regarded the conference as a 'modest success' for the West." As for JFK's outreach, in "1961 he had met with a rather garrulous set of [NAM leaders]: Nkrumah, Nyerere, Keita, Sukarno twice, and Nehru," among others. Rakove, *Kennedy, Johnson, and the Nonaligned World*, 79–80, 86.

33. Robert S. Browne, *Race Relations in International Affairs*, 29.

34. Prashad, *The Darker Nations*.

35. US Embassy-New Delhi to State, September 4, 1961, 396.1-BE/9-161, Box 732, CDF 1960-63, RG 59, NARA. Kennan reported that Nehru "remind[ed the meeting] that issues of colonialism, imperialism, and racialism, while important, were not really burning issues of this moment" as compared to Cold War issues. US Embassy-Belgrade to State, September 3, 1961, 396.1-BE/9-161, Box 732, CDF 1960-63, RG 59, NARA.

36. Report R-12-62, "Role and Trend of Public Opinion in Africa 1961," USIA-IRI, February 16, 1962, Box 7, USIA Office of Research—"R" Reports 1960-63, RG 306, NARA.

37. Even actors who did not foreground the term "Pan-African" followed its currents. See for example Kevin Gaines, *African Americans in Ghana*; Von Eschen, *Race Against Empire*; Meriwether, *Proudly We Can Be Africans*; Singh, *Black Is a Country*; Makalani, *In the Cause of Freedom*; Plummer, *In Search of Power*; and Carol Anderson, *Bourgeois Radicals*.

38. Report RN-2-62, "The Concept of Negritude," USIA-ORI, February 5, 1962, Box 4, USIA Office of Research—Research Notes, RG 306, NARA. Nor, notes Frank Gerits, were "Pan" ideologies strictly limited to race: "Pan-Africanism or Pan-Arabism might have been less universalist, but it was not less interventionist. On the ground they were ranked besides communism or capitalism and not understood in solely racial terms, but viewed as alternative models" of development." Frank Gerits, "The Ideological Scramble for Africa."

39. Goodwin to Kennedy, undated. See also Philip Muehlenbeck, *Betting on the Africans*; and Larry Grubbs, *Secular Missionaries*.

40. Interview of Tom Mboya, Oral History Collection, JFKL; "African Reaction to Inaugural," undated, "Memoranda 1961–64," Box 1, USIA Papers (WHCF), JFKL.

41. USIS-Nigeria to USIA, March 15, 1960; and USIS-Ghana to USIA, June 24, 1960, "Africa #2," Box 1, USIA Office of Research—Foreign Service Despatches 1954-65 Africa & Australia, RG 306; Inspection Report, USIS-Nigeria, May 16, 1961, "Nigeria," Box 7, USIA Inspection Staff—Inspection Reports and Related Records 1954-62, RG 306, NARA; Speech, Murrow to P. R. Society of America, November 13, 1961. Elites in these urban settings were easy to reach compared with the allegedly apathetic masses, who were often geographically dispersed and disproportionately illiterate. But radio, and mobile film trucks carrying "Today" into rural areas, did succeed in expanding the USIA's reach over time. Bowles to Kennedy, March 27, 1961, "Africa—Gen. Mar–May 1961," Box 2, NSF, JFKL; Camp to Schueller, April 13, 1961, "Ghana 1958–," Box 7, USIA Office of Research—Country Project Correspondence, RG 306, NARA.

42. Speech, Murrow to P.R. Society of America, November 13, 1961, 511.00/5-262, Box 1046, CDF 1960-63, RG 59; Document #143, December 19, 1962, in *FRUS 1961–63* Vol. XXV, http://history.state.gov/historicaldocuments/frus1961-63v25/d143. On African views of the United States, for example, Tanzanians "continue to be generally friendly toward the U.S. and the American people. Their impressions of America are often naive, nebulous, and uninformed. There is some awareness of racial segregation in the U.S., but no real tendency to warp or overemphasize it." "Country Plan," USIS-Dar es Salaam to USIA, August 31, 1961.

43. As historian Ryan Irwin writes, the Congo Crisis was "a hotbed of inter-African intrigue, a playground for the superpowers and a turning point in the decolonization process." Irwin, "Sovereignty in the Congo Crisis," in Leslie James and Elisabeth Leake, eds., *Decolonization and the Cold War*, 203.

44. "Examen de la situation internationale à la lumière de la première conférence Afro-Asiatique et appreciation des dix principes de Bandung," early 1965, ANA, MAE, 32/2000, box 24, cited in Byrne, *Mecca of Revolution*, 339, n169. US skepticism bled easily into hostility as the Third Worldist project evolved. See Gettig, "'Trouble Ahead in Afro-Asia.'"

45. Report R-6-61, "Public Opinion in Africa 1960," January 30, 1961.

46. Ibid.

47. Report R-42-61, "Communist Propaganda in Africa 1960," July 27, 1961; Report R-19-62, "Soviet Satellite Propaganda 1961," February 28, 1962; Report RN-17-61, "The Lumumba Symbol in Africa," USIA-ORI, July 13, 1961, Box 4, USIA Office of Research—Notes, RG 306, NARA.

48. Report R-41-62, "Chinese Communist Propaganda," May 3, 1962. Not that it was totally fanciful to blame Hammarskjöld, who told Lodge: "Lumumba must be 'broken.'" "Synopsis of State and Intelligence Material reported to the President," August 10, 1960, Whitman File—Diary Series, Box 52, DDEL, cited in Review by Georges Nzongola-Ntalaja, H-Diplo Roundtable Review 11:28 (2011), 7 fn2.

49. Williams Report on Africa Trip, attached to Rusk to Kennedy, September 9, 1961, "Africa Gen.—Sept. 1961," Box 2, NSF, JFKL; Report RN-17-61, "The Lumumba Symbol in Africa," July 13, 1961; Touré to Kennedy, February 14, 1961, "Guinea, Gen., 1-5/61," Box 102, NSF, JFKL.

50. "Special Report #7," State Department, February 21, 1961, "State Feb. 1961," Box 87, POF, JFKL; Sorensen to Murrow, March 6, 1961, "396.1-BE/9-1561," Box 733, CDF 1960-63, RG 59, NARA. Frustration over this "iron curtain" led the USIS post to seek ways around it via local instead of regional or national publications. Inspection Report, USIS-Nigeria, May 16, 1961.

51. Williams Report on Africa Trip, September 9, 1961; Report RN-17-61, "The Lumumba Symbol in Africa," July 13, 1961.

52. Intercepted letter, cited in Battle to Bundy, February 12, 1962, "Ghana—Dungan File 1960-62," Box 385, NSF, JFKL; Report RN-35-59, "Africa 1958—Communist Activity," February 25, 1959; Jeffrey S. Ahlman, "Nkrumah and the Pan-African Nation: Transnational Politics in Decolonization-Era Ghana," Paper presented January 2013 at AHA Annual Meeting, (New

Orleans). This was very much Nkrumah's vision for his public diplomacy operation: "The BAA wanted to construct a revolutionary Mecca to rival other centres such as Cairo and Dar es Salaam." Gerits, "Ideological Scramble for Africa," 144. See also Ahlman, "Living With Nkrumahism"; and Evan White, "Kwame Nkrumah," 99–124.

53. Rupert Emerson, "Pan-Africanism," 275.

54. Rusk to Kennedy, March 7, 1961, "Kenya 1961," Box 127, NSF, JFKL.

55. Gerits, "Ideological Scramble for Africa," 210; Nyerere, *World Assembly of Youth Forum* 40 (September 1961), 14, cited in Emerson, "Pan-Africanism," 290; Hammarskjöld to Cordier, Cable of August 15, 1960 (UN Archives, New York, File B472), cited in Review by Georges Nzongola-Ntalaja, 17 fn6. See also Nzongola-Ntalaja, "Ralph Bunche, Patrice Lumumba, and the First Congo Crisis," in Robert A. Hill and Edmund J. Keller (eds.), *Trustee for the Human Community*, 148–157. On the "attraction," see Report S-30-60, "Attitudes Study in British East Africa," author unidentified, undated, Box 16, USIA Office of Research—Special Reports 1953-97, RG 306, NARA.

56. Report, "The White Redoubt," attached to Owen to McGhee et al., July 6, 1962, "Africa Gen.—Jun.–Jul. 1962," Box 2a, NSF, JFKL; Battle to Bundy, February 12, 1962. On the place of this outreach (and of Nonalignment) in Nkrumah's diplomacy, see W. Scott Thompson, *Ghana's Foreign Policy, 1957–66*.

57. Report R-165-63, "Ghanaian Propaganda Against the U.S.: Motives and Implications," IRI, August 12, 1963, Box 17, USIA Office of Research—"R" Reports 1960-63, RG 306; Report R-42-61, "Communist Propaganda Activities in Africa 1960," July 27, 1961; Report R-41-62, "Chinese Communist Propaganda," May 3, 1962; Report R-6-61, USIA-IRI, January 30, 1961. On the importance of apartheid, see Irwin, *Gordian Knot*.

58. As an American analyst conjectured after Ghana hosted the World Peace Assembly the next year, after "Belgrade Nkrumah may have been concerned with plans to perpetuate the grouping and to enhance Ghana's role in it." Hilsman to State, April 27, 1962, "World Peace Assembly," Box 50, Records of State Dept. Bureau of Public Affairs (Lot 62D370), RG 59, NARA.

59. Wilkins quoted in Anderson, *Bourgeois Radicals*, 320; Jonathan Rosenberg, *How Far the Promised Land?*, 207; Meriwether, *Proudly We Can Be Africans*, 172–177.

60. Report R-12-62, "Public Opinion in Africa 1961," February 16, 1962.

61. A sizable literature on this subject has blossomed over the last two decades, including Borstelmann, *Cold War and the Color Line* and *Apartheid's Reluctant Uncle*; Dudziak, *Cold War Civil Rights*; Anderson, *Eyes Off the Prize* and *Bourgeois Radicals*; Plummer, *Rising Wind*, and *Window On Freedom*, and *In Search of Power*; Gaines, *African Americans in Ghana*; Von Eschen, *Race Against Empire* and *Satchmo Blows Up the World*; Meriwether, *Proudly We Can Be Africans*; Paul Gordon Lauren, *Power and Prejudice*; Rosenberg, *How Far the Promised Land?*

62. USIS-Ivory Coast to USIA, July 19, 1961, "Africa #2," Box 1, USIA Office of Research—Foreign Service Despatches 1954-65: Africa & Australia, RG 306, NARA; Inspection Report, USIS-Nigeria, May 16, 1961; Report S-30-60, "Attitudes Study in British East Africa," undated.

63. Report S-51-62, "Problems and Processes of Cross-Cultural Communication," undated; Report S-17-61, "Worldwide Reactions to Racial Incidents in Alabama," IRI, May 29, 1961, Box 20, USIA Office of Research—Special Reports 1953-63, RG 306, NARA.

64. Bowles to Murrow, March 3, 1961, "Information Policy," Box 120, Records of PPS 1957-61 (Lot 67D548); Sanger to Jorden, April 26, 1962, 511.00/1-362, Box 1046, CDF 1960-63, RG 59, NARA.

65. Much of this work fell more under the rubric of cultural- than public diplomacy, aimed more at long-term goodwill than at short-term damage control. On the former, see Von Eschen, *Satchmo Blows Up the World*; on the latter, see Krenn, *Black Diplomacy*.

66. Report S-18-61, "African Reactions to Alabama Events," IRI, June 6, 1961, Box 20, USIA Office of Research—Special Reports 1953-63, RG 306, NARA.

67. Minutes, "5th Regional Operations Conference," October 16, 1961.

68. Report R-112-62, "Race Prejudice Mars the American Image," IRI, October 17, 1962, Box 10, USIA Ofc. of Research—Special Reports 1953-63, RG 306, NARA. On

occasion European coverage could outpace both African and domestic: "Often unfavorable U.S. racial developments receive relatively less media prominence in Ghana than in Europe"; USIS-Ghana to USIA, June 24, 1960; Report R-47-62, "Communist Propaganda Activities in Africa 1961," May 24, 1962. Even in noncrisis moments, bloc output highlighted racism, e.g., in a "pamphlet widely distributed entitled 'To Our Dear Friends' purported to be the product of an American Negro organization. The text and photos . . . suggested that beatings and lynchings are the order of the day in the United States. The actual source of the pamphlet [was] the Soviet humor magazine, *Krokodil.*" Report R-42-61, "Communist Propaganda Activities in Africa 1960," July 27, 1961.

69. Report S-41-61, "IRI Background Facts: The Negro American," IRI, July 17, 1961, Box 21, USIA Office of Research—Special Reports 1953-63, RG 306, NARA; Author unidentified to Salinger, August 1, 1961, "FG 296 USIA—Jan. 20–Aug. 31, 1961," Box 184, Subject File—WHCF, JFKL. See also Renee Romano, "No Diplomatic Immunity," 546–579.

70. Report R-12-62, "Public Opinion in Africa 1961," February 16, 1962. On the Airlift, see James Meriwether, "'Worth a Lot of Negro Votes,'" 737–763.

71. Report R-112-62, "Race Prejudice Mars the American Image," IRI, October 17, 1962; Report R-109-62, "Media Comment on the Mississippi Crisis," IRI, undated, Box 10, USIA Office of Research—"R" Reports 1960-63, RG 306, NARA.

72. USACI Report to Congress, January 1963; State to Certain African Posts, May 11, 1963, "Kenya 1963," Box 127, NSF, JFKL.

73. State to Certain African Posts, May 11, 1963; Report R-85-63, "Reactions to Racial Tension in Birmingham," IRI, May 13, 1963, Box 15, USIA Ofc. of Research—R Repts 1960-63, RG 306, NARA.

74. Report R-113-63, "Worldwide Media Reaction to Kennedy Civil Rights Speeches," June 17, 1963, Box 16, USIA Office of Research—"R" Reports 1960-63, RG 306, NARA.

75. Read to Bundy, July 7, 1963, "Africa—General, Students July 1963," Box 3, NSF, JFKL.

76. The Chinese also emphasized "mutual distaste for the *yanqui.*" Browne, *Race Relations in International Affairs,* 29.

77. Emphasis added. Report R-41-62, "Chinese Communist Propaganda," May 3, 1962; and Report R-47-62, "Communist Propaganda Activities in Africa 1961," May 24, 1962, USIA-ORI, Box 8, USIA Office of Research—Research Reports 1960-99, RG 306, NARA. As Byrne puts it, Mao's goal was to exclude the Soviet Union from the Afro-Asian movement; he "told black Africa that white, northern, and industrialized peoples like the Russians and Yugoslavians could never truly share the concerns of the Southern Hemisphere, whereas '[o]ur circumstances are similar . . . we are both of a colored race.'" Byrne, *Mecca of Revolution,* 213.

78. Report RN-34-59, "Egyptian Propaganda Activities 1958," USIA-ORI, February 25, 1959; and Report RN-35-59, "Africa 1958—Highlights of Communist Activity," USIA-ORI, February 25, 1959, Box 3, USIA Office of Research—Research Notes, RG 306, NARA.

79. Report RN-55-59, "UAR Activities in British East Africa," USIA-ORI, March 24, 1959; Report RN-43-59, "UAR Activities in Africa and the Afro-Asian Solidarity Movement," USIA-ORI, March 6, 1959; Report RN-40-59, "UAR Activities in Nigeria 1958," USIA-ORI, March 2, 1959; Report RN-39-59, "UAR Activities in Ghana 1958," USIA-ORI, March 2, 1959, Box 3, USIA Office of Research—Research Notes, RG 306, NARA.

80. Report R-31-4-60, "Communist Propaganda Activities [in] Africa 1959," May 6, 1960. The main bloc theme: "African independence is fictitious until all [especially economic] ties with the West have been broken." See also Report R-7-61, "Developments in Bloc Broadcasting 1960," USIA-ORI, February 10, 1961, Box 4, USIA Office of Research—Research Reports 1960-99; Report S-11-61, "Increased Bloc Broadcasts to Africa," USIA-IRI, April 7, 1961, Box 20, USIA Office of Research—Spec. Reports 1953-63, RG 306, NARA; and Doc. #133, December 5, 1961, in *FRUS* 1961–63 Vol. XXV, http://history.state.gov/historicaldocuments/frus1961-63v25/d133; USIS-Ghana to USIA, June 24, 1960.

81. Report R-42-61, "Communist Propaganda in Africa 1960," IRI, July 27, 1961, Box 5, USIA Office of Research—"R" Reports 1960-63, RG 306, NARA; Report R-47-62, "Communist Propaganda in Africa 1961," May 24, 1962; Bowles to Kennedy, March 27, 1961.

82. Byrne, *Mecca of Revolution*, 100.
83. Report R-39-61, "Ghana: A Communications Fact Book," USIA-IRI, July 24, 1961, Box 5, USIA Office of Research—"R" Reports 1960-63; Report RN-19-61, "UAR Broadcasting," USIA-ORI, August 8, 1961, Box 4, USIA Office of Research—Notes, RG 306, NARA.
84. Bowles to Kennedy, March 27, 1961.
85. "Report on Trip to Africa July–Sept. 1959," Loomis, "Kenya-Correspondence 1960," Box 13, USIA Ofc. of Research—Country Project Corresp. 1952–63, RG 306, NARA.
86. Report R-12-62, "Public Opinion in Africa 1961"; Report R-14-62, "Public Opinion in South Asia, 1961"; Report R-10-62, "Role and Trend of Public Opinion in Latin America 1961"; Report R-13-62, "Public Opinion in Arab States 1961," all February 16, 1962.
87. White to Stephens, April 12, 1962.
88. Report R-12-62, "Public Opinion in Africa 1961," February 16, 1962.
89. USIS-Ghana to USIA, June 24, 1960; "Egyptian Propaganda Activities 1958," February 25, 1959; Rusk to Kennedy, November 28, 1961.
90. Report R-12-62, "Public Opinion in Africa 1961," February 16, 1962; Report S-30-60, "Attitudes Study in British East Africa," undated.
91. Report S-15-64, "The Developing Countries: A Miscellany of Values, Concerns, and Desires," undated. The LDCs studied were Morocco, Nigeria, Malaysia, Philippines, Thailand, India, Iran, Pakistan, Turkey, Argentina, Brazil, Mexico, and Venezuela.
92. USACI Report, January 1963; OPI to USIA Employees, October 28, 1963.
93. Report R-212-63, "Foreign Reactions to Presidential Succession," December 6, 1963; Report R-208-63, "World Reactions to JFK Assassination," IRI, November 27, 1963, Box 18, USIA Office of Research—"R" Reports 1960-63, RG 306, NARA; "Williams Africa Visit," July 15, 1963.
94. Brubeck to Bundy, July 8, 1963, "Africa-Gen., Students July 1963, Box 3, NSF, JFKL.
95. NSC (Gleason), "U.S. Policy Toward Africa South of the Sahara Prior to Calendar Year 1960," August 28, 1958, "NSC-5818," Box 25, WHO-NSC Series, Policy Papers Subseries, DDEL, cited in Gerits, "Ideological Scramble for Africa," 293, fn934.

Conclusion

1. Nico Slate, *Colored Cosmopolitanism*, 200. Antoinette Burton elaborates on the "presumption of Afro-Asian solidarity—as the foundation of a post-imperial political community and as a guarantor of Third World non-alignment—which was at once feared and maligned in the West and so perpetually invoked by people of color and others as the aspirational standard-bearer of radical postcolonial politics." Burton, "The Sodalities of Bandung: Toward a Critical 21st-century History," in Lee, *Making a World After Empire*, 354.
2. Emphasis added. Peter Worsley, *The Third World*, cited in Wolf-Phillips, "Why 'Third World'?," 1313.
3. Report R-47-62, "Communist Propaganda Activities in Africa 1961," May 24, 1962.
4. Most USIA analysts concluded the same—though this is not covered in the present volume—about cultural-diplomacy outreach, with notable high-profile exceptions such as the 1959 Moscow kitchen debate.
5. Cull points out this was ultimately true worldwide, and the USIA adjusted its global operations accordingly. An emphasis on listening also offered the best chance of resolving the "hearts-minds-stomachs-eyeballs" dilemma that made it easier to track overseas sales of American goods than overseas reception of American rhetoric.
6. Emphasis added. US Embassy-Belgrade to State, September 5, 1961, 396.1-BE/9-161, Box 732, CDF 1960-63, RG 59, NARA.
7. Byrne, "Pilot Nation," 342.
8. Odd Arne Westad, "Epilogue," in McMahon, ed., *Cold War in the Third World*, 208. Seth Center confirms the breadth of their vision: Third World actors sought more than just to protest the inherited inequalities of imperialism, "they believed [they] had a compelling vision and a blueprint," which "through persuasion and argument, created sympathy for, and [could] perhaps even convert the world to, the new order." Center, "Supranational Public Diplomacy," 137.

BIBLIOGRAPHY

Manuscript and Archival Collections

National Archives (II), College Park, Maryland
    Record Group 59, Records of the Department of State
    Record Group 84, Records of Foreign Service Posts of the Department of State
    Record Group 229, Records of the Office of Inter-American Affairs
    Record Group 273, Records of the National Security Council
    Record Group 306, Records of the United States Information Agency
    Record Group 469, Records of US Foreign Assistance Agencies
Moorland-Spingard Research Center, Howard University, Washington, DC
    Dabu Gizenga Collection on Kwame Nkrumah
Harry S. Truman Library, Independence, Missouri
    Harry S. Truman Papers as President
    Dean Acheson Papers and Memoranda of Conversation
    Benjamin Hardy Papers
    Oral History Files
    Wilson Beale Papers
    Ralph Block Papers
    Wallace Campbell Papers
    Oscar Chapman Papers
    Clark Clifford Papers
    Robert L. Dennison Papers
    James Earley Papers
    George Elsey Papers
    Gordon Gray Papers
    Kenneth Hechler Papers
    Charles Hulten Papers
    David Lloyd Papers
    Edward G. Miller. Jr., Papers
    Philleo Nash Papers
    Charles G. Ross Papers
    Howland Sargeant Papers
    John Snyder Papers
    Stephen Spingarn Papers
    Charles Thayer Papers
Dwight D. Eisenhower Library, Abilene, Kansas
    Dwight D. Eisenhower Records as President
    Dwight D. Eisenhower Papers as President

White House Office Files
White House Central Files
Records of the President's Committee on International Information Activities (Jackson Cmte.)
Records of the President's Committee on Information Activities Abroad (Sprague Cmte.)
Sherman Adams Papers
Evan P. Aurand Papers
Leonard Burchman Papers
John Foster Dulles Papers
Dennis A. Fitzgerald Papers
James C. Hagerty Papers
John W. Hanes Jr., Papers
Bryce Harlow Papers
Christian Herter Papers
C. D. Jackson Papers and Records
Arthur Larson Records
Edward P. Lilly Papers
Thomas C. Mann Papers
Abbott Washburn Papers
John F. Kennedy Library, Boston, Massachusetts
Papers of John F. Kennedy—Presidential Papers
USIA Audio Recordings Digital Archives
Oral History Files
George Ball Papers
Jack Behrman Papers
Samuel Belk Papers
James Bradshaw Papers
Ralph Dungan Papers
Richard Goodwin Papers
Lincoln Gordon Papers
Teodoro Moscoso Papers
Arthur Schlesinger Papers
William Vanden Heuvel Papers
Seeley G. Mudd Library, Princeton University
Allen W. Dulles Papers
John F. Dulles Papers
George F. Kennan Papers
H. Alexander Smith Papers
Butler Library, Columbia University
Oral History Collection
Bentley Historical Library, University of Michigan
G. Mennen Williams Papers
United Nations Archives, New York
Office for Special Political Affairs
Department of Political Affairs
Branch Registries: Specialized Agencies
Branch Registries: Non-Governmental Organizations

Published Government Documents and Documentary Collections

US Department of State. *Foreign Relations of the United States*, 1947–1962.

Books

Acheson, Dean. *Present at the Creation*. New York: Norton, 1969.
Agyeman, Opoku. *Nkrumah's Ghana and East Africa: Pan-Africanism and African Interstate Relations*. Teaneck, NJ: Fairleigh Dickinson University Press, 1992.

Allison, Roy. *The Soviet Union and the Strategy of Non-Alignment in the Third World.* Cambridge: Cambridge University Press, 1988.

Ampiah, Kweku. *The Political and Moral Imperatives of the Bandung Conference.* New York: Brill, 2007.

Anderson, Benedict. *Imagined Communities: Reflections on the Origin and Spread of Nationalism.* New York: Verso, 1983.

Anderson, Carol. *Bourgeois Radicals: The NAACP and the Struggle for Colonial Liberation, 1941–1960.* New York: Cambridge University Press, 2014.

Anderson, Carol. *Eyes Off the Prize: The United Nations and the African American Struggle for Human Rights, 1944–1955.* New York: Cambridge University Press, 2003.

Andrews, Christopher, and Vasili Mitrokhin. *The World Was Going Our Way: The KGB and the Battle for the Third World.* New York: Basic Books, 2005.

Armah, Kwesi. *Peace Without Power: Ghana's Foreign Policy, 1957–1966.* Accra: Ghana Universities Press, 2004.

Arndt, Richard. *The First Resort of Kings: American Cultural Diplomacy in the Twenty-First Century.* Lanham, MD: Potomac Books, 2005.

Ashton, Nigel. *Eisenhower, Macmillan, and the Problem of Nasser: Anglo-American Relations and Arab Nationalism, 1955–1959.* London: Palgrave Macmillan, 1996.

Aydin, Cemil. *The Politics of Anti-Westernism in Asia: Visions of World Order in Pan-Islamic and Pan-Asian Thought.* New York: Columbia University Press, 2007.

Barrett, Edward W. *Truth is Our Weapon.* New York: Funk & Wagnalls, 1953.

Bayles, Martha. *Through a Screen Darkly: Popular Culture, Public Diplomacy, and America's Image Abroad.* New Haven, CT: Yale University Press, 2015.

Beisner, Robert L. *Dean Acheson: A Life in the Cold War.* New York: Oxford University Press, 2006.

Belmonte, Laura. *Selling the American Way: U.S. Propaganda and the Cold War.* Philadelphia: University of Pennsylvania Press, 2008.

Bernays, Edward L. *Public Relations.* Norman: University of Oklahoma Press, 1952.

Bernays, Edward L. *Propaganda.* New York: H. Liveright, 1936.

Bernhard, Nancy E. *U.S. Television News and Cold War Propaganda, 1947–1960.* New York: Cambridge University Press, 2003.

Bethell, Leslie, and Ian Roxborough, eds. *Latin America Between the Second World War and the Cold War: Crisis and Containment, 1944–1948.* New York: Cambridge University Press, 1997.

Bogart, Leo. *Premises for Propaganda: The United States Information Agency's Operating Assumptions in the Cold War.* New York: Free Press, 1976.

Borstelmann, Thomas. *The Cold War and the Color Line: Race Relations and American Foreign Policy Since 1945.* Cambridge, MA: Harvard University Press, 2001.

Borstelmann, Thomas. *Apartheid's Reluctant Uncle: The United States and Southern Africa in the Early Cold War.* New York: Oxford University Press, 1993.

Bostdorff, Denise M. *Proclaiming the Truman Doctrine: The Cold War Call to Arms.* College Station: Texas A&M University Press, 2008.

Boyd, Richard. *Broadcasting in the Arab World.* New York: Wiley, 1999.

Brands, H. W. *The Specter of Neutralism: The United States and the Emergence of the Third World, 1947–1960.* New York: Columbia University Press, 1989.

Brands, Hal. *Latin America's Cold War.* Cambridge, MA: Harvard University Press, 2010.

Brewer, Susan. *Why America Fights: Patriotism and War Propaganda from the Philippines to Iraq.* New York: Oxford University Press, 2009.

Browne, Robert S. *Race Relations in International Affairs.* Washington, DC: Public Affairs Press, 1961.

Burbank, Jane, and Frederick Cooper. *Empires in World History: Power and the Politics of Difference.* Princeton, NJ: Princeton University Press, 2011.

Byrne, Jeffrey James. *Mecca of Revolution: Algeria, Decolonization, and the Third World Order.* New York: Oxford University Press, 2016.

Campbell, David R. *Writing Security: United States Foreign Policy and the Politics of Identity.* 2nd ed. Minneapolis: University of Minnesota Press, 1998.

Casey, Steven, and Jonathan Wright, eds. *Mental Maps in the Early Cold War Era, 1945–68.* London: Palgrave Macmillan, 2011.

Casey, Steven. *Selling the Korean War: Propaganda, Politics, and Public Opinion.* New York: Oxford University Press, 2010.

Cobbs, Elizabeth A. *American Umpire.* Cambridge, MA: Harvard University Press, 2013.

Cobbs, Elizabeth A. *All You Need is Love: The Peace Corps and the Spirit of the 1960s.* Cambridge, MA: Harvard University Press, 2000.

Cobbs, Elizabeth A. *The Rich Neighbor Policy: Rockefeller and Kaiser in Brazil.* New Haven, CT: Yale University Press, 1992.

Collins, Michael. *Empire, Nationalism, and the Postcolonial World: Rabindranath Tagore's Writings on History, Politics, and Society.* New York: Routledge, 2011.

Connelly, Matthew. *A Diplomatic Revolution: Algeria's Fight for Independence and the Origins of the Post-Cold War Era.* New York: Oxford University Press, 2002.

Cooper, Frederick, and Laura Ann Stoler, eds. *Tensions of Empire: Colonial Cultures in a Bourgeois World.* Berkeley: University of California Press, 1997.

Costigliola, Frank. *Roosevelt's Lost Alliances: How Personal Politics Helped Start the Cold War.* Ithaca, NY: Cornell University Press, 2011.

Cull, Nicholas. *The Cold War and the United States Information Agency: American Propaganda and Public Diplomacy, 1945–1989.* New York: Cambridge University Press, 2008.

Cull, Nicholas. *The Decline and Fall of the United States Information Agency: American Public Diplomacy, 1989–2001.* New York: Palgrave Macmillan, 2012.

Cullather, Nick. *Secret History: The CIA's Classified Account of its Operations in Guatemala, 1952–1954.* Redwood City, CA: Stanford University Press, 1999.

Cullather, Nick. *The Hungry World: America's Cold War Battle Against Poverty in Asia.* Cambridge, MA: Harvard University Press, 2013.

Cumings, Bruce. *The Korean War: A History.* New York: Modern Library, 2010.

Dauer, Richard P. *A North–South Mind in an East–West World: Chester Bowles and the Making of United States Cold War Foreign Policy, 1951–1969.* New York: Praeger, 2005.

Davidson, Basil. *Black Star.* Oxford: James Currey Publishers, 2007.

DeConde, Alexander. *Ethnicity, Race, and American Foreign Policy: A History.* Boston: Northeastern University Press, 1992.

DeGrazia, Victoria. *Irresistible Empire: America's Advance Through Twentieth-Century Europe.* Cambridge, MA: Harvard University Press, 2006.

Dizard, Wilson P. *Inventing Public Diplomacy: The Story of the U.S. Information Agency.* Boulder, CO: Lynne Rienner Publishers, 2004.

Dizard, Wilson P. *Strategy of Truth: The Story of the U.S. Information Service.* Washington, DC: Public Affairs Press, 1961.

Dominguez, Jorge. *To Make a World Safe for Revolution: Cuba's Foreign Policy.* Cambridge, MA: Harvard University Press, 1989.

Dosman, Edgar. *The Life and Times of Raúl Prebisch, 1901–1986.* Montreal: McGill-Queen's University Press, 2008.

Dudziak, Mary L. *Cold War Civil Rights: Race and the Image of American Democracy.* Princeton, NJ: Princeton University Press, 2000.

Eisenhower, Dwight D. *The White House Years: Waging Peace, 1956–1961.* Garden City, NY: Doubleday, 1965.

Eisenhower, Dwight D. *The White House Years: Mandate for Change, 1953–1956.* Garden City, NY: Doubleday, 1963.

Ekbladh, David. *The Great American Mission: Modernization and the Construction of an American World Order.* Princeton, NJ: Princeton University Press, 2009.

Elder, Robert. *Information Machine: The United States Information Agency and American Foreign Policy.* Syracuse: Syracuse University Press, 1968.

Emerson, Rupert. *Africa and United States Policy.* Englewood Cliffs, NJ: Prentice-Hall, 1967.

Emerson, Rupert. *From Empire to Nation: The Rise to Self-Assertion of Asian and African Peoples.* Cambridge, MA: Harvard University Press, 1962.

Engerman, David C., and Nils Gilman, eds. *Staging Growth: Modernization, Development, and the Global Cold War.* Amherst: University of Massachusetts Press, 2003.

Escobar, Arturo. *Encountering Development: The Making and Unmaking of the Third World.* Princeton, NJ: Princeton University Press, 1995.

Espinosa, J. Manuel. *Inter-American Beginnings of U.S. Cultural Diplomacy, 1936–1948.* Washington, DC: Department of State, 1976.

Fanon, Frantz. *A Dying Colonialism.* Trans. Haakon Chevalier, reprint edition. New York: Grove Press, 1994.

Feinberg, Richard E. *The Intemperate Zone: The Third World Challenge to United States Foreign Policy.* New York: Norton, 1983.

Ferrell, Robert, ed. *Off the Record: The Private Papers of Harry S. Truman.* New York: Harper & Row, 1980.

Field, Thomas C. Jr. *From Development to Dictatorship: Bolivia and the Alliance for Progress in the Kennedy Era.* Ithaca, NY: Cornell University Press, 2014.

Fousek, John. *To Lead the Free World: American Nationalism and the Cultural Roots of the Cold War.* Chapel Hill: University of North Carolina Press, 2000.

Friedman, Max P. *Nazis and Good Neighbors: The U.S. Campaign Against the Germans of Latin America in World War II.* New York: Cambridge University Press, 2003.

Friedman, Max P. *Rethinking Anti-Americanism: The History of an Exceptional Concept in American Foreign Relations.* New York: Cambridge University Press, 2012.

Fursenko, Aleksandr, and Naftali, Timothy. *Khrushchev's Cold War: The Inside Story of an American Adversary.* New York: Norton, 2006.

Gaddis, John Lewis. *We Now Know: Rethinking Cold War History.* New York: Oxford University Press, 1997.

Gaddis, John Lewis. *The Long Peace: Inquiries into the History of the Cold War.* New York: Oxford University Press, 1987.

Gaddis, John Lewis. *Strategies of Containment: A Critical Appraisal of Postwar American National Security Policy.* New York: Oxford University Press, 1982.

Gaines, Kevin. *African Americans in Ghana: Black Expatriates and the Civil Rights Era.* Chapel Hill: University of North Carolina Press, 2008.

Garavini, Giuliano. *After Empires: European Integration, Decolonization, and the Challenge from the Global South, 1957–1986.* New York: Oxford University Press, 2012.

Gienow-Hecht, Jessica. *Transmission Impossible: American Journalism as Cultural Diplomacy in Postwar Germany, 1945–1955.* Baton Rouge: Louisiana State University Press, 1999.

Gienow-Hecht, Jessica, and Mark C. Donfried. *Searching for a Cultural Diplomacy.* New York: Berghahn Books, 2010.

Gifford, Prosser, and William Roger Louis. *Decolonization and African Independence: The Transfers of Power, 1960–1980.* New Haven, CT: Yale University Press, 1988.

Gilman, Nils. *Mandarins of the Future: Modernization Theory in Cold War America.* Baltimore: Johns Hopkins University Press, 2007.

Gleijeses, Piero. *Shattered Hope: The Guatemalan Revolution and the United States, 1944–1954.* Princeton, NJ: Princeton University Press, 1992.

Gopal, Sarvepalli. *Jawaharlal Nehru: A Biography.* Vol. 2. London: Jonathan Cape, 1981.

Gordon, Lincoln. *A New Deal for Latin America: The Alliance for Progress.* Cambridge, MA: Harvard University Press, 1963.

Goscha, Christopher and Christian Ostermann, eds. *Connecting Histories: Decolonization and the Cold War in Southeast Asia, 1945–1962.* Redwood City, CA: Stanford University Press, 2009.

Grandin, Greg, and Gilbert Joseph, eds. *A Century of Revolution: Insurgent and Counterinsurgent Violence During Latin America's Long Cold War.* Durham, NC: Duke University Press, 2010.

Grandin, Greg. *Empire's Workshop: Latin America, the United States, and the Rise of the New Imperialism*. New York: Metropolitan Books, 2006.

Grimal, Henri. *Decolonization: The British, French, Dutch, and Belgian Empires, 1919–1963*. Translated by Stephan De Vos. Boulder, CO: Westview Press, 1978.

Grubbs, Larry. *Secular Missionaries: Americans and African Development in the 1960s*. Amherst: University of Massachusetts Press, 2010.

Hahn, Peter, and Mary Ann Heiss. *Empire and Revolution: The United States and the Third World Since 1945*. Columbus: Ohio State University, 2001.

Hannaford, Ivan. *Race: The History of an Idea in the West*. Baltimore: Johns Hopkins University Press, 1996.

Hart, Justin. *Empire of Ideas: The Origins of Public Diplomacy and the Transformation of U.S. Foreign Policy*. New York: Oxford University Press, 2013.

Hayden, Craig. *The Rhetoric of Soft Power: Public Diplomacy in Global Contexts*. Lanham, MD: Lexington Books, 2012.

Henderson, John W. *The United States Information Agency*. New York: Praeger, 1969.

Hill, Robert A., and Edmund J. Keller, eds. *Trustee for the Human Community: Ralph J. Bunche, The United Nations, and the Decolonization of Africa*. Athens: Ohio University Press, 2010.

Hixson, Walter. *Parting the Curtain: Propaganda, Culture, and the Cold War, 1945–1961*. New York: St. Martin's, 1997.

Hogan, Michael J., ed. *The Ambiguous Legacy: U.S. Foreign Relations in the American Century*. New York: Cambridge University Press, 1999.

Hogan, Michael J. *A Cross of Iron: Harry S. Truman and the Origins of the National Security State, 1945–1951*. New York: Cambridge University Press, 1998.

Holsti, Ole R. *Public Opinion and American Foreign Policy*. Ann Arbor: University of Michigan Press, 1996.

Holt, Robert F., and R. M. Van de Velde. *Strategic Psychological Operations and American Foreign Policy*. Chicago: University of Chicago Press, 1960.

Horne, Gerald. *Black and Red: W.E.B. DuBois and the Afro-American Response to the Cold War*. Albany: SUNY Press, 1986.

Hunt, Michael. *Ideology and U.S. Foreign Policy*. New Haven, CT: Yale University Press, 1987.

Husain, Aiyaz. *Mapping the End of Empire: American and British Strategic Visions in the Postwar World*. Cambridge, MA: Harvard University Press, 2014.

Immerman, Richard. *The CIA in Guatemala: The Foreign Policy of Intervention*. Austin: University of Texas Press, 1982.

Immerwahr, Daniel. *Thinking Small: The United States and the Lure of Community Development*. Cambridge, MA: Harvard University Press, 2015.

Iriye, Akira. *Global Community: The Role of International Organizations in the Making of the Contemporary World*. Berkeley: University of California Press, 2002.

Irwin, Ryan. *Gordian Knot: Apartheid and the Unmaking of the Liberal World Order*. New York: Oxford University Press, 2012.

Jacobs, Matthew. *Imagining the Middle East: The Building of an American Foreign Policy, 1918–1967*. Chapel Hill: University of North Carolina Press, 2011.

James, Leslie. *George Padmore and Decolonization from Below: Pan-Africanism, the Cold War, and the End of Empire*. London: Palgrave Macmillan, 2014.

James, Leslie, and Elisabeth Leake, eds. *Decolonization and the Cold War: Negotiating Independence*. London: Bloomsbury, 2015.

Jansen, G. H. *Non-Alignment and the Afro-Asian States*. New York: Praeger, 1966.

Jian, Chen. *Mao's China and the Cold War*. Chapel Hill: University of North Carolina Press, 2001.

Jian, Chen. *China's Road to the Korean War: The Making of the Sino–American Confrontation*. New York: Columbia University Press, 1995.

Johns, Andrew, and Kathryn Statler, eds. *The Eisenhower Administration, the Third World, and the Globalization of the Cold War, 1953–1961*. Lanham, MD: Rowman & Littlefield, 2006.

Joseph, Gilbert, and Daniela Spenser, eds. *In From the Cold: Latin America's New Encounter With the Cold War*. Durham, NC: Duke University Press, 2008.

Kahin, George McT. *The Asian-African Conference*. Ithaca, NY: Cornell University Press, 1956.

Karabell, Zachary. *Architects of Intervention: The United States, the Third World, and the Cold War, 1946–1962*. Baton Rouge: Lousiana State University Press, 1999.

Kaufman, Burton I. *The Korean War: Challenges in Crisis, Credibility, and Command*. 2nd ed. New York: McGraw-Hill, 1997.

Kaufman, Burton I. *Trade and Aid: Eisenhower's Foreign Economic Policy, 1953–1961*. Baltimore: Johns Hopkins University Press, 1982.

Keppel, Ben. *The Work of Democracy: Ralph Bunche, Kenneth B. Clark, Lorraine Hansberry, and the Cultural Politics of Race*. Cambridge, MA: Harvard University Press, 1995.

Khan, Yasmin. *The Great Partition: The Making of India and Pakistan*. New Haven, CT: Yale University Press, 2007.

Kolko, Gabriel. *Confronting the Third World: United States Foreign Policy, 1945–1980*. New York: Pantheon Books, 1988.

Krenn, Michael. *Fall-Out Shelters for the Human Spirit: American Art and the Cold War*. Chapel Hill: University of North Carolina Press, 2005.

Krenn, Michael. *Black Diplomacy: African Americans and the State Department*. Armonk, NY: M. E. Sharpe, 1999.

Krenn, Michael. *Race and U.S. Foreign Policy from the Colonial Period to the Present*. 5 vols. New York: Garland, 1998.

Kroes, Rob. *If You've Seen One, You've Seen The Mall: Europeans and American Mass Culture*. Urbana-Champaign, IL: University of Illinois Press, 1996.

Krugler, David. *The Voice of America and the Domestic Propaganda Battles, 1945–53*. Columbia: University of Missouri Press, 2000.

Kullaa, Rinna. *Non-alignment and its Origins in Cold War Europe: Yugoslavia, Finland, and the Soviet Challenge*. London: I.B. Tauris, 2012.

Kwon, Heonik. *The Other Cold War*. New York: Columbia University Press, 2010.

Kyle, Keith. *Suez: Britain's End of Empire in the Middle East*. London: I. B. Tauris, 2002.

Langley, Lester. *The Americas in the Modern Age*. New Haven, CT: Yale University Press, 2003.

Latham, Michael. *The Right Kind of Revolution: Modernization, Development, and U.S. Foreign Policy from the Cold War to the Present*. Ithaca, NY: Cornell University Press, 2011.

Latham, Michael. *Modernization as Ideology: American Social Science and "Nation Building" in the Kennedy Era*. Chapel Hill: University of North Carolina Press, 2000.

Lauren, Paul Gordon. *Power and Prejudice: The Politics and Diplomacy of Racial Discrimination*. Boulder, CO: Westview Press, 1988.

Layton, Azza Salama. *International Politics and Civil Rights Policies in the United States, 1941–1960*. New York: Cambridge University Press, 2000.

Lee, Christopher, ed. *Making a World After Empire: The Bandung Moment and its Political Afterlives*. Athens: Ohio University Press, 2010.

Leffler, Melvyn. *A Preponderance of Power: National Security, the Truman Administration, and the Cold War*. Redwood City, CA: Stanford University Press, 1992.

Leffler, Melvyn. *For the Soul of Mankind: The United States, the Soviet Union, and the Cold War*. New York: Hill and Wang, 2007.

Lerner, Daniel. *The Passing of Traditional Society: Modernizing the Middle East*. New York: Free Press, 1958.

Lewis, Martin W., and Karen E. Wigen. *The Myth of Continents: A Critique of Metageography*. Berkeley: University of California Press, 1997.

Louis, William Roger. *Ends of British Imperialism: The Scramble for Empire, Suez, and Decolonization*. London: I. B. Tauris, 2006.

Lucas, Scott. *Freedom's War: The American Crusade Against the Soviet Union*. New York: New York University Press, 1999.

Macdonald, Douglas. *Adventures in Chaos: American Intervention for Reform in the Third World.* Cambridge, MA: Harvard University Press, 1992.

Mahoney, Richard. *JFK: Ordeal in Africa.* New York: Oxford University Press, 1983.

Makalani, Minkah. *In the Cause of Freedom: Radical Black Internationalism from Harlem to London, 1917–1939.* Chapel Hill: University of North Carolina Press, 2011.

Makonnen, Ras. *Pan-Africanism from Within.* Edited by Kenneth King. Oxford: Oxford University Press, 1973.

Malik, Kenan. *The Meaning of Race: Race, History, and Culture in Western Society.* New York: New York University Press, 1996.

Malone, Gifford. *Political Advocacy and Cultural Communication: Organizing the Nation's Public Diplomacy.* New York: University Press of America, 1988.

Manela, Erez. *The Wilsonian Moment: Self-Determination and the International Origins of Anticolonialism.* New York: Oxford University Press, 2007.

Manheim, Jarol B. *Strategic Public Diplomacy and American Foreign Policy: The Evolution of Influence.* New York: Oxford University Press, 1994.

Mazov, Sergey. *A Distant Front in the Cold War: The USSR in West Africa and the Congo, 1956–1964.* Redwood City, CA: Stanford University Press, 2010.

Mazower, Mark. *No Enchanted Palace: The End of Empire and the Ideological Origins of the United Nations.* Princeton, NJ: Princeton University Press, 2013.

Mboya, Tom. *Freedom and After.* London: Andre Deutsch, 1963.

McCormick, Thomas J. *America's Half-Century: United States Foreign Policy in the Cold War.* Baltimore: Johns Hopkins University Press, 1989.

McCann, Gerard, and Emma Mawdsley. *India in Africa: Changing Geographies of Power.* Oxford: Pambazuka Press, 2011.

McGarr, Paul. *The Cold War in South Asia: Britain, the United States, and the Indian Subcontinent, 1945–65.* Cambridge: Cambridge University Press, 2013.

McMahon, Robert J. *The Cold War in the Third World.* New York: Oxford University Press, 2013.

McMahon, Robert J. *The Limits of Empire: The United States and Southeast Asia since World War II.* New York: Columbia University Press, 1999.

McMahon, Robert J. *The Cold War on the Periphery: the United States, India, and Pakistan.* New York: Columbia University Press, 1994.

McMahon, Robert J. *Colonialism and Cold War: The United States and the Struggle for Indonesian Independence, 1945–1949.* Ithaca, NY: Cornell University Press, 1981.

McPherson, Alan. *Yankee No! Anti-Americanism in U.S.–Latin American Relations.* Cambridge, MA: Harvard University Press, 2003.

McVety, Amanda. *Enlightened Aid: U.S. Development as Foreign Policy in Ethiopia.* New York: Oxford University Press, 2012.

Medhurst, Martin. *Cold War Rhetoric: Strategy, Metaphor, and Ideology.* Revised ed. East Lansing: Michigan State University Press, 1997.

Meriwether, James. *Proudly We Can Be Africans: Black Americans and Africa, 1935–1961.* Chapel Hill: University of North Carolina Press, 2002.

Meyerhoff, Arthur E. *The Strategy of Persuasion: The Use of Advertising Skills in Fighting the Cold War.* New York: Coward-McCann, 1965.

Mishra, Pankaj. *From the Ruins of Empire: The Intellectuals Who Remade Asia.* New York: FSG, 2012.

Mitrovich, Gregory. *Undermining the Kremlin: America's Strategy to Subvert the Soviet Bloc, 1947–1956.* Ithaca, NY: Cornell University Press, 2000.

Mortimer, Robert. *The Third World Coalition in International Politics.* Boulder, CO: Westview Press, 1984.

Muehlenbeck, Philip. *Betting on the Africans: John F. Kennedy's Courting of African Nationalist Leaders.* New York: Oxford University Press, 2012.

Muller, Joachim, and Karl Sauvant. *The Third World Without Superpowers: The Collected Documents of the Non-Aligned Countries.* Dobbs Ferry, NY: Oceana Publications, 1978.

Namikas, Lise. *Battleground Africa: Cold War in the Congo, 1960–1965*. Redwood City, CA: Stanford University Press, 2013.

Nasser, Gamal Abdel. *The Philosophy of the Revolution*. Cairo: National Publication House Press, 1960.

Nehru, Jawaharlal. *Nehru and Africa: Jawaharlal Nehru's Speeches on Africa, 1946–1963*. New Delhi: Indian Council for Africa, 1964.

Nelson, Michael. *War of the Black Heavens: The Battles of Western Broadcasting in the Cold War*. Syracuse: Syracuse University Press, 1997.

Newsom, David. *The Imperial Mantle: The United States, Decolonization, and the Third World*. Bloomington: Indiana University Press, 2001.

Nichols, David A. *Eisenhower 1956: The President's Year of Crisis—Suez and the Brink of War*. New York: Simon & Schuster, 2012.

Ninkovich, Frank. *The Diplomacy of Ideas: U.S. Foreign Policy and Cultural Relations, 1938–1950*. New York: Cambridge University Press, 1981.

Nkrumah, Kwame. *Africa Must Unite*. New York: Praeger, 1963.

Nkrumah, Kwame. *I Speak of Freedom*. New York: Praeger, 1961.

Noer, Thomas. *Cold War and Black Liberation: The United States and White Rule in Africa, 1948–1968*. Columbia: University of Missouri Press, 1988.

Nwaubani, Ebere. *The United States and Decolonization in West Africa, 1950–1960*. Rochester: University of Rochester Press, 2001.

Nye, Joseph. *Soft Power: The Means to Success in World Politics*. New York: Public Affairs, 2004.

Offner, Arnold. *Another Such Victory: President Truman and the Cold War, 1945–1953*. Redwood City, CA: Stanford University Press, 2002.

Osgood, Kenneth. *Total Cold War: Eisenhower's Secret Propaganda Battle at Home and Abroad*. Lawrence: University Press of Kansas, 2006.

Osgood, Kenneth, and Brian Etheridge, eds. *The United States and Public Diplomacy: New Directions in Cultural and International History*. Boston: Brill Nijhoff, 2010.

Paterson, Thomas. *Contesting Castro: The United States and the Triumph of the Cuban Revolution*. New York: Oxford University Press, 1994.

Paterson, Thomas, ed., *Kennedy's Quest for Victory: American Foreign Policy, 1961–63*. New York: Oxford University Press, 1989.

Parry-Giles, Shawn. *The Rhetorical Presidency, Propaganda, and the Cold War, 1945–1955*. New York: Praeger, 2001.

Pease, Stephen. *Psywar: Psychological Warfare in Korea, 1950–1953*. Harrisburg, PA: Stackpole Books, 1992.

Pierpaoli, Paul G. *Truman and Korea: The Political Culture of the Early Cold War*. Columbia: University of Missouri Press, 1999.

Pirsein, Robert. *The Voice of America: A History of the International Broadcasting Activities of the United States Government, 1940–1962*. New York: Arno Press, 1979.

Plummer, Brenda Gayle. *In Search of Power: African Americans in the Era of Decolonization, 1956–1974*. New York: Cambridge University Press, 2012.

Plummer, Brenda Gayle, ed. *Window on Freedom: Race, Civil Rights, and Foreign Affairs, 1945–1988*. Chapel Hill: University of North Carolina Press, 2003.

Plummer, Brenda Gayle. *Rising Wind: Black Americans and U.S. Foreign Affairs, 1935–1960*. Chapel Hill: University of North Carolina Press, 1996.

Prashad, Vijay. *The Poorer Nations: A Possible History of the Global South*. New York: Verso, 2013.

Prashad, Vijay. *The Darker Nations: A People's History of the Third World*. New York: New Press, 2008.

Puddington, Arch. *Broadcasting Freedom: The Cold War Triumph of Radio Free Europe and Radio Liberty*. Lexington: University of Kentucky Press, 2000.

Rabe, Stephen. *The Killing Zone: The United States Wages Cold War in Latin America*. New York: Oxford University Press, 2011.

Rabe, Stephen. *The Most Dangerous Area in the World: John F. Kennedy Confronts Communist Revolution in Latin America*. Chapel Hill: University of North Carolina Press, 1999.

Rakove, Robert. *Kennedy, Johnson, and the Nonaligned World*. New York: Cambridge University Press, 2012.

Rawnsley, Gary, ed. *Cold War Propaganda in the 1950s*. New York: St. Martin's, 1999.

Reed, Adolph L. Jr. *W.E.B. DuBois and American Political Thought: Fabianism and the Color Line*. New York: Oxford University Press, 1997.

Reynolds, Jonathan T. *Sovereignty and Struggle: Africa and Africans in the Era of the Cold War, 1945–1994*. New York: Oxford University Press, 2014.

Richmond, Yale. *Practicing Public Diplomacy: A Cold War Odyssey*. New York: Berghahn Books, 2008.

Rivas, Darlene. *Missionary Capitalist: Nelson Rockefeller in Venezuela*. Chapel Hill: University of North Carolina Press, 2002.

Romulo, Carlos. *The Meaning of Bandung*. Chapel Hill: University of North Carolina Press, 1956.

Rosenberg, Jonathan. *How Far the Promised Land? World Affairs and the American Civil Rights Movement from the First World War to Vietnam*. Princeton, NJ: Princeton University Press, 2005.

Rotter, Andrew J. *Comrades at Odds: The United States and India, 1947–1964*. Ithaca, NY: Cornell University Press, 1999.

Rusk, Dean. *As I Saw It*. New York: Norton, 1990.

Ryan, David, and Victor Pungong, eds. *The United States and Decolonization: Power and Freedom*. New York: Palgrave Macmillan, 2000.

Sadlier, Darlene. *Americans All: Good Neighbor Cultural Diplomacy During World War II*. Austin: University of Texas Press, 2012.

Saunders, Frances Stonor. *The Cultural Cold War: The CIA and the World of Arts and Letters*. 2nd ed. New York: New Press, 2013.

Savage, Barbara Dianne. *Broadcasting Freedom: Radio, War, and the Politics of Race*. Chapel Hill: University of North Carolina Press, 1999.

Schlesinger, Stephen, and Stephen Kinzer. *Bitter Fruit: The Story of the American Coup in Guatemala*, 2nd ed. Cambridge, MA: Harvard University Press, 1999.

Schmidt, Elizabeth. *Foreign Intervention in Africa*. New York: Cambridge University Press, 2013.

Selverstone, Marc. *Constructing the Monolith: The United States, Great Britain, and International Communism, 1945–1950*. Cambridge, MA: Harvard University Press, 2009.

Sewell, Bevan. *The U.S. and Latin America: Eisenhower, Kennedy, and Economic Diplomacy in the Cold War*. London: I. B. Tauris, 2015.

Shaw, Tony. *Eden, Suez, and Mass Media: Propaganda and Persuasion during the Suez Crisis*. London: I. B. Tauris, 1996.

Shepherd, George, ed. *Racial Influences on American Foreign Policy*. New York: Basic Books, 1970.

Shepherd, George, ed. *Race Among Nations: A Conceptual Approach*. Lexington, MA: Heath Lexington Books, 1970.

Shulman, Holly Cowan. *The Voice of America: Propaganda and Democracy, 1941–45*. Madison: University of Wisconsin Press, 1990.

Sidaway, James. *Imagined Regional Communities: Integration and Sovereignty in the Global South*. New York: Routledge, 2013.

Simpson, Brad. *Economists With Guns: Authoritarian Development and U.S.–Indonesian Relations, 1960–68*. Redwood City, CA: Stanford University Press, 2008.

Singh, Nikhil Pal. *Black Is a Country: Race and the Unfinished Struggle for Democracy*. Cambridge, MA: Harvard University Press, 2004.

Slate, Nico. *Colored Cosmopolitanism: The Shared Struggle for Freedom in the United States and India*. Cambridge, MA: Harvard University Press, 2012.

Smith, Gaddis. *The Last Years of the Monroe Doctrine, 1945–1993*. New York: Hill and Wang, 1994.

Smith, Peter H. *Talons of the Eagle: Dynamics of U.S.–Latin American Relations*. 2nd ed. New York: Oxford University Press, 2000.

Smith, Tony. *America's Mission: The United States and the Worldwide Struggle for Democracy in the Twentieth Century*. Princeton, NJ: Princeton University Press, 1994.

Snyder, Alvin A. *Warriors of Disinformation: How Lies, Videotape, and the USIA Won the Cold War*. New York: Arcade Publishing, 2012.

Sorenson, Thomas. *The Word War: The Story of American Propaganda*. New York: Harper & Row, 1968.

Springhall, John. *Decolonization Since 1945: The Collapse of European Overseas Empires*. New York: Palgrave, 2001.

Sproule, J. Michael. *Propaganda and Democracy: The American Experience of Media and Mass Persuasion*. New York: Cambridge University Press, 1997.

Starr, Paul. *The Creation of the Media: Political Origins of Modern Communication*. New York: Basic Books, 2004.

Stern, John Allen. *C. D. Jackson: Cold War Propagandist for Democracy and Globalism*. New York: University Press of America, 2012.

Stockwell, Sarah. *The Wind of Change: Harold Macmillan and British Decolonization*. London: Palgrave Macmillan, 2013.

Stueck, William. *Rethinking the Korean War: A New Diplomatic and Strategic History*. Princeton, NJ: Princeton University Press, 2004.

Stueck, William. *The Korean War: An International History*. Princeton, NJ: Princeton University Press, 1995.

Taffet, Jeff. *Foreign Aid as Foreign Policy: The Alliance for Progress in Latin America*. New York: Routledge, 2007.

Tan, See Seng, and Amitav Acharya, eds. *Bandung Revisited: The Legacy of the 1955 Asian-African Conference for International Order*. Singapore: National University of Singapore Press, 2008.

Thompson, W. Scott. *Ghana's Foreign Policy, 1957–66*. Princeton, NJ: Princeton University Press, 1969.

Truman, Harry S. *Memoirs: Years of Trial and Hope*. 2 vols. Garden City, NY: Doubleday, 1955–1956.

Tudda, Chris. *The Truth is Our Weapon: The Rhetorical Diplomacy of Eisenhower and Dulles* Baton Rouge: Louisiana State University Press, 2006.

Vaughan, James. *The Failure of American and British Propaganda in the Arab Middle East, 1945–1957: Unconquerable Minds*. London: Palgrave Macmillan, 2005.

Vitalis, Robert. *White World Order, Black Power Politics: The Birth of American International Relations*. Ithaca, NY: Cornell University Press, 2015.

Von Albertini, Rudolf. *European Colonial Rule, 1860–1940: The Impact of the West on India, Southeast Asia, and Africa*. Westport, CT: Greenwood Press, 1982.

Von Eschen, Penny. *Satchmo Blows Up the World: Jazz Ambassadors Play the Cold War*. Cambridge, MA: Harvard University Press, 2006.

Von Eschen, Penny. *Race Against Empire: Black Americans and Anticolonialism, 1937–1957*. Ithaca, NY: Cornell University Press, 1997.

Wagnleiter, Reinhold, and Elaine Tyler May, eds. *"Here, There, and Everywhere": The Foreign Politics of American Popular Culture*. Salzburg: University of Salzburg Press, 2000.

Waller, J. Michael. *Strategic Influence: Public Diplomacy, Counterpropaganda, and Political Warfare*. Washington, DC: Institute of World Politics Press, 2009.

Webb, Alban. *London Calling: Britain, the BBC World Service and the Cold War*. London: Bloomsbury, 2015.

Welch, Richard E. Jr. *Response to Revolution: The United States and the Cuban Revolution, 1959–1961*. Chapel Hill: University of North Carolina Press, 1985.

Westad, Odd Arne. *The Global Cold War: Third World Interventions and the Making of Our Times*. New York: Cambridge University Press, 2005.

Whitfield, Stephen. *The Culture of the Cold War*. 2nd ed. Baltimore: Johns Hopkins University Press, 1996.

Willets, Peter. *The Non-aligned Movement: The Origins of a Third World Alliance*. London: Pinter, 1978.

Wilson, Henry S. *African Decolonization*. London: Edward Arnold, 1994.

Winkler, Allan M. *The Politics of Propaganda*. New Haven, CT: Yale University Press, 1978.

Woods, Randall B., and Howard Jones. *Dawning of the Cold War: The United States' Quest for Order*. Athens: University of Georgia Press, 1991.

Wright, Richard. *The Color Curtain*. Cleveland, OH: World Publishing, 1956.

Wulf, Andrew James. *U.S. International Exhibitions during the Cold War: Winning Hearts and Minds Through Cultural Diplomacy*. Lanham, MD: Rowman & Littlefield, 2015.

Yaqub, Salim. *Containing Arab Nationalism: The Eisenhower Doctrine and the Middle East*. Chapel Hill: University of North Carolina Press, 2004.

Yergin, Daniel. *Shattered Peace: The Origins of the Cold War and the National Security State*. Boston: Houghton Mifflin, 1977.

Young, Charles. *Name, Rank, and Serial Number: Exploiting Korean War POWs at Home and Abroad*. New York: Oxford University Press, 2014.

Zhang, Shu Guang. *Mao's Military Romanticism: China and the Korean War, 1950–53*. Lawrence: University Press of Kansas, 1995.

Articles and Dissertations

Abraham, Itty. "From Bandung to NAM: Non-alignment and Indian Foreign Policy." *Journal of Comparative and Commonwealth Studies* 46:2 (April 2008): 195–219.

Ahlman, Jeffrey S. "Living With Nkrumahism: Nation, State, and Pan-Africanism in Ghana." PhD dissertation, University of Illinois, 2011.

Ali-Dinar, Ali Bahr Aliden. "Contextual Analysis of Dress and Adornment in Al-Fashir, Sudan." PhD dissertation, University of Pennsylvania, 1995.

Allcock, Thomas Tunstall. "Becoming 'Mr. Latin America': Thomas C. Mann Reconsidered." *Diplomatic History* 38:5 (November 2014): 1017–1045.

Anderson, Carol. "From Hope to Disillusion: African Americans, the U.N., and the Struggle for Human Rights, 1944–47." *Diplomatic History* 20:4 (Fall 1996): 531–564.

Berger, Mark T. "After the Third World? History, Destiny, and the Fate of Third Worldism." *Third World Quarterly* 25:1 (2004): 9–39.

Byrne, Jeffrey James. "Pilot Nation: An International History of Revolutionary Algeria, 1958–1965." PhD dissertation, London School of Economics, 2011.

Casey, Steven. "Wilfred Burchett and the UN Command's Media Relation–s During the Korean War, 1951–52." *Journal of Military History* 74:3 (July 2010): 821–845.

Casey, Steven. "White House Publicity Operations During the Korean War, June 1950–June 1951." *Presidential Studies Quarterly* 35:4 (December 2005): 691–717.

Casey, Steven. "Selling NSC-68: The Truman Administration, Public Opinion, and the Politics of Mobilization, 1950–51." *Diplomatic History* 29:4 (December 2005): 655–690.

Connelly, Matthew. "Taking off the Cold War Lens: Visions of North–South Conflict during the Algerian War for Independence." *American Historical Review* 105:3 (June 2000): 739–769.

Cooper, Frederick. "Possibility and Constraint: African Independence in Historical Perspective." *Journal of African History* 49:2 (2008): 167–196.

Cumings, Bruce. "The American Century and the Third World." *Diplomatic History* 23 (Spring 1999): 355–370.

Darwin, John. "British Decolonization Since 1945: A Pattern or a Puzzle." *Journal of Imperial and Commonwealth History* 12:2 (1984): 187–209.

Dudziak, Mary L. "Desegregation as a Cold War Imperative." *Stanford Law Review* 41:1 (November 1988): 61–120.

Dudziak, Mary L. "Josephine Baker, Racial Protest, and the Cold War." *Journal of American History* 81:3 (September 1994): 543–570.

Emerson, Rupert. "Pan-Africanism." *International Organization* 16:2 (Spring 1962): 275–290.

Engerman, David. "The Second World's Third World." *Kritika* 12:1 (Winter 2011): 183–211.

Erb, Claude C. "Prelude to Point Four: The Institute of Inter-American Affairs." *Diplomatic History* 9:3 (July 1985): 249–269.

Espinoza, Cristobal Zuniga. "The Struggle for Promoting Development: An Inter-American Analysis on the Making of the Alliance For Progress, Argentina, Venezuela, and the United States." PhD dissertation, SUNY-Stony Brook, 2014.

Espiritu, Augusto. "'To Carry Water on Both Shoulders': Carlos P. Romulo, American Empire, and the Meanings of Bandung." *Radical History Review* 95 (Spring 2006): 173–190.

Field, Thomas. "Ideology as Strategy: Military-Led Modernization and the Origins of the Alliance For Progress in Bolivia." *Diplomatic History* 36:1 (January 2012): 147–183.

Fraser, Cary. "Crossing the Color Line in Little Rock: The Eisenhower Administration and the Dilemma of Race." *Diplomatic History* 24:2 (Spring 2000): 233–264.

Friedman, Max Paul. "Anti-Americanism and U.S. Foreign Relations." *Diplomatic History* 32:4 (September 2008): 497–514.

Friedman, Max Paul. "Fracas in Caracas: Latin American Diplomatic Resistance to U.S. Intervention in Guatemala in 1954." *Diplomacy & Statecraft* 21:4 (2010): 669–689.

Geary, Brent. "A Foundation of Sand: U.S. Public Diplomacy, Egypt, and Arab Nationalism, 1953–1960." PhD dissertation, Ohio University, 2007.

Gerits, Frank. "The Ideological Scramble for Africa: The U.S., Ghana, French and British Competition for Africa's Future, 1953–63." PhD dissertation, European University Institute, 2014.

Gettig, Eric. "'Trouble Ahead in Afro-Asia': The United States, the Second Bandung Conference, and the Struggle for the Third World." *Diplomatic History* 39:1 (January 2015): 126–156.

Gobat, Michel. "The Invention of Latin America: A Transnational History of Anti-Imperialism, Democracy, and Race." *American Historical Review* 118:5 (December 2013): 1345–1375.

Graham, Sarah Ellen. "American Propaganda, the Anglo-American Alliance, and the 'Delicate Question' of Indian Self-Determination." *Diplomatic History* 33:2 (April 2009): 223–260.

Granville, Johanna. "'Caught With Jam on Our Fingers': Radio Free Europe and the Hungarian Revolution of 1956." *Diplomatic History* 29:5 (December 2005): 811–839.

Haefele, Mark. "John F. Kennedy, USIA, and World Public Opinion." *Diplomatic History* 25:1 (Winter 2001): 63–84.

Hershberg, James. "'High-Spirited Confusion': Brazil, the 1961 Belgrade Conference, and the Limits of an Independent Foreign Policy During the High Cold War." *Cold War History* 7:3 (August 2007): 373–388.

Hess, Gary R. "Accommodation Amid Discord: The United States, India, and the Third World." *Diplomatic History* 16:2 (June 1992): 1–22.

Higgin, Hannah N. "Disseminating American Ideals in Africa, 1949–1969." PhD dissertation, Cambridge University, 2015.

Horne, Gerald. "Race From Power: U.S. Foreign Policy and the General Crisis of 'White Supremacy.'" *Diplomatic History* 23:3 (September 1999): 437–462.

Horne, Gerald. "Who Lost the Cold War? Africans and African Americans." *Diplomatic History* 20:4 (Fall 1996): 613–626.

Immerman, Richard. "Confessions of an Eisenhower Revisionist." *Diplomatic History* 14:3 (July 1990): 11–24.

Jacobson, Mark. "Minds Then Hearts: United States Political and Psychological Warfare During the Korean War." PhD dissertation, Ohio State University, 2005.

Jahanbani, Sheyda. "'A Different Kind of People': The Poor at Home and Abroad, 1935–1968." PhD dissertation, Brown University, 2009.

Jones, Matthew. "A 'Segregated' Asia? Race, the Bandung Conference, and Pan-Asianist Fears in American Thought and Policy, 1954–55." *Diplomatic History* 29:5 (November 2005): 841–868.

Kelley, Robin D. G. "'But a Local Phase of a World Problem': Black History's Global Vision, 1883–1950." *Journal of American History* 86 (December 1999): 1045–1078.

Khalil, Osamah. "The Crossroads of the World: U.S. and British Foreign Policy Doctrines and the Construct of the Middle East, 1902–2007." *Diplomatic History* 38:2 (April 2014): 299–344.

Kirkendall, Andrew J. "Kennedy Men and the Fate of the Alliance For Progress in LBJ-Era Brazil and Chile." *Diplomacy and Statecraft* 18:4 (2007): 745–772.

Krenn, Michael. "'Unfinished Business': Segregration and U.S. Diplomacy at the 1958 World's Fair." *Diplomatic History* 20:4 (Fall 1996): 591–612.

Laville, Helen, and Scott Lucas. "The American Way: Edith Sampson, the NAACP, and African American Identity in the Cold War." *Diplomatic History* 20:4 (Fall 1996): 565–590.

Layton, Azza Salama. "International Pressure and the U.S. Government's Response to Little Rock." *Arkansas Historical Quarterly* 56 (Fall 1997): 257–272.

Longo, Regina. "Marshall Plan Films in Italy, 1948–1955: A Project of Postwar Consensus Building." PhD dissertation, University of California-Santa Barbara, 2012.

Louis, William Roger. "American Anti-Colonialism and the Dissolution of the British Empire." *International Affairs* 61:3 (1985): 395–420.

Louis, William Roger, and Ronald Robinson. "The Imperialism of Decolonisation," *Journal of Imperial and Commonwealth History* 22:3 (1994): 462–511.

Madan, Tanvi. "With an Eye to the East: The U.S.–India Relationship and China." PhD dissertation, University of Texas, 2012.

McMahon, Robert J. "Eisenhower and Third World Nationalism: A Critique of the Revisionists." *Political Science Quarterly* 101:3 (Summer 1986): 456–457.

Meriwether, James. "'Worth a Lot of Negro Votes': Black Voters, Africa, and the 1960 Presidential Campaign." *Journal of American History* 95 (December 2008): 737–763.

Moulton, Aaron Coy. "Guatemalan Exiles, Caribbean Basin Dictators, Operation PBFORTUNE, and the Transnational Counter-Revolution against the Guatemalan Revolution, 1944–1952." PhD dissertation, University of Arkansas, 2016.

Munro, John J. "The Anticolonial Front: Cold War Imperialism and the Struggle Against Global White Supremacy." PhD dissertation, University of California-Santa Barbara, 2009.

Parker, Jason. "'Made-in-America Revolutions'? The 'Black University' and the American Role in the Decolonization of the Black Atlantic." *Journal of American History* 96:3 (December 2009): 727–750.

Parker, Jason. "Cold War II: The Eisenhower Administration, the Bandung Conference, and the Reperiodization of the Postwar Era." *Diplomatic History* 30:5 (November 2006): 867–892.

Plummer, Brenda Gayle. "'Below the Level of Men': African Americans, Race, and the History of U.S. Foreign Relations." *Diplomatic History* 20:4 (Fall 1996): 639–650.

Pullin, Eric. "'Noise and Flutter': American Propaganda Strategy and Operation in India During World War II." *Diplomatic History* 34:2 (April 2010): 275–298.

Rawnsley, Gary. "Overt and Covert: The Voice of Britain and Black Radio Broadcasting in the Suez Crisis, 1956." *Intelligence and National Security* 11:3 (July 1996): 497–522.

Romano, Renee. "No Diplomatic Immunity: African Diplomats, the State Department, and Civil Rights, 1961–1964." *Journal of American History* 87:2 (September 2000): 546–580.

Roth, Lois W. "Public Diplomacy and the Past: The Search for an American Style of Propaganda, 1952–1977." *The Fletcher Forum of World Affairs* 8:2 (Summer 1984): 353–396.

Sackley, Nicole. "Village Models: Etawah, India, and the Making and Remaking of Development in the Early Cold War." *Diplomatic History* 37:4 (2013): 749–778.

Sackley, Nicole. "The Village as Cold War Site: Experts, Development, and the History of Rural Reconstruction." *Journal of Global History* 6:3 (2011): 481–504.

Sauvy, Alfred. "Trois mondes, Une planète." *Le Nouvel Observateur* (118), August 14, 1952, 14.

Schwenk, Melinda."Reforming the Negative through History: The USIA and the 1957 Little Rock Integration Crisis." *Journal of Communication Inquiry* 23:3 (July 1999): 288–306.

Smith, Tony. "New Bottles for New Wine: A Pericentric Framework for the Study of the Cold War." *Diplomatic History* 24:4 (Fall 2000): 567–592.

Tarling, Nicholas. "'Ah-Ah': Britain and the Bandung Conference of 1955." *Journal of Southeast Asian Studies* 23:1 (March 1992): 74–112.

Trask, Roger. "The Impact of the Cold War on United States–Latin American Relations, 1945–1949." *Diplomatic History* 1 (Summer 1977): 283–311.

Tudda, Chris. "'Reenacting the Story of Tantalus': Eisenhower, Dulles, and the Failed Rhetoric of Liberation." *Journal of Cold War Studies* 7:4 (Fall 2005): 3–35.

Vitalis, Robert. "The Midnight Ride of Kwame Nkrumah and Other Fables of Bandung." *Humanity* 4:2 (Summer 2013): 261–288.

Von Eschen, Penny. "Challenging Cold War Habits: African Americans, Race, and Foreign Policy." *Diplomatic History* 20:4 (Fall 1996): 627–638.

Walcher, Dustin. "Missionaries of Modernization: The United States, Argentina, and the Liberal International Order, 1958–63." PhD dissertation, Ohio State University, 2007.

Weathersby, Kathryn. "Deceiving the Deceivers: Moscow, Beijing, Pyongyang, and the Allegations of Bacteriological Weapons Use in Korea." *Cold War International History Project Bulletin* 11 (Winter 1998): 176–199.

Weis, W. Michael. "The Twilight of Pan-Americanism: The Alliance for Progress, Neo-colonialism, and Non-alignment in Brazil, 1961–64." *International History Review* 23:2 (June 2001): 322–344.

White, Evan. "Kwame Nkrumah: Cold War Modernity, Pan-African Ideology, and the Geopolitics of Development." *Geopolitics* 8:2 (Summer 2003): 99–124.

Wolf-Philips, Leslie. "Why 'Third World'?: Origin, Definition, and Usage." *Third World Quarterly* 9:4 (October 1987): 1311–1327.

Yifru, Katema et al. "Africa Speaks to the United Nations: A Symposium of Aspirations and Concerns Voiced by Representative Leaders at the UN." *International Organizations* 16:2 (Spring 1962): 303–330

INDEX